Charles Henry Wright Stocking

The history and genealogy of the Knowltons of England and America

Charles Henry Wright Stocking

The history and genealogy of the Knowltons of England and America

ISBN/EAN: 9783337257477

Printed in Europe, USA, Canada, Australia, Japan

Cover: Foto ©ninafisch / pixelio.de

More available books at **www.hansebooks.com**

OF THE

KNOWLTONS OF ENGLAND AND AMERICA

Volume 1

BY THE

REV. CHARLES HENRY WRIGHT STOCKING, D.D.

Principal of Freehold, N. J., Ladies Seminary

"It were, indeed, a desirable thing to be well descended, but the glory of it belongs to our ancestors."—Plutarch.

NEW YORK

The Knickerbocker Press

1897

The Knickerbocker Press, New York

DEDICATION

IN REVERENT AND LOVING MEMORY

OF

Lieutenant Daniel Knowlton

OF THE CONTINENTAL ARMY,

THE RESOLUTE PATRIOT,
THE FEARLESS SCOUT, THE INTREPID SOLDIER,
THE UPRIGHT MAN,
WHOSE EMINENT SERVICES TO HIS
IMPERILLED STATE AND COUNTRY
AMPLY MERIT THIS
HIS FIRST PUBLIC MEMORIAL,
THIS VOLUME IS
HUMBLY DEDICATED, BY

THE AUTHOR

PREFACE.

THE extraordinary stimulus given to researches in the genealogical field by the various patriotic societies, is one of the happy signs of the times. The activities of commercial, and the blandishments of social life, the mad race for wealth and the pathetic struggle for the necessities of daily existence, the indifference of many to everything outside and beyond their own personal and narrow circle, and the lack of opportunity in others have, until quite recently, made the work of the genealogist an exceptional and unappreciated labor. When men are concerned only about their present condition and individual interests, caring nothing for ancestry or posterity, they live in a very small world, and, like the squirrel playing in its cage, fancy they are happy. But that which now is, is the result of what has been. "No man liveth unto himself and no man dieth unto himself" was the conclusion of an ancient and revered philosopher, and he who cares nothing for those whose transmitted name he bears, and who have written that name high up among the records of of the race, is lacking in the essentials of a self-respecting manhood. And the world has too many of this sort of people.

But because there are others that cherish a legitimate pride of pedigree and of country, this history has been written. It represents the continuous labors of a few persons for about forty years, supplemented by the work of the historian who has sufficiently overcome indifference and discouragement to offer to the members of a large and honorable family this result of his researches. It does not claim to be a perfect and exhaustive record, nor is it likely to be free from errors. The careless manner in which some family records are prepared and kept, the tendency to substitute fiction for fact, the differences in names and dates of the same persons reported by different branches of the same family, and the refusal of other persons to answer inquiries at all, make it inevitable that mistakes will creep into the most carefully prepared genealogy. Accordingly, all persons interested in this particular history are invited to inform the author of any authenticated errors, and he will correct them in a future supplement, adding the names, dates, and pedigree of all who are not herein included. He now submits this interesting result of his labors to the fair judgment of all members of the interesting and honored family whose distinguished record it has been his ambition to preserve, in the hope that it will meet with their cordial approbation.

FREEHOLD, N. J., October, 1897.

CONTENTS.

LIST OF ILLUSTRATIONS.

ERRATA AND ADDENDA

For the "Knowlton Ancestry" verified by the latest information from Correspondents.

Page 21. (5) m, 1651, (14) rem. to Windham. Conn., and m. 2d Abraham Mitchell after 1698. (14 A) Joseph.
Page 22. Mary Kimball was niece of Richard and Mary. (15) b. 1657.
" 23. (26) m. Nov. 15. d 1738.
" 24. (31 A) Deborah (31. B) Susannah (31. C) Hannah, 1672 m. Benj. Baldwin. (31 D) Ezekiel.
Page 27. (62 A) Eli-ha. 1679.
" " (57) m. Barzillai.
Page 32. Erase (130), (131).
" 39. (122) d. 1774.
" 42. For 130 and 131, read (62 A), (C
" 43. (300) Res. Northwood, N.H.
Page 44. [321] Ebenezer and Ruth Smahey had Ebenezer. m. Fiddia Needham, 1844, and had Charles M. Res. Cazenoria, N. Y. ;
Mary A. res. Cazenoria, N. Y.
Annie R. m.---Crandall, of Whitewater, Wis.
" 45. (364) m. June 16, 1776 (366) m. July 19, 1784.
For (132) read (142). Sarah and Barzillai Lamb. (405) Israel, 1737, d. Mar. 26. 1826.
Page 48. (406) Samuel, 1741. m. Cozzens.
" " (408) b, Sept. 16, 1747. (408 A) Isaac, Sept. 12, 1749, d. young.
" 49. (427) m. 1768.
" 51. (222) Stephen m. Abigail. (453), (454) twins, b. Sept. 15, 1765. (455) b. Sept. 20, 1767.
Page 55. Abraham res. in Hardwick.
" 64. (669) Erase Mrs.
Page 70. (782) b. 1763. (792) m. Durgin (794) m. Durgin
" 71. (796) m. Nathan Masters of Deerfield, N. H. Mar. 12. 1797.
" (797) m. Daniel Hoiit (Hoyt) 1802.
" (800) Res. in Northwood also.
" (802) m. Dame He d. Nov. 14. 1851. She d. May 5, 1854.
" (803) b. Sept. 3. (804) m. 2d Dame. (805) m. Dame. (361) Thomas sett. near Lucas Pond. (812) b. 1787. (813) b. March 19.
Page 72. (814) b. Sept. 5, 1795.
" 74. (857) m. Lieut. Amos.
" 81. (1019) b. 1772.
" 82. (1035) m. Elizabeth Noonan, of Pomfert, Conn.
Page 82. [1035] William and Elizabeth Noonan had William.
Laura.
Anna. m. Rev. Thompson Bird, DesMoines, Ia.
William served in the Rev. War for one year from Aug. 9, 1782, and d. at White River Junction, Vt., Jan. 29, 1820. She d. April 25, 1854.
" 83. (1038) For Hill, read Capt. Roswell Preston, Oct 18, 1793, d. Nov. 27, 1854.
Page 83. Mehitable (423) m. 2d Capt. Robert J. Preston, of Hampton, Conn. and d. March 29, 1826.
Page 83. (1041) Capt. of Militia.
" " (1044) He d. Aug. 5, 1821.
" (1048) m. Nov. 24, 1803.
" (1049) m. 2d Rhoda Gage, of Monson, Mass. May 16, 1820.
" 89 (1051) d. Oct. 9, 1851.
" 94 Col. Thomas fell in 1776. After "Remember" insert "friends."
" 98 (1150) Sett. in 1835.
Page 98. [1154] Lyman.
" 99. [1155] Ruth M, m. Stephen White.

The American Knowltons.

Page 99 [1155 A] Read Juliana.
" 104 (1237) Hersey m. Barker.
" 108 Nathan d. at Auburn, Mass.
" 117 (570) m. Daniel. (1460) m. Eliva.
" 120 (1474) Erase, U. S. Senator.
Page 129. (1615) m. Jas. Young and had dau. Caro. m. 2d Wm. Young. m 3rd Chas. H. Dow, and had dau. Frank Belle.
Page 132 (1689) m. Cornelia A Backus.
" 150. (2010) b. Jan. 31, 1791 (791) erase B.
(2011) m. Jan. 4. 1801 (2013). b. Jan. 31, d. July, 20, 1853.
(2016) b. May. 24, m. Apr. 28, 1824.
(2019) b. Jan. 23.
Page 151. (794) read Durgin. (2026) m. Sept. 20.
(2030) m. July 4, 1824. (2032) m. Harvey 1825.
(2034) Res. Northwood, N. H.
Page 152. (802) m. Dame. (2056) b. Jan. 9, 1808, d, Nov. 29, 1897. Abigail. d. May 5, 1854.
" 153. (2099) res. also in Northwood, N. H.
154 (2083) Res. Deerfield, N. H.
(2193) m. Lampson.
164. (2288) Lewis A. m. 1st Caroline Pendleton. He d. 1898.
(2291) d. young. (2292) m. Jeannette Wylie.
Page 169 (2380) Aaron B. b. Dec. 14, 1835, m. Martha Cline, Oct. 20, 1864.
(2393) m. Julia Piper.
Page 169. [2393] Dexter Derby and Julia Piper had [1] Samuel Carroll Mar. 3, 1842, m. Eunice H. Ransom Aug. 29, 1872.
(2)Emily Elizabeth, Nov. 26, 1846.
Samuel C. and Eunice H. Ransom had
Florence Harlow, Nov. 8, 1873.
Alice Greenwood, Oct. 24, 1878.
Eunice d. Nov. 4. 1881, and Samuel C. m. 2d Frances G. Janney, Dec. 27, 1883, and had
[1] Walter Janney, Oct. 23, 1884.
[2] Dorothy Frances, May 2, 1889.
Samuel C. Derby is Prof. of Latin, and Dean of the College of Arts, Philosophy and Science in the Ohio State University at Columbus.
Page 172. (2465) Res. Dublin, N. H.
" 180. Carl was grandson of Joshua.
" 182. (2662) m. Philip Staats.
" 192. (2840 A.) Amos.
" (2851) b. Jan. (2853) b. 1823. (2851) b. April 1828. Daniel m. 2d Mrs. Judith Knowlton Smith, d. 1860.
Page 194. (2864 A) Lucina, m. Frederick Hodgman.
" 195. Robert H, m. Mary A. Butler.
George Gay b. 1825, m, Isabelle Kelsey.
Robert W. and Miriam had also Mary, b. Jan 20, 1835, d. 1842.
For Fairfield N. Y., read Esperance, Schoharie Co.
" 202. (3015) m. Luman Eno. (3017) m. Extein.
Page 206. (3089) m. Chaffee.
" 208. (3097) m. Geraldine Sunderland, of Willington, Conn, June 25, 1891.
" 218. (3213) m. Marilla. (3234) m. Grant.
" 221. (3282) m. Lora Nason.
" 234. (3558) m. Hon. Wm. Burnham Woods.
" " (3558 A.) Willard Jr. m. Eliza W. Woods, U. S. Senator from Alabama.
(3558 B.) Helen, m. J. L. Robbins, Newark, O.
" 267. (4098) Elijah W. (4100) m. Dr. Harwood Wakeman.
" 285. (4424) Mayhew P. (4425) d. Dec. 13, 1891. (4431) March 26. (4434) d. Dec. 18, 1858.
(4435) b. Sept. 21, 1822, d. 1867. (4438) b. Aug. 30, Nancy d 1869.

Page 286. Erase (4447—4450) (4456) b. Mar. 15. (4461) b. 1848. (4462) b. 1841, Res. Northwood, Nathaniel d. Dec. 6, 1886.
Page 289. [4517] b. June 19.
" 291. Read lineally connected with [4543] Edith A. and Ethel S. [4544] Alrie Res. Gloucester.
Page 299. Amos m. 2d Mrs. Rhoda A. Bull and d. May 21.
" 300. Read Louisianna Lampson.
" 305. [4800] [4801] child. of Lewis A. and Lizzie Pendleton, 2d wife, m. June 8, 1859, Res. Belfast Me. He m. 1st, Caroline Pendleton. For [2091] read [2292] Abina and Jeanette. They had also Rita, Almatia, Eva, Cyrus and Roy, Erase line Jeannette d. &c.
Page 312. [4944] b. Oct. 14. [4945] b. April 26, 1869. [4946] William b. Feb. 22, A. B. rem. to Wilbraham, Mass.
Page 316. (2468) Moore d. after 1855, and Elmira m. 2d Coggeshall 1858, and had (5012), (5013).
Page 329. (5242), (5247) Soldiers in Civil War.
" 330. (5254) d. 1871.
" 331. (5267) m. Dec. 31, 1857. (5271 A) Myron N. July 7, 1847, Unm. Nathaniel d. Dec. 19, 1897.
Page 332. (5282) m. 2d Isaac Reid, of Cincinnati.
" 338. (5304) m. David A. Briscoe, of Duxbury, Mass., Aug. 25, 1895.
(Page 342. (5378) Chas. S. Chaffee and Martha B. George had
" (1) Hattie M. July 20, 1866, m. Emil A. Danielson July 6, 1887.
" (2) Frank S. July 19, 1870. m. Kittie Whitney Oct. 1887.
" 346. (5430) Res. St. Augustine, Fla.
" (2850) Sarah d. Nov. 1865.
Page 347. (5448) m. Chrisler (5451) b. 1854.
" 357. Read Orson Moulton.
" 358. Read Chas. L. when twenty-one years.
" 360. She d. April 4. 1885.
" 362. (5626 B) Oct. 14. 1861, (5626 C) Jan. 23, 1865.
" 364. [5645] m. Comee. [5651] m. Dec. 29, 1892.
" [3152] Res. Andover, Mass.,
Page 365. (3178) m. Rev. Kumler. [5658] m. Wm. M.
" 369. [5728] b. May.
" 370. [5742] Unm. [5743] m. J. M. Anthony.
" 380. [5919 A] Frank.
" 387. Nathaniel Pettes, bro. of J. C. presented the Library Building.
" 414 [6349] William, Res. Portland, Me.
" 422 [6451] b. Oct. 11, 1865, d. Sept. 17, 1896.
" " [6452] Lillian F. b. Mar. 8, 1871.
" " [6453] b. Feb. 27, 1873.
" " [6454] b. Mar. 9, 1877.
" " There were also children, Richard W., Horace, Arthur and Grace.
Page 423. first line, Sept. 1862.
" 426. Erase (6508). (6510) Junie. (6511) Bertha m.
" 444. (4721 A.) read Worthby.
" 445. Freeman and Jennie had also Effie, Bessie, and Francis P.
" 452. Edwin F. d. Oct 25, 1898.
" 459. Phineas has been Deacon of First Church, Wilbrahom, Mass. since 1878.
Page 461. (7086) d. Dec 5. 1897, Unm.
" 463. (7104) d. July 5, 1863. (7105) m. George Pratt.
" " (7108) He d. at North Adams. Mass, Aug. 1897.
" " (7110) m. Alfred Johnson, Feb. 20, 1865. She d. July 7, 1897.
" " (7111) m. Chas. Fowler, Apr 9, 1868.
" " [5278] m. 2d. Sophia M; m. 3d Sarah Dan
" 464. (7120) m. Bessie L. Howery.
" " (7127) m. Clara Watson. July 3, 1894.
" 468 Erase "After Dr. Pierce's death."
" " (7146) Surgeon, U. S. N.

Page 468 [7147] m. A. May Angell, Feb. 10, 1891, and had John Angell, Feb. 1, 1892.
" " Dorothia DeWolf, Oct. 16, 1893.
" " Margaret Knowlton, July 26, 1895.
" " Ernest H. was graduated from Brown University in 1888, and from the Boston Institute of Technology in 1890. Res. Providence, R. I.
[7148] Edward Ihara, m. Fannie D. Gladding, Dec. 27, 1897, and and had Roger. Res. in Providence, R. I. A lawyer.
Henrietta Knowlton, Angell Brownell d. Oct. 15, 1897.
Page 474. [7216] m. Ella L. Gilligan, of Plainfield, N. J., and had J. Russell Jr., Elsie L., Walter E., Res. Ridgewood, N. J.
[7218] m. Carrie Huff Anderson, 1884, and had Grace Edna, William Howard, d. young. He m. 2d Mary Hopper of Ridgewood, N. J., and had George E. Jr. 1897. Res. Ridgewood, N. J.
Page 475. [5658] read, Ella L. Kumler and Wm. M. McElvey had [7230 D.] Jeremiah Dwight.
Page 501. [10] Nellie.
" 506. [8] m. Chas. Barton. m. 2d Benjamin Johnson, [12] b. Oct. 10, m. Osborn.
Page 508. See [2143] for Betsey and Amasa.
See [1042] for Elizabeth and Frank.
Page 509. See [3247] for Frederick and Ida.
See [3883] for John C. and Frances.
[5962] for Sophia Knowlton Rice and J. H. Hess.
Page 512. See (2832 B.) for Edwin C. and Mary.
" " " [3649] for Arthur R. and Etta.
" " " [4207] for Isaac and Georgiana Brackett.
" " " [464] for Silas B. and Mehitable.
" " " [1524] for William and Elida.
Page 513. " [1] Chester S. m. Mary Elizabeth Gould.

ERRATA.

Owing to the reception of sundry family records after the body of this work was in type, and individuals numbered, it became necessary to indicate supplemental names alphabetically, and, in a few cases, out of their numerical order.

(45) Benjamin was killed in 1745.
(247) d. young. His brother (250) m. Comfort Holman.
(477) Miriam. m. James Lockhart.
(1680) Edward. m. Cornelia Backus.
(1683) Remove Dorcas Monahan to 1684.
(1897) Erase Timothy from children of Moses.
(1911) Read Anstice instead of Austice.
(2093 c) Read Mehitable True.
(3303) S. B. Slater.
(3554) Erase death date.
(3089) Chaffee, not Chaffer.
(3090) Erase from Miriam's children.
(5614) March 20.
(6237) Froment family misnumbered. See Supplement.

Knowlton

I Henry Farnham Burke, Esquire, F.S.A. Somerset Herald of Arms and Genealogist of the Order of Saint Patrick, do hereby certify and declare that the Arms above depicted, namely:– Argent a chevron between three crowns or ducal coronets sable, are entered to the name of KNOWTON in a manuscript alphabet of Arms which was probably compiled in the time of King George the First.

As Witness my Hand and Seal at London this 27th day of October 1896.

H. Farnham Burke
Somerset Herald

Crest: A Demi-Lion Rampant.
Motto: "Vi Et Virtute."

THE KNOWLTON FAMILY GENEALOGY

CHAPTER I

The Knowltons of England

AMONG the stories of the Middle Ages, there is a tradition of two brothers enlisting in the service of William the Conqueror, and fighting so bravely during his invasion of Wales that they readily won their spurs. Having observed that they resided, the one on a hill and the other on a knoll, or lesser hill, the king, on investing them with the honors and insignia of knighthood, dubbed them Hill-ton and Knoll-ton. Whatever of truth may attach to this tradition, it is certain that the name is an ancient one, born out of its own native soil. A large proportion of English proper names has been suggested by local situations and associations, and of these the name Knowlton is one of the most striking, as it is one of the most ancient. The suffix *ton* is the old Saxon *tún*, town, so that in its primary use it meant the people, or town, on the knoll, but in process of time it lost this collective force, and was applied to the chief family, or personage, resident thereon. For the purpose both of government and revenue, the English people were grouped in Hundreds, so called because one hundred families were made to comprise one district, or borough.

In Domesday Book, that curious and quaint record of estates and surveys which the Conqueror ordered in 1083, that he might know the extent of his realm and provide for the royal revenues, there was a Knowlton Hundred, originally but a mere hamlet in Dorsetshire, which became by royal appointment a Fair Town, and a rural centre of considerable importance. The original hamlet and manor have long since passed away, but the name survives, and its present boundaries include Knowlhill, Long Crichel, Crichel-Govis, Crichel-Lucy, All Saints, Boreson, Week Farm, Phillipston, and Woodlands. This estate was anciently held by Ansgar, and in Domesday Book the name is Chenoltone, while in subsequent books it is indifferently spelled Cnolton, Knolton, Knollton, Knowlton, Knoulton, Knowton, Knowlden,* Nowton, Noulton, and Nelton. A

* Knowlden means, "at the foot of the knoll."

careful inspection of the Wills and Administrations in the Prerogative Courts of Canterbury and York reveals these varied spellings of the one and same name, for it is differently spelled in the same document, and by the same person. When the reader remembers that proper names were until a very recent date spelled phonetically, or according to their sound, he will find a ready explanation of these singular orthographies.

Knowlton Parish and Knowlton Hall still designate a Manor and Baronial Residence in Kent County, six miles from the archiepiscopal city of Canterbury. It originally belonged to Odo, Bishop of Baieux, who was subsequently disgraced, and his property confiscated to the Crown. In the fifteenth year of the Conqueror, the estate was surveyed, and given to one of his followers, from whom it passed by Knight's service to Perot, and thence to other owners. In the thirty-third year of Edward the First, Perot assumed the title of Lord Knollton, an early example of the transfer of a proper name from the soil to its owner. Lord Knowlton left the estate to his daughter Christian, who married William de Langley, High Sheriff under Edward III. (1327–77). His son called himself William Knollton, Esq., during the reign of Henry VI. (1429–71). In the twentieth year of Henry VII. (1505), William's son John (whose son and successor, Edward, married Elizabeth Peyton, daughter of Sir John Peyton, who was the next owner) came into possession, and he married Dorothy Tyndal, daughter of Sir John Tyndal, Governor of the Tower of London. His grandson and heir, Thomas, had children, Dorothy, Catherine, William, and Thomas. From the time when Sir Perot adopted the title Lord Knollton, down to the day of Sir D'Aeth, it is matter of history that the lords of this manor were known indifferently both by their surnames and by their adopted titles, and the Parish and Hall now perpetuate that historic fact. Knowlton Hall is a fine residence situated on a knoll in a beautiful park of two hundred acres, which are kept in a high state of cultivation, and adorned with the choicest creations of the gardener's artistic genius. The land is gently rolling, affording an agreeable diversity of hill and dale, and beautiful walks and paths entice one into the shade of grand old trees that have delighted for ages the eyes that faded out of human life centuries ago.

An examination of the fragmentary histories and ecclesiastical records of the sixteenth century discloses the fact that the names of these Kentish Knowltons are precisely those that appear and reappear, again and again, among the families of the Knowltons of at least five succeeding generations. Every Knowlton of this period was found within, or near, the county of Kent, and the conclusion would appear to be irresistible that the surname itself came from this particular estate. Indeed, the name could never have been used here in its original and wider significance, for there is not at present, nor has there ever been, even a village settlement here. Besides the Hall, there are only the Rectory and two farm-houses on the estate, and the whole parish reports but twenty-six souls.

Thomas Knowlton, the antiquarian hereafter mentioned, was fond of telling of the distinction enjoyed by one of his ancestors, a retainer of the Earl of Warwick, who always appeared in Court dress, with a silver and jewelled sword at his belt, and other insignia of rank, and who stood high with the King He had charge of one of the Earl's castles in Kent, and was a descendant of the Knowltons above referred to. A granddaughter (Mrs. H. S. Perkins, now living) has often heard the above and many other interesting facts told by the Knowltons concerning the position of their ancestors.

There were Knowltons in Canterbury, and in the City of London as early as 1550, and the published "Visitations and Allegations of the Provinces of York and Canterbury" clearly show that they were never a numerous or a scattered family, but that until the year 1728 they were confined entirely to the counties of Middlesex and Kent. They invariably married by license instead of by banns, which as invariably indicates a recognized social position and condition of comfort, for such license could be obtained only from the Archbishop of Canterbury, and at considerable expense—about £50. In these old records the titles of Mr. and Esq. are frequently used, indicating a social status above that of the common people.

The identity of location, the dates of birth, and the constant repetition of the names of children—and the very names which were given to the children in the New World—would seem to fix beyond any reasonable doubt the ancestry of the first emigrants to America, and to derive their descent from the Knowltons of the old Kentish Manor. It is sufficiently clear that the English progenitors were people of substance, and their occupations were by no means menial. Captain William, the first emigrant, sailed his own ship, and George, his probable brother, was a subscriber in 1624 to a fund for repairing the parish church at Chiswick, which Cromwell's troops had desecrated by converting it into a barrack and stable for his men and their horses.

---

1 Richard of Kent, b. 1553, m. Elizabeth Cantize, July 17, 1577, and had:

(2) George, May 6, 1578. He res. in Chiswick.
(3) Stephen, May 1, 1580. d. young.
(4) Thomas, 1582. m.
(5) William, 1584. m. Ann Elizabeth Smith.

The first two children were b. in the parish of Canterbury, Kent. The great Cathedral is but six miles from Knowlton Manor, and the parish boundaries included at that time the latter. The Manor is now in the parochial boundaries of neighboring Sandwich.

4 Thomas and —— had:

(6) John, 1620. m. Dorothy ——, 1643.
(7) Robert, 1622. m. Susan ——; m. 2d Sarah ——
(8) Mary, 1628. m. John Wilson, April 26, 1651.
(9) Sarah, 1630. m. Augustine Ellis, February 23, 1656.

5 William and Elizabeth had:

(10) John, 1610.
(11) Samuel, 1611.
(12) Robert, 1613. Remained in England. Said to have d. young.
(13) William, 1615.
(14) Mary, 1617. d. young.
(15) Thomas, 1620–2.

Captain William emigrated to America about 1632–4

6 John and Dorothy —— had:

(16) Elizabeth, May 26, 1644.
(17) John, January 14, 1649.
(18) James, September 26, 1650.
(19) Mary, December 18, 1652.

John d. in London 1664, and was buried from St. James Church, Clerkenwells. He is styled a householder.

7 Robert and Susan had:

(20) Ann, January 24, 1644. m. Marcus Gilmanothe, April 11, 1768.
(21) John. d. September 30, 1649.
(22) Dorothy. d. January 7, 1650.
(23) William, 1652. m. Maria ——

Susan d. February 10, 1653, and Robert m. 2d Sarah —— and had:

(24) Sara, October 2, 1655.

Robert d. December 30, 1655.

23 William and Maria had:

(25) John, 1688. m. Elizabeth, 1731.
(26) Thomas, 1690. m. Elizabeth Rice, 1726. m. 2d Mrs. Elizabeth Stephenson, November 17, 1744.

William was a West India merchant. He d. in 1713, and Letters of Administration were granted to —— Chadwell, a creditor, by consent of Widow Maria.

---

25 John and Elizabeth had:

(27) John, 1732. m. d. at Londesboro, Yorkshire, October 21, 1813.
(28) Mary. m. Edward Hare.
(29) William. m. Had chil., John, William and Elizabeth.
(30) Ann Gilmanothe.

John's will was probated September 30, 1781, and the following extract shows him to have been a man of substance.

"I, John Knowlton, Quilton, in the County of Northampton, Gardener to the Right Hon. Earl Fitzwilliam, do make this my last will and testament in manner & form following: i. e. I give unto my dear wife Elizabeth Knowlton £500 to be paid to her within one month after my decease, also during her natural life the Interest & Dividends from £500 in stock of South Sea Annuits also £200 to be invested in Lands & Securities. . . . And whereas, I have before given my oldest Son John £300, and to my daughter Mary, wife of Edward Hare £300, and to my youngest Son William £100 and to Ann G. my daughter £80, and in order that they may now have equality in my Substance, it is my wish that William should be paid £200, and my daughter Ann G. £220. . . . I give and bequeath the Interest of £500 to my son William's children, John and Elizabeth, until John shall be 15 years old and be apprenticed, but after that time one half of the income to be given to William's daughter Elizabeth until she is 17 years of age."

A special bequest was made to Edward Hare who was one of the executors, John and William, sons of the testator, being the other two.

John and his brother Thomas early developed a remarkable gift for landscape gardening, and their genius soon attracted the attention and secured the liberal encouragement of noble patrons. John entered the service of the Earl Fitzwilliam of Northumberland. The magnificent estates of the Earl gave ample scope for John's talents, and he spent there the years of a long and successful life, which ended in the summer of 1781. He was 93 years old, and was buried in Londesboro churchyard, Yorkshire.

27 John and ---- had :

(31) Charles, 1765. m. Jane —— Who had :

(32) Frances Hare Knowlton, 1807. m. Clarke Morris, May 28, 1833. They had :

(33) Mary Jane, May 20, 1834. m. Rev. R. Nutt.
(34) John, August 25, 1835. m. Hannah P. Rooke. d. June 1880.
(35) Frances, January 4, 1837. m. W. Keal. M. R. C. S. W.
(36) William Clarke, Jan. 23, 1838. d. March 25, 1895.
(37) Charles Knowlton, March 8, 1841. Res. Oakham.
(38) Susan Elizabeth, June 22, 1844. m. Rev. W. J. Stobart.
Residence, Oakham.

Charles Knowlton (31) d. August 26, 1848. Jane d. May 17, 1848. They were buried in Branston churchyard, Oakham, England.

Frances H. (32) d. April 22, 1878. Aged 71 years.
Clarke Morris d. August 11, 1857. Aged 61 years.

Thomas (1690) had a more conspicuous position, and, consequently, a more public record. At a very early age he entered the service of Dr. Wm. Sherard at Eltham, a suburb of London, where he at once and for a long time after, left the impress of his genius. This country seat was owned by a graduate and Fellow of Oxford University, whose remarkable devotion to the science of botany amounted to a passion. He had been an extensive traveller in foreign countries, while tutor to Lord Howland, subsequently the Earl of Bedford, and, later on, British Consul to Smyrna, and had, therefore, exceptional opportunities of collecting the rarest plants of the Orient. He founded a large herbarium in Smyrna, enriching it with a marvellous variety of floral and botanical wealth, and his reputation soon admitted him to the intimate friendship of Boerhaave, Hermann, Tournefort, Vaillant, and Micheli. So assiduous was he, so fearless and adventurous along the lines of his favorite researches, that he was at one time nearly shot, having been mistaken for a wolf. In the year 1700 he returned to England, and with his brother, a noted physician of London, settled at Eltham, bringing to their charming home the fruits of his exhaustive researches in the East.

It is no small tribute to Thomas Knowlton that he was selected by two such gentlemen to become their landscape gardener when still a very young man. The Earl of Burlington owned, as Duke of Devonshire, large estates in this vicinity, and the gardens of Eltham could not have failed to arrest his admiring attention, for in 1728 he offered Mr. Knowlton the charge of his country seat at Londesboro, Yorkshire. Whoever has had the good fortune to visit this delightful spot will readily understand the inspiration which the natural topography of the country would furnish to a mind keenly appreciative of the beautiful. The estate is situated in a fine rolling country, two and a half miles from the quaint old Fair Town of Market Weighton, whose smooth white roads, hard as adamant, wind over hill and through dale, past greenest pastures where sleek cattle feed, among groups of white cottages whose clustering vines are not a whit more attractive than the unpretentious comfort within, and by the inevitable and picturesque churches, such as the faith and liberality of past generations have planted here and all over Mother England. Arrived at Londesborough one sees a charming foreground, than which there is none in all the Yorkshire Wolds more worth lingering over. Great stretches of crisp lawn, avenues of stately yews, flowers of every tint and species massed in banks on which raindrops are glistening, and flanked by grand old groves in which the woodman's axe has not been heard for many a century, delight the eye.

Londesborough House stands on the summit of a terrace, at the foot of which is a lovely lake, into which the bending trees dip their branches, and the passing clouds are mirrored.

The colossal towers of York Minster, and the graceful spires of Selby, Howden and Goole are all in sight, and at evening one can turn the pages of Gray and read back into the poetic past as he hears "the curfew toll the knell of parting day." Not long before Thomas Knowlton came here the plain around was but a marsh, and the hand of philanthropy found no better or more imperative work than that of building a cell for two pious monks who should serve as guides to strangers. If the author pauses to indulge in this retrospective reverie, it is because the life and character of men are so largely the product of their surroundings. In a less poetic spot Thomas Knowlton might never have been known beyond the sound of his village bells. But Londesborough had been the theatre of tragic events. Romans, Angles, and Saxons, the Bloody Clifford and his chastened son, the "Shepherd Lord," the Burlingtons and their congenial friends, Pope, Garrick, Sydney Smith, Wyatt, and Violette, the Viennese champion danseuse of the world, were all here. The villa of Edwin the Saxon was also here on the Derwent, and, being converted to Christianity, he is said to have destroyed a pagan temple, and on its ruins to have erected the parish church where, centuries after, the Knowltons found their spiritual home, and under the shadow of which they were buried. Here for twenty-four years the "Shepherd Lord" lived in concealment, he having inherited the estate from his mother, the Baroness de Vesoi, of Bromfleet. After his death the estate passed to Richard Boyle, third Earl of Burlington, in whose service and in that of his successors the Knowltons lived for 115 years. Burlington having died without male issue, the estate passed to the Duke of Devonshire, who had married his daughter. This powerful family, then and since the richest in all England, had magnificent estates all over the British dominion, and the Knowltons had ample scope for the exercise of their gifts.

Under the skilful hand of Thomas Knowlton, the Londesborough estate became famous among its English rivals. He was a diligent student for those times, and Frederic the Great was so much his military ideal that he arranged the gardens in the form of Prussian battalions.

His love for his favorite science created a spirit of discovery and adventure that introduced him to the *Savans* of the Royal Society, and he became a valued correspondent of Da Costa, Mark Catesby, and others. He was accustomed to wade for hours in ponds of cold water in his search for rare species of aquatic plants, and on one of these expeditions he discovered the "moor ball," a species of the fresh-water algæ of the *Conferva* family, called by Linnæus "Egagropila," from its resemblance to the hairy balls found in the stomachs of goats. A botanic genus of the *Ranunculaceæ*, comprising five or six species of plants indigenous to the Cape of Good Hope, has been named after him. Mr. Knowlton also discovered the site of Delgovicia, a long buried camp and temple of the Romans under Septimius Severus. In the "Philosophical Transactions of the Royal Society" are found extracts of letters written in 1767. He says:

"We dug in several places, and discovered a circular foundation 5 ft. wide, and the place within 45 ft. in diameter, which, it seems, was a temple to Diana, said to have been at Goodmanham, but no appearance of it there was ever found. There were many other foundations which had Roman pavements within them, by which, after the dissolution of the Temple, it became a Roman station, then called Delgovicia. In this just discovered the ruins and foundations are a demonstration of the once grandeur of the place."

He also discovered the site of a great battle-field in which

"vast numbers fell, and were so laid in heaps, and covered with the chalky soil in little *tumuli* of the space of 2 or 3 square yards, in which were found great quantities of human bones. And now there is an acre covered over with them lying close to each other, and it is one of the greatest curiosities ever seen."

Among the curious treasures of the Museum of the Royal Society of London are two pairs of deer's horns, unearthed by Mr. Knowlton after they had been buried for eight hundred years in the river Rye, a tributary of the Derwent. One measured from the nose to the top of the skull 22 inches, and to the tip of the horn 24 ft. and both skull and horns weighed 68 lbs. The horns of the other are shorter, but the space between them measures six feet; another breadth of the palm or web is 25 inches; enormous as they are, they were not of full growth, as they were covered with "velvet." They were found buried 6 ft. deep.

Londesborough House,
Yorkshire, England.

Mr. Thomas Knowlton, F.R.A.,
Antiquarian and Botanist,
Londesborough, Eng., 1690–1781.

Mr. Knowlton made voluminous contributions to botanical and antiquarian literature, and his taste and judgment were in constant request from other estates than Londesborough. His son Charles entered Cambridge University, being matriculated in St. John's College in 1746, and while on a visit there, Thomas Knowlton wrote, with discriminating eye and characteristic vigor, to Prof. Da Costa :

"I received your most valuable present which I find abounding in plates, and that he (the author) has copied most of 'Rumphus on Shells' in every plate, and well copied they are, and that without taking any notice from whence so taken. I hope ere long to make you some returns. It is said by most people that Yorkshire hams are very much admired, and if you should think so I will send some up if you will let me know whether they will be agreeable.

"I was at Cambridge, but was greatly disappointed in the design of the Physic Garden which is laid out so preposterously that instead of pleasing gives a disgust designed to please the ignorant rather then the curious, and Miller is not often seen in the garden, having a salary for walking about. Of all the gardens I ever saw, it is the worst furnished. I will say no more, truly lamenting that the design is so erroneously conducted."

Mr. Knowlton's home was a favorite resort of Dr. Johnson, Drake the historian, Dr. Fothergill, and the great Garrick, and a stone bench is still shown which was the chosen seat of Pope. The integrity of this remarkable man is illustrated by the following incident :

A young lady of high position had married against her parents' will, and her father promptly disinherited her, and bequeathed his large estates to Thomas Knowlton. On learning the facts in the case, Mr. Knowlton made search for the lady, found her in London, and conveyed to her all that he had received from her father. The grateful lady made the long journey from London to Londesboro in her private carriage—a long journey in those days—to express in person her unspeakable gratitude for this noble act of Knowlton. "Madam," replied Thomas, "I deserve no thanks. The property was yours, not mine. I could never have kept it."

His devotion to his favorite science was so intense and his idiosyncrasies so marked, that he requested to be buried in the pleasure grounds which he had beautified, and for this purpose he selected his own burial plot. But in later years the Parish Wardens enlarged the boundaries of the churchyard, and so took Thomas in.

26 Thomas and Elizabeth Rice had :

(39) Charles, bap. December 9, 1727. m. Sarah Fowler, of Keighley, December 19, 1755.

Elizabeth dying, Thomas m. 2d Mrs. Elizabeth Stephenson, November 17, 1744, and had :

(40) Elizabeth, 1745. m. Robert Wilson, July 19, 1769.

Thomas d. November 28, 1781, aged 91. His 2d wife, Elizabeth, d. April 12, 1797, aged 83. They are both buried in Londesboro churchyard, Yorkshire.

---

39 Rev. Charles and Sarah Fowler had :

(41) Thomas, June 10, 1758. d. 1836.
(42) Elizabeth, March 21, 1760. m. Robert Dawson, August 1, 1793.
(43) Charles S., bap. December 14, 1761. d. December 18, 1761.
(44) Charles, July 6, 1764. m.
(45) Sarah, bap. January 22, 1767. d. June 9, 1845.

Rev. Charles d. January 28, 1814, aged 87.

---

40 Elizabeth Knowlton and Robert Wilson had :

(46) Elizabeth, August 9, 1770. m. Samuel Stavles.
(47) Mary, August 17, 1772. m. Seth Stavles.
(48) Thomas Knowlton, December 23, 1774. m. Elizabeth Lawson.
(49) Robert, October 6, 1777.

Elizabeth d. December 23, 1821, aged 77. Robert Wilson owned and operated a tannery in Pocklington, England, and one of his sons became a reputable physician.

---

42 Elizabeth Knowlton and Robert Dawson had :

(50) Thomas.
(51) Becket.
(52) Charles Knowlton. Graduated at Oxford University.
(53) A daughter. m. —— Gerforth, of Steeton, Eng. She was a famous beauty.

Robert Dawson dying, Elizabeth m. 2d —— Duckitt, of Bardford, England. Both of Elizabeth's husbands were wine merchants. The Duckitt family numbered one son and two daughters, one of whom still resides in Scarboro, England, unm.

Mrs. Elizabeth Knowlton Wilson,
Pocklington, Yorkshire, England.

Reverend Charles Knowlton, M.A.,
Rector of Keighley, and Canon of York,
Yorkshire, England, 1727–1814.

44 Charles and —— had:

(54) Charles. Who m. and had a daughter and son:

(55) Helen.

(56) Arthur.

The former resides at Sydenham, Upper Level, England, where she is a partner in a fancy goods firm. Her father, Charles, was a merchant, and d. in London, 1857.

---

48 Thomas Knowlton Wilson and Elizabeth Lawson had:

(57) Elizabeth. m. Thomas Hopper. He d.

(58) Thomas K. d. young.

(59) Margaret.

(60) Charles Knowlton. d. in the India Mutiny.

Mrs. Elizabeth Hopper has two daughters. They all reside in Princess Crescent, Scarboro, England's most delightful watering-place, where they dispense a gracious hospitality, and both honor, and are honored by, the Knowlton blood.

Rev. Charles Knowlton (39), son of Thomas, graduated from Cambridge University in 1751, and, on taking Holy Orders in 1753, was presented by the Earl of Burlington to the living of Keighley, Yorkshire. This was one of the oldest rectories in England, its first minister having been settled there in 1245. Keighley is an old Saxon proper name, meaning the field of Kihel. In Domesday Book it is surveyed as the property of Ralph de Kighley, Knight, whose son Richard bestowed it on the prior and canons of the neighboring monastery of Bolton. After the dissolution of the monasteries, the parish and ecclesiastical patronage passed into the hands of the Earl of Cumberland, and subsequently to the Earls of Burlington, the third of whom, the Rt. Hon. Sir Richard Boyle, was the owner of Londesborough Manor, and other enormous estates, and the patron of Thomas Knowlton. Five priors had successively been at the head of this ancient parish, and Charles Knowlton was the twenty-first rector. He found here a famous agricultural district, with a widely scattered people, who were more thrifty than cultured. An examination of the parish registers written up by him during his unprecedentedly long rectorship of sixty-one years, reveals the average literary attainment of his people, for, of the great numbers whom he officially admitted to the holy estate of matrimony, only a very few could write their own names, the most of them simply making their mark. Mr. Knowlton ministered in a rude age, and to a rude people, who were the natural product of the country itself. Keighley is situated in a mountainous district, on the side of hills, to climb which habitually both requires and develops a sturdy physique.

The visitor, however, is well repaid for the effort, for a splendid panorama is then unfolded to the delighted eye, and the beauty of the encircling hills as they retreat towards the horizon, standing sentry over the rich pastures between, is enhanced by the waters of the sylvan Aire, that flows through and among them. The character of the people in Mr. Knowlton's time is set forth in the following lines of a poet of that day.

"Thence to Keighley where are mountains
Sleepy, threatening, lively fountains,
Rising hills and pleasant valleys,
Bon Socias and good fellows,
Jovial, jocund, jolly bowlers,
As if they were the world's controllers."

There is here an allusion to a prevailing passion for bowling and other rude sports, in which Mr. Knowlton is said to have participated freely, and thus to have made himself exceedingly popular among the lusty Yorkshiremen. Bull-baiting was a local amusement which was long fostered by a strange superstition. The bull was fastened to a ring in a huge stone, directly in front of the church, and worried by dogs, under the pretence that only thus could the beef be made fit for use, and candles were burned before it day and night as long as it was exposed for sale. Before Mr. Knowlton's death the brutal sport had been discontinued, not unlikely through his influence, for his reputation was that of a generous and kind-hearted pastor, who was not in sympathy with any form of cruelty. He was as great a favorite with the female portion of his flock as with the male, being handsome in person and courtly in manners.

He married Miss Sarah Fowler of Keighley, Dec. 19, 1755, by whom he had

(41) Thomas, June 2, 1758.
(42) Elizabeth, March 13, 1760.
(43) Charles, December 7, 1761. d. in infancy.
(44) Charles, June 29, 1764.
(45) Sarah, January 14, 1767.

During the rectorship of Mr. Knowlton, Keighley became a manufacturing town, large quantities of woollen goods being made for the London market, and it was probably the loss of a part of its rural beauty that caused a crusty old historian to write:

"This parish lyeth immediately North of Bingley in the course of the Arc, without one feature or one fact belonging to it which can interest the eye, the memory, or the imagination. I may then be excused if I betray some anxiety to reach pleasanter scenes, for hard is the fate of a Topographer while he respires the smoak of manufactories, and is stunned by the din of recent populations."

The River Aire, from Keighley Rectory,
Yorkshire, England.

KEIGHLEY PARISH CHURCH,
Yorkshire, England.

Mr. Knowlton was appointed one of the Canons of York Minster, and was widely known and honored. He died June 28, 1814, at the ripe old age of 87, and was buried under the chancel of his venerable parish church, which still remains the one conspicuous architectural feature of old Keighley. His name is cast in the door of an iron safe where the parish registers are kept, and a wooden tablet in black and gold marks the date of his rectorship.

Of his three remaining children, but one married. Elizabeth Knowlton became the wife of Mr. Robert Dawson, August 1, 1793.

Thomas Knowlton (41), son of Rev. Charles, inherited the genius and followed the profession of his grandfather. At an early age he entered the service of the Earl of Burlington, and by a diligent use of his opportunities became not only a famous landscape gardener, but also a man of affairs, and the agent of the Earl of Burlington and of his heir the Duke of Devonshire. Sarah, his sister, had charge of Burlington House at Londesborough, and as such she appears in the letters of Lady Granville. When twenty-four years of age, she was considered by all the great people of Burlington House as a remarkable beauty. Even in middle life, she was declared by the Duke of Devonshire to be the handsomest woman in Derbyshire.

CHATSWORTH.

All travelled Americans know something of "Beautiful Chatsworth," the favorite residence and estate of the Dukes of Devonshire. Their ancestors were lineal descendants from Robert de Gernon of Suffolk, who married the daughter of Lord Cavendish, and whose children, according to the custom of that time, took the name of Cavendish, out of compliment to the mother. Chatsworth was bought by Sir William Cavendish, Privy Councillor to Henry VIII., Edward VI., and Queen Mary, early in the sixteenth century, and on his death his son William, Baron Cavendish and Duke of Devonshire, succeeded to his father's enormous estates. He was a famous man both in statesmanship and letters, and a munificent patron of art. His mother, the celebrated "Bess of Hardwicke," began the building of Chatsworth, and devoted all her life to the work, under the influence of a prophecy that her life would be preserved as long as she should continue that work. A severe frost stopped the workmen, and the mortar was dissolved first in hot water and then in hot ale, but all to no purpose. The building ceased, and she died in 1607. Her son enlarged and improved what she had begun, under the supervision of Sir Christopher Wren, and Sir William Spencer, the ninth Duke of Devonshire, completed the work, making Chatsworth the most magnificent residence in the United Kingdom. The park is twelve miles in circuit, and is laid out with consummate and lavish beauty, and includes an orangery, conservatories covering one acre, an arboretum one hundred acres in extent, a French and a kitchen garden. Chatsworth House itself is a palace of art where have been brought the best creations of the sculptor's and the painter's genius, and through the liberality of its lordly owner a large part of it is open to tourists.

Here lived Thomas and Sarah Knowlton, the former being the agent of the eighth and ninth Dukes in the management of their vast possessions. The fact that Sir Joseph Paxton was his immediate successor sufficiently indicates the importance of the position and the great responsibility of its occupant. So large was the number of officials connected with the care and administration of Chatsworth that the "Great Duke," as he was called, decided to build a model village for their special use, and the result of that determination was

EDENSOR.

This is the most unique spot in all England, and it comprises a village, a parish, and a shire. There are thirty-six houses built in the form of Anglo-Swiss and Italian Gothic villas, each being different from all the others. The equipment is complete, there being besides the pretty residences a handsome church, post- and telegraph-offices, a school, and offices of the agent, or steward as his title is, and whose beautiful residence is the most pleasing architectural feature of Edensor, except the church. The latter is a modern structure built on the foundations of the old church in which the Knowltons worshipped, and preserving a portion of the original. The Lords of the Manor are buried here, and in the adjacent churchyard, the most interesting of whose monumental tablets is the one erected to Lord Cavendish who was cruelly murdered in Phœnix Park, Dublin. This tablet bears a touching inscription, and the following verses of Holy Scripture:

"Blessed Are The Peacemakers, For Theirs Is The Kingdom Of Heaven."
"Blessed Are The Pure In Heart, For They Shall See God."

The training which Thomas Knowlton had received from his grandfather, and the experience gained in the service of his noble patron, naturally made him the Duke's choice when he concluded to build his pet and model village. Mr. Knowlton therefore left Londesboro with his sister Sarah, and the two took up their residence at Chatsworth, the sister being his housekeeper, and having no other relation to the Duke and his family than that of a neighbor and friend. Her beauty and accomplishments had early attracted ardent suitors, one of whom had been accepted, and arrangements were made for the marriage, but a brief illness hurried her lover to his grave. Miss Knowlton resolutely shut, with her own hand, the golden gates of matrimonial affection, and never after permitted the addresses of admiring suitors.

LISMORE.

Among the Devonshire estates was Lismore with its famous castle. The aboriginal toparchs had selected this spot on account of its scenic attractions, calling it Magh-Sgiath, the "Chosen Field," and the earthworks around their

EDENSOR,
Derbyshire, England.
The Model Village of the Duke of Devonshire.

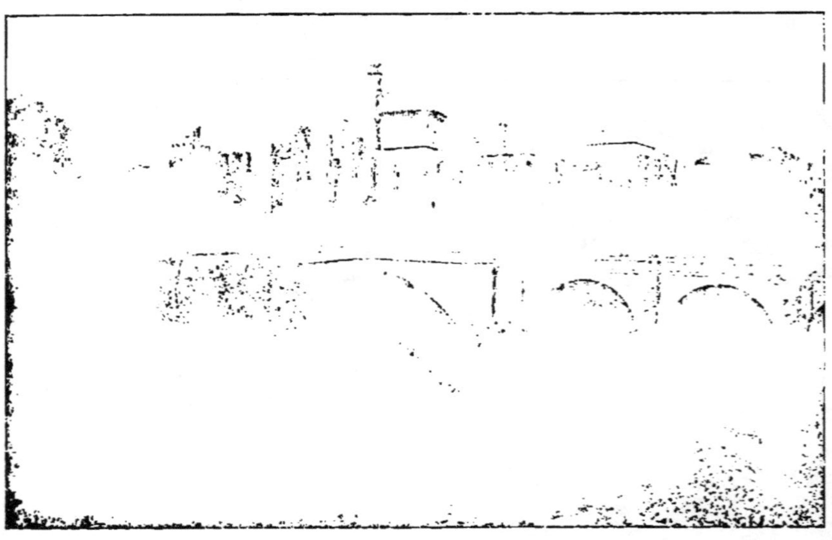

Lismore Castle, Ireland.

dwellings were of such extent that the site was named Lios-mor, the "Great Fortified Habitation." The pagan Lis, or Fort, was the abode of the old Irish chieftains. Saint Carthagh, a refugee monk of noble birth, built a great abbey here in 635, and in 1185 Prince John began the erection of the magnificent castle which now stands above the stream of the beautiful Blackwater, lifting its lofty towers two hundred feet above the deep moat and the murmuring river, one of the grandest fortresses ever devoted to the genius of beauty, and to the security of man in troublous times. Lismore and its castle were for centuries considered so choice a possession that the old Irish chieftains kept the red tide of war rolling through and around it for hundreds of years. The old chronicles say :

"Lis-Mor is a famous and holye Citie, half of which is an asylum into which no woman ever dare enter: but it is full of cells and holy monasteries; and religious men in great numbers abide there: and holy men flock there from all Ireland and Britain, beeing desyrous of going from thence to Christ."

Of the twenty churches once here, but two remain, one of them being the old Cathedral which was evolved from the Abbey of St. Carthagh. Alfred the Great was educated here, and here he gained that fame as a harpist that made him successful in gaining the ear of the Danish Prince. Queen Elizabeth bestowed this great property on Sir Walter Raleigh, who planted here the first potatoes Ireland ever had, and in these lordly apartments he enjoyed the first tobacco brought as a fragrant offering from the New World to the Old. Sir Walter sold this property to the same Sir Richard Boyle, Earl of Cork and Burlington, who became the patron of the English Knowltons, and thus its history is more or less identified with them. His duties as agent and steward of the Dukes of Devonshire called Thomas frequently to Lismore, and his office was at the arch in the great quadrangle shaded by a venerable beech of gigantic dimensions. Sir William Spencer, the ninth Duke, offered the permanent charge of the castle and estate to Thomas Knowlton, who had already had charge for 18 years, but as the family of His Grace resided there but a small portion of the year, and as Chatsworth afforded more scope for his abilities, and more congenial surroundings, Mr. Knowlton declined to hold the position longer. His work at Lismore survives, however, for Sir William interested himself in making Lismore something of an ideal village. He built long streets of stone and adobe cottages for the peasants and laborers, enclosing the highways in high stone walls, and building the cottages flush to the street. Many of them are but one story high, white or of neutral tints, and ornamented with flowers and shrubs, and presenting a tidy and extremely pleasing appearance. To the taste and energy of Thomas Knowlton, Lismore owes not a little of its quaint and picturesque beauty. His declination of the Duke's appointment led to his eventual retirement from active duty, and he retired to Darley Dale, in the famous Peak of Derbyshire, purchasing the estate of Darley House, now owned by the Pagets, where he resided with his sister until his death, in 1836. He was commissioned colonel of the regiment of Chatsworth Rifles, and though living the life of a civilian he always wore his sword and epaulettes even in the privacy of his home. He had a singular aversion to driving in a carriage, and his sister was obliged to enjoy without his company the elegant establishment of which a few remaining old people talk with admiring recollection. His time was spent in the field and gardens of Darley House, directing his laborers in beautifying his estate and in producing fruitful harvests.* He received an ample salary from the Duke until his death, and after making some special bequests, one of which was a perpetual dole of bread to the poor of Londesborough parish from Christmas to Easter, he left all his estate to his sister Sarah. He was buried at his own request with his grandparents, his uncle John, and his cousin John in Londesborough churchyard. He had served the Devonshire Dukes for about 50 years.

His sister survived him nine years. She is still remembered by a few old residents as a remarkably beautiful woman even in her old age, a lady of benevolent spirit, but very exclusive in social life. Her relations with the great people of Chatsworth House were of the most intimate character as appears from her correspondence, for she writes, New Year's Day, 1843:

"The Duke of Devonshire returned to Chatsworth on the 21st Inst, and the day following honored me with a call. I was at dinner, having only taken my Soup, and His Grace would leave the Drawing Room and come into the Dining Room where he carved for me. He is everything that is good and amiable."

Under date of July 6th, 1841, she writes to Hon. Paul Holland, of Knowlton, Quebec:

"I find you are a true Knowlton, never having sought for the arms of the family in the Herald's College. . . My brother and I had them from Mrs Adams who, you will recollect, was descended from my grandfather's brother, her maiden name being Knowlton. She got them from the Herald's Office in order to have them quartered with her husband's Arms to paint on their carriage. Thus we became possessed of them. My brother afterwards ascertained from the College that they were right . . As Ladies have no right to the crest, I have only the Arms cut on a Lozenge on my seal which I will seal this letter with for you to see. I shall be glad to receive a letter with your seal when you have it cut. *You may safely* adopt them. My great grandfather's name was William,

* Thomas was the only one who successfully cultivated pineapples in England.

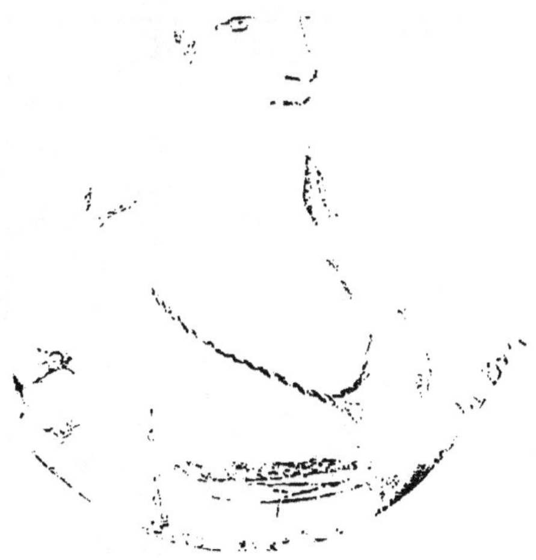

Miss Sarah Knowlton,
Darley Dale, England, 1767–1845.

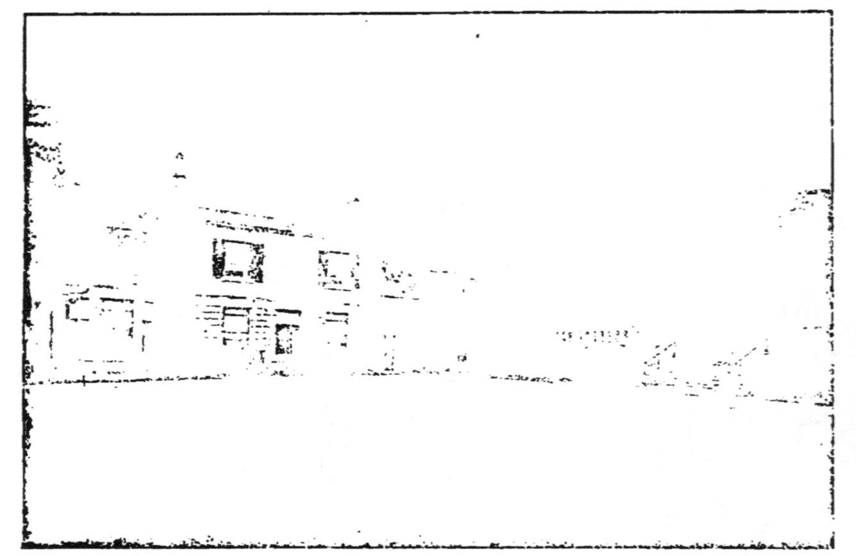

Darley House,
Derbyshire, England.
Residence of the Knowltons.

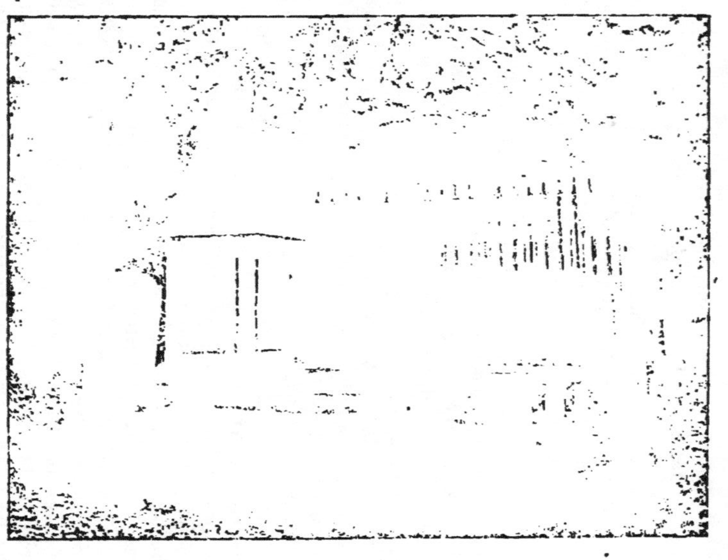

THE KNOWLTON TOMBS,
Londesborough Churchyard,
Yorkshire, Eng.

my grandfather's Thomas, and your relations having kept up those names shows that we are descended from the same source."

Among her personal effects were found a Prayer Book formerly belonging to Elizabeth, wife of Thomas Knowlton (1690), and a paper signed, J. Knowlton, 1582, the only possible inference from which, even were there no other testimony, is that these Knowltons were the kinsfolk of the founder of the American family.

The Darley Dale Knowltons were members of the old parish, whose church is still one of the most venerable and picturesque structures in the land: Its exterior is unaltered, but the interior is modernized, and beautifully treated by ecclesiastical art. It originally had four galleries, to accommodate the parishioners of four different towns, each being assigned its own gallery. During the latter part of his life, Col. Thomas Knowlton had a falling out with the parish officers, and thereafter he read prayers and a sermon twice a day to his own household with pious persistency.

Miss Knowlton had also a marked personal peculiarity. Her affections, which were blighted by the untimely death of her lover, turned to cats, of which she had numerous and remarkable specimens. A room in Darley House was set apart for their exclusive use, and they accompanied her by turns, when she went to drive. It would appear that she thought herself the last of her family, or that between her sister, Mrs. Elizabeth Dawson, and herself some alienation had occurred, for she left her entire estate to Hon. Paul Holland Knowlton, of Knowlton, Province of Quebec, the romantic circumstances of which will be narrated in the Canadian chapter. He visited Darley Dale and was entertained by the Duke of Devonshire, who declared to him that the Knowltons were the best agents Chatsworth and Lismore had ever had. Miss Knowlton died June 9, 1845, aged nearly 79 years, and was buried by her brother's side in Londesborough. With her, the English Knowltons virtually disappear.

CHAPTER II

The Knowltons of New England

CAPTAIN WILLIAM KNOWLTON sailed from the port of London for Nova Scotia in 1632–4, as is usually believed, although this date is only approximate. A record is kept of those emigrants only who, on leaving England, took the oath of loyalty to the English Crown, and promised conformity to the Doctrine, Discipline, and Worship of the Established Church, and who also swore that they were "no subsidy men."

As a large number desired to avoid this enforced allegiance, and to enter the land of their adoption free to follow their own political and religious inclinations, they took no legal departure, but sailed away with more or less secrecy, and were therefore not enrolled in the official records of the government. As no record of Knowlton appears in the Customs Department at London, it must be inferred that William was independent in political action, and a non-conformist in religion. As every resident within the geographical boundaries of an English parish was enrolled in its records, no matter what his faith might be, Capt. Knowlton and family were undoubtedly so enrolled at Chiswick. Unfortunately, the old parish church was seized by Cromwell and his troopers in 1645, and used as a garrison. His horses were stalled in its chancel, the men were quartered in the nave, and all the early parochial records were burned, except a small account book of the church wardens. In this book the name of George Nolleton appears as one of a number obligated to pay for repairs on the church from 1619–1622. Of the children of Capt. William already mentioned, John, William, Dea Thomas, and, probably, Samuel, accompanied him in his voyage to America, for one of this name was found in Hingham soon after the others appeared in Ipswich, and he died in 1655, leaving a will, probated September 1655, in which his "brother John" is named as executor. As John, son of Capt. William, is the only one answering to this relation and date, Samuel must have been the son of Capt. William, following the family to this country at a later date, perhaps.

Capt. William died on the westward voyage, and his widow and children proceeded to Nova Scotia, where they remained but a short time. The next we hear of them is in Ipswich, Mass., where John became a resident in 1639,

William and Thomas following him in 1642. This old town had been organized only the year before John Knowlton selected it for his home. Musconnomet, the Sagamore of the Agawams, deeded to Mr. John Winthrop for a consideration of twenty pounds sterling a tract of land containing several thousand acres, with exclusive right to all timber, game, and fisheries therein comprised. The deed was executed January 28, 1638. Winthrop had begun a settlement here in 1633, and had met with armed interference by the neighboring Indians. For the purpose of securing a well-ordered and godly community, it was provided that no one could become an inhabitant without consent of the freemen, nor could one become a member of this corporate body unless he were a member of some church, or could furnish from his minister a certificate of soundness in the faith and godliness of life.

To each freeman was alloted from the town lands a farm of fifty acres, besides a house lot, and no householder could build his dwelling more than half a mile distant from the meeting house. This provision had in view a surer defence against the savages, and a compulsory attendance on divine service, and when a householder excused himself from such attendance on the ground of living too far to attend in stormy weather, the town promptly sold him out, and transferred him to a nearer location. Bachelors were required to place themselves under the domestic protection and moral influence of their married neighbors. Every inhabitant must have some industrial occupation, and because the chief dependence for daily bread was the farm, mechanics were required to leave their work and assist the farmer whenever the safe housing of the crops was threatened. The Indians gave these early settlers such trouble by their thievish habits that every man was required to choose an ear mark for his cattle and swine, while the Indians were forbidden to mark theirs, and when beef and pork were offered for sale by them, they were required to produce the ears as proof of their rightful ownership. For money they used bullets and wampum, each of the former being equivalent to a farthing, and of the latter, six, four white and two blue, for a penny. This paternal government extended to the private affairs of the household, regulating diet, parental discipline, and personal manners. No buns or cakes could be eaten except at weddings and funerals. Not until 1753 was a carriage owned or used by these hardy people. They were mostly farmers, and in order to keep their farms intact the law of entail from the father to the son was enforced. If one died childless, the law required the devise of his estate to his nearest male kinsman. Not until 1792 did the General Court permit the free disposal of property. Every freeman who was a military or sea captain, minister, doctor, lawyer, teacher, merchant, or graduate of some college, was called Mr. and his wife Mistress, while all others were called by the inferior titles of *goodman* and *goodwife*. The thrift of these Ipswich settlers attracted so many prospecting inhabitants that in 1650 no further grant of farms was possible, there being at this date one hundred and forty-six families in residence.

The first church in Ipswich, 1646, was the "Church of Christ," and it embraced one hundred and sixty souls.

"The Church of Christ, here, consists of 160 souls, being pure in their conversation, and free from epidemicall views of all Reforming Churches, which under Christ is secured by their pious and orthodox ministry."

Patriotic devotion to their new country was a marked feature of these early settlers. Four of the Knowltons, John, Benjamin, Abraham, and William, served in King Philip's war; several of them participated in the siege and capture of Louisburg; the rosters of the Revolutionary troops frequently bear the Knowlton name, and in the subsequent wars of 1812 and of the Rebellion, this same patriotic stock is still at the front. Old Ipswich gave an extraordinary proof of this devotion to country on June 9 1788, when all the commoners, including many Knowltons, surrendered all their lands to pay the town debts incurred during the War of Independence.

Amid such surroundings and influences the Knowltons began their career in America.

---

1 Captain William and Ann Elizabeth Smith had:

(2) John, 1610. m. Marjery Wilson.
(3) William, 1615. m. Elizabeth.
(4) Dea. Thomas, 1622. m. Susannah; m. 2d Mary Kimball.
(4A) Samuel.

Capt. William was at least part owner of the vessel in which he sailed for America. He died on the voyage, probably not far from Nova Scotia, for a land surveyor, Alphonso Wells by name, in the employ of the Canadian Government, brought word to the Canadian Knowltons that, when surveying land in Shelburne in 1839, he had found an ancient head-stone there bearing the name of William Knowlton, 1632. Anneapolis was the first settlement made in Nova Scotia, in 1604. This was captured by the English in 1620, and retaken by the original settlers the following year. In 1632, the French were in possession of portions of New Brunswick and Nova Scotia, and there were here a few families from the Colony of Massachusetts Bay. It was probably here that Capt. William's remains were landed and buried. Tradition also says that his ship was sold here, and that his widow and children proceeded to Massachusetts, probably to Hingham, the following year, where his widow is said to have remarried.

The English tradition is that her name was Ann Elizabeth Smith. On June 9, 1668 one Anne, widow of William Knollton, petitioned for an appraisal of land in Hingham, and she has been thought by some to have been the

JOHN KNOWLTON'S HOUSE.
Old Ipswich, Mass.

2 John and Marjery Wilson had:

(5) John, 1633. m. Sarah Whipple, July 3, 1661.
(6) Abraham, 1635. d. unm.
(7) Elizabeth, 1637.

John was a shoemaker, residing in Ipswich. He became a citizen there in 1639, and a freeman June 9, 1641. On December 19, 1648, he subscribed to a fund for the pay of Major Denison to whom had been entrusted the defence of the townships against the assaults of Indian and other enemies. From the records of sales and transfers of property in Ipswich, it would appear that John had accumulated a considerable property at the time of his death, October 8, 1654/5.

Marjery Wilson was from England; she survived him but a few months. (See Appendix for their wills, and for the inventory of the property.) The following preamble expresses the sentiments of the afore-mentioned subscribers.

"Whereas, the inhabytaynts of this Towne have engaged themselves to paye yearly on ye 10 day of December unto Major Denison soe long as he shall be their Leader the sum of four pounds seven shillings in way of gratuitye as under their hands may appear, and because it is most manifest this Sayd Sum will not be raysed unlesse some better order be taken for the same espechally in respect of the (Al—— and) change of the Inhabytaynts &c."

---

3 William and Elizabeth had:

(8) Thomas, 1640. m. Hannah Green, November 24, 1668.
(9) Nathaniel, 1641. m. Deborah Grant, May 3, 1662.
(10) William, 1642. m. Susannah ——.
(11) John, 1644. m. Bertha (Bethia) Carter.
(12) Benjamin, 1646. m. Hannah Mirick, November 30, 1676.
(13) Samuel, 1647. m. Elizabeth Witt, 1669.
(14) Mary, 1649. m. Samuel Abbe, October 12, 1672. Had s. Johnathan. Res. Wenham.

4 Deacon Thomas, m. Susannah ——, who d. Nov. 20, 1680. And m. 2d Mary Kimball, May 17, 1682.

He was a cordwainer in Ipswich, Mass., and also shoemaker, for he is so called in a deed in which John Knowlton, his brother, and John Baker join him as grantors. He was in Ipswich in 1642, and took a prominent part in the civil affairs of the town, and was Deacon . the old First (Congregational) Church. Having no children, he sent William . "boys to scool from the age of 5 to 8, and a girl from 1½ till she was married," and he also took Nathaniel, his nephew, to live with him. His nephew Thomas ( ), styled "Thomas, Jr.," was given a bequest December 3, 1688, and he conveyed the bulk of his remaining property to his nephew, Nathaniel, by a deed of gift, dated December 5, 1688, for which the said Nathaniel executed a bond of even date for the faithful performance of his trust. As this will and bond expressly declare the legatees to be the children of his brother William, this evidently settles in the negative the disputed question as to whether Dea. Thomas had children. He left a silver vessel to the church, and the rest of his property as mentioned in the Appendix. Deacon Thomas d. April 23, 1692.

Mary Kimball, b. in England in 1625, was the dau. of Richard and Mary (Scott) Kimball, who sailed from Ipswich, Eng., in the ship *Elizabeth*, April 10, 1634. He became an inhabitant of Ipswich, Mass., on February 23, 1637. He was a wheelwright, and he became one of the representative men of the town. Mary d. November 20, 1688.

Samuel (4A) was a mariner. He is commonly supposed to have remained in England, but he certainly was in Hingham prior to September 22, 1655, on which date the inventory of his property was taken by his brother John, as administrator, and who died the following October.

---

5 John and Sarah-Whipple had:

(15) Joseph, 1651. m. Mary Wilson, August 14, 1677.
(16) Samuel, 1653. m. Mary Witt, August 16, 1669.
(17) Daniel, 1655. m. ——. Res. in Holliston, Mass.
(18) John, 1656. m. Sarah ——.

(19) Nathaniel, July 24, 1658/9. m. Deborah Jewett, May 8, 1682.
(20) Elizabeth, March 1, 1659. m. Timothy Dorman, November 30, 1688. She d. September 22, 1788. Res. Ipswich.
(21) Thomas, May 19, 1662. m. Hannah Carter, 1683.
(22) William, 1664. m. Lydia ——, March 16, 1688. Sett. in Wenham.
(23) Johnathan, 1665. m. Elizabeth ——. Settled in Malden.
(24) Susannah, August 15, 1673.

John was a shoemaker. He took the freeman's oath October 16, 1680. On November 30, 1670, he was drafted into the Narragansett Expedition. Sarah was the daughter of John and Sarah Whipple, her father being "feoffee of the Grammar School" in Ipswich, a Deputy to the General Court in 1640, and for a time thereafter a Deacon and Ruling Elder in the Congregational Church.

John's eyesight began to fail him at forty-two years of age, as appears from the following letter, April 5, 1675.

To my Loveing frejnd, Samll
Sayward liveing at Yorke this Deliver.

Loveing and kind freynd, my haerty love remembered, vnto you, & my respects to yourOoncle & Aunt, & so vnto the Selectmen of ye Towne, with the rest of my Loveing frends for whose loves sakes I am obleigded to rend^r vnfayned & haerty thankefulnes / The Occasion of my P^rsent writeing is such, wch I take little pleasure in, or once Conceiud of, w^n I was last with you, which is to let you vnderstand y^t It is best in my opinion for mee not to remoue to you: If I should goe thither seekeing to follow other Imploym^ts then my Trade, will not bee to my Comfort, neither redoun to y^r Contents / & as for my Trade, for the sake of wch you were pleased Lyberrally to accomodate mee, God by his prouidence hath much vnfitted mee the same to follow by reason of an Impediment In my sight, wch doth Inforce mee in great part to leaue it off / Now my reall desire is that Neither your selfe, nor any other P^rson, should bee wronged, so I hope you Samll, & the rest of my frejnds there, will with such prudence Mannage affayrs there, that I may not bee two much damnifyd in the house / I know not vnto whom to surrend^r It better than vnto you selfe, & Dadiver: Yet (it standing vpon the Land my much respect frejnd Capt Davess gaue to mee vpon my settleing there, I thinke it most Convenjent to Conferr with him of this matter, whose Assistance & advise I question not will bee most aduantagious, both to you & alsoe to me / w^t Capt Davees his Accop^t cometh to I purpose to giue in w^n hee comes to this town / I pray you ord^r the rest with as much discretion as may bee, for the content of all men concerned herein, onely let mee not loos all / so at P^rsent I rest yor Loueing frejnd /

John Knoulton.

Aprill 5 : 73 : one thing more I did forget / Two fforks wch I delivered to Mis Sayword wch came to = 00 : 07 : 6 I also left w^{n} I was there at Thom^{s} Symsons, one spade y^{t} Cost mee = 0 : 08 : 6 one shovell 5^{s} 6^{d}, one Mattocke 8^{s}, these things I know in my worke = 13 : 6 were little the worse take y^{m} yo'selfe if you do good they cost me in good pay all 22^{s} / Alsoe the nayls I sent about the house were Two thousand one hundred / one Thousand 2^{s} 6^{d} P C the rest 1^{s} 4^{d} P C y^{e} Hinges 3^{s} 6^{d} /

vera copia of this letter transcribed & compared with ye originall this 11th of Octob^{r} 79 : P Edw: Rishworth Re/Cor :

John's name is connected with so many real estate transactions that he was evidently a man of substance. He was, moreover, a public official, for in January, 1671,

"Y^{e} Selectmen having called John Brown before them, & having had comp^{l} that ye s^{d} John doth neglect his occasions, & spend much time and expense in ordinaries, doe now forewarn him the s^{d} John Brown that he doe not frequent any of the ordinaries upon penalty of the law."

JOHN KNOULTON.

He removed to Wrentham, before 1679, and d. October, 1684.
Sarah d. February 4, 1678.

Abraham Knowlton (6) was born in Ipswich. He was drafted into the Narragansett Expedition November 30, 1672, receiving £2-14s for his services. He removed from Ipswich to Salisbury in 1677, where he

"took the oath of allegiance & fidelity before Tho. Bradbury, Capt of Y^{e} Military Company of Salisbury, Dec 5, 1677."

He was never married. His name is spelt "Noulton." He lived for some time with his uncle Dea. Thomas.

---

8 Thomas and Hannah Green had:

(25) Thomas, May 11, 1670. m. Mercy ——; m. 2d Susannah ——
(26) Robert, 1672. d. unm. See Appendix for his will. He served in the colonial wars under Col. Appleton, and in the Canada Expedition.
(27) Ebenezer, 1674.
(28) Ephraim, 1676.
(29) Zerubbabel, d. September 23, 1684.
(30) Mary, March 29, 1681. m. John Williams, June 26, 1707.
(31) Patience, December 2, 1686. m. William Rollo, March 13, 1706.

Hannah was the second child of William and Hannah (Carter) Green, of Devonshire, England. He was a freeman in 1640. She d. at Norwich, Conn., October 24, 1708.

Thomas, Jr., was b. in Ipswich. He was a cordwainer and the jailor of the town, its jail being the second one erected in the Colony. In 1680 he is mentioned as having carried to Boston for trial one Goody Morse who had murdered Good Wife Ordway's child. There has been not a little conflict of opinion about the movements of Thomas, some having supposed that he lived and died in Ipswich, and others insisting that he removed to Norwich, Conn. This latter view is undoubtedly correct, for on June 4, 1702, Samuel Bliss and Ann, his wife, residents of Norwich, Conn., conveyed to Thomas Knowlton, cordwainer, of Ipswich, and Benjamin Baldwin, of Osborn, Mass., 550 acres of land lying between the Shetucket and Quinnebaug rivers in Norwich. This same property was subsequently sold to John Andrus, Jr., carpenter, of Ipswich, the deed being signed by Thomas, Jr., and the signatures being also witnessed by Patience, and by Thomas Knowlton, Senior. The appearance of Thomas, Jr., the jailor, in both Ipswich and Norwich is readily explained by the fact that his investments in real estate would oblige him to pass a portion of his time in each town. The Ipswich records do not show him to have been the jailor there at the time of his death in 1717, while the Connecticut records do show that at least three of his children, "Thomas ye 3d," Patience, and Mary, were living in the latter city, and with whom he undoubtedly spent a part of his time.

Thomas d. February 28, 1717, in Ipswich. Hannah d. in Norwich, Conn., October 24, 1708.

---

9 Nathaniel and Deborah Grant had:

(32) Samuel, November 9, 1672.
(33) Ebenezer, 1674. m. Sarah Towle, February 14, 1699.
(34) Sarah, 1677. m. William Maxcy, March 6, 1697.
(35) Abraham, February 27, 1679. m. Sarah Fuller, 1701.
(36) Abigail, 1680. m. Charles Crow, February 17, 1706.
(37) Nathaniel, 1682. m. Reform Jewett, April 15, 1717.

Nathaniel became the legatee of his uncle Deacon Thomas' property by virtue of a deed of gift, in return for which said Nathaniel gave his uncle his bond for the faithful performance of his trust. See Appendix.

---

10 William and Susannah—— had:

(38) Thomas, 1667. m. Marjery Goodhue, December 9, 1692; m. 2d Marjery Carter.
(39) Sarah, December 1, 1671.
(40) Joseph, 1677. m. Lucy Whipple.

11 John and Bertha Carter had:

(41) John, 1670. m. Abigail Bachelor (or Batchelder), December 20, 1697.
(42) Robert, 1672. m. Had 5 children.
(43) Ezekiel, 1679. m. Sarah Leach, January 29, 1698.

John resided in Ipswich, from which place he removed to Manchester, Mass., about 1679. He was a captain of the local militia. He was made a freeman in 1669, and took the oath in Manchester in 1680. He was a carpenter, a very enterprising man, and dealt largely in real estate.

---

12 Benjamin and Hannah Mirick had:

(44) Mary, September 17, 1677. m. Increase Licks, October 28, 1697.
(45) Benjamin, December 9, 1679. m. Elizabeth Phelps, May 27, 1703.
(46) Sarah, August 31, 1682. m. Johnathan Taylor, July 26, 1712; m. 2d Abner Hitchcock, 1748.
Mercy, May 19, 1685. d. young.
(47) Joseph, January 3, 1686. Accidentally killed in Norwich, Conn. 1718, leaving an estate of 2 cows.
(48) Mercy, November 11, 1690. m. Wm. Stebbins, March 15, 1718,

Benjamin was born in Ipswich. He served in King Philip's War, being stationed for a time at the Springfield Garrison. He was paid £16,12s for services (September 23, 1676.) He took the freeman's oath January 1, 1678 and received grants of land in Springfield in 1684 and 1717, to which was added another grant in Brookfield 1718. He and Miriam were received as members of the First Cong. Church in 1736.

He removed to Springfield, Mass., where on February 10, 1678, he and Joseph Stebbins were

"ordered to see that swine were rung & yoked if found on y^e / March to ye end of Oct. on streets or commons, in or about town, or in fields, lands, gardens, & meadows."

Benjamin d. at Springfield, August 19, 1690. His widow m. 2d Matthew Crowfoot (Crofut), December 17, 1702.

nection - Made by H. F. Currier

532 Warren Ave.

Increase[3] **Sikes** son of Increase[2] son of Richard & Phebe Sikes of Spring-field Mass (See Savage)

13 Samuel and Elizabeth Wilt (or Witt) had:

(49) Catherine, 1668.
(50) Elizabeth, June 26, 1669. d. young.
(51) Sarah, June 16, 1670. m. Joseph Allen, January 20, 1712.
(52) Samuel, November 2, 1672. m. Sarah Fellows, June 26, 1736.
(53) Benjamin, 1674. m.
(54) Johnathan, March 16, 1677/8.
(55) Nathaniel.
(56) Ebenezer, June 18, 1684. m. Elizabeth Poland, January 11, 1715.
(57) Elizabeth, April 18, 1685/6.
(58) Thomas, 1688. m. Ruth Lord, January 11, 1714.

Samuel resided in Ipswich. He was a shoemaker, and being lame he was specially remembered in his uncle's, Dea. Thomas's will. His own will is dated January 16, 1695.

---

15 Joseph and Mary Wilson had:

(59) Abraham, 1678. m. Sarah Lord, 1699.
(60) Joseph, February 1, 1680.
(61) A dau., April 30, 1686. d. 1693.
(62) Daniel, April 1, 1693. d. young.

---

16 Samuel and Mary Witt had:

(63) Elizabeth, May, 1669/70.
(64) John, 1673.
(65) Rice, 1676. m. Mary Dodge, January 2, 1699.
(66) Susannah, 1678. m. John Dennis, July 24, 1702.

Samuel took the freeman's oath in Wenham, October 13, 1680.

---

17 Daniel and —— had:

(67) Daniel, 1688. m. Dorgullia Lamb.
(68) Johnathan, 1690. m. Rebecca ——.
Residence, Holliston, Mass.

---

18 John and Sarah —— had:

(69) Sarah, September 19, 1685. m. Daniel Ringe, March 22, 1711.
(70) John, 1686. m. Rebecca Young, May 29, 1704.
(71) Timothy, 1687. m. Hannah Storey, August 10, 1713.

(72) Thomas, May 13, 1689. m. Martha Conant, March 10, 1 ....
Ipswich.

(73) Abigail, 1690. m. Isaac Giddings; m. 2d Lieut. Wm. Dodge.

John removed from Ipswich to Wenham, and on the

"10th of ii month 1669, John Nowlton Vpon the condition he ...eth 4s pr yeere Contributon to ye Ministry, sh! have liberty to Joy ... pternership in a galiry & in the meantime to have liberty of a S... belowe in witness whereof he have set to his hand

JOHN KNOWLTON."

John d. September 11, 1720. Sarah d. January 24, 1712.

---

19 Nathaniel and Deborah Jewett had:

(74) Nathaniel, May 3, 1683. m. Mary Bennett, pub., February 13, 1703.
(75) John, December 7, 1685. m. Susannah Hutton.
(76) Joseph, April, 1687. d. young.
(77) Thomas, November 8, 1692.
(78) Abraham, February 27, 1698, m. Mary Smith Knowlton, September 20, 1722.
(79) Elizabeth, September 15, 1702.
(80) David, May 15, 1707. m. Esther Howard, February 25, 1731.

Nathaniel "was a man of consequence" in Ipswich. He was a Commoner, February 18, 1678, Deacon of the First Congregational Church in 1697, for many years its treasurer, and a Deputy to the General Court in 1700, '02, '03, '05, '09, '14, '15 and '20. His record is thus laconically and eloquently expressed by an old historian, "Though honored by men he did not forget to honor his God." Deborah was from Rowley, Mass. Her father Benj. Jewett conveyed land to his son-in-law, December 26, 1684. Nathaniel d. September 18, 1726. Deborah d. 1743.

---

20 Elizabeth and Timothy Dorman had:

(81) Timothy, September 18, 1689. d. 1712.
(82) Elizabeth, December 7, 1691. m. John Daggett, November 30, 1721.
(83) Mary, October 28, 1693. m. Joseph Stavely, March 29, 1716.
(84) John, February 9, 1696. m. Rebecca Smith, June 28, 1730.
(85) Hannah, December 22, 1698. m. Israel Daggett, April 25, 1724.

Residence, Ipswich, Mass., where she d. September 22, 1738.

21 Thomas and Hannah Carter had:

(86) Thomas, 1684. m. Mary ——

---

22 William and Lydia (2d Wife) had:

(87) William, March 7, 1706.

Wm., sen., resided in Wenham, where he d., March 16, 1718.

---

23 Johnathan and Sarah E. —— had:

(88) Elizabeth, April 22, 1688. d. young.

Sarah dying, he m. 2d Elizabeth —— and had:

(89) Elizabeth, February 4, 1702. m. Nathan Brown, August 15, 1737.
(90) Johnathan, June 9, 1705. m. Mary Maxwell, April 15, 1731. She is styled, "An Anciente Mayde." Res., Malden, Mass.
(91) Isaac. m. Mary Dear, pub., October 12, 1723.

---

25 Thomas and Mercy —— had:

(92) Mercy, August 7, 1694. m. John Bates, November 30, 1714.

Mercy d. August 23, 1694, and Thos. m. 2d Susannah ——, and had:

(93) Susannah, March 14, 1698.
(94) Thomas, March 31, 1699. m. Susannah Cone, December 24, 1724.
(95) Lucy, bap. December 11, 1705. m. Thomas Holmes, June 9, 1732.

Susannah d. 1708, and Thomas m. 3d Sarah Benjamin, of Norwich, Conn., December 31, 1708, and had:

(95A) Hannah, bap. December 7, 1712. d. young.
(95B) Hannah, bap. September 4, 1715.

Thomas, 3d, was born in Ipswich, Mass., removed to Norwich, Conn., after Mercy's death, and bought a farm in East Haddam, Conn., March 20, 1705, in the deed of which he is designated as Thomas Knowlton, Junr., of Norwich. At the General Assembly holden at Hartford, May 9, 1706, he was commissioned lieutenant of the Train Band in East Haddam, "on the east side of the great river." This Thomas has frequently been supposed to have been the son of

William (3), and the Thomas who married Marjery Goodhue has been considered the son of Thomas and Hannah Green. This point the historian has settled by finding a document of which the following is an extract (Salem Records):

"July 2, 1692. Thomas Knowlton, son of William Knowlton to his son Thomas, Shoemaker, gives his parlor new chamber, a part of his cellar, and the privilege of using water from the well-pump.

May 26, 1698. "* * * that ye sd Thomas Knowlton Senr & Thomas Knowlton Junr, his Sonne, and Benjamin Baldwin of Woburne and Mary Knowlton of sd Ipswich, children of sd Thomas Senr and ye sd Thomas Senr as Guardian to his two other children, viz Ebenezer & Patience, for & in consideration of ye summe of 147 pounds to them payd and Secured by (——) by Joseph Cliffe of sd. Ipswich clothier ye receipt whereof they ye sd Thomas Senr & Thomas Junr & Mary & Thomas Senr as Guardian aforesd doth acknowledge themselves therewith fully satisfied therewith & doe therefore hereby fully acquit ye sd Cliffe for eve haue withe ye consent of their now wives viz, Hannah ye now wife of sd Thomas Senr and Susanna ye now wife of sd Thomas, Junr, and Hannah ye now wife of ye sd Benjamin " &c.

This, then, settles the parentage of Thomas, who m. Mercy and Susannah, and also the parentage of his sisters, Mary and Patience. Thomas 3d d. September 20, 1730.

Robert (26) was in the Canada Expedition, and

"being by God's providence in an Exposition against a potent enemy whose eminent danger"

etc., might make his return uncertain, he made his will April 30, 1690 (see Appendix). His company was commanded by Major Samuel Appleton.

---

28 Ephraim and —— had:

(96) Ephraim, 1700.
(97) Thomas, 1702.
(98) Hannah and eight others, history unknown. Hannah. m. ——Storey

Ephraim rem. to Norwich, Conn. Samuel Storey, who left Ipswich in 1726, removed to Norwich, and left his entire estate to Ephraim's children, one of whom, Hannah, married his son. Ephraim had then deceased.

30 Mary Knowlton and John Williams had :

(99) Mary, February 17, 1714. m. Nathaniel Giddings of Norwich, Ct. ; 2 children.

(100) Benjamin, July 4, 1715. d. July 15, 1732.

(101) Joseph, January 22, 1718. d. young.

(102) Zipporah, July 28, 1720. m. James Geer, of Groton, Conn. ; 1 child.

(103) Joseph, April 23, 1723. m. Hannah Lathrop ; m. 2d Eunice Wheeler, 1746.

Mary was born in Ipswich, Mass., and was married in Norwich, whither her father Thomas had removed. Capt. John Williams was of Welsh descent, b. in Haverhill, Mass., February 17, 1679, and removed to Foquetannock, then a part of the township of Norwich, Conn. He d. in 1742, leaving an estate of five negroes valued at £600, and real and personal property valued at £21,727. Mary made benevolent use of her wealth, for in addition to her more private charities, she supported and endowed the chapel at "Long Society" which she and her husband had built for the convenience of many who lived too remotely from the parent church to attend its services with regularity. Mary died March 9, 1749, and her many virtues are recited in an "Elegy" or funeral lamentation very common in those days. It was probably composed by her pastor, and it comprises fifty-six four-line verses printed in heavy black type. This worthy couple are buried in the cemetery hard by, and their epitaphs are still perfectly legible. Mary's will was probated August 1, 1749, in which she bequeathed to Nathaniel Giddings £2.10, James Geer of Groton, £2.10, to her granddaughters, Mary and Sarah Giddings, and Zipporah Geer, £100 each, and to her beloved son Joseph the residue of her property.

The mother of John Williams was Mary Fuller, dau. of Samuel Williams of the *Mayflower*. Among the distinguished descendants of this worthy couple were Gen. Joseph Williams of the Revolution, Hon. James H. Phelps of Brattleboro, Vt., Gen. Chas. Edward Phelps, Baltimore, Hon. Fred. Nichols of Brattleboro, Vt., and T. Dwight Williams, Esq., of Brooklyn, N. Y.

---

31 Patience Knowlton and William Rollo had :

(104) Zerubbabel, January 11, 1707.

(105) Elizabeth, March, 7, 1709.

(106) Alexander, April 26, 1711.

(107) Hannah, March 5, 1713.

(108) Mary, April 25, 1715.

(109) Ebenezer, February 26, 1717.

(110) John, February 26, 1720.

Patience and William removed to East Haddam, Conn., being "admitted to full communion" in the First Congregational Church there, August 15, 1714.

33 Ebenezer

Married and had children, of whom no account can be found. A strip of land was given him by the town of Newbury, Mass., for setting up a tannery.

---

35 Abraham and Sarah Fuller had:

(111) Abraham, 1702. m. Mary Fuller, 1722.

Sarah d. July 29, 1724.

---

37 Nathaniel and Reform Jewett had:

(112) Mary, May 10, 1719.
(113) Margaret, March 17, 1720. d. 1730.
(114) Elizabeth, July 15, 1722. d. young.
(115) Elizabeth, August 23, 1725. d. young.
(116) Anna, February, 23, 1728. d. young.
(117) Thomas, December, 13, 1730. d. 1730.
(118) Ebenezer, January 25, 1732. d. 1736.
(119) Sarah, May 30, 1735. d. young.
(120) Thomas, October 30, 1737.
(121) Samuel, June 26, 1726.

Reform was the dau. of Benj. and Reform (Prescott) Jewett, of Milton, Mass.

---

38 Thomas and Marjery Goodhue had:

(122) Robert, September 7, 1693. m. Hannah Robinson, November 21, 1717.
(123) Marjery, August 27, 1694. d. same day.
(124) Marjery, March 25, 1695. m. Jabez Dodge, November 25, 1718.
(125) Joseph, March 9, 1696/7. m. Abigail Bird, November 25, 1718.
(126) Deborah December 31, 1697/8.

Marjery d. August 23, 1698/9, and Thomas m. 2d Marjery Carter, 1702, and had:

(127) Abraham, April 30, 1703. m. Martha Lamson, January 16, 1734.
(128) Sarah, March 5, 1705. m. John Woodbury, April 2, 1723.
(129) Ezekiel, March 5, 1707. m. Susannah Morgan, 1728.

Marjery Goodhue was a granddaughter of Deacon William Goodhue, a prominent citizen of Ipswich, and one of its earliest settlers. He was Representative in the Colonial Assembly in 1666, '67, '73, '76, '77, '80, '81, and '83. For

of Roxbury Col. [14] 3

Lamb. Thomas - Abial - Samuel - 1

Barzillai Lamb b. 9-12-1712 in
Framingham Mass. M. 2-28-1734
Sarah Knowlton b.
dau. of Robt (prob) Removed 1740 to
Hopkinton Mass. and late in life to
Templeton " where he settled on
a large farm.

Issue

1 John b. 9-23-1734

2 Israel " 1737 d. 3-26-1826 at 89
set. in Philipston

3 Samuel bap. 4-5-1741 M. 3-18-1762 Rebecca Cozzens

4 Joshua b. 11-30-1743
set. in Templeton

5 Joseph " 9-10-1747 M. Relief Cobleigh, his
wife Patty d. 2-20-1830 buried at

6 Isaac " 9-12-1749 d. 10-8-1829 Philipston
he d. soon after m.

7 Barzilla bap. 1752 M. Zebah Bigelow

8 Dau. died young.

was mother of his ch. 9 of them.
Israel M. (1) Lucy Wheeler (dau John 2d)
(2) Hannah Piper wid. of Lieut. Abner Sears
of Rev. Army). J. Walter Lamb, g.g. of Israel.
3357 Indiana Av. Chicago.

[illegible]

resisting illegal taxation he was imprisoned by Governor Andros. Marjery's father was Joseph, who m. Sarah Whipple, daughter of Elder John Whipple, who d. in Ipswich 1683, leaving an estate of £3000. Marjery's grandfather was a captain in the colonial wars, and his descendant, Wm. Whipple, was a signer of the Declaration of Independence, and a brigadier-general at the capture of General Burgoyne.

---

40 Joseph and Lucy Whipple had:

(130) Elisha, 1693.
(131) Joseph, December 1, 1699.

Joseph resided in Ipswich.

---

41 John and Abigail Batchelder had:

(132) John, April 30, 1699. m. Elizabeth Hilton, October 18, 1720.
(133) Joseph, December 20, 1701. m. Emma ——.
(134) Abigail, May 2, 1705. m. Solomon Parsons, April 7, 1730.
(135) Churchill, March 5, 1707.
(136) Marion, September 17, 1711.
(137) Lucy, February 28, 1714. m. Joseph Knight, November 4, 1787.
(138) Prudence, April 15, 1718. m. Joseph Giddings, December 28, 1737.
(139) Andrew, March 5, 1720. m. Lucy Stone, 1741.
(140) Hannah, March 13, 1723. m. Daniel Lufkin, August 8, 1747.

John was a carpenter. Residence, Manchester, Mass.

---

42 Robert and —— had:

(141) Lydia.
(142) Sarah. m. Borzillai Lamb.
(143) Mary. m. Abijah Foster, December 13, 1733. Rem. to New Ipswich, N. H., in 1734.

---

43 Ezekiel and Sarah Leach had:

(144) Deborah, October 29, 1699. m. Thos. Adams, April 17, 1722.
(145) Robert, July 17, 1701. m. Lydia Bishop, December 24, 1724.
(146) Ezekiel, February 7, 1703. m. Emma Foster, December 23, 1724.
(147) Sarah, October 24, 1704. m. John Woodbury, February 2, 1722.

Ezekiel was a weaver, res. in Manchester, Mass., and d. 1706. His widow was appointed administratrix of his estate, November 4, 1706.

45 Benjamin and Elizabeth Phelps had:

(148) Mary, April 4, 1709. m. Samuel Stebbins, Jr., May 20, 1734.
(149) Elizabeth, September 15, 1711. m. Hugh Evans, January 9, 1732.
(150) Miriam, May 12, 1716. pub. to Moses Bartlett, April 11, 1735.
(151) Ebenezer, 1718.
(152) Benjamin, December 8, 1720. m. Sarah Mann, June 9, 1743; m. 2d wid. Joanna Taylor, March 7, 1746; m. 3d Rebecca Brooks, January 30, 1749.

Benjamin was killed at the siege of Louisburg, 1750. Residence, Springfield, Mass.

---

51 Sarah Knowlton and Joseph Allen had:

(153) Catherine, December 27, 1713.
(154) Moses, October 7, 1715.
(155) Sarah K., December 8, 1717.
(156) Elizabeth, February 24, 1719. m. Stephen Cross.

---

52 Samuel and Sarah Fellows had:

(157) Samuel, 1737. m. Esther Dane, July 9, 1759.
(158) Nathaniel. m. Elizabeth Dane, December 25, 1742.

---

53 Benjamin and —— had:

(159) Benjamin, 1718. m. Abigail Dodge; m. 2d Abigail Dean.
(160) Susannah. m. —— Brown, of Ipswich.

---

56 Ebenezer and Elizabeth Poland had:

(161) Abraham, 1716.

Ebenezer d. March 11, 1743.

---

58 Thomas and Ruth Lord had:

(162) Thomas, August 3, 1718.

Thomas d. and Ruth m. 2d —— Medes, as appears from her mother's will, dated December 4, 1738.

59 Abraham and Sarah had:

(163) Abraham, 1700. m Sarah Caldwell, December 9, 1721; m. 2d Sarah Lull.

(164) Susannah, 1702.

Abraham was a capt. of militia. He d. in Ipswich, May 21, 1751. Sarah d. July 29, 1724.

---

60 Joseph and —— had:

(165) Elizabeth, February 14, 1702. m. Nathan Browne, August 17, 1737.
(166) Isaac, 1704.
(167) Johnathan, June 9, 1705.

---

64 John and —— had:

(168) Margaret, 1700. m. Moses Mitchell, December 10, 1723. Res. Wenham.

(169) Thomas, January 6, 1708. m. Amy Chase.
(170) Ebenezer, 1710. m. Jane Philbrick, 1736.
(171) Benjamin, 1712.
(172) Miriam, 1714. m. Joseph Day, March 26, 1733.

John resided in Hampton, N. H. His sons were noted for their extraordinary height, being, on the average, about 6 ft. 4 in. tall.

---

65 Rice and Mary Dodge had:

(173) Paul, September 11, 1704. d. young.
(174) Rice, Jr., January 27, 1705. m. Lydia Woodbury, December 12, 1727; m. 2d —— Adams; m. 3d Elizabeth Smith, 1750.
(175) Bethia, September 12, 1709. m. Robert Annable, November 27, 1729; m. 2d Andrew Foster. Res., Ipswich.
(176) Nancy M., April 3, 1716. m. Paul Knowlton. Res. in N. H.
(177) Churchill, February 16, 1720. m. Jane Rogers, July 4, 1741.
(178) Deborah, January 10, 1723. m. John Austin, September 24, 1754.
(179) Abraham, February 8, 1725. m. Miriam Cole, December 6, 1745.

Rice rem. from Ipswich to Wenham. He and the Dodges signed an agreement February 24, 1731, to build a stone wall around the cemetery, and to keep the latter in order. The Dodges were a very prominent family of Ipswich and Wenham, and owned contiguous estates. Rice d. November 15, 1766, aged 90.

67 Daniel and Borguilla Lamb had :

(180) Ruth, 1715. m. Edward Carlyle, September 27, 1733.
(181) Daniel, 1717. m. Abigail Almy, February 17, 1743.
(182) Sarah. m. —— Knowlton.
Residence, Hopkinton, Mass.

---

68 Johnathan and Rebecca had :

(183) Johnathan, 1739.
(184) John. m. 2 children.
(185) Rebecca.
Residence, Holliston, Mass.

---

70 John and Rebecca Young had :

(186) Elizabeth, September 22, 1704. m. Thomas Hurd.
(187) Mary, December 17, 1706. m. Robert Butler
(188) George, May 22, 1711.
(189) John, January 24, 1717.
(190) Ruth, 1713. pub. to John Mead of Stratham, N. H., July 23, 1732.
Residence, Ipswich and Belchertown, Mass.

---

71 Timothy and Hannah Storey had :

(191) Silas, 1712. m. Res., in Belchertown, Mass.
(192) Paul, 1714. m. Mary Knowlton of Wenham, March, 1744.
(193) Benjamin, 1716.
(194) Timothy, 1720, in Medway. m. in 1744.
(195) Rosel, 1722.

Timothy res. in Plantation No. 5, now Hopkinton, N. H. He served in the Port Royal Expedition, June 17, 1707, in Col. F. Wainwright's Regt. In 1739, and for many years thereafter, the town meetings were held at his house. He was one of a committee to lay out the township in lots, and to construct highways.

---

73 Abigail Knowlton and Isaac Giddings had :

(195 A) Joseph. m. Prudence, dau. of John and Abigail Knowlton, December 28, 1738.

Isaac d. March 26, 1737, and Abigail m. 2d Lieut. Wm. Dodge, She d. in 1756.

74 Nathaniel and Mary Bennett had:

(196) Mary, June 3, 1704.
(197) William, February 8, 1706. pub. to Martha Pinder, of Boxford, February 13, 1728.
(198) Nathaniel, June 30, 1708. m. Mary Fuller.
(199) Jeremiah, July 13, 1712. d. young.
(200) Jeremiah, August 2, 1713. m. Sarah Allen, of Sudbury, July 24, 1735. Rem., Concord, N. H.
(201) Martha. m. Dr. Flint.

Residence, Ipswich.

---

x75 John and Susannah Hutton had:

(202) Susannah. m. Josiah Dodge, March 30, 1739.

Residence, Wenham.

---

78 Abraham and Mary Smith Knowlton had:

(203) Mary, May 13, 1723. m. John Hart, August 10, 1746.
(204) Paul, January 17, 1724.
(205) Ruth, March 12, 1726. d. young.
(206) Elizabeth, July 20, 1729.
(207) Ebenezer, October 20, 1731.
(208) Abraham, October 24, 1732.
(209) John, August 9, 1734. d. young.
(210) Nathaniel, December 15, 1740. m. Mary ——.

Mary was from Woburn, Mass. Abraham was ensign of militia.

---

80 David and Esther Howard had:

(211) David, 1732. d. young.
(212) Esther, June 16, 1734. d. 1739.
(213) David, July 16, 1735.
(214) John, August 28, 1737.

David was drowned with six other fishermen off the Ceado Banks, April 7, 1737, and Esther m. 2d David Rose, January 29, 1741.

86 Thomas and Mary had :

(215) Thomas.
(216) Joseph.
(217) Hannah.

---

91 Isaac and Mary Dear had :

(218) Mary, December 18, 1726. d. October 16, 1727.
(219) Isaac, bap. July 13, 1729. d. young.

Residence, Malden, Mass.

Isaac d. and his wid. m. Capt. Robert Choate, a lineal descendant of the family of that name, emigrating from England in 1643 and settling in Chebasco, Ipswich, Mass. Capt. Robert purchased of Widow Mary Dear Knowlton the house left her by her husband Isaac, and it stood for many years on the present site of the town house.

Capt. Robert and Widow Mary Knowlton had :

Unity, May 4, 1799. m. Timothy Knowlton, February 10, 1826.

---

94 Thomas and Susannah Cone had :

(220) Jared, July 18, 1726.
(221) Thomas, September 30, 1728.
(222) Stephen, August 26, 1730. m. 2d Rebecca —— ; m. 3d Mary Purple.
(223) Lucy, March 6, 1733.
(224) Rosel, July 15, 1735. m.
(225) Hannah, November 19, 1737. m. —— Gates, of Gates Mills, Ohio.
(226) Joseph. bap. July 7, 1749. m. Ruth Dodge ; m. 2d Reliance Cole, 1779.
(227) Susannah, bap. July 7, 1749. m. —— Potter.
(228) Mary, bap. July 7, 1749. m. Sheldon Potter. Sett. in Maine.
(229) Alexander. unm. d. in Marietta, Ohio.

Thomas d. June 14, 1781. Susannah d. August 14, 1787. Residence, East Haddam, Conn.

---

96 Ephraim and Charity —— had :

(229 A) Thomas, 1726. m. Jane Carter, 1746.
(229 B) Ephraim, 1728. m. Elizabeth Butler.

Removed to Conn. and thence to N. Y. State.

Knowlton Pond,
Old Ashford, Conn.

97 Thomas and —— had:

(229 C) William, 1722.
(229 D) Thomas, 1724.

---

111 Abraham and Mary Fuller had:

(229 E) Mary, March 26, 1723. m. Francis Sawyer, October 26, 1751.
(229 F) Ruth, March, 1727.
(229 G) Elizabeth, July 20, 1729.
(229 H) Abraham, October 24, 1731. m. Mrs. Elizabeth Wise, January 8, 1750.
(230) John, August 16, 1734. d. young.
(231) Jacob, June 10, 1744.

Residence, Ipswich.

---

122 Robert and Hannah Robinson had:

(232) Daniel, 1726. m. Zerviah Wadkins, November 7, 1745.
(233) Esther, November 25, 1727. d. young.
(234) Sarah, August 17, 1731. d. October 28, 1739.
(235) Thomas, April 26, 1733. m. Bridget Bosworth, December 8, 1756.
(236) Robert, May 27, 1735. d. 1739.
(237) Abraham, April 3, 1740. m. Molly Knox, March 21, 1763.

Robert was b. in Ipswich, removed to Sutton N. H., and from there to Ashford, Conn., in 1725, being the first Knowlton to settle there. He bought a large farm and engaged also in the manufacture of salt. He was Representative in the Colonial Assembly of Conn. from 1739 to 1755.

He and his wife Hannah were received into the Ashford church from that at Sutton, December 11, 1726, and he became a prominent leader in ecclesiastical affairs.

On January 7, 1762 he was chosen deacon (the duties of which office he had for many years discharged), but

"he offered such reasons for being dropped, as age, inability for the service, etc., that he was excused."

He was repeatedly chosen as a committee to examine candidates for the pulpit "as to their principles and discipline," and his strong religious feeling and patriotic ardor seem to have been inherited by his descendants, who were firm supporters and loyal members of the Ashford church, and among the first to respond to the call to arms.

Robert d. December 29, 1794. Hannah d. December 7, 1777.

124 Marjery Knowlton and Jabez Dodge had:

(238) Anne Dodge, February 26, 1720. m. Ebenezer Maynard, of Westboro, February 15, 1743.
(239) Ezekiel, April 21, 1723. m. Mary Goddard, of Sutton.
(240) Deborah., August 26, 1725. m. Solomon Rund, September 25, 1741. Res., Shrewsbury, Mass.
(241) Anna, April 27, 1730. d. young.
(242) Mary, April 27, 1735. m. —— Knowlton. Res., Ipswich.

Jabez and Marjery removed from Ipswich to Manchester, and thence to Shrewsbury, Mass.

---

125 Joseph and Abigail Bird had:

(243) Marjery, April 30, 1720. d. February 5, 1740, in Shrewsbury.
(244) Abigail, September 17, 1722. d. at Hardwich, Mass., March 4, 1807, unm.
(245) Thomas, November 10, 1724. Killed at Hoosac Fort, August 17, 1745.
(246) Joseph, October 18, 1726. m. Mary Knowlton, September 21, 1749.
(247) Abraham, November, 1727. m. Comfort Holman; m. 2d Susannah Jordan.
(248) Jacob, October 29, 1729. m. Sarah Pratt, November 21, 1759; m. 2d Sarah Smith.
(249) Nathan, June 28, 1733. Mentioned in his father's will, April 17, 1756.
(250) Abraham, January, 1731, in Shrewsbury.
(251) Samuel, January 21, 1737. Rem. West.
(252) Nathaniel, January, 21, 1737. Rem. West.
(253) Israel, January, 28, 1740.

Joseph was born in Ipswich, Mass., from which place he removed to Shrewsbury, in 1733. He was admitted to the Church there, with Abigail, that year. He was a farmer and weaver, and it marks the superstitious spirit of that day that he was ploughing in the field, when Molly G., a reputed witch, came to him soliciting some special favor. This being denied, she left him in a towering rage, and for the rest of the day the oxen stood still in the furrows, refusing to move, a circumstance which confirmed prevailing superstitions.

In his will probated September 2, 1760, he leaves to each of his children except Joseph, £28:

"To my son Joseph I give and bequeath all my lands, meadows and buildings in said town and elsewhere, and all my stock and husbandry tools and tackling. Furthermore, my will is that . . . my daughter

Abigail shall have a good comfortable room and fire wood, either in my own dwelling or my son Joseph's, so long as she shall live a single woman."

Abigail d. July 3, 1748, and Joseph m. 2d Anna ——. He d. 1760.

---

127 Abraham and Martha Lamson had:

(254) Paul, April 17, 1736. m. Lucy Forbush, 1769
(255) Silas, September 9, 1737.
(256) Sarah, March 6, 1740. d. young.
(257) Abraham, September 19, 1742. d. young.
(258) Robert, March 18, 1744. d. young.
(259) Sarah, January 24, 1746. m. David Drury, 1765.
(260) Martha, January 24, 1748. m. Thomas Drury, 1769.
(261) Abraham, November 25, 1750. m. Lydia Batchelder.

Martha was from Ipswich; Abraham was b. in Marlboro, Mass., rem. to Shrewsbury, and was admitted to the church there in 1735. He d. November 3, 1768.

---

129 Dea. Ezekiel and Susannah Morgan had:

(262) Mary, May 16, 1731. m. Joseph Knowlton, Jr., 1749. Res. Wardsboro, Vt.
(263) Susannah, April 19, 1733. m. Gershom Wheelock, 1757.
(264) Deborah, December 23, 1734. m. Jabez Bigelow, October 5, 1761. Sett. in Westminster, Mass.
(265) Ezekiel, May 11, 1736. m. Anna Miles, October 4, 1759. Res., Westminster.
(266) Luke, October 28, 1738. m. Sarah Holland, July 29, 1760.
(267) William, April 29, 1741. m. Hannah Hastings, October 26, 1764.
(268) Sarah, January 28, 1745. m. James Simonds, May 19, 1766. Res., Templeton, Mass.
(269) Marjery, June 1, 1747. m. Joshua Bigelow, April 11, 1764. Res., Westminster, Mass.
(270) Capt. Thomas, April 27, 1750. m. Elizabeth Batchelder, April, 1771.

Susannah was the daughter of Captain Morgan and Susannah Pitts, his wife, who came from England. Captain Morgan died on the voyage. Deacon Ezekiel and Susannah were dismissed from the church in Manchester, Mass., to that in Shrewsbury, in 1731. He was Deacon of the Shrewsbury church from 1743-74. At a church meeting called to settle a pastor, March 2, 1762, Ezekiel was made chairman of a committee to extend a call to Rev. Joseph Sumner, and on May 19th following he prepared Articles of Discipline to bind pastor and people. He was Selectman from 1743-49. He d. March 4, 1774; Susannah d. March 17, 1784.

130 Elisha

settled in Providence, R. I., before 1720. He was lieutenant in the local militia at that date, a surveyor in 1728, and a Justice of the Peace in 1734. He was made a freeman there in October, 1720, and a deputy from Providence to the General Court in 1719, '21, '24, '29, '31, and '33.

---

131 Joseph,

brother of Elisha, resided in Providence, Newport, and Gloucester, R. I

---

132 John and Elizabeth Hilton had:

(271) John, June 29, 1723. m. Lucy ——
(272) Anna, June 14, 1725. m. John Glover, November 14, 1742.
(273) Mary, December 17, 1726. m. Solomon Lufkin, January 18, 1745.
(274) Elizabeth, August 28, 1728. m. Lieut. Wm. Dodge of Wenham, April 24, 1754. He died, October 20, 1763, aged 87.

Residence, Manchester, Mass.

John removed to Wenham, and died there in 1738. He contributed towards the erection of a schoolhouse, and he is styled Capt. John Knolton. His widow Elizabeth m. 2d John Hassen. She d. in Manchester, Mass., 1692, aged 90.

---

134 Abigail Knowlton and Solomon Parsons had:

(275) Abigail, February 21, 1731.
(276) Marion, November 16, 1732.
(277) Sarah, August 5, 1734.
(278) Lucy, September 20, 1736.
(279) Solomon, July 10, 1739.

---

138 Prudence Knowlton and Joseph Giddings had:

(280) Hannah.
(281) Joseph.
(282) Isaac.
(283) Abigail.

Joseph d. 1752.

---

139 Andrew and Lucy Stone had:

(284) Robert, May 26, 1743. m. —— Perry; m. 2d —— Pratt.
(285) Jeremiah, 1745. m. Ann Pierce.

(286) Andrew, 1742. m. Ruth Ridlow. Soldier in Revolutionary War.
(287) Johnathan, July 28, 1750. m. Widow Mary Blunt Oakes, 1777.
(288) Betsey. m. —— Preble.
(289) Molly. m. —— Jameson.
(290) Rachel. m. —— Chapman.
(291) Lydia. m. —— Hall.
(292) Abigail. m. —— Linscott.
(293) Sally. m. —— Cothlene.
(294) Anna, August 21, 1759. m. Thomas Hitchcock, 1779.

Residence, Machias, Maine.

---

145 Robert and Lydia Bishop had:

(295) Lydia, July 24, 1725. m. Jeremiah Andros of Chebasco, May 11, 1750.
(300) Sarah, May 11, 1726. m. Abraham Masters, April 14, 1754.
(301) Anna, September 22, 1728. m. Zebulon Foster, April 7, 1750.
(302) Rachel, Feb. 23, 1730. m. Andrew Low, November 9, 1752.
(303) Robert, April 22, 1733.
(304) Mary, April 21, 1735. m. Johnathan Masters, February 17, 1757.
(305) Ezekiel, April 1, 1740. m. Elizabeth Woodbury, February 5, 1762.
(306) John, July 22, 1742. d. 1748.

Robert was a carpenter. Residence, Manchester, Mass. He d. 1775.

---

146 Ezekiel and Emma Foster had:

(307) Emma, June 25, 1725. m. Benjamin Leach.
(308) Ezekiel, December 2, 1726. d. 1734.
(309) Anna, August 8, 1728. m. Edmund Jumper, August 25, 1753.
(310) John, November 29, 1730. m. Mary Herrick, May, 1753.
(311) Elizabeth, June 25, 1732. m. Nathaniel Lee.
(312) Margaret, November 5, 1734. m. Edward Hovey.

Ezekiel resided in Manchester, Mass., and was probably shipwrecked off Sable Island, March 18, 1734. Emma was a celebrated doctress. She d. 1788.

---

149 Elizabeth Knowlton and Hugh Evans had:

(313) John, June 2, 1743.
(314) Robert, July 3, 1744.
(315) Elizabeth, August 5, 1746.

Residence, Gloucester, Mass.

152 Benjamin and Sarah Mann had:

(316) Benjamin, June 9, 1743.
(317) Elizabeth, February 18, 1745. m. Daniel Murphey, November 17, 1768.
Residence, Springfield, Mass.

---

157 Samuel and Esther Dane had:

(318) Esther, September, 1761. m. William Kinsman.
(319) Samuel, 1764. m. Jane Linscott.
(320) Joseph, May 17, 1767. m. Fannie Stevens, September 14, 1794.
(321) Ebenezer, August 5, 1770. m. Ruth Smalley.
(322) Mary. m. Michael Kinsman, pub., September 27, 1783.
(323) Martha, July 29, 1772. m. Isaac Moore, 1798.
Residence removed to Farmington, Maine.

---

158 Nathaniel and Elizabeth Dean had:

(324) Nathaniel. m. Lucy Chapman.
(325) Joseph. m. Martha Dean; m. 2d Martha Wheeler.
(326) Nathan. m. Eliza Dodge, April 18, 1829.
(327) Lucy. m. Joseph Cummings, June 21, 1790. Topsfield, m. 2d Daniel Cummings.
(328) Lydia. m. James Burnham, November 6, 1798.
(329) John, 1750. m. Mary A. Dodge of Beverly, June 28, 1776.
(330) Isaac. m. Patty Woodbury, 1800.
(331)
Nathaniel d. 1811. Elizabeth d. September 14, 1798.

---

159 Benjamin and Abigail Dodge had:

(332) Ezra. m. Abigail Dodge, February 11, 1762.
(333) Edmund. m. Mary Austin, September 7, 1784.
(334) Benjamin. d. young.
(335) Neamiah. m. Elizabeth Potter, November 14, 1769.
(336) Susan.
(337) Moses. m. —— Cummings.
(338) James. Deputy to General Court of New Hampshire, 1777.

Abigail d., and Benj. m. 2d Abigail Dane, April 22, 1756. They had:

(339) Malachi. m. Abigail Patch, May 19, 1782.
(340) Ephraim. m. Mary Murphy, September 4, 1780.

(341) Hannah. m. Oliver Norton, October 22, 1792.
(342) Esther. m. —— Rush of Ipswich. Ten children.
(343) Betsey. m. —— Woodbury ; m. 2d D. Cummings, January 16, 1804.
(344) Hepsibah. m. Thomas Cummings, August 25, 1787.
(345) Abigail. m. Benjamin Larcom.
(346) Benjamin. m. Abigail Larcom (or Lawrence), December 1, 1789.
(347) Annie. m. Wm. Foster, May 29, 1797.

Benjamin lived on the Ayres farm in Hamilton, Mass., in Salem, and in Ipswich, where he d. April 3, 1781. Abigail d. May 20, 1790.

---

163 Abraham and Sarah Caldwell had :

(348) John, October 23, 1722. m.
(349) Priscilla, January 24, 1724. m. Joseph Smith, January 20, 1744.

Sarah dying, Abraham m. 2d Sarah Lull, and had :

(350) Abraham, August 26, 1726. m. Sarah Lord, November 29, 1754. Res. in Ipswich. d. October 2, 1797.
(351) Thomas, February 4, 1728. d. 1729.
(352) Sarah, August 30, 1730. d. 1731.
(353) Thomas, May 28, 1732. m. Sarah Stacey, August 16, 1755.
(354) Sarah, November 24, 1734. d. 1750.
(355) Isaac, September 26, 1736. d. 1737.

Residence, Ipswich.

---

169 Thomas and Amy Chase had :

(356) Sarah, August 18, 1735. d. young.
(357) Ebenezer, June 24, 1737. d. 1749.
(358) Johnathan, June 16, 1739. m. Ruth Page, April 29, 1762.
(359) Sarah, 1741. m. David Shaw.
(360) Molly, 1742. m. John Shaw.
(361) Nathan, October 29, 1743. d. young.
(362) William, April 19, 1746. m.
(363) John S., May 10, 1748. d. young.
(364) Thomas, May 10, 1749. m. Betsey Giles.
(365) Anna, July 13, 1753. m. Andrew Baker.
(366) Ebenezer, August 14, 1759. m. Elizabeth Rawlings.

Thomas was b. in Hampton, and rem. to Kensington, where he m. Ruth. He rem. to Northwood, N. H., in 1759, where he d. March 23, 1774. Amy d. there October 6, 1791. Thomas was a very large and powerful man, six feet four and a half inches in height, and of corresponding weight. His sons resembled him, for they were over six feet tall, and their average weight was 225 pounds. Northwood was incorporated October 6, 1773, and Thomas was elected surveyor. He was active in establishing schools, and his name, with that of his son Johnathan, is signed to the following resolution :

"We the subscribers, do solemnly engage and promise that we will to the extent of our power at the risque of our lives and fortune with arms oppose the hostile proceedings of th [so in the original] British fleets and armies against the United American Colonies."

---

170 Ebenezer and Jane Philbrick had :

(367) Marian, July 30, 1737.
(368) Johnathan. He served in Captain Marston's company during the French and Indian War, was allowed pay for doctor's bill at Albany Flats in 1759.
(369) Peter. Soldier in the colonial wars. Was paid £7 10 s. for military service, on June 26, 1761.

Ebenezer was a blacksmith. Residence, Hampton, N. H.

---

171 Benjamin and —— had :

(370) David, November 14, 1740. m. Mary A. Green.

---

174 Rice, Jr., and Lydia Woodbury had :

(371) Benjamin, December 10, 1728. m. Phoebe Wright, 1750.
(372) Francis, May 4, 1732. m. Hannah Trewlett.
(373) Joseph, April 22, 1734. m. Elizabeth Carbery, September 30, 1772.
(374) John, November 20, 1737. d. 1763.
(375) Rice 3d, August 27, 1740. m. Sarah Coey, January 28, 1757 ; m. 2d Judith Lane, 1763.
(376) Ezra, 1744.

Lydia dying, Rice m. 2d —— Adams in 1745, and had:

(377) Charles A., 1747. m. Eunice Pickard, 1769.
(378) Lydia W., 1749. m. Elkanah Babbitt.

This wife, —— Adams, d. 1749, and Rice m. 3d Elizabeth Smith, November 26, 1750. Residence, Wenham, Mass.

---

177 Churchill and Jane Rogers had:

(379) Reuben, July, 1744. m. Mary Morse, April 19, 1765.
(380) Joseph, August 11, 1742. m. Rachel Patch, November 4, 1762.
(381) Amos, July 6, 1746. m. Mary Warren, December 30, 1765. He was killed in the Revolutionary War.
(382) Lucy, June 4, 1748. m. John Osment, March 31, 1768.
(383) Abraham, September 1, 1750. m. Rhoda Tennant, December 17, 1771.
(384) John, August 18, 1752. m. Res. in Wenham, Mass. He d. 1797.
(385) William, September 12, 1754. m. Elizabeth Smith. Rem. to Northport, Me., and thence to Isle of Haute.
(386) Robert, June 28, 1757. Changed his name to Rogers. m. Betsey Dane. Rev. soldier. Rem. to Maine.
(387) Thomas, January 28, 1760. m. Joanna Martin, January 29, 1782. Rem. to Northport, Me. d. October 10, 1827. A colonel.
(388) Parker, March 8, 1762. Disappeared.
(389) Benjamin, June 18, 1766. m. Susanna Woodbury, December 21, 1786. Rem. to Beverly, Mass. d. August 5, 1822. A captain. She d. December 20, 1824.

Churchill was b. in Ipswich, and removed to Maine, in, or near, Belfast.

---

179 Abraham and Miriam Cole, of Beverly, Mass., had:

(390) Caleb, February 24, 1752. m. Elizabeth Bailey. Rem. to Canada.
(391) Johnathan, December 19, 1755. m. Hannah Morgan.

Residence, Wenham, Mass.

---

180 Ruth Knowlton and Edward Carlyle had:

(392) Amos.
(393) Louisa.
(394) Lucy.

Residence, Hopkinton, Mass.

181 Daniel and Abigail Almy had:

(395) William. m. Julia ——.
(396) Mary.
(397) Asa. m. Sarah Hadley.
(398) Elias, 1744. m. Elizabeth Jennings. Res. in Hopkinton. d. 1837.
(399) Anna. m. Phillip Metcalf, 1790.
(400) Daniel. m. Abigail Marshall, 1781.
(401) Nathan. m. Patience Miller; m. 2d —— Jennings.
(402) John, January 24, 1745. m. Martha Jennings, April 20, 1769.

Daniel d. September 15, 1782. Residence, Framingham, Mass.

---

182 Sarah Knowlton and —— Knowlton had:

(403) Borguilla.
(404) John, September 23, 1734.
(405) Isaac. m. Lucy Wheeler; m. 2d Hannah Sawyer.
(406) Samuel. m. Rebecca Coggins, March 18, 1762.
(407) Joshua.
(408) Joseph. m. Relief Cobleigh.

Residence, Hopkinton, Mass.

---

184 John and —— had:

(409) John, February 28, 1763. m. Susannah Jennings, 1789.
(410) Isaiah, May 22, 1767. m. Jemima Johnson, May 25, 1796.

Residence, Holliston, Mass.

---

189 John and —— had:

(411) John, 1740.

---

191 Silas and —— had:

(412) Rosel, m. Ann Dutton; m. 2d Sophia Goodall.
(413) Gideon, 1739.
(414) Jared. m. Lydia.
(415) Ascnath. m. Asa Wilson.
(416) Anna. m. Nathan Wilson. She d. insane.
(417) Dorothy. m. Joshua Whitney, January 14, 1781; m. 2d —— Hartshorn.

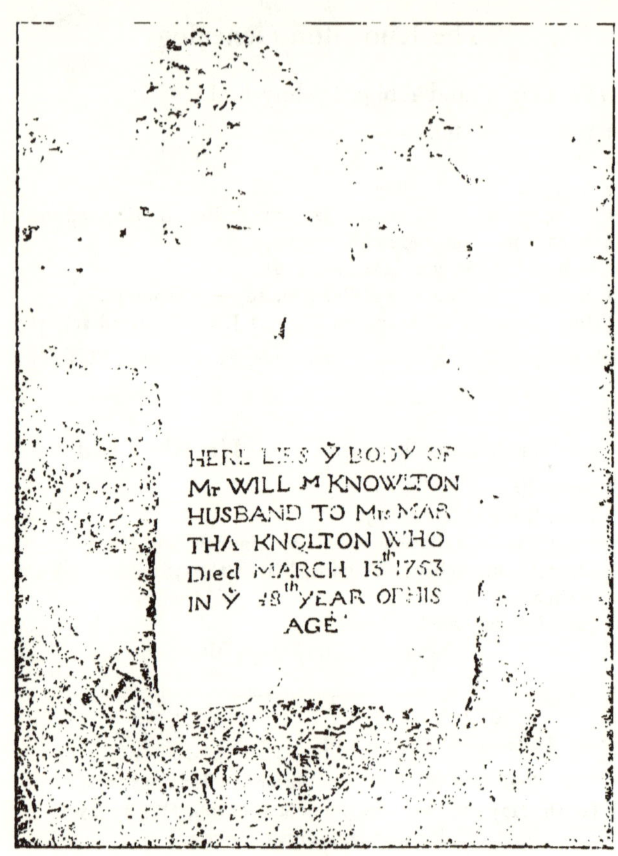

THE GRAVE OF WILLIAM KNOWLTON,
Ashford, Conn.

(418) Joshua, 1772. m. Elizabeth Shattuck.
Alice. m. Thomas Squires.

Residence, Belchertown, Mass.

---

192 Paul and Mary Knowlton, of Wenham, had:

(419) Amy.

Residence, Wenham, Mass.

---

194 Timothy and —— had:

(420) Timothy, 1745. m. Sarah Mansfield; m. 2d Eunice ——.
(420 A) Ebenezer, 1752. m. Mary Barber, August 28, 1765.

Residence, Medway and Rowe, Mass.

---

197 William and Martha Pinder had:

(421) Lucy. d. young.
(422) Lucy, February 20, 1736. m. Dea. Abijah Brooks, of Ashford.
(423) William, December 23, 1738. m. Mehitable Eaton, of Ashford, Conn.
(424) Daniel, December 23, 1738. m. Elizabeth Farnham, December 3, 1763; m. 2d Rebecca Fenton, April 24, 1788.
(425) Thomas, November 30, 1740. m. Anna Keyes, April 5, 1759.
(426) Nathaniel, May 9, 1746. d. young.
(427) Mary, May 9, 1746. m. Ezekiel Tiffany of Ashford, March 9, 1748/9.
(428) Sarah. m. Joshua Kendall of Ashford.
(429) Priscilla. unm.

William was a "housewright." He was b. in Ipswich, Mass., whence he removed to West Boxford, where he m. Martha Pinder, and from there he went to Ashford, Conn., late in the year 1748. He purchased a farm of four hundred acres which he divided among his sons. Martha was admitted to the church by letter, January 24, 1749, but it does not appear that William ever became a member, though he liberally sustained the local institutions of religion. Martha was a granddaughter of John Pynder, of Pynder, England, "a Soldier in yᵉ Countrie's Service," and a subscriber to the fund for the services of Major Dennison in King Philip's War. She was the great-granddaughter of Henry Pynder, who with his wife Mary sailed for America from London in the ship *Susan and Ellen*, 1635. Said Henry was a lineal descendant of the Pynders of Lincoln County, England, to whom the following arms were granted in 1538, as registered in the Herald's College, London:

"Azure, a chevron between three lions' heads, erased argent, guttae de poix, ducally crowned or. Crest, a lion's head erased or, ducally crowned azure."

William d. in Ashford, March 13, 1753, and Martha m. 2d Colonel Dean of Taunton, and removed there.

---

198 Nathaniel and Mary Fuller had:

(430) Nathaniel, 1730. m. Elizabeth Parks, February 15, 1762.
(431) Mary, September 15, 1733. m. Thomas Messer, January 20, 1758.
(432) Ebenezer, September 15, 1733.
(433) Lydia, 1747.

Residence, Sudbury, Mass.

---

202 Susannah Knowlton and Josiah Dodge had:

(434) Josiah, September 8, 1740. m. Hannah Conant, November, 1761.
(435) Susannah, 1742. m. Israel Fellows, March 29, 1762.
(436) Rhoda, August 25, 1744. m. Benjamin Hinds, 1762.
(437) Sarah, May 24, 1749. m. Johnathan Leonard, November 1, 1764.
(438) Asahel, August 26, 1752. m. Ada Walker, 1773.
(439) Benjamin, May 1, 1754. m. Tabitha Perkins, December 26, 1776.
(440) Phoebe, September 23, 1759.

Susannah and Josiah were m. in Ipswich. Their parents resided in Wenham, from which place they removed to Nova Scotia, where they d. in 1805, at or near, Annapolis.

---

207 Ebenezer and —— had

(441) Gideon, 1754. m. Mary Gibson, 1796.
(442) Abner, 1756. m. Elizabeth Knowlton, January 20, 1780.
(443) Antipas, 1758. d. in Ipswich, May 20, 1785.

Ebenezer was a soldier in the Colonial War of 1755, and his powder-horn, marked "Sargent Ebenezer Nolton, Fort William Henry, Nov. 17, 1775," is in the possession of a descendant, Mr. Abner Knowlton, of Chico, Cal. His sons Abner and Antipas served in Capt. Richard Dodge's company, Colonel Baldwin's regiment, in the Revolutionary War. Ebenezer d. in Ipswich, September 27, 1777.

210 Nathaniel and Mary —— had :

(444) Nathaniel, m. Mary ——. Res. Brattleboro, Vt.
(445) Jeremiah, m. Susan Whitney. Res. Brattleboro, Vt.

---

221 Thomas and —— had :

(446) Thomas, 1760. m. Susannah Hollis, 1783.

---

222 Stephen and —— had :

(447) Stephen, July 15, 1753. m. Diodema Chubb, February 1. 1780.
(448) Abigail. m Ebenezer Rowley, 1776.
(449) Azubah.
(450) Susannah.
(451) Deborah.
(452) Levina.
(453) Mary.
(454) Hannah.
(455) Joshua.

Stephen's first wife dying, he m. 2d Rebecca —— and had :

(456) Sarah.

Rebecca d. September 8, 1795, and he m. 3d Mary Purple, widow of Edward Purple, December 31, 1795, and d. January 29, 1814, aged 84. Res. East Haddam, Conn.

---

226 Joseph m. 1st Ruth Dodge. He m. 2d Reliance Cole, 1786, and had :

(456 A) Joseph, March 1, 1787. m. Ruth Richardson, January 2, 1808. m. 2d Jemima Holden. m. 3d Sarah Richardson.
(456 B) Benjamin, September 23, 1792. m. Olive Pillsbury, April 3, 1809. m. 2d Polly Ketcham, January 11, 1816.
(456 C) Reliance. m. —— Clarke. Res. Sudbury, Vt.
(456 D) Thomas. m. Susan Oney. 7 children.

Joseph m. 3d Thankful Gates and had :

(456 E) Thankful, 1796. m. Ivery Bragdon, January, 1819. m. 2d Wm. Tucker, 1832. She d. October 22, 1839.
(456 F) Betsey, July, 1800. m. Benj. Tupper, 1822.
(456 G) Ruth. m. John Willoughby, November 15, 1807. She d. 1832.

Joseph was born at East Haddam, Conn. He served in the Havana Expedition in 1762, and also in the Revolutionary War. He d. at Pillar Point, N. Y., May 1, 1834, aged 95.

---

229 A Thomas and Jane Carter had:

(457) John, August 17, 1747. m. Mary Manning.
(458) Thomas.
(459) Daniel, 1750.
(460) Ephraim, 1756. m. Elizabeth Butler.
(461) Sarah, 1758. m. —— Talcott.
(462) Robert, February 10, 1759. m. Mary Gay, February 3, 1787
(463) Enoch, 1760.
(464) Silas B., 1762. m. Mehitable Kendrick.
(465) Caroline. m. —— Collins.
(466) Ruth. m. —— Duff.
(467) Jerusha. m. —— Lyon.

Thomas removed from Sharon Springs, Conn., to Bethlehem, N. Y.

---

229 B Ephraim and Elizabeth Butler had:

(468) Robert, 1745. m.
(469) Stephen, 1749.
(470) Elizabeth, 1749. m. John Woolsley, 1772. She d. 1815.

Ephraim settled in Bedford, N. Y. He was a soldier of the Revolution, and fought at White Plains, the battle-field being a portion of his estate. Elizabeth d. 1801.

---

229 H Abraham and Mrs. Elizabeth Wise had:

(471) Sarah, December 8, 1751. m. Wm. Longfellow, April 7, 1781.
(472) Elizabeth, October 27, 1753.
(473) Abraham, September 12, 1756. m. Mrs. Esther Russell, August 22, 1777; m. 2d Sarah Fitts; m. 3d Hannah Fitts.
(474) Mary, September 5, 1758.

Residence, Ipswich, Mass.

After Abraham's death, his widow Elizabeth m. 2d Daniel Heard, June 22, 1762, by whom she had several children. She d. at the age of ninety-two, and at the residence of her son, William Heard East Concord, N. H., in 1819. Abraham was a Minute-man in the Revolution, enlisting January 24, 1775.

232 Daniel and Zerviah Wadkins had:

(475) Stephen, July 8, 1746. m. Anna Fletcher, September 20, 1783.
(476) Robert, February 6, 1748.
(477) Miriam, 1750. m. —— Tupper.
(478) Eleanor, 1752. m. —— Upham.
(479) Esther, 1754. m. —— Marsh.
(480) Daniel, 1757. m. Rachel Olney.
(481) Mehitable. m. John Hall, 1772.

Daniel lived in Ashford, Conn. He was a soldier, and served at the siege of Louisburg. His subsequent career is narrated in the Nova Scotia chapter. Zerviah was the daughter of Capt. William Watkins (or Wadkins) of the Colonial Army, who also was a Representative from Ashford, in the Connecticut General Assembly. She is buried at Fort Belcher, Nova Scotia.

---

235 Thomas and Bridget Bosworth had:

(482) Mary, June 15, 1758. m. Nathaniel Bosworth, of Mansfeld, Conn.
(483) Jemima, April 22, 1759. m. Isaac Abbey.
(484) Ezra, December 21, 1760. m. Abigail Bostwick.
(485) John, April 17, 1762. m. Jemima Barrow.
(486) Hannah, February 13, 1764. m. James Perkins.
(487) Daniel, February 8, 1766. d. young.
(488) Keziah, August 21, 1768. d. September 6, 1777.

Bridget d. in Ashford, Conn., June 9, 1777, and Thomas m. 2d Hepsibah Peak, of Ashford, September 24, 1778, and had:

(489) Johnathan, June 27, 1779. m. Zerviah Sanger, April 4, 1802.
(490) Thomas, June 18, 1781. Lost at sea when young.
(491) Jesse, October 12, 1784. m. Joanna Hale. Sett. in N. Y. State.
(492) Chester, October 12, 1787. m. Priscilla Sanger, July 1, 1807.

---

237 Abraham and Molly Knox had:

(493) Amasa, February 26, 1764. m. Margaret Topliff, 1834.
(494) Sarah, June 20, 1765. d. 1775.
(495) Miriam, December 15, 1766. m. Abner Woodward, April 15, 1790.
(496) Stephen, September 7, 1768. m. Hannah Heath, January 8, 1795.
(497) Persis, April 2, 1770.
(498) Abel, April 9, 1772. m. Barbara Dimock.

(499) Abraham, December 17, 1774. d. young.
(500) Abraham, July 11, 1776. d. young.
(501) Nathan, August 11, 1778. m. Lydia Leonard.
(502) Daniel, March 17, 1781. m. Hannah Knowlton, November 24, 1803.
(503) Amos, March 20, 1783. m. Nancy Webb, September 13, 1804.

"Abraham, Sen's mark for his creatures was a crop on right ear, a half penny crop on back side of left ear."

He d. in Ashford, Ct., June 14, 1821. Molly d. July 8, 1819.

---

246 Joseph and Mary Knowlton had:

(504) Abigail, June 29, 1750.
(505) Asa, September 21, 1752. m. Had s. Jesse.
(506) Anna, October 7, 1754.
(507) Grace, July 23, 1756. m. Josiah Goulding, of Grafton, Mass., 1777.
(508) Nathan, May 15, 1760. m. Abigail Maynard, January 8, 1782.
(509) Joseph, May 4, 1761. m. Priscilla Howe, May 11, 1784.
(510) Mary, August 23, 1763. m. Joseph Boyden, December 15, 1785. Res., Guilford.
(511) Rachel, March 15, 1765. m. Jasper Rand, 1783.
(512) Samuel, July 6, 1769. Res., Shrewsbury, Mass.
(513) Asahel, November 23, 1773. Res., Shrewsbury, Mass.

Mary d. August 21, 1796, and Joseph m. 2d Miss Cheney, of Ward (Auburn), Mass. Mary was the daughter of Deacon Ezekiel Knowlton. Joseph was admitted to the church in Shrewsbury, 1774, and to that in Ward in 1790. He conveyed his farm to Josiah Goulding, his son-in-law "to see him through," his daughter, Grace, returning his considerate provision for her by making a happy home for him in her own house, where she ministered to his needs with loving fidelity until his death, August 22, 1816.

---

247 Abraham and Comfort Holman had:

(514) Comfort, 1761. m. George Haskell, April 25, 1782. She d. 1837.

Comfort d. in 1761, and Abraham m. 2d Susannah Jordan, May, 1764. They had:

(515) Sarah, June 13, 1765. m. Elijah Bangs, April 21, 1791. She d. 1834.
(516) Israel, January 11, 1767. m. Abigail Carter, 1794.
(517) Thomas, January 23, 1769. d. September 8, 1777.
(518) Lucy, December 21, 1770. m. Nathan Haskell, June 2, 1795.

(519) Abraham, May 6, 1774. d. young.
(520) Phillip, July 30, 1776. d. young.
(521) Thomas, February 9, 1782. m. Susan Heywood, December 6, 1806.

Abraham was a tanner, residing on the old Petersham road, in Templeton. He was a lieutenant of the 10th Company, Worcester County Regiment, his commission dating May 3, 1776. In his old age his appearance was most striking, for his long white hair falling to his shoulders gave him a very venerable appearance. Susannah d. April 27, 1816. He rem. to Hardwick and m. 2d there, and d. June 9, 1812. He was a Selectman and on Committee of Correspondence.

---

248 Jacob and Sarah Pratt had:

(522) Joseph, November 20, 1760. m. Huldah Warren, December 25, 1784; m. 2d Relief Stratton, December 21, 1797.

Sarah dying, Jacob m. 2d Sarah Smith, November, 1762, and had:

(523) Sarah, September 29, 1763. m. Ebenezer Rich. Rem. to Ohio.
(524) Jacob, June 16, 1764. d. young.
(525) Elizabeth, June 16, 1765.
(526) Elijah, March 2, 1767. Drowned December 2, 1790.
(527) Anna, July 17, 1769.
(528) Abigail, June 26, 1771. m. —— Mills. Sett. in N. Y. State.
(529) Jacob, October 6, 1776. m. Rhoda Smith, June 10, 1800.

Jacob was a blacksmith and farmer. He rem. to Hardwick, Mass., in 1752, and served during two campaigns in the French and Indian War, with rank of corporal, in Capt. Samuel Robinson's company. He d. not later than 1788, for his widow m. 2d Deacon Joseph Allen, August 6, 1789.

---

249 Nathan and —— had:

(530) James, July, 1774. m. Betsey Tracey.
(531) Samuel, November 13, 1778. m. Aurilla Coates.

---

254 Paul and Lucy Forbush had:

(532) Paul, October 23, 1770. m. Lovie Whipple, 1801.
(533) Lucy, February 28, 1772. m. Elijah Hale, of Grafton, February 14, 1799.

(534) Robert, December 7, 1773. m. Lydia Thurston, of Westboro, Mass., 1807.

(535) Daniel, December 9, 1775. m. Mary Hemmingway, 1803.

(536) Sarah, November 11, 1777. m. Samuel Thurston, June 24, 1802. Res., Westboro, Mass.

(537) John, January 6, 1780. m. Diodemia Duncan.

(538) Marjery, October 25, 1781. m. Zarun Perkins, February 18, 1810. Res., Wallingford, Vt.

(539) Joel, November 1, 1783. m. Mary Brooks.

(540) Beulah, September 25, 1785. m. Jonas Baker.

(541) Ruth, January 5, 1788. m. Isaac Cutler, April 8, 1823.

(542) Anna, September 9, 1789. m. Jona Newton, February 22, 1818; m. 2d Zarun Perkins.

(543) Jacob, May 17, 1791.

(544) Levi, June 9, 1797. m. Louisa Divoll, 1822.

Paul was Selectman in Shrewsbury four years, and d. there June 27, 1799. Lucy d. May 18, 1837.

---

261 Abraham and Lydia Batchelder had:

(545) Silas, June 3, 1773. m. Mercy Wakefield.

(546) Martha, June 1, 1775. m. Nathan Munroe, March 31, 1805.

(547) Sarah, July 24, 1777. m. John White, 1798.

(548) David, November 14, 1779. m. Lucy Brigham.

(549) Lydia, October 21, 1781. d. June 28, 1808.

(550) Abraham, August 4, 1784. m. Lucy Faulkner.

(551) Thankful, October 25, 1789. d. January, 1872.

Lydia was from Upton, Mass. She d. September 28, 1803, and Abraham m. 2d Lucy Whitney, of Upton, 1805. He was a soldier of the Revolution in Capt. Thomas Baker's company, Col. Nathaniel Tyler's regiment, in the Rhode Island Alarm, July, 1780. He d. September 12, 1807. Res., Shrewsbury.

---

263 Susannah Knowlton and Gershom Wheelock had:

(552) Asa, June 10, 1758.

(553) Gershom, February 7, 1761.

(554) Susannah, November 17, 1762. m. Barlow Carpenter, 1803.

(555) Abigail, September 30, 1765. m. David Harris, February 24, 1788.

(556) Elizabeth. m. Capt. John Rice, November 16, 1790.

(557) Martha. d. August 28, 1840.

(558) Alice. d. young.

Residence, Shrewsbury, Mass.

265 Ezekiel and Anna Miles had :

(559) Joseph, June 27, 1760. m. Betsey Sprague.
(560) Stephen, May 28, 1762. m. Comfort White, January 24, 1796. He d. January 16, 1853.
(561) Ezekiel, 1764. m. Had s. Geo. W. d. October 5, 1823.
(562) Miles, March 27, 1766. m. Tryphena Sprague. He d. September 25, 1824.
(563) Jemima, 1768. m. Thomas Wright, February 7, 1791 ; m. 2d Batchelder Bowker, February 1, 1798.
(564) Levi, 1769. m. Polly Morse, 1801 ; m. 2d Mrs. Butterfield. He d. 1842.
(565) Lucy, May 27, 1776. m. Amasa Clymer or Elmer. No chil. She d. 1850.
(566) Anna, April 7, 1778. m. John Brill. No chil. She d. April 30, 1860.
(567) Asaph, September 1, 1781. m. Betsey Sawyer, December 23, 1806. He d. February 12, 1844.
(568) Lyman, January, 1774. m. Lepha Whitcomb, 1795. He d. July 28, 1832.

Ezekiel and Anna lived in Templeton, Mass. Joseph rem. to Gardner, Mass., Stephen to West Gardner, Jemima to Fitzwilliam, N. H., Levi, Lyman, Lucy, Anna, and Asaph to Canada. The history of the last five is included in the Canadian chapter.

Ezekiel Knowlton, Sr., was one of the most conspicuous men of his day and State. He was commissioned Captain, April 6, 1776, Colonel Dyke's Worcester County regiment, and served in the Revolutionary War until March 1, 1777. He d. December 1, 1810. Anna d. April 8, 1826. Res., Templeton, Mass.

---

266 Luke and Sarah Holland had :

(569) Calvin, January 22, 1761. m. Sophia Willard.
(570) Patty, December 5, 1762. m. Daniel Warner.
(571) Silas, December 9, 1764. m. Sarah Holbrook.
(572) Sarah, May 2, 1767. m. John Holbrook.
(573) Alice, July 22, 1769. m. Nathan A. Stone, April 24, 1788.
(574) Lucinda, August 8, 1771. m. Samuel Willard.
(575) Luke, Jr., May 24, 1775. m. Charlotte Kenny.

HON. LUKE KNOWLTON,

the fifth child and second son of Deacon Ezekiel, was born in Shrewsbury, November 4, 1738. From his youth up he displayed those traits of character that made him so conspicuous a figure years afterwards in his adopted State. Ambitious and enterprising by nature, he early fitted himself to become by education and observation a leader of men in the stirring events that lay before him. When but twenty-one years old he enlisted in the regular service of the Continental Army, and in Captain Fay's company, of Shrewsbury, and served during the French and Indian War in 1759 at Crown Point, Fort Ticonderoga, and other points. From a journal of each day's events kept by him with pathetic simplicity of style we get a graphic picture of the sufferings and privations to which the patriotic soldiers of that troublous time were subjected. The cover of his journal bears the following inscription.

"Luke Knowlton
His Book
Bought att Bostown, May 25
Anno Domini 1759.

Luke Knowlton, His Hand
wrote at the Landing Place,
Near Ticonderoga Fort——
July 26th Anno Domini, 1759.

Luke Knowlton
His Book
Shrewsbury June 3,
1759."

This journal covers a period from June 4th, to November 18th, the last entry of which is:

"Lord's Day. I travelled to Shrewsbury, home to my father's and found my honored parents well."

Knowlton writes of the avidity with which they ate raw turnips and, when they could get it, raw pork, and at one time they were in such extremities that they killed and ate one of their pack horses. When their time of enlistment had expired, the officers refused to give the men their discharge, whereupon Luke Knowlton gathered two hundred of them on the parade ground, armed and loaded with their personal effects, determined to assert their rights. The officers threatened to fire upon them, but the men were calmly resolute, and the officers were obliged to yield. Knowlton's sense of personal rights and his firmness in defending those rights, were made the more effective by a quiet dignity and judicious reserve that marked his subsequent career in public life.

At the close of the war he and a few associates petitioned the Government for a grant of 20,000 acres of land, and subsequently for 37,000 more, in what

Hon. Luke Knowlton,
Judge of the Supreme Court,
Newfane, Vt., 1738-1810.

was then known as Goncester, now Brookfield and Fairfield, beginning at a line twenty-three miles east of Lake Champlain, on the northwest bank of the river Le Moyle. The petition was granted, the tract was named Knowlton's Gore, and thus was laid the foundation of Knowlton's subsequent prosperity.

He married Sarah, daughter of Ephraim Holland, of Shrewsbury, January 5, 1760, and removed to Newfane, Vt., February, 1773, where thirteen families had already settled. At the organization of the town in the following year, he was chosen Town Clerk, holding the position for fourteen years. Knowlton was from the day of his removal to Newfane *facile princeps*, for he represented the town in the State Legislature during seven terms, was a member of the Old Council from 1787 to 1793, Judge of the Windham County Court, and was elected Judge of the Supreme Court in 1786. In published sketches and histories of Newfane it is freely admitted that the town owed its original prosperity and subsequent importance chiefly to the sagacity, enterprise, and ability of Judge Knowlton. His rare perception gave him an intuitive knowledge of men, and his liberality to the poor, gravity of deportment, suavity of manner, and personal godliness won for him the general appellation of "Saint Luke." * He gave the land for a public Common, and contributed largely towards the erection of the first court-house and jail in Newfane.

As Judge Knowlton had been a staunch Loyalist during the ante-revolutionary period, he received from the British Government a liberal grant of land in Lower Canada, upon a portion of which is now located the town of Sherbrooke. This, with the other fact of his well-known Tory sentiments, placed him under the ban of suspicion, even after he had given in his adherence to the Government of Vermont, and he was so fiercely threatened by his neighbors that he fled from Massachusetts, where he was then living, to Vermont. On his return he had an experience of which the records of the Supreme Court held at Westminster, February term 1784, are the evidence. The case is known as that of Freeman *vs.* Prouty: an indictment for burglary.

Although Knowlton had abundantly proved his loyalty to the new Government and order of things, the "Yorkers" believed him to be still secretly negotiating with the British Government, and in its pay. So stoutly did they continue their charge of treason that Congress in secret session, November 27, 1782, ordered his arrest, and, as already stated, he fled for safety. Returning the following year, he was kidnapped one November night by Francis Prouty, Thomas Whipple, Johnathan Dunkely, John and Darwin Wheeler, and others,

"armed with pistols, clubs, guns, swords and bayonets,"

and conveyed beyond the border. General Fletcher under whom Knowlton had fought in 1759 ordered the militia to assemble to the rescue, but the fearless return of Knowlton made further operations unnecessary. The rioters were

* His piety is evidenced in every page of his war journal, for he has carefully recorded the services on the Lord's Day, giving always the text and name of the preacher.

subsequently tried and convicted, and Prouty as ringleader was fined £30, with costs and forty days' imprisonment.

It would appear that his traducers left no stain upon his reputation, for he was chosen Deacon of his church, and it fell to him to "set the psalm," reading off two lines at a time for the congregation to sing. He died December 12, 1810. His wife died September 1, 1797.

---

267 William and Hannah Hastings had :

(576) Hannah, 1765. m. Capt. Thomas Harrington, October 14, 1784.
(577) Asa, 1767. m. Olive Waite, February 2, 1789.
(578) Susannah, 1771. m. John S. Whitney, May 4, 1799.
(579) Artemus, 1774. m. Huldah Lyon, 1798. m. 2d Rhoda Smith.
(580) William, June 20, 1777. m. Clorinda Smith, 1802.
(581) Seth, May 11, 1781. m. Relief Howe.
(582) Joseph H., March 22, 1785. m. Chloe Forbush, 1806.

William was a Deacon in the Shrewsbury church 1784–1820, where he rem. from Templeton in 1776. He was a Selectman 1785–7, and was admitted to the church in Shrewsbury, with his wife, June 1778. He d. there September 13, 1820. Hannah was a lineal descendant of Capt. Thomas and Susannah Hastings, members of the old English family of that name, who sailed to America from Ipswich, Eng., in the ship *Elizabeth*, April 10, 1636. They settled in Watertown, Mass., where Hannah d. October 25, 1832.

---

270 Capt. Thomas and Elizabeth Batchelder had :

(583) Susannah, March 22, 1772. d. 1776.
(584) Cynthia, July 9, 1773. d. 1776.
(585) Elizabeth, September 26, 1775. m. Noyes. d. 1848.
(586) Dea. Ezekiel, April 28, 1777. m. Eleanor Brown, 1828.
(587) Susannah, May 2, 1779. m. Thomas Witherbee, Jr., 1800.
(588) Luke, July 30, 1782. m. Hetty Rand, September 3, 1804.
(589) Thomas, November 17, 1784. m. Rebecca Whitney, November, 1809.
(590) Amasa, March 10, 1787. m. Sarah Parks, 1816.
(591) Cynthia, March 19, 1789. d. October 19, 1861. unm.
(592) Mark B., October 9, 1791.
(593) Hannah W., February 10, 1795. m. Daniel G. Noyes, 1817.

Capt. Thomas was elected Selectman of Shrewsbury twenty-one times, and Town Clerk ten times. In 1777 the expediency of having a bass-viol to assist in the music was solemnly discussed by the congregation, and Capt. Thomas was selected to "sett the psalm," an office which he held for six years. He served in the Revolutionary War, his commission as 2d Lieut. dating December 6, 1777. He was promoted December 3, 1778, and was Capt. of the 6th Company, Worcester Co. Regiment. He received pay for the loss of personal effects at the evacuation of New York, September, 14, 1776, and was probably at the battle of Harlem Heights, where his kinsman and namesake, Col. Thomas, fell. He d. August 22, 1829, and his widow, Elizabeth, d. January 7, 1833.

---

271 John and Lucy —— had:

(594) Abraham, 1756. m. Anna Taylor.

---

284 Robert and —— Perry and 2d —— Pratt had:

(595) Chauncey. m. Annie Phillips.
(596) Levi.
(597) Lydia. m. —— Mc'George.
(598) Daniel. m. Ruth Meritt.
(599) William. m. Barbara Ritz.
(600) Sophia.
(601) Lottie.

Robert was a sailor. He removed from Machias, Me., to Vermont, and engaged in farming. He served in the Revolutionary War, in Captain Allin's company, Colonel Bradford's regiment, having enlisted for the whole war. He also served in the War of 1812. He married at, or near, Sackett's Harbor, N. Y., and removed west.

---

285 Jeremiah and Anna Pierce had:

(602) Ezekiel, 1765. m. Mary Knowlton, 1795.
(603) Mehitable, 1779. d. 1869.
(604) Anna.
(605) John. m. Sally Knowlton, 1804.
(606) Johnathan. d. 1858.
(607) Samuel. m. Lucy Knowlton. m. 2d Mercy Knowlton.
(608) Andrew.
(609) Sally. m. —— Williams. She d. 1870
(610) Betsey. m. James Cupps.
(611) Jeremiah. m. Deborah Stetson, December, 1820.
(612) Fellows. d. at sea, 1825.
(613) David.

286 Andrew and Ruth Ridlow had:

(614) John, 1799. m. Lydia Hall. m. 2d Mary Meseroe.
(615) Joseph. m. Susan Redlaw.
(616) Andrew, 1796. m. Mary Maddocks.
(617) Sarah. m. E. Johnson.
(618) Susan. m. Samuel Rice, soldier in War of 1812.
(619) Anna, 1792. d. 1872.

Andrew was a Revolutionary soldier. He served with the rank of corporal at the defense of Machias, Me., in Capt. Jacob Ludwig's company; re-enlisted in Colonel Jones' Third Regiment, Maine Militia, to assist Colonels Wade and Ludwig in the operations around Providence, R. I. He d. aged 95.

---

287 Johnathan and Mary Blunt Oakes had:

(620) Sarah, May 25, 1778. m. Jeremiah Butler, November 25, 1802.
(621) Johnathan, December 4, 1780. m. Deborah Tufts, August 20, 1801.
(622) Samuel, January 4, 1783. m. Olive Butler, March 6, 1806.
(623) Gilbert, January 26, 1785. pub. to Sarah Odell, November 27, 1806.
(624) Lydia A., October 17, 1787. m. Thomas Wellman; 12 chil.
(625) Francis. m. Lovie Butler, November 26, 1812. m. 2d Rosanna Hunter, November 17, 1841.
(626) Katherine. m. Joseph Dennett, September 3, 1832. They rem. to Indianapolis, Ind.
(627) Hannah, March 25, 1795. d. young.

Johnathan was b. in Ipswich, and resided for a time in Walpole (Malden) Mass., from which place they removed to Damariscotta, Me., in 1787. After a brief stay here, Johnathan pushed on to the Sandy River, a tributary of the Kennebec, and effected a settlement on Lot 17, where he built a log house There being no mills on the river at this early date, Johnathan was obliged to shoulder his bag of corn, and carry it through an unbroken wilderness to the mill at Winthrop, a round trip of fifty-two miles, with only a pocket compass, or spotted trees, as a guide, and involving an absence of a week from the isolated log house in which his wife remained entirely alone with her infant son Johnathan, Jr. The great freshet of October 22, 1785, drove the family from their rude quarters, and they were with difficulty rescued, being taken out of the top window, and ferried across the river to the house of his brother-in-law. He subsequently erected mills at Farmington Falls, and, although they were swept away by floods, his indomitable energy and perseverance revived his fortunes, and at his death, November 5, 1819, he was a principal owner of real estate and milling property. His humane and generous disposition endeared him to all classes, and he passed the latter years of his life in the serene enjoyment of public confidence and neighborly regard. He was an ardent Methodist, and, with Stephen Titcomb, he was mainly instrumental in building the first meeting-house at Farmington Falls.

His widow, Mary, d. October 2, 1825.

---

294 Anna Knowlton and Thomas Hitchcock had:

(628) Joseph, December 9, 1780.
(629) Martha, March 21, 1782. d. 1788.
(630) Hannah, August 12, 1785. m. 12 child. She d. 1834.
(631) Martha, May 14, 1788. m. Zacharias Butterfield.
(632) Mary, August 17, 1789. m. Isaac Butterfield.
(633) Anna, October 16, 1791. m. William Adams.
(634) Thomas, April 2, 1795. m. Sally Parker; m. 2d Ruth Thomas.
(635) Samuel, December 19, 1796.
(636) Sarah, June 10, 1801. m. Ebenezer Knowlton, December 28, 1818.

---

305 Ezekiel and Elizabeth Woodbury had:

(637) Robert, 1761. m. Jemima Smith.
(638) Sarah, April 15, 1763. m. Moses Trussell, December 18, 1786.
(639) Ezekiel, May 9, 1768. m. Susan Smith, November, 1793. ~~m. 2d Gordon.~~
(640) Elizabeth, October 9, 1770. d. at Hopkinton, ~~Mass.~~ unm.
(641) John, December 8, 1773. d. at Hopkinton.
(642) Mary, October 3, 1775. d. at Hopkinton. unm.
(643) Levi, October 7, 1777. d. at Hopkinton.
(644) Nathaniel, 1780. m. Susan Greely; m. 2d. Mary Connor.
(645) James, March 17, 1782. d. in Hopkinton. School teacher.
(646) Lydia, February 20, 1784. m. Wm. K. Storey.

Ezekiel enlisted in the Colonial Army when but eighteen years old, served in the French and Indian War, and endured great privations and sufferings. At the close of the war he returned, and m. his cousin Elizabeth. He d. January 6, 1818. Elizabeth d. May 6, 1826.

---

309 Anna Knowlton and Edward Jumper had:

(647) John, August 16, 1757.
(648) Elizabeth, September 2, 1758.
(649) Rebecca, August 12, 1761.
(650) Abigail, January 10, 1762.

310 John and Mary Herrick had:

(651) John, Jr., November 29, 1755.
(652) Ezekiel, 1757. m. Mehitable Fisk. He d. 1806.
(653) Robert, February 24, 1759. m. Eda Allen, November 12, 1780.
(654) Mary, July 11, 1761. m. Moses Hill.
(655) Sarah, June 17, 1763. m. Benjamin Leach, September 1, 1784.
(656) Anna, December 31, 1765. m. Daniel Trussell.
(657) Daniel, August 25, 1768. m. Mary Stocker, January 13, 1793.

Residence, Manchester and Gloucester, Mass. John, Jr., sailed from Newburyport, as Prize Master on the ship *Bennington*, sent home one prize, and was never heard of afterwards.

---

317 Elizabeth Knowlton and Daniel Murphey had:

(658) Daniel.
(659) Sarah.
(660) Elijah. m. Mrs. Elizabeth Bliss.

Daniel was a corporal in Captain Colton's company, Colonel David Brewer's and Colonel Rufus Putnam's regiments. He fought at Bunker Hill, and served for three years and eight months in the Revolutionary War.

---

319 Samuel and Jane Linscott had:

(661) Samuel, August 9, 1788. m. Betsey Butler, February 20, 1812.
(662) John, December 7, 1789. m. Sally Green; m. 2d Sarah Butler.
(663) Betsey, February 6, 1791. m. James Cummings, October 28, 1813.
(664) Joseph, September 20, 1792. m. Mary Tufts of Indiana, January 22, 1818. 3 chil.
(665) Ebenezer, October 10, 1794. m. Sally Hiscock, December 28, 1818.
(666) Esther, March 25, 1796. m. Richard Maddock, March 27, 1819. She d. May 30, 1832. He d. 1863.
(667) Joshua, September 8, 1797. m. Lydia Lowell, November 16, 1820.
(668) Jane, April 23, 1799. m. Oliver Lowell, April 30, 1820. She d. December 5, 1821.
(669) Benjamin, January 15, 1801. d. December 5, 1827. unm.
(670) Martha, July 5, 1802. m Ebenezer Stowers, December 22, 1823. d. June, 1859.
(671) Sally, September 3, 1804. d. young.
(672) Dean, July 23, 1807. m. Mehitable Graves, November 17, 1831. Shoemaker.

Samuel rem. from Ipswich to Sandy River Township, Maine, in 1786, where by farming in summer and shoemaking in winter he acquired a considerable fortune. He was noted for his geniality and benevolence, and many of the old settlers recall with a delight which age has not diminished the old red wagon of "Uncle Sam" which he always filled with fruit for free distribution among them in their boyhood days. He d. February 17, 1844. She d. May 22, 1857, aged 93.

---

320 Joseph and Fanny Stevens had:

(673) Fanny, August 19, 1795. m. Francis Lynch, April, 1815. Ten chil.
(674) Nancy, December 29, 1796. d. unm.
(675) Samuel D., January 5, 1800. m. Nancy Shattuck, April 1, 1824.
(676) Eliza, April 4, 1801. m. William Ames, August 20, 1832. She d. February 29, 1872. He d. 1868.
(677) Maria B., April 1, 1806. m. Joseph Clark, October 11, 1825. She d. October 6, 1892.
(678) Hannah E., June 3, 1807. m. Geo. W. Carne. She d. January 5, 1885.
(679) Elizabeth A., November 5, 1809. d. young.
(680) Emeline K., December 29, 1811. m. Joshua Burns. Three chil. She d. March 19, 1884.

Joseph was a shoemaker. He rem. from Ipswich, Mass., to Amherst, N. H., where he d. March 7, 1842. Fanny was from Amherst, N. H., and d. November 25, 1834.

---

321 Ebenezer and Ruth Smalley had:

(681) Edmund, October 1, 1800. m. Caroline Parsons, December 17, 1822.
(682) Mary A., June 13, 1808.
(683) Dean O., June 16, 1812. m. Marilla Wood, September 6, 1836.
(684) Ebenezer, June 1817. d. young.
(685) Ebenezer, August, 1822. m. Fidelia Needham, April 16, 1844.

Ebenezer settled in Hanover, N. H. He rem. from there in 1806, to Cazenovia, N. Y., where he d. February 22, 1842. Ruth d. March 21, 1861.

---

323 Martha and Isaac Moore had:

(686) Mary B., January 11, 1800. m. —— Woolson, 1826.
(687) Joseph, March 3, 1803. m. Mrs. Lovie B. Cram, May 20, 1832.
(688) Dean, February 8, 1805.

(689) Esther D., January 18, 1808. d. October 30, 1831.
(690) Isabel, May 10, 1810. m. Joseph Crosby, September 7, 1835.
(691) Christiana, July 28, 1815.

Residence, Milford, N. H.

Martha d. July 23, 1871, aged 99.

---

318 Esther and William Kinsman had:

(692) Samuel, October 22, 1785. m. Rachel Carter.
(693) Mary, October 2, 1787. m. Ephraim Annable.
(694) Thomas, June 19, 1789. m. Sally ——.
(695) William, December 13, 1791. m. Hannah Shotwell.
(696) Esther, July 1, 1793. m. Moses Sanborn.
(697) Ebenezer, October 21, 1799. d. July 6, 1816.
(698) Martha, October 22, 1801. d. young.
(699) Elmira, December 28, 1804. m. Ezekiel Roberts.

Esther d. May 31, 1807. William d. July 17, 1806. Residence, Ipswich.

---

324 Nathaniel and Lucy Chapman had:

(700) Martha. m. James Thompson.
(701) Polly. m. Ezekiel Knowlton.
(702) Eunice. m. Jonah Folsom, Jefferson, Maine.
(703) Joseph. Sett. in Daramiscotta.
(704) Ezra.

---

325 Joseph and Martha Dean had:

(705) Martha. m. Nathaniel Thompson.
(706) Sally, 1754. m. John Knowlton.
(707) Lucy. m. Samuel Knowlton.
(708) Benjamin.
(709) Mercy. m. Samuel Knowlton.
(710) Joseph W., August 18, 1780. m. Nancy ——.
(711) Priscilla. m. Chas. Hilton.
(712) George W. m. Susan —— ; m. 2d Martha Wheeler, March 11, 1832.

---

329 John and Mary Dodge had:

(713) Mary. m.
(714) John, 1781. m. Mary Dodge, December 26, 1818. He d. March 18, 1834.

(715) Elizabeth, 1783. d. October 28, 1861.
(716) Joseph, 1787. m. Lucretia H. Brigham.

John, Sen., d. March 25, 1834. Mary d. March 23, 1824.

---

330 Isaac and Patty Woodbury had:

(717) Isaac, June 15, 1801. m. Nancy Dodge Knowlton, December 1, 1836.
(718) Martha, June 18, 1802. m. Epps Farr, November 27, 1823. She d. August 23, 1876. One dau., Martha.
(719) Eliza, February 19, 1807. m. Isaac Patch, December 8, 1827.
(720) Esther, June 24, 1812. m. Joseph Knowlton.
(721) Lucinda, September 26, 1816. m. Francis Allen, March 3, 1842. Had s. Albert.

Isaac d. July 28, 1843. Patty d. September 20, 1870.

---

332 Ezra and Abigail Dodge had:

(722) Susannah, April 18, 1763.
(723) Ezra, November 5, 1768.
(724) Levi, May 5, 1782. m. Margaret Woodbury, March 4, 1809.
(725) Susan. m. Timothy Higgins.
(726) Nancy.
(727) Emma. m. —— Topliff.
(728) Fanny.
(729) Abigail. m. 6 chil.
(730) Joseph, January 23, 1780. d. at sea, 1820.

Abigail d. October 25, 1812.

---

333 Edmund and Mary Austin had:

(731) Moses, July 22, 1779. m. Eunice Cummings, October 20, 1805.
(732) James, June 2, 1785. m. Nancy Allen, May 22, 1813.
(733) Edmund, December 31, 1790. m. Lydia Patch, December 10, 1818.
(734) Mary. m. Benjamin Burnham, February 11, 1799.

Edmund d. November 24, 1827. Mary d. October 12, 1841. Residence, Ipswich, Mass.

335 Neamiah and Martha Tilton had:

(735) Neamiah, August 10, 1775. m. Patience Parsons, July 26, 1797.
(736) Asa, May 5, 1777. m. Anna D. Farr, 1802. He d. November 27, 1859. She d. November 1, 1859.
(737) Martha, November 9, 1779. d. October 7, 1851.
(738) Josiah, August 12, 1783. m. Elizabeth Woodbury, March 11, 1815.
(739) Benjamin, November 6, 1784.
(740) Charles, October 5, 1789. d. January 22, 1867.

Neamiah m. 1st Elizabeth Pott, and 2d Susannah Fellows, October 11, 1771, having no issue by either.

He m. 3d Martha Tilton, November 22, 1774, who d. August 10, 1832. He d. at Boylston, Mass., August 13, 1834.

---

337 Moses and —— Cummings had:

(741) Moses, 1784. m. Abigail Lufkin.
(742) Elizabeth. m. —— Curtis.
(743) David. m.
(744) Benjamin. d. unm.
(745) Esther. m. —— Bugby.
(746) Susan. m. —— Foster.
(747) Mary. m. —— Hoyt.

Residence, New Gloucester, Maine, whence Moses and his family removed to Essex, Mass.

---

339 Malachi and Abigail Patch had:

(748) Michael, July 7, 1782. m. Margaret Boyd, pub., April 6, 1805.
(749) Azor, February 15, 1787. m. Lois Chamberlain, December 27, 1810.
(750) Ivers, February 15, 1790. m. Sarah Patch, October 15, 1814.
(751) Lavinia, bap. August 28, 1785. m. Thomas Moore.
(752) Mercy, November 12, 1800. m. Aaron Dodge, September 22, 1827.
(753) Anna, February, 1802. m. Andrew Woodley, April 13, 1830. She d. December 24, 1874.

Residence, Salem, Mass.

Malachi served in the Revolutionary War as a Fifer, from September 4, 1776, to November, 1777. He enlisted at Beverly, Mass., and in October, 1777, was under General Gates. He was run over by his wagon, and died from his injuries at Ipswich, September 14, 1830. Abigail d. August 22, 1839.

340 Ephraim and Mary Murphy had:

(754) Temple, May 12, 1793. d. 1811.
(755) Fannie, May 12, 1798. m. Antonio Ferrandero, May 20, 1821. 4 chil.
(756) Katie. m. —— Richardson. 3 chil.
(757) Mary A. m. 1 dau. Susan.
(758) Brackett.
(759) George.
(760) Eunice, August 12, 1787. m. Jona Smith. 3 chil.
(761) Polly, October 14, 1781.
(762) Ephraim, June 26, 1785. m. Mrs. Hannah Barrett, May 17, 1806.
(763) Lucy. m. 6 chil.
(764) Sarah. m. 6 chil.
(765) Benjamin.
(766) Enos, January 1, 1791.

Removed from Ipswich, and settled in Thomaston, Me.

---

345 Abigail Knowlton and Benjamin Larcom had:

(I) Sally, September 23, 1795. m. Sheldon Dodge, February 23, 1819.
(II) Abigail, September 3, 1797.
(III) Benjamin, December 31, 1799.
(IV) Theresa, November 5, 1801.
(V) Joseph, December 3, 1803.
(VI) Neamiah, September 9, 1806.
(VII) Ezra, December 19, 1808.
(VIII) Catherine, December 25, 1815.

Abigail d. February 21, 1870.

---

346 Benjamin and Abigail Larcom had:

(766 A) David, October 11, 1790.
(766 B) Abigail, December 17, 1792.
(767) Ira, January 8, 1797. m. Molly ——; m. 2d Elizabeth Perry. He committed suicide.
(768) Hezekiah, March 15, 1801.
(769) Hannah, August 19, 1803.

Benjamin d. May 28, 1839. Abigail d. December 18, 1824.

347 Annie Knowlton and William Foster had:

(770) William, August 25, 1798.
(771) Ives, August 24, 1800.
(772) Cynthia, March 3, 1804. m. —— Gibbs.
(773) A son, 1809.
(774) Abigail, August 28, 1814. m. —— Witham.

---

348 John and —— had:

(775) Thomas, 1756.

---

350 Abraham and Sarah Lord had:

(776) Abraham, January 25, 1756.
(777) Mary, August 16, 1758. m. Abraham Wyatt, 1782.
(778) Nathaniel, February 22, 1761.
(779) Elizabeth, March 17, 1764. m. Daniel Stearns, September 17, 1783.
(780) Ebenezer, June 18, 1767. He built the pulpit in the Ipswich church.
(781) Lucy, July 13, 1771. m. —— Oliver.
(782) John, January 1774. m. Dorcas Shapleigh, August 4, 1790.
(783) Cyrus, June 4, 1780.

---

353 Thomas and Sarah Stacey had:

(784) Sarah, February 27, 1757. d. young.
(785) Dea. Thomas, October 26, 1760.
(786) Jacob, August 14, 1766. m. Abigail Hodgkin.
(787) Sarah, January 10, 1768. m. James Lord.
(788) Mary, August 15, 1775. m. Thomas Lord, September 29, 1795. 10 chil. She d. March 15, 1855. He d. February 21, 1853.
(789) Rebecca. m. Thomas Lane. 8 chil.

---

358 Johnathan and Ruth Page had:

(790) Susannah, February 16, 1763.
(791) William B., August 25, 1764. m. Mary Wallace, July 19, 1784.
(792) Sarah, May 22, 1766. m. Ebenezer Dustin. 6 chil.
(793) Betty, April 12, 1768.
(794) David, September 10, 1770. m. Drusilla Deague.
(795) Lydia, January 10, 1772.

(796) Patience, April 12, 1776.
(797) Dolly, December 12, 1778.
(798) Johnathan, May 10, 1781.
(799) Polly, September 15, 1784.

Johnathan was b. in Kensington. In 1767, he bought fifty acres of land in the Province of Nottingham for which he paid thirty pounds, lawful money. In the summer of 1768, he built him a log house. He bought fifty acres more in 1774, and in 1777 he and his brother Thomas added one hundred and fifty acres more, paying for the tract only twelve shillings. He was one of the signers to a protest against the hostility of Great Britain, and one of a Committee of Safety in 1777. He lived in Northwood, N. H., many years, and d. there in June, 1814. Ruth d. October, 1825.

---

364 Thomas and Betsey Giles had:

(800) Asa, February 2, 1777. m. Ruth Knowlton; m. 2d Sally Knowlton, 1812. He d. October 10, 1861. Res., Danbury, N. H.
(801) Sally G., April 14, 1778. m. Samuel Gerrish. She d. September, 1849.
(802) Nathan, April 8, 1780. m. Abigail Dane.
(803) Stephen C., September 9, 1782. m. Mary Greene.
(804) Sherburne, October 29, 1784. m. Sally Knowlton; m. 2d Betsey Dane, September 21, 1831; m. 3d and 4th; and d. January, 1875.
(805) Hannah, April 24, 1787. m. Samuel Dane. She d. 1881.
(806) Nancy Ann, April 22, 1789. d. April, 1876.
(807) Jeremiah, July 17, 1791. Drowned July 9, 1810.
(808) Joseph, January 25, 1794. m. Susan Dearborn, September 8, 1819.
(809) Ebenezer, September 17, 1796. m. Lydia Harris.

Thomas was born in Kensington, Mass., and rem. to Northwood when young, and eventually settled on land formerly called Lucas Pond. He d. March 7, 1832. Thomas served in various companies during the Revolution, and was promoted from a private to sergeant, ensign, and lieutenant. See Appendix.

---

366 Ebenezer and Elizabeth Rawlings had:

(810) Charlotte, August 3, 1785. m. Nathan Holt. 7 chil.
(811) James, October 16, 1788. m. Sally Demerritt, April 30, 1815. He d. 1824.
(812) Shuah, March 19, 1790. m. Dominicus Griffin. 3 chil.
(813) Sally B., May 19, 1793. m. Asa Knowlton.

(814) Nancy, September 13, 1794.
(815) Betsey, October 18, 1797.
(816) Hosea C., March 31, 1799. m. Betsey Seavey, 1825. Res. in Chichester, N. H.
(817) Ruth, October 12, 1801. m. Ezra Baxter. 2 chil.
(818) Lydia, April 18, 1803. m. J. C. Johnson. 1 chil.

Ebenezer settled in Nottingham, at the foot of Saddleback Mountain. Like his father and brothers he was over six feet tall.

---

370 Rev. David and Mary A. Green had :

(819) Jane, September 17, 1768. m. Capt. E. Brown.
(820) Betsey, July 27, 1770.
(821) Mary, March 15, 1773. m. Thomas Blake. 3 chil.
(822) Johnathan, April 1, 1776.
(823) Jemima, June 23, 1777.
(824) (Rev.) David, October 9, 1780. m. Hannah True. Res., Pittsfield, N. H. He d. March 11, 1817.
(825) Ebenezer, April 6, 1782. m. Abigail True, November 28, 1802. d. November 18, 1891.
(826) Nathan, December, 1783.

David was a clergyman. He m. Mary A. in Seabrook, Mass., and rem. to Fairfield, N. H., March, 1770. He d. March 11, 1815. Mary d. November 29, 1817.

---

371 Benjamin and Phoebe Wright had :

(827) Phoebe, June 21, 1751. d. young.
(828) Benjamin. September 26, 1753. m. Abigail Wright, 1776.
(829) Henry, April 16, 1756. m. Sybil ——.
(830) Lydia, October 31, 1758. m. Ephraim Adams.
(831) Esther, August 10, 1761. d. in Potsdam, N. Y., April 16, 1777.
(832) Sarah, August 26, 1764. m. Obadiah Coolidge.
(833) John, January 18, 1766. m. Sally Holden.
(834) Eunice, January 28, 1769. m. Luke Rice. 2 chil.
(835) Bertha, April 8, 1771. d. young.
(836) Hannah, September 18, 1776. m. Ishmael Holcomb. 5 chil.

Benjamin was b. in Ipswich, and rem. to New Ipswich, N. H., about 1751, for in the following year he was a proprietor of that town, and included in the tax list, being rated as the seventh out of ninety-five in point of wealth. There is scarcely a record of public enterprise, patriotic spirit, or private worth with which his name is not prominently associated. He was tithing-man of the first council meeting in 1762, and at the last town meeting held under the rule of George III. he was chosen a

"Committee of Correspondence and Inspection to Promote the General Safety."

Largely through his energy a company of militia was formed, of which he was first lieutenant, Capt. Thomas Fletcher commanding, in 1771, and he served in this rank in the Lexington Alarm. He d. July 21, 1809. Phoebe, his wife, d. January, 1813.

---

375 Rice 3d and Sarah Coey had:

(837) Judith, January 9, 1766. m. —— Dodd.
(838) Lydia, May 1, 1768.
(839) Lucy, October 11, 1769. m. John Gott, Jr.
(840) John, November 20, 1771. m. Mary Gott, August 18, 1793. He d. 1325. She d. 1827.
(841) Ruth, June 30, 1774. m. William Pierce, 1799.

Rice served in the Revolutionary War from Gloucester, Mass., though residing in Wenham.

---

376 Ezra and —— had:

(842) Susannah.

---

377 Charles A. and Emma Pickard had:

(843) Johnathan, May 28, 1770. m. Dolly Prouty, 1790.
(844) Mary, December 30, 1771. m. Josiah Bush, December 11, 1792.
(845) Francis, August 13, 1775. d. at No. Brookfield, Mass., August 26, 1838.
(846) Eunice, February 10. 1778. d. March 11, 1798.
(847) Hannah, 1780. d. May 22, 1789.
(848) Judith, May 26, 1782. m. Bela C. Stoddard, June 12, 1812.
(849) Capernium, December 11, 1787. m. Marshall P. Wilder, of Sterling, Mass.
(850) Charles, October 10, 1790. d. July 11, 1826.

Charles A. was a farmer. He and his sister Lydia, b. in Ipswich, were taken when quite young to the home of their uncle Chas. Adams, in North Brookfield, after whose death Charles A. inherited the farm. He was a Minute-man of the Revolutionary Army. He d. August 1, 1820. Eunice d. December 20, 1826.

379 Reuben and Mary (Mercy) Morse had :

(851) John. m. Mary Curtis. He d. April 4, 1844. She d. May 12, 1853.
(852) Andrew. m. Olive Curtis.
(853) Stephen. m. Betsey Curtis, 1795.
(854) Lucy. m. —— Harney.
(855) Jane. m. Moses Kenney.
(856) Annie. m. William Flanders. 8 chil.

Reuben removed from Beverly, Mass., to Maine.

---

380 Joseph and Rachel Patch had :

(857) Anna, October 9, 1764. m. Lieut. Wm. Atkinson.
(858) John, October 29, 1766. m. Elizabeth Parker of Accomac, Va.; m. 2d Martha Parker.
(859) Mark. m. 2d Nancy Lovett. m. 3d.
(860) William, 1773. m. Lucy Woodley, September 28, 1799; m. 2d Sally Woodley, 1802.

Residence, Wenham, Mass.

---

381 Amos and Mary Warren had :

(861) Daniel, December 8, 1767. m. Lucy Freeman.
(862) Eunice. m. James Woodbury, October 13, 1791.
(863) Mary. m. ——Powers.
(864) Robert. m. —— Loomis.
(865) Polly, 1774. m. Ebenezer Moulton of Wenham. 8 chil. She d. May 30, 1858. He d. May 13, 1847.

Mary Warren was the sister of Gen. Warren of Bunker Hill fame. Amos was a soldier of the Revolution. He enlisted in 1775, in Capt. Richard Dodge's company, Col. Baldwin's regiment, and on December 8, received pay and subsistence, being then at Chelsea. He also received pay for losses at the evacuation of New York. On February 14, 1777, he re-enlisted for three years in Col. Benj. Tupper's regiment, being credited to Wenham. He held the rank of private at Bunker Hill, being subsequently promoted to be a sergeant, and dying in the war, June 30, 1778.

---

383 Abraham and Rhoda Tennant had :

(866) Abraham, November 21, 1773.
(867) Caleb, June 29, 1777.

Abraham dying, his widow m. John West, 1788.
Residence, Wenham, Mass.

384 John and —— had:

(868) John, December 3, 1780. Res. in Ipswich.
(869) Elizabeth, June 29, 1783.
(870) Joseph, March 19, 1786.

Residence, Ipswich.

---

385 William and Elizabeth Smith had:

(871) Robert. m. Sarah Buckmaster (or Buckminster).
(872) Benjamin. m. Esther Lindsay.
(873) Joseph, April 6, 1799. m. Rhoda Buckmaster.
(874) Elizabeth. m. Samuel Hamilton. She died at the age of 100 years.
(875) Nancy. m. Aaron Matthews; 8 chil.
(876) Jane. m. Joseph Curtis; 4 chil.
(877) Sarah. m. George Smith; 7 chil.

William removed to Northport, Me., and thence to the Isle of Haute.

---

384 John and —— had:

(877 A) John, 1773. m. Isabella Bailey, 1796.
(877 B) Mark, 1774. m. 3 times; 3d Nancy Thorndyke.

John d. 1797.

---

386 Robert and Betsey Davis had:

(878) Robert. d. young. Res. in Maine.
(879) Lucy. m. Joseph Savage. Res. in Maine.
(880) William. res. in Maine.
(881) Mercy. m.
(882) Sarah. m. Asa Parlin.
(883) Cyrus, October 25, 1799. m. Celia Bostwick.
(884) Anna, 1802. m. Daniel Savage.
(885) David F., 1802. m. Susannah Knowlton.

---

387 Thomas and Joanna Martin had:

(886) Thomas, October 23, 1783. Lost at sea.
(887) Parker, January 18, 1785. Disappeared. Last seen in a southern port.
(888) Jeremiah, February 24, 1788. m. Betsey Rhodes, 1813.

(889) Amos, April 25, 1789. m. Betsey Knowlton, 1820.
(890) Harriett, May 9, 1791. m. Daniel Collins ; m. 2d Robert Moore.
(891) Lewis, June 10, 1793. Killed in War of 1812.
(892) George, November 15, 1795. m. Ruth Holmes, September 20, 1816.
(893) Susannah, July 22, 1798. m. Daniel F. Rogers.
(894) Nathaniel, February 23, 1805. m. Rachel Pottle, August 18, 1834.
(895) Abraham, February 4, 1803. m. Lucinda Billings May 21, 1824.

Col. Thomas served in the Maine Militia during the war of the Revolution, being promoted rapidly from the rank of lieutenant through the various grades to that of colonel. He resided in Northport Me.

While on a visit to Great Britain at the close of the war, he was presented with what was then believed to be the coat-of-arms of the Knowltons embroidered on a household ornament. His patriotic ardor expressed itself in such antipathy to England that he removed the lion which formed the crest, and substituted an American flag. He d. October 10, 1827.

---

389 Capt. Benjamin and Susanna Woodbury had:

(896) Bernard. m. Betsey Sargent, August 10, 1810.
(897) Benjamin, April 25, 1787. m. Lydia Haskell.
(898) Susannah, September 12, 1788.
(899) Ebenezer, December 9, 1789.
(900) Issachar, January 1, 1792.
(901) Joanna. m. Thomas Preston.

Residence, Beverly.

Capt. Benjamin d. August 5, 1822. Susannah d. December 20, 1824.

---

391 Jonathan and Hannah Morgan, of Beverly, had :

(902) Jonathan, 1777. m. Mollie Knowlton.
(903) Hannah, 1780. m. John Cleaves ; m. 2d —— Barnet.
(904) Barnet, June 19, 1788. m. Betsey Sargent, October 13, 1814.

Residence, Ipswich, Mass.

---

395 William and Julia —— had :

(905) Josiah, 1770. m. Miriam Draper.
(906) Kate, November 30, 1773.
(907) Oliver, July 8, 1779. m. Mary Dodd, April 20, 1802.

Residence, Holliston, Mass.

397 Asa and Sarah Hadley had:

(908) Asa, Jr., 1765. m. Alice Divoli.
(909) Sarah. m. Joel Johnson. She d. 1808.
(910) Deborah. m. —— Thiers. She d. 1809.

---

398 Elias and Elizabeth Jennings had:

(911) Rebecca, October 3, 1765. m. David Morse, June 29, 1790. Rem. to Holland Purchase. He d. 1843. She d. 1840.
(912) Elisha, June 5, 1767. m. Polly Chamberlain, of Dublin, N. H., January 1, 1795; m. 2d Hannah Chamberlain.
(913) Elias, May 14, 1769. m. Lydia Fisk, August 2, 1789; m. 2d Hannah Fisk. Sett. in Warwick, Mass.
(914) Daniel. m. Lucinda Blake, September 9, 1803.
(915) Jesse. m. Polly Blake, May 7, 1794.
(916) Luther, February 14, 1773. m. Prudence Dadman, 1800.
(917) Elizabeth, April 19, 1776.
(918) Gilbert, March 6, 1778.
(919) Simeon, October 31, 1779. m. Hannah Wrisley, November 26, 1829.
(920) Jason.
(921) James, June 6, 1791.
(922) Sally, February 27, 1795.
(923) Leonard, 1796. m. Angeline Coleman, 1823.
(924) Lucinda, 1798.

---

399 Anna and Philip Metcalf had:

(925) Philip.
(926) Daniel.
(927) Anna.
(928) Mary.

---

401 Nathan and Patience Miller had:

(929) Micah, July 8, 1782.
(930) Susannah, May 4, 1784.
(931) Rebecca, March 12, 1786.
(932) Philena, May 20, 1788. m. Solomon Hopkins.
(933) Sophia, October 6, 1790.
(934) Nancy, 1792. m. Ebenezer Knowlton.
(935) Nathan, July 16, 1794. m. Eunice Randall, February 18, 1816. He d. 1873. She d. 1864.

402 John and Martha Jennings had:

(936) Martha, August 16, 1769. m. Isaac Hunt, of Hancock. Res. in Hancock, N. H.
(937) John, October 7, 1771. m. Polly Rowell. Rem. to Dunnerton, Vt. He d. November 14, 1875.
(938) Elizabeth, January 11, 1774. d. young.
(939) James, July 25, 1776. d. 1778.
(940) Abigail, December 18, 1778. m. Samuel Moore, November 16, 1815.
(941) Betsey, May 14, 1781. m. Samuel Derby, February 23, 1806.
(942) Thaddeus, December 6, 1783. m. Rebecca Bishop, Dublin, N. H., February 23, 1806. He d. January 14, 1826. She d. March 28, 1833.
(943) Simeon, August 3, 1786. d. August 2, 1813.
(944) Henry, March 5, 1789. m. Polly Learned, October 14, 1829.
(945) James, November 25, 1791. m. Sally Adams, of Richland, N. Y.

Martha d. April 7, 1797, and

John m. 2d Elizabeth Wright, February 19, 1798, and had:

(946) Eliza, February 28, 1799. m. Barzillai Davis. Rem. to Nelson, N. H.
(947) Luke, August 1, 1801. m. Mercy Bemis, December 28, 1826.
(948) Ira, March 30, 1803. m. Eliza Lovekin. Rem. to Worcester. d. October 25, 1845.
(949) Mary, July 2, 1804. m. Cornelius Towne. She d. May 19, 1836.
(950) Levi, March 31, 1806. d. 1854. m. Mrs. Lucy Hadley, Worcester, Mass.

Residence, Dublin, N. H.

---

410 Isaiah and Jemima Johnson had:

(951) Isaiah, July 20, 1797. m. Clarissa Spooner; m. 2d Lydia Pelland. He d. March 5, 1875.
(952) Leonard, September 22, 1799. m. Lauretta Low.
(953) William, December 12, 1800. m. Jeanette Waterman, November 26, 1829.
(954) Nancy, June 18, 1803. m. Asa Jackson, March 28, 1830.
(955) Henry, October 9, 1805. m. Hannah Downs, 1831.
(956) Mary, March 1, 1808. m. Wm. Burgess, May 2, 1830.
(957) Jemima, April 2, 1810. m. Daniel Spooner.
(958) Royal, April 18, 1812. d. 1815.

(959) Jared, April 15, 1814. m. Hannah G. Upton ; m. 2d Ada Jackson.
(960) Julia, August 8, 1816. m. Paul Demerritt.
Residence, Holliston, Mass.

Isaiah d. November 24, 1842. She d. March 6, 1854.

---

409 John and Susannah Jennings had :

(961) Ebenezer, June 26, 1790. m. Nancy Knowlton. Res. in Hopkinton, N. H. d. July 20, 1871.

(962) Jesse, July 22, 1791. m. Sarah Wight, 1816.

(963) Silas, August 1, 1793. m. Susannah Nutting, April 6, 1817 ; m. 2d Elizabeth Hardy.

(964) John, September 30, 1795. m. Lois Bemis. Rem. to Sandy Creek, N. Y. d. January, 1832.

(965) Jeremy, March 15, 1798. m. Elizabeth Farnham, of Marlborough, N. Y., May, 1819.

(966) Eunice, April 3, 1800. m. James Upton, 1827. 3 chil.

(967) Mary, September 3, 1803. d. July 18, 1826.

John was a soldier of the Revolution, and served in Capt. Joseph Lealand's company, Col. Abner Perry's regiment, in the Rhode Island Alarm, July, 1780, and for three years previous.

Susannah was the daughter of Daniel and Elizabeth (Cozzens) Jennings. John was b. in Dublin, N. H., and d. there April, 1835.

---

411 John m. —— Tarbox. m. 2d Hannah Flanders, and had :

(968) John, 1765.

(969) Philip, April 9, 1769. Rem. to Wentworth, N H.

(970) Benjamin, February 12, 1771. m. Polly Jackman.

(971) Joseph, June 4, 1773. m. Lois Flanders, December 29, 1796.
Residence, Hancock, N. H.

---

412 Rosel and Sophia Goodall had :

(972) Rosel, October 20, 1788. m. Prudence Cocklin, 1809. Res. in Pelham, Mass.

(973) Warren, September 4, 1790. m. Mary A. Dunbar.

(974) Nancy, March 10, 1793. m. James Bartlett, November 11, 1816. 10 chil.

(975) Elisha, July 23, 1796. m. Nancy Hubbard, April 28, 1817.
(976) Susannah, June 9, 1798. m. Josiah Dunbar, October 25, 1815.
(977) Dutton, December 5, 1800. Res., Belchertown, Mass.

Rosel d. in Belchertown, Mass., 1806.

---

413 Gideon and —— had:

(978) Rev. Gideon K., 1759. m. Polly Hayden. d. August 15, 1810. She d. August 29, 1822.
(979) Lydia.

---

414 Jared and Lydia —— had:

(980) Roswell, 1771. m. Lydia Stone, 1795.
(981) Jane. m. —— Coon, Troy, N. Y.

---

415 Asenath and Asa Wilson had:

(982) Roswell, July 29, 1781.
(983) Phineas, August 15, 1785.
(984) Sylvester, April 9, 1787.
(985) Sophia, May 3, 1789.
(986) Susan, April 27, 1794.
(987) Asenath, August 29, 1796.
(988) Asa W., September 4, 1798.
(989) Clarissa, July 4, 1800
(990) Peter, June 22, 1802.

Residence, Belchertown, Mass.

---

416 Anna Knowlton and Nathan Wilson had:

(991) Estes, May 14, 1796.
(992) Horace, January 15, 1798.
(993) Violet, January 20, 1799.
(994) Russell, March 16, 1800.

---

418 Joshua and Elizabeth Shattuck had:

(995) Joshua.
(996) Isaac.

(997) Welcome.
(998) Friend, January 26, 1794. m. Alice Hammen. d. April 27, 1868.
(999) Betsey. m. Martin Wheelock. d. 1874.
(1000) John, 1802. m. Roxana Wheeler.
(1001) Sylvia, 1805. m. Samuel Bradford.
(1002) Oren, 1807. m. Jane Fuller.
(1003) Madison, March 7, 1809. m. Anna Berne.
(1004) Sally. m. Joshua Shumway. 6 chil.
(1005) Polly. m. John Bidwell. 4 chil.
(1006) Elijah. m. Sally Brown.

Residence, Belchertown, Mass.

---

420 Timothy and Sarah Mansfield had :

(1007) Ebenezer, 1770. m. Mehitable Welch, of Boston, January 3, 1799.
(1008) Joseph, 1771. m. Betsey Johnson, December 6, 1804.
(1009) Benjamin, 1773. m. Betsey Grant, June 3, 1798.
(1010) Mary, February 28, 1776. m. James Clark. Rem. to Mich. 6 chil.
(1011) Rachel, 1777.
(1012) Hannah, 1779. m. —— Keyes.
(1013) Paul, June 2, 1780. m. Eunice Shaw, February 22, 1802. m. 2d Esther Anthony.
(1014) Rhoda, March 3, 1782. m. Ebenezer Fisher, 1802.
(1015) Huldah, July 12, 1783. m. Robert Bratton. 6 chil.
(1016) Sarah, 1784. m. —— Kentefield.
(1017) Ephraim. d. young, 1786.
(1018) Aaron, September 30, 1787. d. 1800.
(1019) Timothy, 1792. m. Eunice Rice. Res. Buxton.

Timothy removed from Medway, to Rowe, Mass., before 1770, for four children were born there between that year and 1776.

He bought a small farm in a very rugged spot, the cultivation of which was so difficult that he left it, and removed to Belchertown, where the rest of his children were born. He suffered from a sunstroke which clouded his mind exactly one year to a day, after which he recovered his usual mental powers.

He d. June 20, 1815. Sarah d. March 20, 1820.

---

420 A Ebenezer Knowltown

Served in the Rhode Island Alarm from December 8, 1776–December 29, at the rate of 4s. 6d. per day. The following receipt is on file at the Archives of Commonwealth of Mass.

"We, the subscribers, have rec^{d} of Capt. Lovell, of Medway in full of our Wages, Travelling Fees, and Back Allowances of Provisions and Sarse which was due to us upon the Alarm, when in ye State of Rhode Island Stationed at Warwick, Dec^{m} ye 8th 1776. We say rec^{d} by us in full, as Witness our Hands."

Signed by EBENEZER KNOWLTON.

"Marching Orders, Dec. ye 26, 1776.

"To Joshua Partridge, One of ye Selectmen of medway.

"I have rec^{d} Orders from Capt. Fairbank to march with all ye men draughted in medway, and to be at David Man's, Innholder, in wrentham on Monday, ye 30th day of this Instant at Nine o'clock in the morning. There is a Carrage Provided to Carry the Soldiers' Packs to David Man's and it is to be at your house tomorrow at 12 o'clock at noon and you are hereby Desired to Notifie the men Draughted in the East Company in Medway to appear at your house at the time above mentioned.

"MOSES THOMPSON."

Ebenezer served eight years, and was in the battles of Bennington, Rutland, Vt., and many other engagements.

---

422 Lucy Knowlton and Dea. Abijah Brooks had:

(1020) Samuel. m. Eunice Bass.
(1021) Patty, January 5, 1755.
(1022) Lucy, September 1, 1756.
(1023) Esther, May 29, 1758.
(1024) Nathaniel, March 18, 1760.
(1025) Abijah, November 22, 1761.
(1026) Roxalena, December 3, 1763.
(1027) Theophilus, January 24, 1766.
(1028) Simon, December 22, 1767. d. June 4, 1844.
(1029) Joseph, March 6, 1770.
(1030) Thomas, April 19, 1775.
(1031) Lemuel, April 19, 1775.

Residence, Ashford, Conn.

---

423 William and Mehitable Eaton had:

(1032) Joshua, October 21, 1760.
(1033) Harney, November 12, 1762. m. —— Wheeler.
(1034) Fanelia, February 2, 1765. m. —— Wheeler, of N. Y.
(1035) William, January 1, 1767.

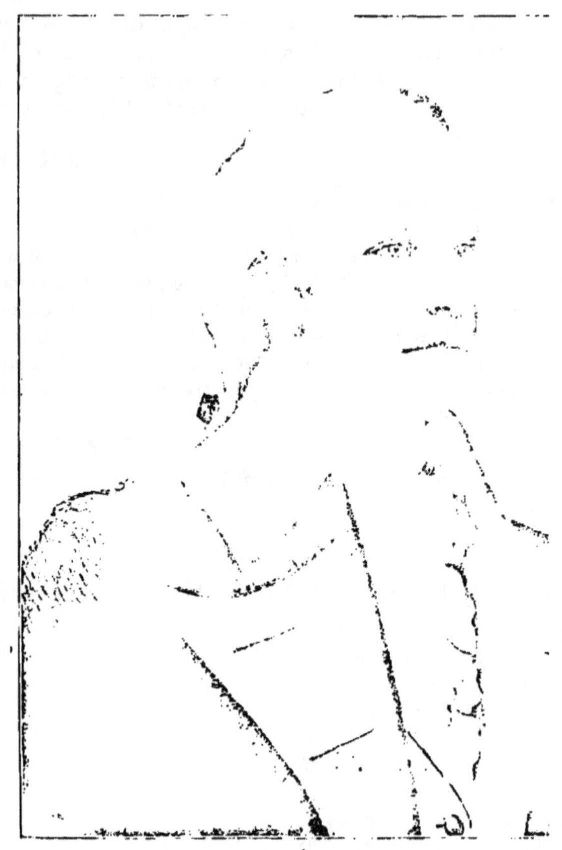

Lieutenant Daniel Knowlton,
Connecticut Line, Continental Army.

(1036) Stephen, November 10, 1768. m. Eunice Swan. Res., Stonington, Conn.
(1037) Achsah, August 29, 1772.
(1038) Mehitable, April 27, 1774. m. —— Hill, of N. Y. 8 chil.
(1039) Ephraim, April 27, 1774. d. April 6, 1797.
(1040) Ann. m. —— Delamater. Lived in N. Y.

William and wife were admitted into the church in Ashford on "confession," August 5, 1770. He committed suicide when insane, January 9, 1784.

---

424 Lieut. Daniel and Elizabeth Farnham had:

(1041) Daniel, December 17, 1765. m. Betsey Burchard, April 4, 1793. d. February, 1834.
(1042) Elizabeth, March 24, 1768. m. Fred. Chaffee, of Ashford, Conn.
(1043) Nathaniel, December 24, 1770. m. Sarah Leach, November 25, 1798.
(1044) Manassah, December 24, 1770. m. Lydia Burton, b. March 19, 1773, She d. January 15, 1806; m. 2d Elizabeth Card, August 5, 1821; m. 3d Clarissa Cogswell, She d. November 23, 1841.
(1045) Ephraim, October 3, 1773. m. Jemima Farnham, of Ashford, Conn.
(1046) Martha, February 24, 1777. m. Chas. W. Brandon, of Ashford.
(1047) Keziah, February 9, 1781. m. Amasa Lyon, January 3, 1805.
(1048) Hannah, April 19, 1783. m. Daniel Knowlton.

Elizabeth d. June 1, 1786, and Lieut. Daniel m. 2d Rebecca Fenton, and had:

(1049) Erastus Fenton, January 29, 1790. m. Waite Windsor, February 20, 1814.
(1050) Marvin, September 3, 1794. m. Calista Leonard, April 19, 1820.

LIEUT. DANIEL KNOWLTON was baptized in the West Parish of Boxford, Mass., December 31, 1738. He was but two years old when his father removed to Ashford, Conn. Daniel's early training was calculated to have a powerful influence upon his military career afterwards, and it probably laid the foundation for some of those deeds of heroism which have made his name revered among his descendants. When only nineteen years old he enlisted in the colonial regiments for service in the French and Indian War, together with his brother Thomas. From the very first he distinguished himself for bravery and daring, particularly as a scout, being often sent in command of small parties to reconnoitre in the forests. No duty connected with the long and bloody war upon the frontiers required more skill, or tact, than that of scouting, where the slightest indiscretion might betray the venturesome explorer to the cruelty of the savage. On one of these occasions, while serving in Capt. John Slapp's company, Phineas Lyman's 1st Connecticut regiment, in Lord Loudon's expedition to Fort Edward, between the 15th of March and the 17th of October, 1757, Daniel saved the life of his companion and friend, Israel Putnam, who, in venturing into the dense forest outside the ramparts of Fort Edward, was attacked by an Indian who was about to tomahawk him. Knowlton came to his friend's relief, and brought down the redskin by a timely shot from his musket. This incident explains the life-long friendship which existed between Putnam and Daniel Knowlton. The bravest troopers and fiercest fighters in the bloody encounters of the French and Indian War within New York State, were men of Connecticut regiments. Knowlton did most of his fighting in this campaign in Northern New York, in and around the ramparts and forts of Fort Edward, Ticonderoga, and that vicinity.

In June, 1758, he served in Col. Eleazer Fitch's 3d Connecticut regiment and Capt. Jedediah Fay's company, at Crown Point. About this time Knowlton captured three men belonging to a gang of bloodthirsty desperadoes, whose numerous atrocities had made them as odious as they were terrible. With a small force on hostile territory, it was unsafe either to retain or dismiss the prisoners, and the captors decided that the crimes of the offenders entitled them to halters, and that there must be no delay. Halters were accordingly made from the bark of hickory saplings, by Knowlton's orders, from which the culprits were soon dangling between heaven and earth. From May 7, 1761, to December 30, 1761, Daniel served as a sergeant in Capt. Robert Durkee's company, Phineas Lyman's Connecticut regiment, and from March 17, 1762, to December 4, 1762, in Capt. Hugh Ledlie's company, Lyman's regiment, the above companies being mustered and serving in the Crown Point Expedition. The original muster-rolls, showing his services in these campaigns, are on file in the State Library, at Hartford, Conn. It is not known positively that Daniel rendered service in the Havana expedition, as most of the muster-rolls of these regiments were lost, or destroyed. We have very good reasons, however, for believing that he did, as we have proof of his brother Thomas's service there, and also proof that they served side by side in nearly every campaign of the French and Indian War.

Upon returning to Connecticut, and to Ashford, in 1763, he m. November 3d, Elizabeth Farnham, the daughter of Manassah Farnham, of Windham. Elizabeth was b. at Windham, March 10, 1742. Her mother was Keziah Ford daughter of Joseph Ford, a brave soldier in King Philip's War. Daniel's wife, Elizabeth, was the granddaughter of Henry Farnham and Phebe (Russell) Farnham, and great-granddaughter of Ralph Farnham and Sarah Sterling. Ralph, father of said Ralph, m. Elizabeth Holt, and was sixth son of Sir John Farnham of Quorndam, County Leicester, England, who lived in the reign of Edward I. His arms are registered in the Heralds' College.

Lieut. Daniel Knowlton's House,
Ashford, Conn.

Daniel now enjoyed a brief respite from the hardships of war, and turned his attention to the affairs of his home and family. His appearance at this time is said to have been that of a very tall, wiry man, slightly stooping shoulders, high brow, prominent nose, serious, though gentle features, and blue eyes, in one of which there was a slight cast, the result of a laceration in the French War while chasing a band of savages. A projecting bramble, or prickly branch, tore the eye partially out of the socket, but the indomitable will of the soldier paid little heed to the annoyance, and he pushed on, disregarding the pain. His light brown hair was powdered and dressed after the fashion of the period. The gentleness and humanity of the man are illustrated by the following incident, which has erroneously been ascribed by some to his younger brother Thomas. One day, as Daniel was riding past the Presbyterian Church at Ashford, he noticed a large crowd congregated about the whipping-post, planted in the vicinity according to the harsh custom of the day. Upon inquiry, he learned that a culprit was to be flogged for non-attendance at church and non-payment of dues. When the sentence was read preparatory to laying on the stripes, observing that the usual clause was omitted requiring the stripes to be applied to the bare back, he jumped from his horse and threw his own coat over the shoulders of the culprit, thus mitigating the force of the blows.

Four sons and a daughter were born to Daniel and Elizabeth during this temporary period of domestic peace and happiness at Ashford, but the clouds of Revolution were gathering in the Colonies, and at the first call to arms Knowlton promptly responded.

It is related that the night before the Putnam men marched to the relief of Boston, "Old Put," as he was called, was noticed to leave his house and silently walk over to a field adjacent, and there look towards Ashford for some little time, shading his eyes with his hand. Being followed by a neighbor, and being asked for whom he was looking, the old General ejaculated, "Gad, Zounds, had I only Daniel Knowlton to take with me, I 'd lick Hell itself." To this "Lexington Alarm" Daniel responded by leaving his plough in the furrow, like Cincinnatus of old, though he was, probably, not at the battle of Bunker Hill, and the precise nature of his service at this date is matter of tradition rather than of history. He was, however, one of the very first in the field, and was commissioned Ensign of Col. John Chester's Connecticut regiment, Sixth Battalion, Wadsworth brigade, Capt. Reuben Marcy's company, in June, 1776. Stationed with this regiment at Flatbush Pass, August 26th, he participated in the memorable battle of Long Island, August 27, 1776, where his entire regiment narrowly escaped capture.*

* The "Espadata," or ensign's staff, which was carried by Knowlton, is in the possession at the present time of one of his great-grandsons, Mr. Miner Knowlton, of Poughkeepsie, N. Y., and the musket which Sergeant Knowlton carried during the French and Indian War and the first year of the Revolution, and which saved the life of Putnam, is now in possession of his great-great-grandson, Mr. William Herrick Griffith, of Albany, N. Y.

Subsequently he was detached from Chester's regiment and Wadsworth's brigade, and after the battle of Long Island assigned to Knowlton's Rangers, which his brother Thomas commanded. He participated with the Rangers at the battle of Harlem Heights, 16th September, 1776, at which place, and during which engagement, his brother was slain. It was related by Trumbull of Connecticut, an intimate friend of Col. Thomas Knowlton, that upon his death the news was carried to his brother Daniel, who was fighting bravely in another part of the field. Upon hearing the sad news he exclaimed, "We will retrieve my brother's loss," and before the day was over the loss was partially retrieved by that glorious victory at Harlem Heights.

When Col. Thomas Knowlton led the Ashford company to the American headquarters near Boston, shortly after the battle of Lexington, General Putnam, the early friend of Daniel, asked the Colonel where his brother Daniel was. Being informed that he had gone in another direction, the General remarked: "I am sorry that you did not bring him with you; he alone is worth half a company. Such is his courage and lack of fear, I could order him into the mouth of a loaded cannon, and he would go."

After the battle of Harlem Heights Knowlton returned to Chester's regiment, and participated in the battle of White Plains, N. Y., October 28, 1776. For bravery on the field, he was appointed by the State Assembly Second Lieutenant of one of eight battalions of troops ordered to be raised. He again rejoined Knowlton's Rangers on the Harlem lines after the White Plains engagement, continuing with them and being in the thick of the fight at Fort Washington, where, with the entire garrison, he was made a prisoner. For about two years he was in the hands of the enemy, being confined a portion of the time in the old prison-ship *Jersey*, anchored in Wallabout Bay, during which period he met with abuse, privation, and persecution. On one occasion, it is related, while he was on the *Jersey*, pacing back and forth, with his eyes lowered to the deck, one of his jailers, a British officer, pompously asked him why he did not hold up his head like a man and a soldier? Knowlton quietly replied:

"In passing through fields of grain, Sir, I have noticed that the valuable ears or heads bow toward the earth, only the empty and worthless stand erect."

The officer thereupon showed appreciation of the answer by bowing his own head, and leaving the prisoner to pursue his meditations undisturbed. The infamy and inhuman treatment of American patriots confined on the *Jersey* and other prison-ships are too well known to need repetition. The indignities and cruelties to which Knowlton was subjected during these terrible months were never forgotten. The very name of "Briton" fired his soul ever after. Long years after the war, when at his home in Ashford, he was accustomed to attend Divine Service at a Congregational church at Westford. One Sunday

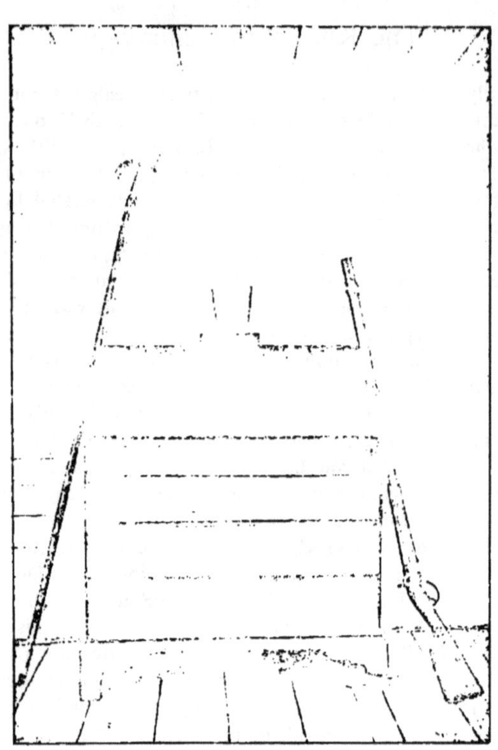

Bureau, Musket, Ensign, Battle-Axe, and Drinking Glass of Lieut. Daniel Knowlton.

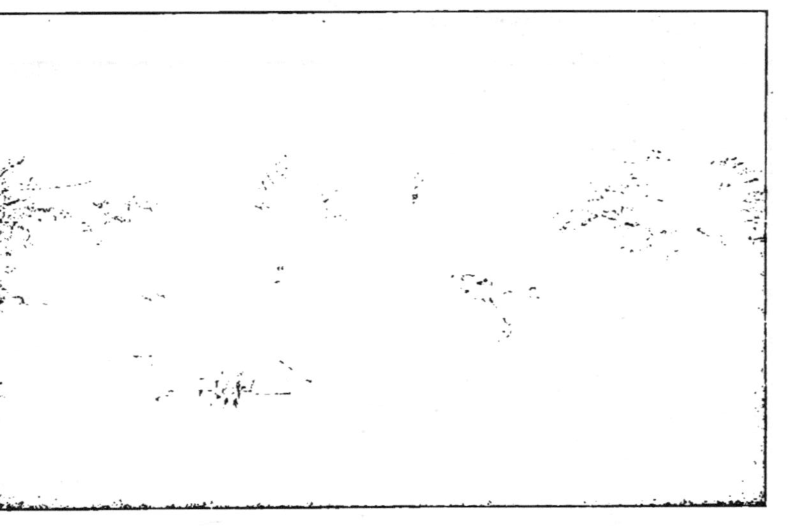

THE SPOT WHERE LT. DANIEL KNOWLTON HEARD THE LEXINGTON ALARM.
Ashford, Conn.

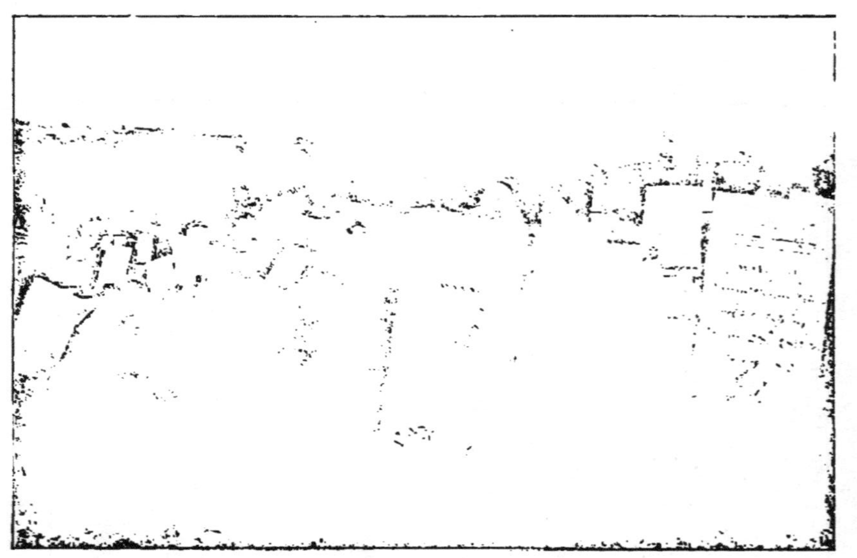

The Grave of Lieut. Daniel Knowlton,
Ashford, Conn.

when the minister gave out a hymn having for its refrain "Give Britain praise," Lieutenant Knowlton immediately rose up in his seat, and requested that this hymn should be omitted, and another sung in its stead; but the minister paying no attention to his request, and the choir beginning to sing, the old soldier marched deliberately out of church, saying that he could not worship with a congregation that "gave Britain praise for anything." And he never entered that church again.

While imprisoned by the British, in an old meeting-house on Long Island, for the space of four days he was allowed neither food nor drink. At length a compassionate woman, hearing of his condition, concealed food and a bottle of water in her clothing, and prevailed upon the guard to allow her to visit the meeting-house. She found Knowlton almost in a dying condition, and but for her timely relief he would soon have perished. It was about this time that Lieutenant Colonel Selah Hart, of Farmington, presented a petition to the Connecticut Assembly for aid in behalf of Ethan Allen, Daniel Knowlton, and a few others, which was granted.

This quaint old document, alluding to our men as "captivated by their enemies," is preserved in the Archives of Connecticut to this day. The petition reads as follows:

"*Whereas* Lieut. Colonel Selah Hart of Farmington hath preferred his memorial to this Assembly, for himself and about thirty-eight other continental officers *captivated by the enemies* of the United States of America, and confined by them on Long Island, showing to this Assembly that said officers and their families are reduced to great distress by means of said officers being held in captivity, the most of them ever since the 15th of September last, since which they have received no wages or allowances from the United States or either of them, and that they have spent all their money, are considerably in debt, and have no means of subsistence; that they are unable to procure hard money; that paper money or bills will not pay them; praying for relief etc. as per memorial and a list of said officers' names lodged in the files of this Assembly appears.

"*Resolved* by this Assembly. That the Committee of the Pay-Table be and they are hereby directed to adjust and settle said officers' accounts, when produced to them, and to allow to them, the same waged since their captivity as was allowed to officers of their rank in the continental army at the time they were captured; and that the committee pay to them, or to said Selah Hart for their use, the balance due to each of said officers or such part thereof as on consideration of their case may appear necessary for their relief: Provided such evidence shall be produced as shall satisfy said committee that said officers have not received their wages already. And said committee are directed if possible to make said payment, or considerable part thereof, in hard money, and for that purpose to draw on the Treasurer of this State for the same, or bills of credit to exchange for the same, and the Treasurer is directed to pay the same accordingly; and said committee are to charge the sum so paid to the United States, and transmit an account thereof to General Washington with the names and offices of the persons to whom, or for whom, the same is paid, and the Battalion and Company to which they belonged, as soon as they can ascertain the same, and request the General to give orders that said sum may be ordered and paid to the Treasurer of this State for the use of this State."

Upon being exchanged with other prisoners, Daniel was assigned as Lieutenant to Capt. Joshua Bottom's company, Lieutenant-Col. Levi Well's regiment, and participated with them in the battle of Horseneck, 9th December, 1780, where he was again taken prisoner. Upon being released he was given brief leave of absence to visit his home in Ashford, soon after which he enlisted again, being commissioned First Lieutenant.

He served with that rank in Capt. Benjamin Durkee's company of Matrosses in the Provisional Regiment stationed at Fort Trumbull, New London, Ct., from July 16, 1782, until the war was ended and the army disbanded. He was given occasional leave of absence.

That Knowlton did not receive the military rank which was his due was owing to the fact that he was a prisoner of war much of the time, and chiefly because he refused advancement on one or two occasions, preferring to serve in that station where he could serve his country best. Bold, stern, and intrepid as a lion in the battle-field, he was retiring, non-assertive, in private life, and inclined to belittle his achievements. Nothing was more distasteful to his mind than display or ostentation.

When a descendant had read the simple inscription on his grave-stone in the Westford Hill cemetery ("A Patriot of the Revolution"), he turned to one of Knowlton's oldest kinsmen and inquired why a more fitting monument had not been erected over the grave of the hero. The answer was characteristic of the Knowltons:

"The best acknowledgement of a man's services to his race is rendered when his countrymen demand with surprise and wonderment why his deeds are not more publicly appreciated."

After the war was over he retired to private life at Ashford, and occupied himself with the humble pursuits of his farm life. He met with a severe affliction in the death of his wife Elizabeth, on June 1, 1786. He married a second

Colonel Thomas Knowlton,
At Bunker Hill.

time, 24th April, 1788, Rebecca Fenton of Willington, by whom he had two sons, Erastus Fenton and Marvin. He is also said to have performed military service in the war of 1812. He met his death from the effects of a fall in the barn attached to his farm at Ashford, 31st May, 1825. His grave-stone in the cemetery at Westford bears the following inscription:

"Lieutenant Daniel Knowlton
A Patriot of the Revolution
Died May 31st 1825 aged 86 years."

---

425 Col. Thomas and Anna Keyes had:

(1051) Frederick, December 4, 1760.
(1052) Sally, November 23, 1763. m. Samuel Utley, of Ashford, Ct., December 16, 1781.
(1053) Thomas, July 13, 1764/5. m. Martha Marcy, of Willington, Ct., 1807.
(1054) Polly, January 11, 1767. m. Stephen Fitts of Ashford, January 1, 1793.
(1055) Abigail, June 20, 1768. m. Thomas Chaffee, of Ashford, November 21, 1781.
(1056) Sampson, February 8, 1770. d. September 10, 1777.
(1057) Anna, June 8, 1771. d. young.
(1058) Anna, March 19, 1773. m. Dr. John Kittredge, January 1, 1804.
(1059) Lucinda, November 10, 1776. d. February 16, 1805.
Wife Anna d. May 22, 1808.

COLONEL THOMAS KNOWLTON,

the seventh child of William and Martha Pinder Knowlton, was born in Boxford, Mass., about November 22, 1740. Like his elder brother Daniel, the songs to which his cradle was rocked were the patriotic hymns of a people called daily to defend their liberties, and the staple of current conversation was furnished by personal adventure and military exploits. The various French and Indian wars had left the colonies but brief intervals of repose for many years, and the New England farmer was as skilful with the musket as with the plough. When scarcely sixteen years of age, Thomas Knowlton had accompanied his elder brother Daniel, the famous scout, in the campaigns which were terminated by the conquest of Canada, and in August, 1758, he fought in the battle of Wood Creek, in which he had hair-breadth escapes, now outwitting the cunning of his savage foe, and again, by strength and agility, making him bite the dust. Nature had cast him, like his elder brother, in a military mould, and set her prophetic seal on him from birth. More than six feet in height, sinewy, erect, handsome as an Apollo, he was a veritable Anakim in physical presence, and commanded the admiration of all who knew him. Trumbull, the great painter, who enlisted in the War of Independence for the express purpose of leaving on his glowing canvas the accurate features of its heroes, caught the gleam of patriotic inspiration that lighted up Knowlton's face at Bunker Hill, and from that faithful portraiture we can readily construct the actual soldier.

In the capture of Ticonderoga, July, 1759, several Knowltons had their honorable share, Luke, Ezekiel, and Benjamin of Massachusetts, and Thomas of Ashford with them, and when the siege of Havana was ended by the surrender of the city, Thomas was one of the victors whom neither war nor disease had mastered.

He had married, three years before, Anna, daughter of Sampson Keyes of Ashford, with whom, after the capture of Havana, he settled down into the uneventful life of an average Connecticut farmer. As David was fitted for the leadership of Israel amid the solitude of the Judæan hills, so was Thomas Knowlton the better prepared for the struggle of '75 and '76 by that contest with the untamed forces of nature which an Ashford farm necessitated. Whoever visits the old town to-day will be as much impressed by its comparative sterility as he will be captivated by its rugged beauty. Unless this region have degenerated since William of Boxford transplanted here his domestic vine and fig-tree, the Knowltons must have found but a stubborn soil, fruitful in rock, sand, and straggling vine, but yielding slowly to persistent cultivation. That they supported families of generous numbers here is presumptive proof that they owned both fair and fertile acres, but the general appearance of the old town is that of a hard field in which to earn one's bread by farming. Thomas Knowlton spent here sixteen years of quiet domestic joy and useful industry. His taste for arms, however, had been whetted in the four campaigns of his earlier life, and when a local militia force was formed he was naturally elected ensign, 3d Company, 1st Regiment. In 1761 he joined the 10th Company, Capt. Robert Durkee, and in the following year was made its 2d lieutenant, Capt. Hugh Ledlie, commanding. In civil affairs he was equally and early prominent, being made a Selectman of the town at the unprecedented age of thirty-three, and stories have been related, again and again, illustrative of a walk and conversation that made him honored for his integrity, admired for his personality, and beloved for his humanity.

A false rumor of British insolence brought him and his company promptly to arms in September, 1774, and when the touch of fate gave immortality to Lexington and Concord the following year, Knowlton was in his element. The captaincy of the Ashford company was vacant, and he was chosen by acclamation. So spontaneous was the patriotic uprising that, when the volunteers poured into the camp at Pomfret, only one fifth were considered necessary, and the Ashford company being at once recognized as superior in material and tactics, it was promptly drafted into the 5th Regiment, and before night was on

THE BATTLE OF BUNKER HILL.
(From the original painting by Trumbull.)

its way to Cambridge. Subsequently, this company was reorganized and increased to two hundred men by members from other companies, with Capt. Knowlton in command, and on June 16, 1775, they marched to Breed's Hill for their first baptism of blood. Against Knowlton's remonstrance, and in the face of his more intelligent judgment, Gen. Israel Putnam had decided to occupy an untenable position exposed to the enemy's batteries, and that could readily be captured by the land and naval forces which the British would inevitably combine. Knowlton was so much a soldier that he obeyed even a suicidal order of his superior, and occupied a small redoubt near the Mystic River. Anticipating the tactics of the British General Howe, he constructed a stone and rail fence parallel with an already existing one a little back of the redoubt, filled the space between the two with hay, and thus prepared for the onset of the red-coats. Behind this extemporized breastwork over which the British made merry, less than one thousand raw, imperfectly disciplined, and scantily equipped Americans awaited the very flower of British soldiery several times their own numbers. When the fight was over, the British had lost 1054 killed and wounded, the Americans but 449. Knowlton commanded the Connecticut forces, handling them with such skill that only three of the Ashford troops were killed. He saved the retreat from becoming a rout, and his heroic valor was the more to be praised because he fought against what he saw from the first were overwhelming odds. A ball striking his gun curved it into the form of a semi-circle, but he grasped another, and without hat or coat led on his men to desperate deeds of valor. For his part in this memorable and initial battle in open field for independence, Knowlton was presented by an admiring friend with a gold-laced hat, a sash, and a gorget, the last being now in the possession of a relative, Mr. Geo. T. Chaffee, Rutland, Vt.

Knowlton's record at Bunker Hill commended him at once to the regard of Washington, with whom he was ever after a great favorite. As evidence of this, the first countersign given by Washington to the army after Bunker Hill was "Knowlton," and the Ashford company became virtually the bodyguard of the Commander-in-chief. A night march to Charlestown and the capture of five English officers under the very eyes of the enemy, gave Knowlton both diversion and reputation. When the 20th Regiment of the line was organized, Knowlton became its major and, immediately after, its acting colonel and paymaster. He was appointed Lieut.-Colonel, August 12, 1776, and fifteen days later, at the disastrous battle of Long Island, he saved, by a timely and masterly retreat, his regiment from capture. Soon after, the famous corps known as "Knowlton's Rangers" was formed from picked men of five Connecticut, one Rhode Island, and two Massachusetts regiments, for special, delicate, and hazardous duty.

This corps was attached to the person of General Washington, receiving its orders directly from him, and appealing to those only who found satisfaction in "leading a forlorn hope."

On September 16, 1776, the battle of Harlem Heights was fought, and the first victory in the open field was won by the Americans, despite the overwhelming numbers of the British. In the thick of the fight Knowlton fell, mortally wounded.

The force under his command had mistaken the order of their commander, at which it is said Knowlton turned pale, fearing the day was lost. The splendid courage of our troops, however, retrieved the disaster, though at a terrible price. A ball pierced the brave Colonel, and he lived just long enough to give to his son Frederic, who was a private in his father's corps, the last benediction, and to his country and the world the assurance that he died content to buy, even with his life, the precious treasure of human freedom.

It is one of the compensations in human life that, sooner or later, posterity will do the honored dead justice. In the General Orders of the following day, Washington declared that "the brave and gallant Colonel Knowlton was an honor to any country." General Reed wrote:

"Our greatest loss was a brave officer from Connecticut, whose name and spirit ought to be immortalized, one Colonel Knowlton. I assisted him off, and when gasping in the agonies of death all his inquiry was if we had drove the enemy."

Capt. Stephen Brown, his successor, adds more explicitly:

"I took hold of him and asked if he were badly wounded. He told me he was, but, says he, 'I do not value my life if we do but get the day.' He desired me by all means to keep up this flank. He seemed as unconcerned and calm as though nothing had happened to him."

And history, calmly writing out this verdict, pronounces him one of the noblest soldiers ever claimed by any country, and whose death cut off a man otherwise destined to be a great general. Original letters now in possession of the Hon. P. H. Woodward, Hartford, Conn., express the sober convictions of such eminent men as Colonel Burr, General Dearborn, and others, all of whom paid high tribute to the worth and virtues of the dead hero. In his own town there was a great lamentation, for the whole community joined their tears to those of the disconsolate widow and eight fatherless children. Colonel Knowlton was buried with military honors on the field of battle, 143d Street, N. Y. Not until September, 1893, did even a mural tablet indicate that the great metropolis, for whose safety he had given his life, remembered and honored him. On November 13, 1895, his native State paid formal tribute to the memory of one of her greatest sons. A superb bronze statue was then unveiled in the Capitol grounds at Hartford, to tell the citizen of the present and the future what a modest headstone in old Ashford has long been repeating,—the glory of self-sacrifice for God and Country. The statue was erected by the State of Connecticut, largely through the efforts of the Hon. P. H. Woodward, of Hartford, and Dr. J. Knowlton

Statue of Col. Thomas Knowlton,
Capitol Grounds, Hartford, Conn.

Marcy, of Windsor, Conn. At the ceremony of unveiling, the Hon. Charles Dudley Warner, Chairman of the Commission of Sculpture, delivered an appropriate and eloquent address, in which he declared that "Colonel Knowlton was a great man. Judged by what he did, and by what his rare talents promised, I doubt if the State has produced a greater military genius, or a more unselfish patriot. The official recognition of his services and of his great qualities comes late; but his fame is permanent, and it will increase, for it is of the sort of heroism that the people take to heart long after 'the flags are folded and the drums silent.'" The historic address—a notable one—was delivered by the Hon. P. H. Woodward, and was printed and widely circulated.

The inscription on the modest tombstone in the old cemetery at Warrenville, Conn., reads thus:

THIS MONUMENT
IS ERECTED IN MEMORY OF
COLONEL THOMAS KNOWLTON AND HIS WIFE.

That brave Colonel, in defense of his Country, fell in battle September 16, 1766, at Harlem Heights, Island of New York. Age 36 years. Mrs. Anna, the amiable Consort of Colonel Knowlton, died May 22, 1808. Age 64, and is buried beneath this Monument.

"Remember God did us part;
Accept it with a willing heart."

---

430 Nathaniel and Elizabeth Parks had:

(1060) Betty, March 17, 1764.
(1061) Sarah, September 7, 1765.
(1062) John, January 18, 1767.
(1063) William, July 30, 1769. d. young.

Nathaniel was b. in Ipswich, rem. to Sudbury, m., and d. there.

---

441 Gideon and Mary Gibson had:

(1064) Gideon, November 18, 1798. d. 1800.
(1065) Gideon, December 16, 1800. m. Mildred Curtis. He d. June, 1863.
(1066) Ruel, January 8, 1803.
(1067) Abner, May 7, 1807. m. Nancy Sweet.
(1068) Ann, June 14, 1808. m. Ira Moulton.
(1069) Louisa, April 23, 1809. m. George Ring. 6 chil.
(1070) Franklin, September 14, 1811. m. Persis Stacey.

(1071) A daughter, September 17, 1813. d. young.
(1072) Sophronia, November 19, 1815. m. Gordon Ring. 4 chil.
(1073) Ira, February 17, 1818.
(1074) Harriet, July 26, 1820. m. Nathaniel Mitchell.

Gideon res. in New Boston, Windsor, and Stoddard, Mass. He d. May 2, 1859. Mary d. June 12, 1860.

---

442 Abner and Elizabeth Knowlton of Wenham had:

(1075) Betsey, September 16, 1781.
(1076) Olive, August 4, 1782.
(1077) Abner, March 27, 1785.

Abner res. in Ipswich. He enlisted in the Revolutionary Army May 9, 1775, and served in the East and at the battle of Trenton. He d. at sea November 3, 1784.

---

443 Antipas

res. in Ipswich, and was a soldier of the Revolution. He served in the Lexington Alarm, April 19, 1775, and from that date until the close of 1776. His company was in the military operations in New England, and in those for the defense of the Hudson River.

---

444 Nathaniel and Mary —— had:

(1078) Moses, 1806. m. Caroline Whitaker. He d. 1858. She d. 1877.

---

445 Jeremiah and Susan Whitney had:

(1079) Abraham, July 5, 1801. m. Lucy Hildreth.
(1080) Mary. m. Ira Robbins.
(1081) Anna. m. —— Staniels.
(1082) Eliza.
(1083) Sallie. m. —— Oliver.
Residence, Brattleboro, Vt.

Jeremiah d. 1805.

---

446 Thomas and Susannah Hollis had:

(1084) Joshua, 1785.
(1085) Susan, 1788.

(1086) John, 1789. m. Charlotte Holmes.
(1087) Sarah, 1790.
(1088) Alvin, 1796.
(1089) Polly.
(1090) Warren.

Thomas rem. to Maine.

---

447 Stephen and Diodemia Chubb had:

(1091) Rachel, March 3, 1781. m. Cephas Case.
(1092) Calvin, May 23, 1783. m. Betsey S. Peck, of New Lyme, O.
(1093) Diodemia, October 6, 1785. m. Moses Camp of Winsted, Conn.
(1094) Laura, September 21, 1788. m. David Wright, June 1, 1810.
(1095) Stephen, August 25, 1791. m. Lydia Dudley, of Austin, O.
(1096) Samuel, June 6, 1793. m. Fanny Beach, November 15, 1814.
(1097) Deborah, 1795. m. Caleb Chapman.
(1098) Harriet. m. Isaac Cutler.

STEPHEN KNOWLTON

resided in Chatham, Conn. He served in the Revolutionary War from May 8 to December 18, 1775, as a private in the 5th Company, Colonel Spencer's 3d. Regiment Connecticut Militia. His widow received a pension in 1844. In 1804 Stephen and his family removed to Morgan, Ashtabula County, Ohio, making the long journey in an ox-cart. His daughter, Diodemia, was followed by her ardent lover, Moses Camp, overtaken at Albany, and married and settled in Winsted, Conn. Stephen built the first frame house in Morgan, and lived in it to a good old age, He d. May 30, 1830. Diodemia was of Huguenot descent and was born in New Hartford, Conn. She was a woman of remarkable energy of body and mind, and she imparted her force of character to her children. The latter portion of her life was passed in the home of her daughter, Mrs. Wright, where she died at the advanced age of 94.

Their son Calvin located near them, and his house was the favorite stopping-place for travellers on their way to the lake to procure salt.

Stephen, Jr., lived near them on lot 125, where he made a clearing and planted an orchard, removing subsequently to lot 417, where he lived for the rest of his life.

Samuel was unfortunate in his domestic relations, a fact which seemed to interfere with the permanence and prosperity of the rest of the family, for he removed not long after marriage, and his record is unknown.

Deborah's husband, Caleb Chapman, came to Morgan, Ohio, in 1804, bought land of Stephen Knowlton, and paid for it by "chopping" and by clearing certain acres of land. He built for himself a dwelling-house, barn, and cider-mill,

448 Abigail and Ebenezer Rowley had :

(1099) Reuben, February 10, 1777. m. Polly ——.
(1100) Abigail, November 5, 1779. m. Hazael Durham. Res., Utica.
(1101) Erastus, April 17, 1782. d. 1845.
(1102) Diantha, July 10, 1784. m. Thos. R. Bull, April 3, 1806. Residence Winsted, Conn. Served in 8th Conn. Regiment, 9th Company, 1812.
(1103) Ada, June 26, 1786.
(1104) Flora, April 15, 1789. m. John Westlake, June 1, 1809.
(1105) Betsey, June 10, 1791.
(1106) Adna, 1793.
(1107) Alpheus, 1795. m. Lydia Rawson.
(1108) Almira, 1798. m. Halsey Bailey.
(1109) Beulah, 1800. m. Benjamin Fowler, May 27, 1829.
Residence, Winsted, Conn.

Ebenezer was a soldier of the Revolution, serving in the 9th Company, 2d Regiment Connecticut Militia. He d. August 25, 1834. He was an industrious and thrifty man, and a great favorite with his fellow pioneers, being jovial, and fond of practical jokes. He d. August 25, 1834.

---

456 A Joseph and Ruth Richardson had :

(1110) Monroe, November 15, 1811. m. Susan Bryan, 1835.
(1111) Maria, October 30, 1814. m. David H. Weller. 3 chil. He d. 1875
(1112) Perry, March 14, 1817. m. Caroline H. Weller, November 2, 1846
(1113) Asa, August 19, 1819. m. Rachel Adams, 1845.

Ruth d. August 19, 1819, and Joseph m. 2d Jemima Holden, December 18, 1819 They had :

(1114) Ruth A., February 19, 1822. m. Edwin Riggs, 1845. She d. [illegible].
(1115) Henry A., January 12, 1828. m. Vastaline Alger, 1849.

Joseph m. 3d. Sarah Richardson, August, 1856. She d. June, 1864. Joseph d. at Sackett's Harbor, N. Y., April 26, 1869.

456(B) Benjamin and Olive Pillsbury had :

(1116) Benjamin, July 13, 1810. m. Eliza Smith, April 18, 1833.

Benj., Sen., m. 2d Polly Ketchum, January 11, 1816, and had :

(1117) Harriet E., October 23, 1816. m. Charles Weller, August 16, 1876.
(1118) Margaret, October 23, 1816. m. Hiram Blackman.
(1119) Rosetta, January 17, 1818. d. March 17, 1835.
(1120) Polly, November 15, 1820. d. January 1850.
(1121) Darwin, January 17, 1823.
(1122) Bernard K. January 10, 1825. m. Amanda ——
Residence, Clarendon Vt. and West Stockholm, N. Y.

Benj. d. February 17, 1827.

456(E) Thankful Knowlton and Ivory Bragdon had :

(1123) Laura S., April 9, 1820. m. Lamb Willoughby.
(1124) George W., June 23, 1823. d. 1829.
(1125) Baron D., December 14, 1826. m. Rhoda Powell.
(1126) Philander, December 14, 1828. m. Lucy Snow, 1852.
(1127) Albert.

456(F) Betsey Knowlton and Benjamin Tupper had :

(1128) Dolphus.
(1129) Julia. m. Ezekiel Smith.
(1130) Pitt, 1830. m. Marinda Bostwitch (Bostwick).

Benjamin d. in Parishville, N. Y., 1876.

456(G) Ruth Knowlton and John Willoughby had :

(1131) Sarah.
(1132) Olive.
(1133) Douglass.
(1134) Ruth.

Ruth d. 1832. John d. 1834.

457 John and Mary Manning had:

(1135) Ephraim, March 19, 1777. m. Louisa Rexford. He d. May, 1871. 6 chil.

(1136) Robert, February 9, 1779. m. Sally Brown.

(1137) Sally, August 12, 1781. m. Neal Gow. She d. 1830.

(1138) John, May 26, 1783. m. Louisa Evans.

(1139) Daniel, July 26, 1786. m. Susannah Vedder; m. 2d Mrs. Judith Knowlton, March 27, 1830.

(1140) Elizabeth, February 24, 1788. m. Daniel Shepard; m. 2d Elijah Ferguson; m. 3d Isaac Lewis. 7 chil.

(1141) Lucretia, February 23, 1792. m. Thomas Peters.

(1142) Esther, July 17, 1794. m. John Evans. She d. August 1878. 6 chil.

Residence Clifton Park, Saratoga Co., N. Y.

John d. July 19, 1838. Mary d. October 7, 1836. John was ensign in Captain Rawling's company, —— Regiment N. Y. State Militia, serving in the War of the Revolution. He was buried in Vale Cemetery, Schenectady, N. Y.

---

460 Ephraim and Elizabeth Butler had:

(1143) Mary, December 31, 1776. m. John Townsend.

(1144) John B., March 21, 1781. m. Polly Rexford.

(1145) David, May 7, 1783. m. Achsah Barnes, 1804.

(1146) Ephraim, June 26, 1785. m. Rem. to Janesville, Wis.

(1147) William, February 15, 1789. m. Almira Parkhurst.

(1148) Betsey, April 15, 1792.

(1149) Dyer, March 16, 1795. m.

(1150) Alvah. Settled in Albany, N. Y., 1855.

Ephraim was b. in Bethlehem, Albany Co., N. Y., and rem. to Rexford Flats, Saratoga Co., where he d.

---

462 Robert and Mary Gay had:

(1151) Judge Hiram, March 25, 1788. d. September 6, 1863. Res., Little Falls, N. Y.

(1152) Robert W., November 27, 1792. Carriage maker and salt inspector. m. Miriam Gaylord, November 17, 1816. Syracuse, N. Y.

(1153) Dr. Josiah, December 17, 1794. Res., Cazenovia and Rochester, N. Y. d. March 26, 1858.

(1154) Lymon, December 19, 1797. Res., Syracuse. Carriage maker. d. March 17, 1882.

(1155) Ruth M., September 30, 1799. m. —— Smith. d. December 10, 1882.
(1155 A) Julian, June 29, 1802. d. young.
(1156) Daniel, May 29, 1804. m. Catherine Burrell, of Little Falls, N. Y. d. February 2, 1890.
(1157) Jerusha Caroline, February 16, 1807. m. Henry Graves. d. May 27, 1891.

Robert was born at Sharon Springs, Conn., February 10, 1759. When but seventeen years old he enlisted in the army, serving during most of the Revolutionary War. He was at Fort Edward and witnessed the massacre of Jane McCrea, in the battles of Stillwater and Saratoga, and at Valley Forge with Washington. His son changed the name to Nolton, a change suggested, perhaps, by a spelling of the name which was at one time adopted by his English ancestors. His descendants resumed the former spelling a few years since. Robert removed to Saratoga Co., N. Y., either to Greenfield or Milton, as is shown by a deed dated October 28, 1793, in which he spells his name Knowlton. He also lived in Fairfield, N. Y. He d. in Boonville, N. Y., December 10, 1851.

---

468 Robert and —— had :

(1158) Stephen, 1776. m. Phoebe Russell, 1796.
(1159) Abijah, July 26, 1782. m. Abigail Ann Russell.
(1160) Phoebe.
(1161) Elizabeth.

Robert owned a large farm of 1600 acres in Bedford, Westchester Co., N. Y., the original deed of which was given by Queen Anne. He was a signer to the following petition. Dated North Castle, N. Y.

"To the Right Honorable George Clarke Esq Commander in Chief of the Province of New York, &c.

The Petition of the Inhabitants of North Castle and bordering neighbors Humbly Sheweth, That your poore petitioners are greivously oprest by francies pellem Esqr Justice of the peach for this county for that the said Justice Is a man that is given to Drinking and for the most part apears a party and Is very Rash In way of Speaking in Liccor that If it Was not for the Law of man he would kill a man before night, and he will have Special warrants and Send for poore men and then perswade them it Will be Charge to them and If they would not give him some money In pocket and treat him with punch which Is his usal drink, and ye s^d compleaner was fors^d so to do and when money has been paid and a Receit given he has given Judgment again for some of that money by these and many other Like actions wee are much oprest therefore wee your Honours poore petione's pray you would Suspend him from acting as a Justice any Longer that we may Injoy peace and wee shall Ever pray for your long administration ouer us, and In the main time beg Leive to subscribe our Selves your Honours most obedient Humble Servants.

WILLIAM DUSINBERRE,
RYCHARD WOOLEY,
REUBEN HALLAM,
DAUID FEBE,
ROBERT KNOULTON,
JACOB FORMAN,
ROBERT CARPENTER,
JOSEPH SARLS,
JOSEPH FOWLER,
RICHARD HONEYWELL,
HENERY DUSINBERRE."

---

471 Sarah Knowlton and Wm. Longfellow had :

(1162) Elizabeth, June 10, 1785. m. Stephen Williams, December 1812.
(1163) William.
(1164) Susan.
(1165) Abraham.

William Longfellow had a most honorable Revolutionary record. He was of that New England family to which the American Poet Laureate belonged. At the age of twenty, he enlisted in a company of Minute-men under Capt. Nathaniel Wade, Col. Moses Little's regiment, May, 1775, marched to Cambridge, and was in the battle of Bunker Hill. He served during the whole of that year, and reinlisted the next year, having the rank of Sergeant. His health being impaired he returned home to Canaan, N. H., in 1777, and after recovery he enlisted on the Privateer *Fancy*, Captain Lee, commanding. The *Fancy* was captured by the English man-of-war *Fordroyant*, and Longfellow was taken to England where he was imprisoned until the end of the war, when he returned home.

---

473 Abraham and Sarah Fitts had :

(1166) Ebenezer K. m. Margaret Bass, December 16, 1802.
(1167) Lucy, 1772. m. Richard Lakeman, December 3, 1796.
(1168) Hannah. m.

Abraham and Mrs. Esther Russell had no children. He was for several years a shoemaker in Boston. He enlisted in the War of the Revolution, fought at Lexington and Bunker Hill, and served on the sloop *Republic*, a privateer. He was captured and impressed into the British service. When his release was secured, he returned from England, and in 1805 bought a farm near Canaan N. H. His wife, Esther, died in 1812. In 1819 Abraham went to Allentown Pa., where he d. of cancer July 25 of that year. He was subsequently reinterred at Enfield, N. H., by his grand-nephew, Abraham L. Williams, Esq. Sarah Fitts was the dau. of Abraham Fitts (or Fitch) and Mary Rose of Salisbury, b. March 15, 1697.

---

475 Stephen and Anna Fletcher had :

(1169) Seth, August 6, 1784. m. Jerusha Lewis, March 20, 1818. Sett. in Malone N. Y. He d. September 24, 1857.
(1170) Daniel, May 19, 1786. m.
(1171) Sylvia, January 31, 1788. m. Caleb E. Maxham, April 20, 1826.
(1172) Thomas, November 12, 1790. m. Jerusha Newell, February, 1826.

Stephen was a carpenter and farmer. He was b. in Ashford, Conn. and rem. to Bridgewater Vt., in 1803. He served in the Revolutionary War. He made all the hand looms for the domestic weavers of the town, many of which are in good preservation at the present time. He d. November 28, 1816. Anna d. December 2, 1826.

---

480 Daniel and Rachel Olney had :

(1172 A) Zerviah, 1787.

---

482 Mary and Nathaniel Bostwick had :

(1173) John.
(1174) Nathaniel.

---

484 Ezra and Abigail Bostwick had :

(1175) Reuben.
(1176) Ezra. m. Anna Loomis ; m. 2d Abigail Hoar.
(1177) Roxana.

---

485 John and Jemima Barrow had :

(1178) Achsah, January 2, 1789. m. Jesse Marsh. 2 chil.
(1179) Jemima, May 12, 1792.

(1180) John, 1795. m. Almira Chaffee, November 30, 1815. m. 2d Polly Crab.
(1181) Guerdon, June 2, 1797. m. Laura Pickett.
(1182) Tamsen, July 16, 1800. m. Ezra W. Crawford, November 18. 1828
(1183) Laura, 1804. m. Washington Blackley, 1827.
Jemima d. 1856 aged 89.
Residence Ashford, Conn.

489 Johnathan and Zerviah Sanger had:

(1184) Johnathan, January 21, 1803. d. young.
(1185) Armanda, August 27, 1805. m. D. B. Reed, March 27, 1825.
(1186) Palmer, December 29, 1807. m. Harriet Conant, December 29, 1824.
(1187) Almena, September 7, 1811. m. L. P. Rowley. She d. September 6, 1895.
(1188) Johnathan W. November 1, 1817. m. Harriet M. Bottom, April 3, 1842.
Res. West Ashford, Conn.

491 Jesse and Joanna Hale had:

(1189) John. m. Had son Edward. d. in Michigan, 1855.
(1190) Jesse L., October 12, 1819. Res. in Peoria, Ill.
(1191) Albert. m. and res. in Ida, Kansas.
(1192) Laura M. m. Rev. A. W. Baker, June 2, 1837.

492 Chester and Priscilla Sanger had:

(1193) Philena, M., September 25, 1808. m. W. A. Locke, March 16, 1835. 7 chil.
(1194) Minerva, January 17, 1811. m. Harry C. Locke, November 29, 1834. 2 chil.
(1195) Sophronia, May 29, 1813. m. J. C. Laubson, March 15, 1839. 2 chil. She d. March 9, 1871.
(1196) Alvina, November 17, 1815; d. young.
(1197) Orissa, June 7, 1818. m. Chas. Torry, June 5, 1844. 3 chil.
(1198) Jane, April 19, 1821. m. Dorester Torry, May 3, 1845. 3 chil.
(1199) James, April 19, 1821. m. Clarinda Wheat, March 11, 1845.
(1200) Adelia, December 10, 1826. m. Isaac Torry, June 3, 1848. 2 chil.
(1201) Elizabeth, June 21, 1829. m. Wm. H. Ashley, May 17, 1862.
Residence, Centreville, N. Y.

Chester d. April 30, 1871. Priscilla d. November 17, 1877.

493 Amasa and Margaret Topliff had:

(1202) Persis, April 12, 1788. d. February 25, 1794.
(1203) Polly, March 12, 1793. d. February 12, 1821. unm.
(1204) Peggy, September 13, 1796. d. September 26, 1818. unm.
(1205) Amasa, July 5, 1798. d. September 28, 1828. unm.
(1206) Lucinda, November, 6, 1800. d. February 12, 1820. unm.
(1207) Merrick, August 29, 1802. m. Fatima Perrin.
(1208) Persis, March 23, 1805. m. Mace Moulton, 1824.

Residence, Monson, Mass.

Amasa d. April 19, 1825. Margaret d. March 27, 1834.

---

495 Miriam Knowlton and Abner Woodward had:

(1209) Hiel, September 20, 1791. m. Anna H. Andrews.
(1210) Joseph, December 30, 1792. d. young.
(1211) Jahiel, 1793.

Abner Woodward was a soldier in the Revolutionary War, serving during several campaigns. He was a lineal descendant of the original Woodward family who sailed from Ipswich, England, on the ship *Elizabeth*, William Andrews, master, April 10, 1634. The family consisted of Richard Woodward (b. 1589), his wife Rose, and two sons, and it is a curious fact that among their fellow passengers were other families who also intermarried with the Knowltons in various parts of New England.

Abner resided in Willington (now Enfield), and Ashford, Conn., and was the ancestor of Dr. Ashbel Woodward the biographer of Gen. Nathaniel Lyon, son of Amasa Lyon and Keziah Knowlton, and to the son of Dr. Ashbel, the Hon. P. H. Woodward of Hartford, Conn., were assigned the honor and the privilege of delivering the oration at the unveiling of the statue of Col. Thomas Knowlton, in the Capitol grounds in Hartford, November 13, 1895.

Miriam Knowlton Woodward d. in Willington, Conn., August 24, 1793.

---

496 Stephen and Hannah Heath had:

(1212) Stephen, April 17, 1797. m. Cassandra Hester, August 17, 1821. Rem. to N. York.
(1213) Arnon, January 28, 1800. m. Susan Wentworth, March 11, 1830.
(1214) Orson, November, 10, 1803. d. 1807.
(1215) Marcus, February 26, 1806. d. May 30, 1843.
(1216) Luke, March 22, 1808. d. October 12, 1846.
(1217) Ebenezer, April 2, 1810. m. Elizabeth Lyon, April 3, 1838.

(1218) Samuel, November 3, 1813. m. E. Fay Woodward, October 5, 1839.
(1219) Hannah Minerva, September 15, 1816. m. John S. Dean, May 16, 1838.

Residence, Ashford, Ct.

Stephen d. September 15, 1849.

---

498 Abel and Barbara Dimock had :

(1220) Abraham, February 25, 1795. m. Huldah Hastings, September 16, 1829.
(1221) Lucinda, January, 1797. m. David Mufford. 3 chil.
(1222) Giles, 1798. d. 1822.
(1223) Laura, 1800. d. young.
(1224) Miles, 1802. m. Mrs. Tucker.
(1225) Cephas, 1804. m. Julia E. Ludlow, 1850.
(1226) Mary, 1806.
(1227) Eliza, 1808. m. Dr. Reuben Mufford. 6 chil.
(1228) Abel, 1810. d. April 20, 1866.
(1229) Stephen, 1812. d. 1847.
(1230) Melissa, 1815. d. 1847.

Abel m. 2d Eunice Fuller of Mansfied, Conn. They had :

(1231) Joseph.
(1232) Jerusha.
(1233) Johnathan.
(1234) Jelina.

Abel removed to Arkansas, and d. 1844.

---

501 Nathan and Lydia Leonard had :

(1235) Permelia, March 17, 1801. m. Lysander C. Frost, March 8, 1831.
(1236) Dennis, September 8, 1802. pub. to Eliza Weatherby, February 29, 1828. Res., Wilbraham, Mass.
(1237) Hessey, June 6, 1804. m. William S. Baker.
(1238) Nathan, August 6, 1806. m. Lucy Murdock, June 8, 1840. No chil. He was a jeweller, and d. September 2, 1864. Thorndike, Mass.
(1239) Lydia, April 29, 1808. m. Thomas Glover, December 1, 1831.
(1240) James, June 29, 1814. d. young.
(1241) Abraham, April 5, 1816. m. Emily Wilt.

Residence, Wilbraham, Mass.

Nathan d. May 13, 1862. Lydia d. December 3, 1859.

Deacon Daniel Knowlton,
Ashford, Conn., 1781–1852.

502 Daniel and Hannah Knowlton had :

(1242) Miner, September 25, 1804. d. December 23, 1870. unm.

(1243) Amanda, June 24, 1807. m. Lewis Topliff, July 20, 1836. She d. July 20, 1836.

(1244) Miriam, March 16, 1809. m. Hiram Cady, November 24, 1831. 4 chil.

(1245) Danforth, May 5, 1811. m. Miranda H. Rockwell, September 26, 1837.

(1246) Elvira, September 14, 1816. m. Asher Knowlton, her cousin, March 25, 1840.

(1247) Edwin, June 24, 1825. m. Mary F. Woodward.

Residence, Ashford, Conn.

DANIEL KNOWLTON.

Daniel Knowlton (Daniel Knowlton 2d as he was known until the death of Lieut Daniel Knowlton, and in later years known by his neighbors as Deacon Knowlton) was the son of Abraham Knowlton and Molly Knox, and was born in Ashford, Conn., March 17, 1781, on premises long owned and occupied by his father, and previous thereto by his grandfather Robert Knowlton. His early educational facilities were meagre, being such as were afforded by the district school which he attended during the winter months, assisting in the labor of the farm in summer. On November 24, 1803, he married Hannah Knowlton, daughter of Lieut. Daniel Knowlton, and settled down as a farmer on premises adjoining his father's farm, where all of his children were born, and where he lived until his death in 1852. The title and occupancy of this large and productive farm have continued in certain descendants to the present time.

From early manhood he took a lively interest in the welfare of the town, and was often elected to office, always serving with credit. He served on Board of Relief seven times ; Selectman, three times ; "Agent of town to commence and defend suits," twice ; Member of the General Assembly, three times ; Judge of Probate, seven times ; beside filling several minor offices.

He early became a member of the Baptist Church located in the west part of the town, organized in 1775 largely through his father's efforts, and in which he took a decided interest ; giving it liberal financial support ; serving on the Society Committee eighteen times, and as Deacon for thirty years, or more.

He was an earnest and exemplary member of this church, and a man of genial disposition, sound judgment, and sterling traits of character. The children of Daniel and Hannah were all of marked ability and character, and while the women naturally took a less conspicuous part in life they inherited the sterling qualities of their parents.

HANNAH KNOWLTON, WIFE OF DANIEL,

was the daughter of Lieut. Daniel Knowlton, a Revolutionary hero, by his first wife Elizabeth Farnham, and she was a niece of Col. Thomas Knowlton, and an aunt of Gen'l Nathaniel Lyon, who fell at the battle of Wilson's Creek, Missouri, in the War of the Rebellion.

She was born at Ashford, Conn., April 19, 1783, and married Daniel Knowlton, Esq., November 26, 1803. She died December 24, 1854.

It is said by her descendants that her early life was severe, as the father, Lieut. Daniel, was fighting, or a prisoner, during the Revolutionary War, and the farm was consequently neglected. The women of those days had much to do caring for the family, and beside the household labor, did spinning, weaving, and making of silk to provide for daily needs, and to exchange for the necessaries that could not be raised on the farm.

They found their highest glory *in the home*, and in the training of the sturdy race of men to whom they gave birth. Hannah's life was quiet and unassuming, and full of love and devotion to her family and friends.

She was a woman of a keen and bright mind, affectionate disposition, and generous to the poor, as far as her means would allow, always feeding some unfortunate outcast. "Aunt Hannah" as she was always called by neighbors, was very fond of their children as well as of her own, and beloved by them in return. The children called her "Grandma Deacon," and were fond of her sweetmeats, which she freely dispensed.

---

503 Amos and Nancy Webb had :

(1248) Sally, April 23, 1805. m. Chauncey Warren, April 9, 1823. 4 chil. she d. February 9, 1874.
(1249) Asher, January 3, 1807. m. Elvira Knowlton, March 25, 1840.
(1250) Jabez, January, 16, 1809. m. Susan Bickford, June 1839.
(1251) Mary Ann, February 26, 1811. d. 1821.
Residence, Ashford, Conn.

Amos d. February 23, 1864. Nancy d. April 25, 1864.

---

507 Grace Knowlton and Josiah Goulding had :

(1252) Joseph. m. Sally Dalrymple, 1850. Rem. to Maine.
(1253) Justus. d. young.
(1254) Relief. m. Joseph Henshaw, of Auburn. 8 s.
(1255) Polly. m. Ebenezer Dunbar. 3 dau.
(1256) Sally. m. —— Warren. 6 s. and 1 dau.
Residence in Ward, now Auburn, Mass.

Grace d. 1824.

---

508 Nathan and Abigail Maynard had :

(1257) Sarah, July 16, 1783. m. —— Gleason ; m. 2d Aaron Sibley. She d. April 10, 1871. Had s. Freeman. Res., Waltham, Mass.

Mrs. Hannah Knowlton,
Ashford, Conn., 1783-1854.

(1258) Benjamin, August 3, 1782. m. Olive Stone, December, 1807. d. August 23, 1865, at Jamaica, Vt.
(1259) Nathan, January 23, 1785. m. Sally Gates. d. March 12, 1848.
(1260) Maynard, October 20, 1787. m. Susannah Gates. d. July 18, 1868.
(1261) Abigail, March 13, 1790. m. Johnathan Stone, of Auburn. 7 chil. She d. February 15, 1874.
(1262) Lucretia, March 3, 1792. d. young.

Abigail d. December 21, 1790, and Nathan m. Olive Pomeroy, of Warwick, Mass. They had:

(1263) Joanna, July 23, 1793. m. David Rockwood. 11 chil. She d. August 16, 1857. Res., Bennington, Vt.
(1264) Pomeroy, August 1, 1794. m. Marcia Palmer. 1 dau. He d. June 1, 1874.
(1265) Lucinda, February 3, 1796. d. young.
(1266) Olive, February 1, 1797. m. C. Fay, April 2, 1824. 6 chil. She d. March 3, 1886. Res., Lawrence, Mass.
(1267) Arad, December 29, 1798. m. Sophia Wilkinson, October, 1825.
(1268) Mary, February 16, 1800. m. Luther Waters. She d. September 13, 1866.
(1269) Lucy, December 10, 1801. m. N. S. Clark, of Auburn.
(1270) Asahel, February 22, 1803. m. Sophronia C. Cummings, January 19, 1832.
(1271) Swan, April 21, 1804. m. Mrs. Sarah Eddy Baird, January 24, 1799. d. November 27, 1883.
(1272) Luthera, July 31, 1808. m. Ezra Rice, of Auburn, Mass., November 14, 1832.

NATHAN KNOWLTON

was b. in Shrewsbury, Mass., and rem. to Newfane, Vt. In November, 1776, he enlisted in Capt. Moses Harrington's company, Colonel Dyke's regiment, and was stationed at Dorchester from December until the following May. Re-enlisting in Captain Inglesbury's company, Col. Job Cushing's regiment, he served as corporal and musician in the campaign against General Burgoyne. He was present at the surrender of that General, and heard him insultingly call General Gates "Granny Gates," to which the latter replied:

"I will own the title, for I have just delivered Great Britain of ten thousand men."

Knowlton again enlisted and marched to Rutland, to Enfield, Conn., and Providence, R. I., with several divisions of prisoners, after which he was honorably discharged. Nathan was commissioned Lieutenant in the 1st Company, 3d Regiment, 2d Brigade, Vermont State troops, by Gov. Thos. Chittenden. August 29, 1792, and for his Revolutionary service he received a pension at the age of 96. He d. from a fall on the ice, March 24, 1856, at Newfane, Vt.

---

509 Joseph and Priscilla Howe had:

(1273) Relief, March 17, 1785.
(1274) Mary J., June 11, 1787.
(1275) Samuel, May 1, 1791.
(1276) Hollis, June 18, 1793.
(1277) Sarah, August 26, 1795.
(1278) Samuel, January 14, 1798.
(1279) Walter H., August 10, 1800.
(1280) Caroline, May 20, 1803.
(1281) William, July 2, 1805.

Joseph owned and operated mills in Shrewsbury, Mass., from which place he rem. to Ohio.

---

511 Rachel Knowlton and Jasper Rand had:

(1282) Anna, February 14, 1784. m. Lyman Converse, February 20, 1810. Res., Bridport, Vt.
(1283) Mehitable, January 28, 1787. m. Luke Knowlton, September 23, 1804.
(1284) Candace, August 8, 1788. m. Johnathan Rice, April 26, 1815. 2 chil. Res., Amherst, Mass.
(1285) Elizabeth, October 21, 1789. m. Abisha Larned, February 27, 1816.
(1286) Mary, June 24, 1791. d. young.
(1287) Mary, October 18, 1794.
(1288) Wareham D., June 22, 1796. m. Hannah Underwood. Rem. to Galena, Ill. She d. August 22, 1836.
(1289) Jasper R., June 6, 1801. Sett. in Westfield, Mass.

Rachel d. March 7, 1802.

---

514 Comfort Knowlton and George Haskell had:

(1290) Abraham.
(1291) Charles.
(1292) Mark.
(1293) Franklin.

(1294) Bela B.
(1295) Comfort.
(1296) Deborah. m. —— Whipple.
Residence, Winchendon, Mass.

---

516 Israel and Abigail Carter had :

(1297) Israel, March 12, 1795. d. young.
(1298) Calvin, September 2, 1797. m. Abigail Powers, September 20, 1822. d. January 30, 1878 Res., in Rye, N. H.
(1299) Israel, December 22, 1799. d. young.
(1300) Abraham, March 5, 1802. d. young.
(1301) Maria, June 8, 1804. m. Wm. Dexter, June 3, 1828.
(1302) Abraham, June 12, 1807. unm. Res. in Cambridge, Mass. A mason.
(1303) Timothy C., August 14, 1810. m. Susan Locke, February 18, 1836.
(1304) Lucy, July 25, 1815. unm. She d. September 1, 1878, at Cambridge.

Israel d. in Brighton, Mass., October 12, 1842.

Abigail d. in Cambridgeport, Mass., October 9, 1851. Their dau. Lucy was struck by lightning, and was made deaf and dumb for life.

---

521 Thomas and Susan Heywood had :

(1305) Mary H., August 31, 1807. unm.
(1306) Elizabeth, July 8, 1809. unm.
(1307) Lucy, August 20, 1811. unm.
(1308) Thomas, May 20, 1813. m. Eliza A. Brand, December 10, 1845.
(1309) Amos, April 27, 1815. m. Mary J. Hodge, 1842 ; m. 2d Ann M. Stone.
(1310) Susan, June 24, 1821. m. Francis Gerald, November 10, 1844.
(1311) Charles G. December 24, 1824. d. young.
(1312) Charles H., June 4, 1830. m. Annie C. Root.

Residence, Winchendon, Mass. Thomas d. there September 1, 1835.

---

522 Joseph and Huldah Warren had :

(1313) Polly, August 13, 1793. m. Artemus Mann, November 7, 1816.

Huldah d. July 25, 1796, and Joseph m. 2d Relief Stratton, December 20, 1797. They had :

(1314) Relief, October 13, 1798. d. July 3, 1807.

(1315) Cynthia, November 28, 1799. m. Jason Goulding, March 3, 1829.
(1316) Rosanna, June 24, 1802. d. young.
(1317) Joseph, September 6, 1804. m. Abigail Canuth, May 20, 18— ; m. 2d Harriet Bowker, June 16, 1830.
(1318) Frances E., November 24, 1808. m. Rev. J. W. Chickering, November 9, 1830.

Residence, Gerry and Templeton, Mass.

Joseph was a physician and a man of deserved prominence. He was Deacon of the Congregational Church for many years, Town Clerk for seven years, and Selectman for fourteen years. Relief d. March 6, 1840.

---

529 Jacob and Rhoda Smith had :

(1319) Stephen S., November 22, 1800. m. Sally Atwood.

Rhoda dying, Jacob m. 2d Rosetta Robinson and had :

(1320) Rhoda, 1809. d. at Stockbridge, Vt., August 6, 1829.
(1321) Jonas, July 30, 1811. m. Eliza Pinney. 2 chil.
(1322) Rosetta, May 24, 1814. m.
(1323) Emmons, August 4, 1816. m. Abigail Taggart ; m. 2d Harnie Taggart.

Jacob m. 3d Nabby Taggart, and had :

(1324) Agnes, 1818. d. September 15, 1842.
(1325) Phoebe, September 3, 1822. m. Joseph Taggart of Stockbridge.
(1326) Abigail, December 5, 1826. m. Alonzo Keyes.

Jacob was a corporal in Capt. Samuel Robinson's Company, serving March 13–December 2, 1757, also in the Crown Point Expedition and in the Eastern Provinces. He m. 2d Rosetta Robinson. He held the office of Deacon in the Congregational Church at Hardwick, Mass., and Stockbridge, Vt., whither he removed. He d. April 29, 1861.

---

530 James and Betsey Tracy had :

(1327) George. m. Betsey E. Brummell, 1840.
(1328) John, 1796. m. Rebecca Sperry.
(1329) Julius.
(1330) Betsey. m. Joel Finch.
(1331) Polly. m. John Sanford.
(1332) Laura.
(1333) Rebecca.

531 Samuel and Aurilla Coates had:

(1334) Roxana, February 21, 1802. d. young.
(1335) Erastus, March 7, 1804. m. Mary Moore.
(1336) Sewell, February 13, 1806. m. Maria Quance, January 22, 1834.
(1337) Roxana, November 22, 1808. m. W. H. Day. Res., Huntington, Mass. Had s. William. Res., Topsfield, Mass.
(1338) Myron, March 31, 1811. d. November 20, 1815.
(1339) Orlando, May 30, 1813. d. September 17, 1820.
(1340) Fannie, May 7, 1815. d. young.
(1341) Fannie, September 7, 1816. m. A. B. Jones, March 21, 1838. Res., Chicopee Falls, Mass.
(1342) James M., November 21, 1819. m. Nancy Kendall, October 15, 1846; m. 2d Susan A. Lincoln, October 7, 1860. Res., Noblesboro, Mass.
(1343) Samuel H., December 4, 1822. m. Marietta Howard, April 6, 1843.
(1344) John H., April 22, 1727. d. young.

Samuel d. June 10, 1831. Aurilla d. December 12, 1869.

---

532 Paul and Lucy (Lovie) Whipple had:

(1345) Catherine, May 29, 1802. m. Levi Whitcomb, May 31, 1827. Res., Marion, Ia. She d. July 8, 1876. 4 chil.
(1346) Levi W., June 11, 1803. m. Amanda Hollister, March 18, 1832. Res., Utica, Ohio.
(1347) Joel, April 25, 1805. d. August 3, 1839, at Albany, Ill.
(1348) Elijah, February 7, 1807. d. November 8, 1838, at Chatham Centre, Ohio.
(1349) Lucy, November 2, 1810. m. Thomas Carter, October 13, 1845. She d. October 24, 1865, Fairfield Co., Ohio.
(1350) Orilla, December 27, 1811. m. John Lusk, 1840. She d. October 22, 1842 at Marion, Ia. 1 dau.
(1351) Robert, January 5, 1814. d. at Crawford, Neb., February 16, 1888.
(1352) Edward, December 28, 1815. m. Abigail Williams, February 18, 1845. He d. July 6, 1891, at Marion, Ia.
(1353) Francis P., February 16, 1818. m. Nancy Wilson, October 31, 1848. d. May 11, 1871.

Residence, Hoosac Falls (now Florida), Mass.

Paul d. August 31, 1847. Lucy d. April 11, 1845.

---

534 Robert and Lydia Thurston of Westboro

removed from Shrewsbury, to North Brookfield, Mass., where, on November 18, 1818, he was found dead by the roadside. He had been in the woods to cut a well-pole, and was probably the victim of heart disease. His widow m. 2d Josiah Bush, October 2, 1819, and returned to Westboro.

---

535 Daniel and Mary Hemmingway had:

(1354) Mary, July 5, 1804. m. Edward Wright, October 16, 1825. Res. Bethany, N. Y.

(1355) Fermelia, November 9, 1805. m. Chauncey Barry, 1829.

(1356) Adaline, September 22, 1807. m. Apollos Kenny, 1834.

(1357) Venus, 1809.

(1358) Daniel, September 12, 1811. m. Chlorine Bowker, March 2, 1850.

(1359) Hepsabeth, September 27, 1813. m. Edward Wright, May, 1, 1836.

(1360) Thaddeus, March 31, 1822. m. Mary Stewart (or Stevens,) May 28, 1845.

(1361) Levi P., May 9, 1824. m. Alicia Dickerson, January 26, 1852. Res., Wisconsin.

Daniel and family removed from Shrewsbury, Worcester Co., Mass., to N. Y. in 1808, and settled in Pavillion, 1816. He d. at Bethany N. Y., July 4, 1847. Mary d. October 8, 1874.

---

537 John and Diodema Duncan had:

(1362) Elbridge G., May 19, 1806. m. Artelissa Robinson, November 15, 1831.

(1363) Diodema, July 12, 1809. m. Elijah Wyman, November 19, 1831.

(1364) Sarah D., November 14, 1811. m. Franklin Dortt, 1833.

(1365) Lucy A., June 19, 1815. d. February, 1842.

John d. in Rochester, Vt., August 5, 1848. Diodema d. there May 12, 1842.

---

539 Joel and Mary Brooks, of Grafton, Mass., had:

(1366) Ruel F., January 10, 1810. m. Sarah Luther, April 9, 1838.

(1367) Laura, January 10, 1810. m. Isaac Crosby, December 2, 1830.

(1368) John C., December 6, 1812. m. Louisa Goddard, September 18, 1839.

(1369) Daniel H., July 31, 1817. m. Aurilla Pinkham, January, 1845.

(1370) Elijah B., January 31, 1815. m. Mehitable Hall, March 31, 1843.

(1371) Chas. H., October 9, 1819. m. Martha Boyden, April 14, 1844.

(1372) Harriet, August 13, 1826.

(1373) Samuel, June 27, 1824. d. young.

Residence, Shrewsbury, Mass.

Joel d. August 14, 1839.

545 Silas and Mercy Wakefield had :

(1374) Irene, January 20, 1799. m. Washington Wakefield.
(1375) Perrin, August 22, 1801. m. Elizabeth Carter, May 2, 1826.
(1376) Newell, April 27, 1803. m. Sophia Wallace, January 1, 1827.
(1377) Dexter, February 22, 1805.
(1378) Lydia B., March 7, 1807. m. Elisha A. Briggs. 3 chil.
(1379) Mary D., March 7, 1807. d. in Mt. Vernon, Ohio.
(1380) Calvin F., February 11, 1810.

Silas was b. in Shrewsbury, Mass., and removed to Mt. Vernon, Ohio, where he d. about 1798.

Mercy was from Sutton, Mass. She was the daughter of Samuel Wakefield, who was a soldier in the Revolutionary War, Capt. John Putnam's company, Col. Ebenezer Larned's regiment, which served in the Lexington Alarm.

546 Martha Knowlton and Nathan Munroe had :

(1381) Luther.
(1382) Caroline.
(1383) Eliza.

547 Sarah Knowlton and John White had :

(1384) Asa.
(1385) John.
(1386) Moses.

548 David and Lucy Brigham had :

(1387) Julia Ann, December 4, 1800. m. Seth Baker, March 10, 1816.
(1388) Eli, October 28, 1802.
(1389) Artemus, September 11, 1804. m. Fanny Spencer, March 20, 1824.
(1390) Elbridge G., October 6, 1806.
(1391) Abraham, December 8, 1808. m.
(1392) Lucy, September 3, 1811.
(1393) David, August 2, 1816. m. Harriet Hamilton, August 2, 1843.
(1394) Marietta, Dec. 3, 1817. m. Chester Keyes, Sept. 2, 1837. She d. March 27, 1849.
(1395) Harriet. d. young.

Residence, Shrewsbury. Rem. to N. York City.

Lucy was from Northboro, Mass. David d. September 6, 1823.

550 Abraham and Lucy Faulkner had:

(1396) Mary E., December 18, 1808. m. Lewis Brown, April 29, 1829.

(1397) James F., November 1, 1810. m. Olive Brown, September 30, 1832. m. 2d Margaret Dickey, September 27, 1838.

(1398) Nancy F., August 19, 1812. m. Chas. H. Ide, October 6, 1834.

(1399) Sarah W., March 15, 1815. m. John Brown, November 20, 1840. 3 chil.

(1400) Thankful, July 9, 1817. d. 1855.

(1401) Charles A., July 31, 1819. m. Sarah Crouch, December 18, 1845; m. 2d Caroline Crouch; m. 3d Nancy Cooper.

(1402) Charlotte, July 31, 1819. m. Williamson D. Vanoter, November 1., 1852. Res., Santa Monica, Cal.

(1403) Henry G., November 16, 1822. m. Martha Miller, February, 1846.

Lucy was from Grafton, Mass. Rem. from Shrewsbury to Brownsville, Ind., 1838, where Abraham d. October, 1843, and Lucy in 1867.

---

559 Joseph and Betsey Sprague had:

(1404) Elmer, March 4, 1792. d. July 3, 1867. unm.

(1405) Melinda, July 4, 1794. m. Simon Flint.

(1406) Lucy, June 23, 1796. m. Moses Haskell, April 15, 1817.

(1407) Mary, 1798.

(1408) Stillman, March 17, 1802. m. Lydia Cheney, 1828; m. 2d Emily Thorpe, December 29, 1831.

(1409) Cynthia, June 28, 1805.

(1410) Clarissa, March 8, 1810. m. Geo. W. Hatch; m. 2d Calvin Childs.

(1411) Elizabeth, January 13, 1813. m. Joseph Blood.

Residence, Templeton, Mass.

Joseph was a Revolutionary soldier, serving in his father's, Captain Ezekiel's, company, Colonel Dyke's regiment. He is mentioned in the roster of Massachusetts militia as having received a gun, blanket, and soldier's pay at Dorchester, Mass., March 31, 1777. He d. March 28, 1836. Betsey d. April 20, 1854.

---

560 Stephen and Comfort White had:

(1412) Montgomery, October 31, 1796. d. young.

(1413) Emery, September 8, 1798. m. Polly Fisher. He d. January 1, 1857.

(1414) Charles, May 10, 1800. m. Tabitha F. Stuart, 1821.

(1415) Augustus, October 19, 1803. m. Anna Murray Sims, November 26, 1835. d. 1862.

Residence, Templeton, Mass.

Stephen was a Revolutionary soldier, and served in his father's company from December 4, 1776, to March 1, 1777. He d. January 16, 1853. Comfort d. February 8, 1831.

---

561 Ezekiel and —— had:

(1416) George W., November 10, 1802. d. April 3, 1867.

Ezekiel was a soldier of the Revolution.

---

562 Miles and Tryphena Sprague had:

(1417) Justus, July 3, 1791. m. Chloe Hanruven, December 11, 1815.
(1418) Sullivan, June 23, 1793. m. Isabel Bezold, January 30, 1817.
(1419) Chester, February 6, 1796. m. Sally Bixby, March 9, 1818; m. 2d Susan Underwood, June 5, 1842.
(1420) Samantha, January 20, 1798. m. Luther Johnson.
(1421) Miles J., January 17, 1800. m. Lemyra Bartlett; m. 2d Abigail Howard; m. 3d Betsey Jones.
(1422) Tryphena, June 3, 1801. m. Nathaniel Kidder, January 11, 1820. 14 chil. Rem. to Warren, Pa.
(1423) Roxanna, July 8, 1803. m. Simeon Hungerford, April 7, 1838. He d. February 20, 1877.
(1424) William, December 7, 1807. Rem. to Kentucky, 1837.

Miles Rem. from Templeton to Wardsboro, Vt. and d. in Gardner, Mass., September 25, 1824. Tryphena d. October 14, 1824.

---

563 Jemima Knowlton and Thomas Wright had:

(1425) Lyman, March 8, 1793.
(1426) Betsey, December 28, 1795. m. Dexter Whittemore.

Thomas d. June 8, 1796, and Jemima m. 2d Batchelder Bowker. They had:

(1427) Wright, November 1, 1798. d. December 29, 1831.
(1428) Luke, October 28, 1800.
(1429) Elijah, January 28, 1803. Res., Keene, N. H.
(1430) Lucy, November 3, 1804. d. October 13, 1827.
(1431) Cynthia, February 12, 1807.
(1432) Roxana, July 28, 1809.
(1433) Hannah, March 25, 1815.

Residence, Fitzwilliam, N. H.

564 Levi and Polly Morse had:

(1434) Polly, 1802. m. —— Coolidge. No chil.

Levi m. 2d Mrs. Butterfield. They had:

(1435) Miles E., 1809. m. Belena Ellis, 1831.
(1436) Ephraim, 1812. d. young.
(1437) Eliza, 1816. d. 1827.

Levi rem. to Potton, Province of Quebec, in 1800, and d. in 1842 at Knowlton Landing, P. Q., Canada.

---

567 Asaph and Betsey Sawyer had:

(1438) Hannah A., May 2, 1808. m. Amasa Lewis, January 24, 1830.
(1439) Amasa E., September 10, 1810. m. Harriet Lewis, February 14, 1836.
(1440) Mary, March 5, 1812. d. young.
(1441) Harriet A., March 27, 1813. m. Hial Curtis.
(1442) Asaph A., April 7, 1815. m. Mary Peaseley, February 3, 1845.
(1443) Luke Holland, August 7, 1816. m. Elizabeth Spinney, October 15, 1840.
(1444) Cynthia Holbrook, July 5, 1818. m. Roswell Sargent, December 29, 1836.
(1445) Ezekiel L., June 20, 1820. m. Nancy Bryan, January 6, 1841.
(1446) Lucy E., April 24, 1822.

Asaph rem. to So. Stukely, P. Q., where he d. February 12, 1844.

---

568 Lyman and Relief Whitcomb had:

(1447) Czarina, March 22, 1796. m. Stephen Parker, July 18, 1815.
(1448) Rosetta, July 11, 1799. m. Aaron Frost, 1820.
(1449) Lee, April 16, 1801. m. Maria Sargent, February 3, 1828.
(1450) Stephen P., June 8, 1807. m. Elizabeth Halliker, March 18, 1833.
(1451) Jane, June 27, 1809. m. Jacob Shephard, February 28, 1825.
(1452) Whitcomb, July 14, 1814. d. August 23, 1843.
(1453) Newton, September 8, 1815. m. Laura Turner.
(1454) Anna, June 21, 1818. m. Luther Libby, October 9, 1835.

Lyman rem. from Templeton, Mass., to South Stukely, P. Q., Canada. He served in the militia from 1806 as captain and major, was for many years a magistrate, and was the first member of Parliament elected from Shefford

County, November 4, 1829. He gave an extraordinary impulse to educational matters, and his public and private charities were numerous. His death in 1832 was an irreparable loss.

---

569 Calvin and Sophia Willard had:

(1455) George Willard, June 19, 1795. m. Elizabeth Carroll.
(1456) John Calvin, March 9, 1799.

Calvin was b. in Newfane, Vt. He graduated from Dartmouth College in 1788, and studied law with his father, Hon. Luke. He became a distinguished lawyer.

---

570 Martha (Patty) Knowlton and David Warner had:

(1457) Sally K., April 1, 1788. m. James Miller.
(1458) Lyman, April 24, 1790.
(1459) Harriet, October 27, 1794.
(1460) Willard, June 24, 1797. m. Elvira Williams.
(1461) George, May 29, 1799.
(1462) Calvin, 1801.
(1463) Daniel, May 15, 1803.
(1464) Luke, 1805.

CHAPTER III.

The Canada Knowltons

SOON after the cessation of hostilities between the American Colonies and the mother country, and the establishment of the United States as a separate and independent nation, the government of Great Britain offered by public proclamation a free grant of land to all who remained of the Tory party, if they would leave the States and settle in Canada. This offer was prompted by the evident belief that the new and infant nation was but one of those numerous political experiments which have ambitiously struggled into life, and almost as quickly died out of it. Among the considerable numbers who shared in this sober conviction of the English Government, was Judge Luke Knowlton, of Newfane, Vt. His Tory sentiments will excite less surprised comment when it is remembered that he lived near the northern boundary line, and that contiguity to one's neighbors effaces, more or less, sharp lines of distinction and separation. The American nation was not only an experiment, it was doubly so for being a republican one. Judge Knowlton was too sensible and too honorable a man not to accept the logic of arms, even though results might not be permanent. Moreover, he was no longer a young man, and he felt unequal to a stout grapple with the untamed forces of the great northern wilderness, in a desperate effort to found a new home. His children, however, he encouraged to take advantage of the offer of the English Government, and thus secure a permanent home and influence. Silas, the second son and third child, was the first to accept the parental advice. He had married, in 1786, Sarah Holbrook, the sister of his brother-in-law, John Holbrook, by whom he had born to him Paul, then but nine years old, and Luke, an infant. He "took up" a section of land in the County of Brome, Province of Quebec, the tract now known as the township of Stukely, and then returned to Newfane for his family. Through his influence, a neighbor, one Whitney, with wife and infant daughter, accompanied the Knowltons on their trying journey to Canada.

When the little band of emigrants reached the boundary line of Stukely, the two women engaged in an amicable dispute as to which should have the honor of being the first white female to settle in the new township. Mr. Whitney settled the matter by suddenly lifting his child in his arms, and depositing her on the farther side of the line. The formation of a township in Canada at this par-

Knowlton, P. Q., Canada.

ticular time was regulated by somewhat peculiar provisions. The area was one hundred square miles, and forty settlers, called "Associates" were required, their names to be entered in the "Letters Patent" from the Crown, and all of them to go into actual residence.

There was something of Greek flavor in the policy which conferred peculiar privileges on the fathers of male children, and Quebec imitated Athens in its prudent forecast of its civil and military welfare. Eastern Canada was fortunate in having among its pioneers such people as these Knowltons. Silas came of a sturdy stock that had rounded and hardened its muscle and sharpened its mental faculties in frontier life and border warfare. The boy had sung, many a time, the battle songs that stirred the father's blood, and the tales in which he had revelled were those of daring exploit and Indian foe during the troubled years between 1740 and 1764. But, as every emigrant to the wild North learned to his cost, a calmer and sturdier courage was required in the harder battle of civilization. Canada was a wild and trackless forest, and the victory to be won there was a victory over unutterable hardships and almost insurmountable obstacles. Enormous forests filled with fierce beasts and pestilent insects had to be cleared. Not a single road invited communication between widely separated hamlets, and the making of one to the French settlements was an era. The accumulated snow and ice of a very long winter left but a short season for agriculture, and when famine threatened it was no unusual thing for the "Associates" to tramp twenty, thirty, even forty miles, each in his turn, carrying a bag of corn to the mill, that he and his neighbors might have bread. When Silas Knowlton took two barrels of potash to Montreal, it required two sleds with two yoke of oxen for each, and a journey of eighteen days, and although the profits were one hundred dollars, invested in household necessities, the money was well earned.

Their meal was prepared in "plumping mills," a rude contrivance of an upright log bored out, and a pestle attached to a spring pole. One quart only could be pounded at a time, and the meal was eaten mixed with pumpkin.

The life of Silas Knowlton and his brave wife is, as yet, an unwritten story of heroic courage and splendid self-sacrifice, out of which have come, long years ago, thrift and happiness to many who have "entered into their labors."

Going to market was the one great event of the year, and this, too, over a road constructed through bogs and swamps, because that was the shorter and the only feasible way. The Knowltons were their own architects and cabinet makers, and their original homes were rude in construction and appointment. Good digestion must have waited on appetite, for they were a healthy and sturdy race, and during the long absences of their husbands and brothers the women reared and defended their children with consummate courage.

These Knowltons were not altogether at an advantage over their fellow settlers, for of the latter all who had remained loyal to the Crown during the Revolutionary struggle, and who had professed fidelity to "the United Empire of

Great Britain," were styled the U. E., and to them and to each descendant forever was to be given a grant of two hundred acres of land, free from expense of survey, and of tax. Under this act of Parliament, or royal proclamation, the public lands of the Province are still granted to all who can prove their descent from a U. E. The Knowltons soon became, as they still remain, quite as loyal to the British, as they had been to the American, flag.

---

571 Silas and Sally Holbrook had:

(1465) Paul Holland, September 17, 1787. m. Laura Moss.
(1466) Luke, April 26, 1795. m. Mary Ware.
(1467) Samantha, 1797. m. Samuel Stone.
(1468) Samuel W., 1798. m. Amanda Loomis.

Silas rem. from Newfane, Vt., in February, 1798, to Stukely, P. Q., where Sally d. in 1800. He d. November 18, 1843 or 1844.

---

572 Sarah Knowlton and John Holbrook had:

(1469) Patty, March 22, 1788. m. William Fessenden.
(1470) Franklin, February 27, 1792.
(1471) Sybil, June 15, 1794.
(1472) Sally, March 28, 1796. m. Geo. W. Hall; m. 2d Isaac Coale of Baltimore. 8 chil.
(1473) Sophia, March 15, 1798. d. young.
(1474) Lucinda, March 25, 1800. m. Hon. Willard Warner, U. S. Senator from Alabama.
(1475) Eliza, April 15, 1804. d. 1853. unm.
(1476) Rev. John C., January 7, 1808. m. Cynthia Tuttle.
(1477) William, April 20, 1810. d. young.
(1478) Frederick, February 15, 1813. m. Harriet ——.

Sarah was a woman of uncommon beauty and grace, and one of the most prominent figures in Brattleboro society. Her early home was in Newfane, Vt., where she became so familiar with the privations and simplicity of pioneer life that she was intimidated by no subsequent perils. Indians and wild beasts were the familiar enemies of her childhood, and she became as courageous as she was handsome. She married John Holbrook, a country merchant, who carried his produce and goods for barter on a pack-horse through West River Valley, from Newfane to Greenfield, Mass., returning with other goods gotten by exchange. Their daughter, afterwards Mrs. Fessenden, was the first woman to ride in a wheeled conveyance in that part of the country.

Mr. and Mrs. Holbrook removed to Brattleboro, Vt., and bought the dwelling-house now known as the "American House," a public inn, a portion of which was used for a country store. To secure a proper depot for his produce and a convenient place for exchange, Mr. Holbrook formed a partnership with David Porter, a leading merchant of Hartford, Conn., and the firm thereafter conducted the two stores as branches of the same house. Mr. Holbrook became a director of the old Phœnix Bank, Hartford, and brought the first bank notes ever circulated in Brattleboro.

He also built a large slaughter house, where he cured large quantities of beef, pork, hams, and tongue for the West Indian market, transporting these to the seaboard on a line of flat boats which he had established on the Connecticut River.

In 1809 he sold out all his property and removed to Warehouse Point, Ct. His commanding figure, positive manner, and sonorous voice gave him so powerful an influence over his fellow-men, that it was said that a request or command from him was likely to be obeyed as quickly as if shot from a gun. He was by faith a Congregationalist, and a Deacon of the church, though not a predestinarian. On one occasion, his pastor, having called on him, engaged him in an earnest argument, in which the spiritual guide asserted the truth of infant damnation. The worthy Deacon rose, opened the door, and drove the parson into the street, declaring that any one who held such "damnable" doctrines could not stay under his roof.

Mr. Holbrook was postmaster of Brattleboro, 1794–1804, and the second original member of the Vermont Asylum under the Marsh bequest. He died 1838. Sarah d. March 22, 1851.

573 Alice Knowlton and Dr. Nathan A. Stone had :

(1479) Edson S., August 2, 1789.
(1480) Jasper, April 20, 1791.
(1481) Benjamin, April 23, 1793. d. young.
(1483) Benjamin, August 28, 1795.
(1484) Lucinda, November 19, 1797.
(1485) Alice K., August 10, 1800.
(1486) Sophia K., January 24, 1802.
(1487) Sarah, May 15, 1804.
(1488) Nathan F., January 28, 1806.

Alice d. in Newfane, Vt., November 14, 1865, aged 96.

574 Lucinda Knowlton and Samuel Willard had :

(1489) David, 1797.
(1490) Lucinda, 1799.

Samuel was from Petersham, Mass. They removed to Canada, Prov. of Quebec. Lucinda d. there in 1800.

575 Luke and Charlotte Kenney had:

(1491) Seleucia, May 21, 1800. m. Hezekiah Robinson, June 3, 1817.
(1492) Marcia, October 2, 1801. m. Clarke Fisher, June 24, 1820.
(1493) Sally, July 9, 1803. m. Daniel W. Sanborn, January 2, 1820. m. 2d Dr. Rotus Parmalee.
(1494) Infant, 1805.
(1495) Charlotte S., April 14, 1806. m. Austin Wheeler, December 18, 1825.
(1496) Luke M., February 5, 1808. m. Laura A. Wheeler, October 6, 1832.
(1497) Abigail, December 16, 1809. d. January 25, 1834. unm.
(1498) Rosetta, August 20, 1811. d. young.
(1499) Katherine A., September 18, 1812. m. Merrick Cummings, January 21, 1838.
(1500) Hanson, September 14, 1814. m. Mary Soles, March 18, 1839.
(1501) Patty W., September 11, 1816. m. John Jackson, September 1, 1848.
(1502) Merab A., October 7, 1818. m. Wm. Willard, July 12, 1842.
(1503) Goodloe H., April 14, 1821. m. Julia Duboise.
(1504) Almus A., November 8, 1827. m. Lucy Newton.

Residence, Waterloo, P. Q.

LUKE KNOWLTON, Jr.,

seventh child of Hon. Luke, was born in Newfane, March 24, 1775., where he resided for more than forty years. He received his education at Westminster, Vt., and Chesterfield, N. H., after which he entered the office of his brother Calvin as a law student. His subsequent career was that of a very successful and eminent lawyer. He married, in 1799, Miss Charlotte Kenney of the same town. An incident connected with this marriage illustrates the character of this extraordinary man. Miss Kenny was little more than a child, being under sixteen years of age. Her father, an active and enterprising man, owned a large estate of one thousand acres, six hundred and fifty of which were under careful cultivation, and he passed for a rich man in those earlier and simpler times. When young Knowlton asked him for his daughter there was a stormy interview. The father formulated his objections in true business style by three propositions: (1) She was too young; (2) he could not spare her; (3) she would have no dower, there being eleven other children to share his property. To these the ardent young advocate promptly replied, (1) that Charlotte would grow older every day, and as rapidly in his hands as in those of her father; (2) that her father had a wife and other daughters, while he (Luke) had none, and that Kenny could therefore do without her better than he could; (3) that he wanted the daughter, and not the dowry. The young lawyer won his case, and it was not long before the objections of the father disappeared, for Luke was soon and for many years a member of the State Legislature, and Assistant Judge of Windham County Court. His ability won the business confidence of his father-in-law, and the two became investors in wild lands, out of which they made handsome fortunes. Luke Knowlton often rode on horseback five hundred miles on tours of purchase and inspection, enduring fatigue and privation with characteristic perseverance. In 1821 he removed from Newfane to Stukely, P. Q., where he settled on the same farm that his brother Calvin had purchased and improved in 1798. He d. September 17, 1855. She d. 1843.

---

576 Hannah Knowlton and Capt. Thomas Harrington had:

I. Capt. Thomas, March 13, 1785. m. Relief Mixer, 1805.
II. Hannah, May 2, 1786. m. Lewis Pratt, 1802.
III. Grace, September 18, 1789. m. Asa Mixer, Jr., 1804.

Captain Thomas was a lineal descendant of Robert Harrington, of the ancient family of Errington, Arrington, Harrington, of England, and who was one of the proprietors of Watertown, Mass., as early as 1642, owning an estate presented to him by his kinsman, Deacon Thomas Hastings. Captain Thomas served in the Indian wars as captain of the Shrewsbury militia. He d. December 20, 1834. Hannah d. March 8, 1793.

---

577 Asa and Olive Waite had:

(1505) William, 1790. Rem. to Illinois.
(1506) Asa, Jr., 1792. m. Damaris Howe, 1819.

Asa d. Widow Olive m. Lewis Smith in 1826.

---

578 Susannah Knowlton and John S. Whitney had:

(1508) William, April 3, 1795.
(1509) Artemus, January 4, 1797.
(1510) Joseph H., December 25, 1799.

---

579 Artemus and Huldah Lyon had:

(1511) Seth, August 29, 1799. m. Volma Shepard ; m. 2d —— Palmer.
(1512) Deborah, February 25, 1804. m. Chas. Dix. Res., Holden, Mass. 2 chil.
(1513) Huldah. m. John Hart. Res., Sutton, Mass. 6 chil.
(1514) Rhoda. d. young.
(1515) Tamsen. d. young.
(1516) Artemus, February 15, 1809. m. Maria Kenny, September 27, 1836.

Artemus rem. to Charlton, Mass. He m. 2d Rhoda Lathe, and d. May 16, 1834.

580 Dea. William and Clorinda Smith had :

(1517) Julia, September, 1799. m. Jesse Pirkes, March 3, 1821.
(1518) Harriet, March 26, 1801. m. —— Foster, February 27, 1817.
(1519) Freeman, June 12, 1803. m. Hannah Murphy, October 9, 1825.
(1520) Joseph E., February 19, 1805. m. Sarah Fitts.
(1521) Martha, January 26, 1807. m. Seth Follett, April 3, 1826.
(1522) Abigail, April 9, 1809.
(1523) Clorinda, November 5, 1811.
(1524) William, September 26, 1814. m. Elida P. Ramsdell, August 13, 1850.
Deacon William res. in Shrewsbury, Mass.

Clorinda d. November 1, 1860.

---

581 Dr. Seth and Relief Howe had :

(1525) Darwin, August 8, 1802. m. Sarah Harrington.
(1526) Charles, November 4, 1803. Drowned, December, 1822.
(1527) Eunice, April 4, 1806. d. young.
(1528) Artemus, February 19, 1809. m. Emeline Smith, 1835.
(1529) William S., September 28, 1810. m. Hannah Harrington ; m. 2d Miriam Dresser.
(1530) Eunice, January 6, 1813. m. E. G. Putnam, April 26, 1831.
(1531) Nancy, November 23, 1814. m. Horace Stowe ; m. 2d E. B. Rice ; m. 3d C. C. Felton.
(1532) Calvin, January 2, 1817. m. Mary Warren, January 25, 1837.
(1533) Dolly, December 2, 1818. m. Jos. P. Leland, January 30, 1837.
Residence, Shrewsbury, Mass.

Dr. Seth was a physician, and is still quoted as one of the celebrities of Old Shrewsbury. He was an original character, and his personal eccentricities seem to have contributed to his professional success. Among his *materia medica* were such singular ingredients as pulverized toads, beetles, and other unmentionable matter, not uncommon among the practitioners of that early day. The surprising cures with which he is credited are a curious illustration of the subtle influence of the mental on the physical condition, for the faith of his patients in his skill was absolute. He d. April 12, 1832.

---

582 Joseph H. and Chloe Forbush had :

(1534) Wm. H., March 8, 1807. m. Susan Brigham, March 3, 1828.
(1535) Hannah W., September 16, 1808. m. S. Haven, August 24, 1829.
(1536) Mary A. B., May 12, 1810. m. J. Newton, 1832.

(1537) Joseph F., August 20, 1811. m. Huldah Newton, June 2, 1833. m. 2d Sarah E. Johnson, November 26, 1840.
(1538) Susan W., February 20, 1814. m. John Rice, 1837.
(1539) Relief M., February 7, 1816.
(1540) Lorenzo C., April 23, 1818.
(1541) Caroline E., September 3, 1820.
(1542) Francis A., June 26, 1823.
Residence, Shrewsbury, Mass.

Joseph was Deacon of the Congregational Church.

---

586 Dea. Ezekiel and Eleanor Brown had:

(1543) Lincoln B., December 15, 1805. m. Charlotte Spooner; m. 2d Lucretia Wolcott.
(1544) William A., April, 1809. m. Nancy ——.
Residence, Shrewsbury, Mass.

Ezekiel d. November 29, 1828.

---

587 Susannah Knowlton and Thos. Witherbee, Jr., had:

(1546) Calvin K., December 9, 1800.
(1547) Thomas H., June 25, 1802. m.
(1548) Elizabeth, March 3, 1804. m. Elijah A. Brigham.
(1549) Luke, December 19, 1809.
(1550) Josie C., November 11, 1815.
(1551) Susan P., November 26, 1818.

---

588 Luke and Hetty Rand had:

(1552) Charles L., February 15, 1809. m. Alma A. Damon, November 27, 1834.

Removed from Shrewsbury to Bridport, Vt., where Luke d. September 9, 1809.

---

589 Thomas and Rebecca Whiting had:

(1553) Rebecca W., October 9, 1810. m. Dr. A. Brigham, June 15, 1832.
(1554) Nancy F., April 12, 1812. m. Asa Davis.
(1555) Harriet A., September 3, 1818. m. John Hatton, August 17, 1841. m. 2d Robert Slade. 14 chil.
(1556) Calvin W., October 22, 1820. d. young.

(1557) Thomas W., May 1, 1823. d. December 31, 1854.
(1558) George L., October 1, 1824. m. Olive Haskins.
(1559) Charles L., March 25, 1832. d. young.
Residence, Shrewsbury, Mass.

Rebecca d. May 17, 1812. Thomas m. 2d Martha Giles, December 11, 1817, and d. in Detroit. Mich., August, 1832.

---

590 Amasa and Sarah Parks had :

(1560) Sarah E., May 19, 1817. m. Rufus A. Blood.
(1561) Catherine, March 18, 1818. m. Osman S. Rice, January 27, 1848. m. 2d Moses Swain, January 19, 1859.
(1562) Asa B., April 17, 1825. m. Adeline Sturges, October 18, 1855.
Residence, Shrewsbury, Mass.

Amasa d. March 30, 1876.

---

592 Mark B. and Elizabeth Smith had :

(1563) Sarah, February 25, 1824.
(1564) Caroline, February 25, 1824. m. Geo. Stebbins, December 12, 1848. 3 chil.
(1565) Thomas H., August 28, 1833. m. Susan Hall, March 3, 1863.
(1566) Nancy M., October 29, 1836. m. Horace Nichols, June, 1, 1859. 2 chil.
Residence, Shrewsbury, Mass.

Mark d. March 28, 1860.

---

593 Hannah Knowlton and Daniel G. Noyes had :

(1567) Cynthia, April 21, 1818.
(1568) Sarah M., July 12, 1820.
(1569) Calvin W., November 13, 1827.
(1570) Susan A., January 21, 1832.

---

594 Abraham and Anna Taylor had :

(1571) Molly, 1776. m. Jonathan Knowlton.
(1572) Caleb, January 15, 1778. m. Anna Sargent.
(1573) William, December 1, 1779. m. Betsey Andrews.

(1574) John, April 21, 1781. d. young.
(1575) Anna, May 30, 1784. m. Mark Sexberry.
(1576) Abigail, May 30, 1784. m. William Young.
(1577) Abraham, February 9, 1790.
(1578) Charity, November 20, 1787. m. Neamiah Stanley, November 26, 1807. Res., Jamesville, N. H.
(1579) John, November, 13, 1796. m. Betsey Buckley Andrews, September, 1826.

Residence, Manchester and Beverly.

Abraham was a Revolutionary soldier. Served as Minute-man, April 19, 1775, commissioned 2d lieut., May 7, 1776. Paid for losses at Bunker Hill. He d. February 13, 1829. Anna d. March 18, 1836.

---

595 Chauncey and Annie Phillips had :

(1580) Amasa. m. Anna Tuttle.
(1581) Levi. m. Amy Tuttle.
(1582) Hannah. m. D. W. Harper. Res., Panora, Ia.
(1583) Perry. m. Melinda Mapes.
(1584) Rosanna. m. John Grames, Dundee, Oregon.
(1585) Frederick. m. Susan Powers. Res., Panora.
(1586) Sophronia. m. John Odell, Vandalia, Mich.
(1587) Chauncey. m. Kate Carmichael.
(1588) Robert.
(1589) Electa. m. Nathan Odell.
(1590) Lydia. m. Wm. Allen, Linden, Ia.

Chauncey and Annie d. in Shanesville, Ohio, and were buried in Mishawaka, Ind.

---

599 William and Barbara Ritz had :

(1591) Francis M., 1857. m. Etta Morrison, October 24, 1886.
(1592) Elias, 1860. m. Ida E. Vail, June 18, 1882.
(1593) Charles, 1864. m. Alice Hyatt, February 10, 1891.
(1594) Cora, 1871.
(1595) Lovina M., 1874. unm.
(1596) Lovena M. d 1874.

---

602 Ezekiel and Polly Knowlton had :

(1597) Abigail, March 21, 1795. d. 1883. unm.
(1598) Polly, May 29, 1797. m. Asa Fogg. She d. 1877. 7 chil.

(1599) Sally, August 23, 1799. m. Henry Erskine.
(1600) Hiram, November 14, 1803. m. Lorena Hunt. He d. 1889.
(1601) Amy, January 30, 1806. m. Edward Stevens, 1825. 8 chil.
(1602) Joseph W., August 2, 1808. m. Julia Davis.
(1603) Lucinda, January 13, 1811. m. Daniel Carey. She d., 1860.
(1604) Levina, January 7, 1814. d. June 20, 1894. unm.
(1605) Isaac C., September 6, 1819. m. Mary S. Wellington.

EZEKIEL KNOWLTON

was a foster child of an English naval officer, named Eastman, who died at sea.

Polly was the sister of Joseph Knowlton, who fought in the battle of Bunker Hill, and who died July 7, 1845, aged ninety-six.

The following letter will show that Ezekiel was eminently practical, and, withal, not wanting in facetiousness.

DAVISTOWN, April 14th, 1795.

DEAR POLLY:—

I embrace the present opportunity to inform you, if in the land of the living, that I, through the infinite goodness of a merciful God, am in good health, and am making shooger, and hope these lines will find you enjoying the same blessing.

I expect to come down before planting, and if you and your babe are able to come up I shall be glad to have you be ready in about three weeks. Its tedious living here alone. It is a great time of scarcity here, and I must go down after seed corn, for there is neither corn or grain to be had here in this place. It will be very difficult getting Bread here, but it is very difficult and costly living alone, and maintaining two families—so I think "of the two evils," as the saying is, "it is best to choose the least," and as we shall both enjoy more satisfaction by living together than apart, I think it best to move you up as soon as posable. I suppose you will be loth to leave your friends, but you may remember what I have often told you—that I am the only friend that you have on earth's world according to the laws of matrimony, and if there is any other that you set more by than you set by me I must look out for another housekeeper, for I cannot live alone. I don't write this to grieve you, my Dear, but because I would wish to be just. I look very plain.

But being in haste I must close by subscribing myself your loving friend and partner till death.

EZEKIEL KNOWLTON.

605 John and Sally Knowlton had:

(1606) George, November 4, 1806. m. Louisa Bowker (or Bolles).
(1607) Rosanna, June 30, 1808. m. James Grant; m. 2d —— Hatch.
(1608) Freeman, April 26, 1809. m. Abbie Bowker.
(1609) Martha, January 7, 1811. m. ——Prince; m. 2d ——Johnson; m. 3d John Safford. Res., Towner.
(1610) John C., February 2, 1814. m. Eveline Bacon; m. 2d Lucy Tanner.
(1611) Ann, September 5, 1816. m. J. Kendall Brown.
(1612) David, June 8, 1819. m. Susan M. French.
(1613) Sally, April 5, 1822.
(1614) Charles H., April 11, 1825. m. Delinda Davis, December 26, 1847; m. 2d Victoria Speer.
(1615) Caroline, November 15, 1828. m. Jas. Terry; m. 2d Thos. Young; m. 3d Chas. Davis. No chil.

Residence, Liberty, Maine.

John d. 1853.

---

607 Samuel and Lucy Knowlton had:

(1616) Lucy, August 3, 1812.
(1617) Joseph F., August 3, 1812.

Lucy d. at the birth of her twins, and Samuel m. 2d Mercy Knowlton. They had:

(1618) Clarissa, March 5, 1814. m. William Sanborn. Sett. in Liberty, Me.
(1619) Alfred, April 2, 1816. m.
(1620) Benjamin.
(1621) Mary J., August 12, 1818.
(1622) William A., August, 1819.

Mercy d. 1820. and Samuel m. 3d Esther Kenniston. They had:

(1623) Samuel, January 14, 1823. m. Hannah B. Lewis, July, 1846.
(1624) Jeremiah, February 22, 1828.
(1625) Sarah, June 3, 1829.
(1626) Lot M., November 6, 1832. m. Alice Dolen.
(1627) Bainbridge, March 2, 1834. m. Augusta Ozier, 1866.

Esther d. 1834, and Samuel m. 4th Julia Howard. They had:

(1628) Andrew J., March 2, 1835.
(1629) Henry, January 10, 1837. m. Mary A. Semms, April 5, 1861.

(1630) George F., September 2, 1838.
(1631) Julia A., November 3, 1840. m. —— Davis.
(1632) Angeronia, April 22, 1842. m. —— Cotton.
(1633) Carrie B., March 28, 1844. m. A. A. Brown.
(1634) Amijah, September 28, 1846.

Residence, Maine.

---

611 Jeremiah and Deborah Stetson had:

(1635) David, November 12, 1822. d. 1833.
(1636) Susan F., August 27, 1824. m. Joseph F. Knowlton, July 3, 1842.
(1637) Sarah A., August 5, 1826. m. Everett Stetson.
(1638) Martha, September 9, 1828. m. Abner Robinson, December 2, 1852.
(1639) Henry S., March 8, 1831.
(1640) Jeremiah, November 27, 1833.
(1641) Mary H., August 20, 1836. m. Captain Martin Tukey.
(1642) Melissa, January 11, 1837. m. Henry Tukey.
(1643) Lucy S., June 7, 1844. m. Mercy S. Gammons.

Residence, Nobleboro, Me.

Jeremiah d. March 1, 1871. Deborah d. November 4, 1871.

---

614 John and Lydia Hall had:

(1644) Magnus. m. Olive Grover, 1875.
(1645) Jane, 1823. m. Thomas Alling, 1849; m. 2d Abraham Hart, 1861. Thomas was lost at sea.
(1646) Sarah.
(1647) Samuel. m. Roxana Burtsell.
(1648) Susan. m. James Endres.

John d., 1856. Lydia d., 1845, and he m. Mary Meseroe.

---

615 Joseph and Susan Redlaw had:

(1649) Joseph. m. Matilda Clark.
(1650) Mary. m. David Hodgkins.
(1651) Ephraim. d. young.
(1652) Jackson.
(1653) Adoniram. m. Susan Barstow.

Joseph d. aged 70.

616 Andrew and Mary Maddocks had:

(1654) Ruth. d. young.
(1655) Sally R.. m. Benj. B. Barstow, 1848. 4 chil.
(1656) Mary A. d. young.
(1657) Rufus M., 1828. m. Mary A. Hodgkin.
(1658) Edwin W., 1832. Res., California.
(1659) Martin, 1835. m. Nancy A. Dunbar, 1857.
(1660) Mary M., 1838. m. Nelson C. Glidden.

Andrew was a soldier in the War of 1812.

---

617 Sarah Knowlton and E. Johnston had:

(1661) Ephraim.
(1662) Reuben.
(1663) Warren.

---

618 Susan Knowlton and Samuel Rice had:

(1664) Sally. m. Zaccheus Hodgkin.
(1665) Samuel. m. Sally Hodgkin.
(1666) Andrew. m. —— Noyes.
(1667) David. m. —— Stubbs.

Samuel Rice was a soldier in the War of 1812. Susan d. at the age of 94.

---

620 Sarah Knowlton and Jeremiah Butler had:

(1668) Ephraim.
(1669) Jeremiah.
(1670) Francis.
(1671) Olive.

Residence, Shrewsbury, Mass.

---

621 Johnathan and Deborah Tufts had:

(1672) Josiah B., September 29, 1802. m. Deborah Weeks, of New York City, May 28, 1828.
(1673) Rebecca, March 18, 1804. m. Francis Butler, January 19, 1826.
(1674) Caroline, October 30, 1805. m. E. S. Butler, February 16, 1830.
(1675) Sophronia, July 14, 1808. m. Solomon Luce, June 10, 1844.
(1676) Sumner, May 11, 1810. m. Marianna Gilbert, November 4, 1831.
(1677) John Adams, February 5, 1812. m. Sylvia Brown, October 28, 1841. Res., Chesterville, Me.

(1678) Jason, September 15, 1813. m. Rachel R. Preston, July 10, 1842. Res., Fairbanks, Me.

(1679) Selden, May 2, 1815. m. Abigail Hodgkins, December 12, 1842. m. Cordelia Backus, 1856.

(1680) Edward A., August 11, 1819. m. Joanna Wright.

Residence in Industry, Me., from which place they rem. to the old homestead in Farmington, Me.

Johnathan served as a private in the War of 1812, and at its close he received a land warrant as bounty for such service. This he sold for $170. He was for many years a teamster between Farmington and Hallowell, and by the judicious investment of the profits of this business he became an extensive operator in lumber.

Deborah was born in Lee, N. H., in 1782, and d. October, 1871. Johnathan d. May 1, 1864.

---

622 Samuel and Olive Butler had :

(1681) Francis H., April 20, 1807. m. Frances J. Foster, December 18, 1837.

(1682) Hiram, November 6, 1809. m. Mary Stephenson, September 10, 1835.

(1683) Parmelia, September 9, 1812. m. Benjamin Tufts, October 17, 1833. m. Dorcas Monahan, May 13, 1848.

(1684) Sherman, August 20, 1820. m. Martha Stevens, August 23, 1850.

(1685) Samuel, August 28, 1822. m. Julia Hadley, August, 1845. m. 2d Harriet Ellis.

(1686) Sarah Ann, July 27, 1826. m. Temple Fouche, May 10, 1849. Res., Fosters, O.

(1687) George W., December 9, 1829. m. Nancy Hunter, September 9, 1858.

Samuel was the second male child born in the township of Farmington, Me. He was a millwright by trade, and operated mills at Farmington Falls for several years in company with his father, Johnathan. In 1823 he removed to Phillips, on the Sandy River, where he united the occupation of farming with that of milling. In September, 1831, he started for the west, taking his wife and five children in covered wagons, and arrived after a six-weeks journey at a point thirty miles from Cincinnati, in a wild country. Their only possessions now were four worn-out horses, two wagons, and fifty cents in money. Out of such adverse circumstances Samuel and his brave wife conquered a subsistence, built up a comfortable and thrifty home, and left to their family a respectable fortune. The place of their residence is now known as Mainville, Ohio. Samuel d. January 4, 1857.

624 Lydia A. Knowlton and Thomas Wellman had:

(1688) Lydia W., September, 1804.
(1689) Mary W., October, 1806.
(1690) Hannah, October, 1808.
(1691) Emeline, August, 1810.
(1692) Susan, October, 1812.
(1693) Thomas B., August, 1814.
(1694) John K., March, 1816.
(1695) Sarah B., July, 1818.
(1696) Lovie, May, 1820.
(1697) Samuel, June, 1822.
(1698) Gilbert, August, 1824.

Residence, Shrewsbury, Mass.

Lydia d. December 23, 1834.

---

625 Francis and Lovie Butler had:

(1699) William B., August 16, 1813. d. young.
(1700) Mary B., July 28, 1817.
(1701) Lovie B., December 13, 1821. d. young.
(1702) Martha, January 20, 1824. d. September 9, 1838.
(1703) Jeremiah, April 9, 1826. m. Sarah A. Fassett, November 21, 1851.
(1704) William F., July 20, 1830. m. Irene Carrick, October 24, 1862.
(1705) Rev. Francis B. January 12, 1832. m. Mrs. Louisa Butterfield.

Lovie d. October 6, 1840, and Francis m. 2d Rosanna Hunter, November 17, 1841. They had:

(1706) David H., December 21, 1844. m. Clara Hinckley, March 17, 1875.
(1707) Mary B., July 6, 1847. m. Henry C. Johnson, February 3, 1869. Res., Chicago.

Francis inherited a portion of his father's estate, which he greatly enlarged by purchases of neighboring land, and by skilful management he became wealthy. He was prominent in public affairs, and Treasurer of Franklin County in 1855. He d. at Farmington Centre, March 9, 1871. Rosanna d. 1894.

---

637 Robert and Jemima Smith had:

(1712) Robert. m. Betsey Bixby.
(1713) Samuel. m. Elizabeth Pike.
(1714) Josiah S., March 12, 1796. m. Sarah Smith; m. 2d Rosanna Wilcox.

(1715) Sophronia, January 6, 1803. m. Josiah Flanders.
(1716) John.
(1717) Julia.
(1718) Sally.
(1719) Eliza.
(1720) Sophia.
(1721) Daniel.

Robert was a sergeant in the War of 1812. He rem. to Vevay, Ind.

---

638 Sarah Knowlton and Moses Trussell had:

(1722) Moses T., August 25, 1788. d. young at Dumbarton, N. H.
(1723) Sarah, March 24, 1790. d. October 1, 1855. Res., New London, N. H.
(1724) Ezekiel, September 27, 1795. m. Emily Colburn, February 9, 1823.
(1725) Luther, November 9, 1802. m. Eliza Story, October 14, 1840.
Residence, Manchester, Hopkinton, and Dumbarton, N. H.

Moses fought at Bunker Hill, and lost a hand by a cannon-ball which struck him when carrying off the wounded. Sarah d. April 20, 1841.

---

639 Ezekiel and Susan Smith had:

(1725 A) Nathaniel W., September 23, 1794. m. Ruth Herrick.
(1725 B) Samuel S., February 22, 1796. m. Martha Witherspoon, September 2, 1822.
(1725 C) Susannah, May 14, 1798. d. 1806.
(1725 D) Mary, May 22, 1800. m. John Hastings of Newburg.
(1726) Rachel, May 25, 1807. m. Gideon Wilkins, May 15, 1839. She d. Mansfield, Mass., October 25, 1893.
(1727) Belinda, December 14, 1811. m. Stephen Gordon, August 18, 1831. He d. September 24, 1879, at Lawrence, Mass.

EZEKIEL KNOWLTON

was a man of indomitable perseverance and resolution. He rem. to Hopkinton, N. H., when ten years old, working on his father's farm, for which he received a lot of land in Wendell, now Sunapee. By his industry he gradually bought other and larger farms, the buildings and woods of which were destroyed by a great whirlwind which swept over the town in 1821.

He paid great attention to the raising and sale of "neat-stock," furnishing, with characteristic unselfishness, his less fortunate neighbors with what they needed, and waiting patiently for his pay. His sterling character and proverbial honesty were such that, in a certain lawsuit in which he was the defendant, the witness for the plaintiff was adjudged by the court to be a perjurer, and the decree and record were ordered to be so entered. When his father was dying of a fever, and had been given up by three physicians, he killed several sheep, wrapped the patient in their pelts, and the father recovered.

Susan Smith, wife of Ezekiel, came from Manchester, Mass., being brought on horseback when very young in her mother's arms. Her father, Samuel, was a soldier of the Revolution, and left his widow with two small children. Susan went out at service when but seven years old, and being compelled to go into the fields barefoot on a frosty morning she took refuge with her grandparents until nineteen years of age, when she married Ezekiel Knowlton, her wedding-dress being of homespun flannel.

Ezekiel d. at New London, N. H., January 16, 1850. Susan d. March 27, 1869.

---

644 Nathaniel and Susan Greely had no children. She d. September 12, 1813, and Nathaniel m. 2d Mary Connor, September 17, 1816. They had:

(1728) Susan G., April 13, 1819. d. young.
(1729) Nathaniel W., June 24, 1820.
(1730) Susan G., July 27, 1822. d. June 14, 1841.
(1731) Elizabeth, April 19, 1825.
(1732) Mary C., April 8, 1827. m. E. G. Starr.
(1733) Sarah T., April 5, 1830. d. young.
(1734) Sarah T., September 5, 1832. d. October 11, 1850.

HON. NATHANIEL KNOWLTON

was one of the most prominent and influential citizens of Hopkinton, N. H. He was Captain in the militia, a Selectman for twelve years, Moderator of the town meeting in 1815 and '16, Representative to the General Court in 1821, '24, '25, '27, '28, and State Senator in 1831 and '32. The "Reminiscences of Hopkinton," says of him:

"About 1809 he built a house, such as an Englishman said all Yankees built, 'a great house to look at, and a little one behind to live in.' He was a man of great influence in town and State, and had the confidence of all who knew him."

---

646 Lydia Knowlton and Wm. K. Story had:

(1735) Eliza, April 19, 1812. m. Luther M. Trussell, October 14, 1840. She d. September 8, 1877.

(1735 A) James, August 17, 1814. m. Sarah Story, October, 1835.
(1736) Sarah, June 2, 1820. m. Daniel A. Gale, October 14, 1840.
(1737) William, October 15, 1824. m. Mary Bartlett.

---

651 John Knowlton

was a Prize Master in the Revolutionary War. He sailed from Newburyport in the ship *Bennington*, and sent home one prize captured from the British. Having never returned home, he is supposed to have died at sea.

---

652 Ezekiel and Mehitable Fisk

resided in New London, N. H., where he d. September, 1806. Mehitable d. there, 1828.

---

653 Robert and Eda Allen had:

(1738) Samuel, January 6, 1785. m. Sarah Dimond, February 17, 1808.
(1739) John, August 27, 1786. m. Experience Hardy. He d. Nov. 4, 1840.
(1740) Robert, August 27, 1786. m. Hannah Dimond.
(1741) Benjamin, April 13, 1792. m. Lucinda Allen.
(1742) Allen, June 5, 1793. m. —— French.
(1743) Daniel, January 14, 1795. m. Rhoda Abbott.
(1744) Hazen, March 16, 1797. m. Anna Clough.
(1745) Nathaniel, February 12, 1798. m. Ruth Sargent, December 28, 1820.
(1746) Gilman, May 6, 1802. m. Sarah Sargent.

Eda d. January 17, 1812, and Robert m. 2d. Judith Hoyt, August 22, 1813. He was a Revolutionary soldier, in Captain Jabez Cottle's company. Served from April 21, 1775–1778. He d. in Concord, N. H., July 2, 1836.

---

654 Mary Knowlton and Moses Hill had:

(1747) John.
(1748) Samuel.
(1749) Rosannah.
(1750) Samuel.
(1751) Mary.
(1752) Franklin.
(1753) Hannah.
(1754) Ruth.
(1755) Moses.

(1756) Jefferson.
(1757) Sally.
(1758) Huldah.

Residence, Hopkinton, N. H.

Moses d. in Canaan, N. H., 1836.

---

655 Sarah Knowlton and Benj. Leach had :

(1759) Benjamin, December 11, 1785. m. Susan Cheever, February 21, 1811 ; m. 2d Lucy Allen, January 7, 1830.
(1760) Sarah, August 24, 1789. m. Amos H. Mills, March 9, 1803. She d. March 31, 1882.
(1761) Mary, June 18, 1794. d. March 30, 1873. Unm.
(1762) Richard, September 18, 1798. d. December 14, 1817.

Residence, Manchester, Mass.

Sarah d. September 18, 1798. Benj. d. December 20, 1838.

---

656 Anna Knowlton and David Trussell had :

(1763) Mary. d.
(1764) William.
(1765) Mary.
(1766) Nancy.
(1767) Benjamin.
(1768) John.

Family residence, Hopkinton, N. H.

Anna d. in Oxford, N. H.

---

657 Daniel and Mary Stocker had :

(1769) Nancy, March 4, 1794.
(1770) Ariel P., February 27, 1795. m. Abigail Lee, December 19, 1820.
(1771) Sarah L., March 2, 1797.
(1772) John S. C., December 11, 1798. m. Anna W. Hartwell, September 27, 1829.
(1773) Emma, October 29, 1800. d. 1803.
(1774) Daniel H., August 26, 1806. m. Ann Billings, April 25, 1832.
(1775) Lucy P., March 20, 1808. m. John M. Bailey, April 9, 1829.
(1776) William M., July 25, 1810. m. Mary Ferguson.
(1777) Francis P., December 1, 1811. m. Mary Hartwell, October 25, 1838.

Daniel d. September 13, 1842. Mary d. January 10, 1850.

660 Elijah Murphey and Elizabeth Bliss had:

(1778) Ann.
(1779) Hector. m. Helen ——. 2 chil.
(1780) Susan. m. Enos Howland. 7 chil.
(1781) Coolidge B. m. Mary Ann Atkins.

---

661 Samuel and Betsy Butler had:

(1782) Elizabeth, January 14, 1813. m. S. E. Jannings, January 23, 1833.
(1783) Jane L., January 14, 1815. m. Moses Tufts.
(1784) Lucy P., May 15, 1817. m. David Mitchell, February 3, 1847. She d. October 22, 1874.

Residence, New Sharon, Me.

Samuel d. January 25, 1825. His widow m. Ebenezer Weltman.

---

662 John and Sally Green had:

(1785) Sarah, August 23, 1813. m. John Lowell, January 9, 1829.
(1786) John L., August 17, 1818. d. young.
(1787) John, June 16, 1820. m. Lucy Vaughn, November, 1841.
(1788) Joseph, June 13, 1822. m. Sarah Pratt, 1850. He d. November 17, 1857.

Residence, "Knowlton's Corners," Me.

Sally d. May 12, 1854, and John m. 2d Sarah Butler, July 22, 1855. He was by trade a carriage maker, but he also acted as a Methodist local preacher. He d. July 16, 1862. Sally d. July 15, 1872.

---

664 Joseph and Mary J. Tufts had:

(1789) John Morrison, 1836. m. Angeline Tufts, at Maineville, Ohio, 1868. He was a soldier in Company D., 2d Regiment, U. S. Sharpshooters, and after serving two years, re-enlisted in Company I, 4th Regiment, August 21, 1863, serving during the entire War of the Rebellion. Res., Battle Ground, Ind.
(1790) Mary. m. —— Eastman.

Joseph rem. from Maine to Lafayette, Ind., 1845, and died there in 1878. Mary J. d. 1852.

665 Ebenezer and Sally Hiscock had:

(1791) Sarah, September 28, 1819. d. young.
(1792) Samuel, December 29, 1821. m. Hepsie Mitchell, July 12, 1857.
(1793) Jane, November 9, 1823. d. 1827.
(1794) Ebenezer, July 26, 1825. m. Emily Perry, September 8, 1855.
(1795) Joseph, September 14, 1827. d. young.
(1796) Sally, February 21, 1829. m. John R. Adams, December 6, 1849.
(1797) Nancy, May 29, 1832. m. John R. Adams, September 24, 1857.

Ebenezer was a farmer and carriage maker. He resided in Farmington Me., where he d. July 1, 1852.

---

667 Joshua and Lydia Lowell had:

(1798) Joshua, May, 1821. m. Anlacia Colby.
(1799) Russell, April 1, 1823. m. Clarinda Blaisdell. She d. October 14, 1859. He d. April 5, 1861.
(1800) Sylvanus, March 17, 1827. m. Rebecca Colburn, January 23, 1851.

Lydia d. November 5, 1843, and Joshua m. 2d Belinda Pillsbury, May 23, 1844. He was a harness maker, and lived on a part of the family estate in Farmington, Me. He d. April 15, 1873.

---

672 Dean and Mehitable Graves had:

(1801) Samuel D., September 19, 1832. m. Irene Reed, February 23, 1851; m. 2d Martha Tyler, September 20, 1864.
(1802) Esther J., August 23, 1834. m. Leander Burbank.
(1803) Clarissa B., November 8, 1839. m. Aaron Taylor, November 27, 1857.
(1804) Mary, September 23, 1842. d. young.
(1805) Martha, September 23, 1842. d. young.
(1806) Martha, January 14, 1845. m. Henry W. Bailey.
(1807) John, August 10, 1848. d. young.
(1808) Joshua, August 10, 1848. d. young.

Dean lived on a part of the old family estate in Farmington, Me. He d. October 17, 1849. Mehitable d. September 25, 1848.

---

675 Samuel D. and Nancy Shattuck had:

(1809) Harriet, December 24, 1824. d. young.
(1810) Samuel, January 20, 1826. d. young.

(1811) Caroline, October 20, 1827. m. John Bass, January 23, 1852.
(1812) Nancy J., September 7, 1829. m. Elnathan Brewer, August 20, 1851.
(1813) William, January 4, 1832. m. S. J. Brown, October 1, 1854.
(1814) Alonzo, November 18, 1834. d. young.
(1815) Harriet A., October 23, 1838. m. Andrew Fuller, June 6, 1858.
(1816) Mark D., October 5, 1840. m. Abbie E. Currier, October 5, 1863.
(1817) George P., August 11, 1844. m. Helen B. Gibbs, March 12, 1868.

SAMUEL D. KNOWLTON

was b. at Amherst, N. H., where he resided all his life, excepting eighteen months spent in Salem, Mass. He was a boot- and shoe-maker, his shop being the original porch of the old Congregational Church, subsequently converted into a Town House. He was a lieutenant of militia in the Milford Light Infantry. During the turbulent days of the old Anti-Slavery movement, his house was one of the termini of the "underground railroad," where runaway slaves found refuge. He was a very intelligent man, an omnivorous reader, and upright citizenship and humane disposition made him beloved by all. He d. December 23, 1877. Nancy d. June 4, 1870 (another date given is January 3, 1869).

---

673 Fanny Knowlton and Francis Lynch had:

(1818) Agnes, October 28, 1815. m. D. C. Rich, August 15, 1838.
(1819) Alfred, July 31, 1818. m. Ann H. Hewes.
(1820) Eliza, September 22, 1820. m. Wm. H. Osgood.
(1821) Henry, June 24, 1823. m. E. G. Vanderbilt.
(1822) Alice, May 15, 1825. d. young.
(1823) Samuel, June 6, 1827.
(1824) Martha, August 1, 1829. m. Geo. P. Kimball.
(1825) Nancy, May 9, 1833. m. Albert Chamberlain.
(1826) Alonzo, March 3, 1836. m. S. B. Le Sure; m. 2d Minnie Fisk.
(1827) Herbert, May 3, 1838. m. Mary Rowell.

---

678 Hannah Knowlton and Geo. W. Carne had:

(1828) Sarah E., May 3, 1833. m. S. G. Putnam.
(1829) Adaline, June 8, 1837. d. 1853.
(1830) Edward G., March 21, 1851.

---

680 Emeline Knowlton and Joshua Burns had:

(1831) Fannie E., June 3, 1836. d. 1859.
(1832) Clifford, February 25, 1838. m. Susie P. Harvey.
(1833) Sophronia, February 12, 1840.

681 Edmund and Caroline Parsons had :

(1834) Esther, May 3, 1824. d. August 23, 1846.
(1835) Daniel, May 28, 1827. d. young.
(1836) Mary, March 12, 1830. d. February 3, 1845.
(1837) Daniel C., February 6, 1840. Killed in the War of the Rebellion, October 17, 1864.

Residence, Cazenovia, N. Y.

---

683 Dean Owen and Marilla Wood had :

(1838) William, November 4, 1842. d. young.

Marilla d. May 4, 1843, and Dean m. 2d Hannah B. Ehle, June 6, 1846. They had :

(1839) Willis, August 7, 1847. m. Ida L. Orr, August 25, 1885.

Residence, Cazenovia, N. Y.

---

685 Ebenezer B. and Fidelia Needham had :

(1840) Charles M., November 30, 1849. m. Martha J. Bradley, June 29, 1868.
(1841) Annie R., April 17, 1856. m. E. Bowen Crandall, September 17, 1874.
(1842) Mary A., April 15, 1858. m. Walter C. Jackson, September 26, 1877.

Residence, Cazenovia, N. Y.

---

710 Capt. Joseph W. and Nancy had :

(1843) Alice, February 18, 1802. d. 1825.
(1844) William, July 1, 1804. m. Mary Chapman.
(1845) Joseph, July 14, 1806. m. Hannah Sanborn.
(1846) Isaac, May 20, 1808. m. Ruth Butts, April 15, 1835.
(1847) John, February 15, 1809. m. Caroline Churchill, October 10, 1842.
(1848) Martha, February 11, 1810. m. George Howes.
(1849) Mary, April 11, 1812. m. Mark Lichenns.
(1850) Sarah, July 24, 1814. m. David McKenny.
(1851) Nancy, April 19, 1816. d. 1820.

Residence, Strong, Me.

Joseph was a captain in the militia. He d. January 17, 1862. Nancy d. March 31, 1818.

712 George W. and Martha Wheeler had:

(1852) Albion, 1822. m. Ellen Poland, May 5, 1844.
(1853) Thomas, 1825. d. 1851.
(1854) Daniel, 1829. m. Vienna Holbrook, January 28, 1852.
(1855) Sarah, March 14, 1834. m. Thomas Mann, February 5, 1854.

George m. 1st Susan ——. He m. 2d Martha Wheeler, who d. August 14, 1858. He d. December 3, 1841.

---

716 Joseph and Lucretia Brigham had:

(1856) John D., October 29, 1822. m. Adelaide Marshall, December 20, 1846.
(1857) Joseph L., January 26, 1824. d. young.
(1858) Joseph, June 26, 1826. m. Adaline C. Preston, October 8, 1854.
(1859) Mary E., June 27, 1828.
(1860) Lucretia, June 12, 1830.
(1861) George K., July 8, 1840. m. Irene M. Pullins, October 6, 1861.

Joseph d. January 12, 1859. Lucretia d. December 22, 1855.

---

717 Isaac and Mrs. Nancy Dodge Knowlton had:

(1862) Belinda, June 24, 1837. d. young.
(1863) Isaac F., February 3, 1839. m. Sarah W. Dodge, February 2, 1865.
(1864) Augusta, June 27, 1840. d. young.
(1865) John H. m. Sarah A. Knowlton, April 13, 1871.

---

724 Levi and Margaret Woodbury had:

(1866) Joseph, May 29, 1810. m. Esther Knowlton, May 25, 1836.
(1867) Edmund, October 12, 1811. m. Amanda Saunders, July 2, 1836.
(1868) Abigail, October 9, 1813.
(1869) Margaret, June 7, 1816. m. Josiah Woodbury, June 25, 1846.
(1870) Eliza, December 10, 1820. d. October 23, 1840.
(1871) Sarah, November 2, 1822. d. young.
(1872) Jacob, June 7, 1824. d. young.
(1873) Nancy. m. Jeremiah Woodbury.
(1874) Emma. m. Abraham Hobbs.
(1875) Fanny. m. Richard Dorloff.
(1876) Abigail. m. Benj. Preston.

Margaret d. August 3, 1832, and Levi m. 2d Bethiah Poland, August 21, 1853. He d. May 26, 1871.

729 Abigail Knowlton and —— had:

(1877) Benjamin.
(1878) Nehemiah.
(1879) Joseph.
(1880) Ezra.
(1881) Abigail.
(1882) Sally.

---

731 Moses and Eunice Cummings had:

(1883) Permelia, May, 1810.
(1884) Eunice, May 5, 1816. d. October 17, 1841.
(1885) Aaron, December 27, 1819. m. Laura M. Brown.

Moses d. 1829. Eunice d. August 21, 1831.

---

732 James and Nancy Allen had:

(1886) Harriet, January 6, 1815. m. Brainerd Stanwood, April 24, 1840.
(1887) Nancy, October 22, 1816. m. E. B. Phelps. She d. January 11, 1838.
(1888) Mary, October 9, 1818. m. 4 chil.
(1889) James A., February 3, 1821. m. Clarissa Fuller, March 8, 1847.
(1890) Allen, October 25, 1827. m. Frances Farr, 1868.

James d. April 9, 1861. Nancy d. September 26, 1874.

---

733 Edmund and Lydia Patch had:

(1892) Ira P., May 23, 1819. m. Esther Appleton, August 8, 1846.
(1893) Enoch F., May 2, 1821. m. Elizabeth M. Patch, May 14, 1842.
(1894) Richard D., January 29, 1822. m. Mary A. Means, September 3, 1851.

Edmund d. November 18, 1867.

---

735 Neamiah and Patience Parsons had:

(1895) Walter, April 7, 1798.
(1896) Charles, June 1, 1800. m. Mary W. Tuttle.
(1897) Timothy, March 2, 1802. m. Hannah Farr.

(1898) Harvey, August 6, 1803. m. Lucy Davis, November 12, 1824.
(1899) Nehemiah, January 18, 1805. m. L. G. Farr, December 18, 1828; m. 2d Harriet Coley, November 5, 1836.

Patience d. May 2, 1846, and Nehemiah m. 2d Widow N. Colby, September 13, 1846. He was prominent in civil and political life, taking an active part in local matters, and was a Representative to the General Court in 1831. He d. November 25, 1847.

---

736 Asa and Annie D. Farr had:

(1900) Louisa, October 14, 1803. m. George Foster, December 20, 1826.
(1901) Asa, Jr., June 22, 1806. m. Eliza Porter; m. 2d Anna E. Trask, 1842. He d. June 25, 1857.
(1902) Susannah, March 28, 1811.

Residence, Gloucester, Mass.

Asa d. November 27, 1859. Annie d. August 28, 1856.

---

738 Josiah and Elizabeth Woodbury had:

(1903) Thomas W. m. Mary Giles, February 9, 1848.

Residence, Gloucester, Mass.

There were six other children whose names and records are unknown.

---

740 Charles and —— had:

(1904) Charles, Jr., 1819.

Charles, Sen., d. in Rockport, Mass., January 22, 1867.

---

741 Moses and Abigail Lufkin had:

(1905) Hannah, July 25, 1806. m. Joseph Andrews, March 28, 1821.
(1906) Abigail, January 20, 1808. m. Noah Story, June 10, 1837.
(1907) Susan, January 29, 1810. m. Jeremiah Henderson.
(1908) Moses, August 1, 1812. m. Mary Lufkin.
(1909) Esther, June 27, 1814. m. William Allen Andrews.
(1910) Mary L., October 7, 1816. m. Luke Boswell Burnham, December 25, 1860.
(1911) David, June 30, 1819, m. Austice C. Norton.

(1912) Aaron, March 4, 1821. m. Harriet Choate Norton, January 3, 1854.
(1913) Elizabeth, August 12, 1822. m. John P. Lufkin ; m. 2d Jessie Burnham.
(1914) Minerva, July 27, 1824. m. Jonathan M. Richardson, March 26, 1851.
(1915) Perry, March 4. 1829. m. in Canada.
(1916) Cassandra, February 17, 1831. m. Chas. T. Littlefield, January 6, 1856.

MOSES KNOWLTON

was born in New Gloucester, Me., and removed to Essex, Mass., when a boy, where he spent the remainder of his life, on what is known as Hog Island. He was a very successful farmer, and owned one of the four farms into which the island is divided. The Hon. Rufus Choate was born on one of these farms, a lawyer of national celebrity, whose extraordinary career added lustre to the fame of the Old Bay State.

Moses Knowlton removed from Hog Island to the town proper where he continued actively in farming until extreme old age obliged him to retire. His physical strength was phenomenal, and he was often seen to lift a barrel of cider over the tail board of his farm wagon with perfect ease. His mental activity was no less remarkable, and only the lack of early educational advantages prevented him from occupying the prominent public position for which he was by nature eminently fitted.

He was a Director in the Cape Ann National Bank of Gloucester, Mass., and a highly esteemed citizen of Essex.

---

748 Michael and Margaret Boyd had:

(1917) Louisa, September 26, 1806. m. George Norwood, December 20, 1826.
(1918) Margaret, September 16, 1809. m. d. October 4, 1828.
(1919) Michael, September 16, 1809. m. Louisa Hodgkins, November 15, 1849.
(1920) Clementia, January 3, 1811. m. Philander Currier.
(1921) Huldah, February 22, 1813. m. Jonah Patten.
(1922) Mercy, August 27, 1812. m. Ebenezer Cleaves. 1 dau.
(1923) Addison, March 4, 1815. m. Mercy Willey.
(1924) Mary A., March 12, 1817. m. Wm. Lane, Jr., October 14, 1838.
(1925) Desire Ann, May 20, 1824.

Residence, Salem, Mass.

Michael d. February 11, 1865. Margaret d. February 22, 1834.

749 Azor and Lois Chamberlain had:

(1926) George, December 18, 1811. m. Mary Dodge, June 1, 1835.
(1927) William H., April 2, 1814. m. Mary Clarkson, May 21, 1845.
(1928) Andrew, October 24, 1816. m. Mary O. Fulton, April 17, 1838.
(1929) Azor, January 18, 1819. m. Martha Turner, May 4, 1845.
(1930) Ivers, April 1, 1821. d. young.
(1931) Eben, May 3, 1823. m. Elizabeth Mathews, August 12, 1850.
(1932) Lois J., August 21, 1825. m. Reuben Farr, March, 1843.
(1933) Jane H., February 21, 1827. m. Ezekiel Andrews, December 7, 1851.
(1934) Abbie S., May 28, 1829. m. D. G. Gott, May 13, 1855.
(1935) Laura, September 15, 1833. m. Alvin Hale, November 1, 1857.

Lois d. June 12, 1835, and Azor m. 2d Amelia Hale, April 19, 1836. They had:

(1936) Frank P., May 19, 1837. m. Phœbe ——

Residence, Salem, Mass.

Azor d. February 24, 1876. Amelia d. August 26, 1856.

---

750 Ivers and Sarah Patch had:

(1937) Martha L., August 20, 1815. m. Augustus Dodge, March 22, 1834.
(1938) Sarah D., January 10, 1819. m. Zebulon Burnham, February 21, 1837. He d. October 15, 1848.

Sarah d. April 5, 1838, and Ivers m. 2d Sarah Shepard, September 24, 1842. He d. December 31, 1842.

---

755 Fannie Knowlton and Antonio Ferrando had:

(1939) Daniel.
(1940) A dau.
(1941) Henry.
(1942) Jane.

---

756 Katie Knowlton and —— Richardson had:

(1943) Mary.
(1944) Cynthia.
(1945) James.

760 Eunice Knowlton and Johnathan Smith had:

(1946) Mary B.
(1947) William.
(1948) Henry.

---

762 Ephraim and Mrs. Hannah Barrett had:

(1949) Ephraim, 1814. m. Catherine Holmes, April 1834.
(1950) Benjamin, 1817. m. Margaret Spaulding, November 11, 1835; m. 2d Caroline McMullen, October 5, 1851.
(1951) Hannah, 1819. m. Benjamin Stone, July 22, 1841.
(1952) Lucy. m. William Spaulding.
(1953) Sarah. m. Mark Dodge of Isleborough, Me.; m. 2d Sumner Allen; m. 3d Moses Nickerson.

Ephraim rem. from Salem, Mass. to Rockland, Me., in 1805. He was a cooper.

---

775 Thomas and —— had:

(1954) James, 1788. Res., Columbus, O.
(1955) Thomas, 1791. m. Lucy Blanchard; m. 2d Almira ——.
(1956) John, 1793.
(1957) William, June 15, 1795. m. Maria Barney, December 2, 1818. She d. February 11, 1874.
(1958) Sewell, 1800. Res. in Belvidere, Ill.

---

776 Abraham and —— had:

(1959) Mary. m. Ira Robbins.

---

779 Elizabeth Knowlton and Daniel Stearns had:

(1960) Isaac, October 11, 1784. m. Lucinda Rice 1804. He d. April 12, 1858. Res., Vt.
(1961) Sally, August 17, 1786. m. Darius Norcross, February 1, 1804. She d. November 1, 1863. He d. December 27, 1838. Res., Lockport, N. Y.
(1962) Abigail, December 27, 1787. m. Stephen Norcross of Lockport, N. Y. She d. April 7, 1873. He d. June 17, 1850. 8 chil.
(1963) Daniel, November 12, 1789. m. Mary Benson, February 14, 1811. 4 chil. He d. March 20, 1872.

(1964) Lydia, September 30, 1791. m. Wm. S. Marsh, December 18, 1810. She d. May 5, 1814. He d. August 18, 1867.

(1965) Betsey, January 30, 1793. m. Isaac Barker, September 12, 1816. She d. in Guilford, Vt., November 7, 1874. He d. March 10, 1867.

(1966) Lucy, June 29, 1796. m. Joel Brown, April 7, 1818. She d. in Lowell, Mass., September 3, 1868. He d. September 20, 1870.

(1967) Charles, July 17, 1800. m. Almira Bancroft, July 2, 1829. Res., Lowell, Mass.

(1968) Charlotte, July 17, 1800. m. Leavitt H. Gibbs, June 13, 1824.

(1969) Samuel, August 27, 1802. m. Mary F. Moore.

(1970) Selinda, November 8, 1805. m. Luther Streeter, December 23, 1834. 7 chil.

(1971) Harriet, February 25, 1808. m. Moses Seavey, June 4, 1833. Res., Springfield, Mass. 4 chil.

(1972) Daniel, February 14, 1811

Elizabeth was b. in Ipswich, and after her marriage rem. to Dimmerston, Vt., in 1795, and thence to Brattleboro in 1809, where she d. August 6, 1820. She was a woman of resolute character, in which strong convictions were tempered by a cheerful and happy temperament.

Daniel was a soldier of the Revolution. He was the son of Isaiah and Elizabeth Stearns of Cambridge, Mass., a lineal descendant of the Stearnses of Watertown who were the first of that name to emigrate to America in 1636. He enlisted June 12, 1777, in Capt. Thomas Barnes's Light Infantry, Col. Nixon's regiment, and was subsequently transferred to Capt. Holden's company. Although severely wounded at Stony Point, he remained in the service until 1781, or later, and subsequently received a pension. He died at Brattleboro, Vt. June 19, 1824.

---

782 John and Dorcas Shapleigh had:

(1973) Nathaniel, May 26, 1791. m. Rosanna Goodwin, January 1, 1817.

(1974) James, January 16, 1793. m. Isabel Tobey, February 24, 1821.

(1975) John, December 8, 1794. m. Nancy Frye, June 28, 1833.

(1976) Lucy, September 6, 1796. m. James Bartlett.

(1977) Hannah, February 4, 1799. m. Joshua W Kenny, November 8, 1825. She d. April 23, 1870.

John was born in Ipswich, and was a tailor by trade. When but a youth he enlisted in the army, in the year 1780, and for the full term of three years, serving in Col. John Yeaton's 3d Mass. Regiment. The following is a copy of his discharge at Albany, N. Y.——:

"John Knowlton, Soldier in the Third Massachusetts Regiment, being enlisted for three years, is hereby honorably discharged from the Service of the United States.

Given in the State of New York, the 22d day of Dec. 1783. H. Knox, M. Genl.

By the General Command.

Registered in the books of the Regiment

John C. Strafford, Adjt."

Knowlton removed to Kittery, Me., in 1788, and two years later married Dorcas Shapleigh of Eliot, Me. and of a prominent family, after whom one of the townships of the State was named.

She received a pension for John's services, and a bounty of $50 from the State of Maine, July, 1837. John d. October 18, 1798. Dorcas d. October 16, 1842.

---

786 Jacob and Abigail Hodgkin had:

(1978) Mary, September 17, 1799.
(1979) Abigail, March 14, 1801. m. Joseph G. True.
(1980) Thomas, August 31, 1802. m. Cynthia Savage.
(1981) David, March 14, 1804.
(1982) Joseph. m. Rachel Lowe. Res., Watsonville, Cal.
(1983) Jacob, August 18, 1807. m. Mary Rogers, December 11, 1834.
(1984) Caroline, November 6, 1810.
(1985) Francis, September 9, 1814. m. Caroline Billings.

Jacob rem. from Ipswich to Litchfield, Me., and d. there July, 1814.

---

787 Sarah Knowlton and James Lord had:

(1986) Sally, June 22, 1796. m. Chas. H. McClausland, December 5, 1830.
(1987) James, November 1, 1797. d. young.
(1988) Thomas H., January 13, 1799. m. Hannah Woods, January 16, 1825.
(1989) Abigail S., March 15, 1802. m. Daniel Gilman, December 19, 1824.
(1990) Deborah W., February 4, 1806. d. May 9, 1824.
(1991) James, May 12, 1808. d. young.
(1992) Mary C., January 10, 1811. m. Oliver Johnson, 1836. She d. June 11, 1848.

James Lord was a soldier of the Revolution, enlisting in April, 1775, and participating in many battles. He d. February 16, 1847. Sarah d. January 8, 1820.

788 Mary Knowlton and Thomas Lord had:

(1993) Mary, June 22, 1796. m. Joseph True, March 18, 1820.
(1994) Abigail K., January 20, 1798. m. Jonathan Folsom, November 19, 1821.
(1995) Phoebe, January 1, 1800. d. young.
(1996) Thomas, September, 1802. m. Eliza Munroe, January 9, 1825.
(1997) Elizabeth, December 31, 1804. m. E. G. Smith, November 27, 1824.
(1998) Lucy P., May 2, 1807. m. Eliphalet Parker, November 26, 1828.
(1999) James H., February 11, 1810. m. Anna K. Rich, July 14, 1836.
(2000) Daniel D., July 27, 1812. m. Sarah Blackwell, January 1, 1840.
(2001) William, July 10, 1815. m. Ellen D. Smith, March 1, 1845.
(2002) Joseph E., October 14, 1817. m. Emiline True, March 19, 1844.

Thomas d. February 21, 1858. Mary d. March 1, 1855.

---

789 Rebecca Knowlton and Thomas Lane had:

(2003) Endvey.
(2004) Polly.
(2005) Rebecca.
(2006) Abigail.
(2007) Sally.
(2008) Elbridge.
(2009) Thomas.
(2010) Joseph.

---

791 William B. and Mary Wallace had:

(2011) Ruth, March 19, 1786. m. Asa Knowlton.
(2012) John, June 18, 1788. d. young.
(2013) Jonathan, July 31, 1791. m. Lydia Palmer. Res. in Deerfield, N. H.
(2014) Miles, November 25, 1792. m. Nancy Demeritt, November 28, 1816. He d. February, 1874. She d. July 3, 1870.
(2015) Samuel, April 3, 1796. d. young.
(2016) Thomas, March 24, 1798.
(2017) William, July 2, 1800. m. Betsey Drake.
(2018) David, July 2, 1800. d. young.
(2019) Jane, May 23, 1803. m. Miles Durgin, April 28, 1824.
(2020) Nathaniel, May 23, 1805. m. Eliza Hoyt, March 7, 1829.
(2021) David, May 23, 1805. d. young.

Res., Northwood, N. H.

792 Sarah and Ebenezer Dustin had:

(2022) Nancy.
(2023) Irene.
(2024) Betsey.
(2025) David.

---

794 David and Drusilla Deague had:

(2026) Oliver, March 12, 1792. m. Lucinda Batcheller, September 8, 1825; d. March, 1872.
(2027) Mehitable, August 18, 1793. m. Lewis Fiske, April 14, 1817.
(2028) Samuel, May 15, 1795. m. Sally Danforth, August 29, 1818.
(2029) Rhoda, February 7, 1797. m. O. P. Littlefield, 1827; m. 2d —— Libby. Rem. to Quincy, Ill.
(2030) Eliphalet, January 23, 1803. m. Susan Swain. Res. in East Northwood, N. H.
(2031) Harriet, August 30, 1806. m. F. C. Morrill, 1827.
(2032) Lydia, December 15, 1808. m. Jacob Harver, October 3, 1824. d. October, 1848.
(2033) David, January 23, 1811. d. young.
(2034) George W., February 9, 1815. m. Eliza Garland, January 31, 1837; m. 2d Mary Virgin, 1839.

David was the first Knowlton b. in Northwood, N. H. He d. August 3, 1850. She d. January 28, 1867.

---

797 Dolly Knowlton and Daniel Hoyt had:

(2035) Lydia D., November 6, 1803.
(2036) Irene, July 16, 1806.
(2037) David, September 12, 1807. m. Mary Foss.
(2038) Jonah K., January 19, 1811. m. Nancy Woodman.
(2039) Jeremiah B., February 25, 1815.

Dolly d. September 4, 1857.

---

800 Asa and Ruth Knowlton had:

(2040) Olive, October 12, 1804. m. David Smith.
(2041) Thomas, February 24, 1809.
(2042) John, November 25, 1811.

Asa m. 2d Sally Knowlton. They had:

(2043) Asahel, June 22, 1815. m. Eliza Shaw, 1839; she d. December 27, 1850.
(2044) Samuel, February 27, 1817. d. January 29, 1841.
(2045) James, July 17, 1823. m. 2 chil.
(2046) Asa, April 20, 1825. m. Lydia ——, 1854.
(2047) Andrew B., December 19, 1819. m. Mary E. Blake.
(2048) Adoniram, July 5, 1828. d. 1835.
(2049) William, March 25, 1835. m. Merinda Bailey; m. 2d Lydia Currie.

Asa d. October 10, 1861.

---

801 Sarah and Samuel Gerrish had:

(2050) Benjamin.
(2051) David.
(2052) Samuel.
(2053) Betsey.
(2054) Ebenezer.

Sarah was a woman of remarkable nerve. Her husband became periodically insane, and at such times was dangerously violent. On one occasion, when he had sharpened his knives for the customary hog-slaughter in the early winter, he suddenly appeared before his wife Sally with the announcement that he had come to kill her. Though her heart almost ceased to beat from the terror of the situation, she replied instantly, opening her arms at the words:

"Go ahead! I would rather die than lead such a life as I am leading with you!" "You would, hey," shouted the excited husband. "Well, you can't have your way *this* time. You 've got to live with me."

So Sally was left to congratulate herself on that shrewdness and nerve that had come so promptly to her relief.

---

802 Nathan and Abigail Dane had:

(2055) Betsey. m. George Haley.
(2056) William H. H. m. Eleanor Norris.

Nathan d. November 14, 1851.

803 Stephen C. and Mary Greene had :

(2057) Jeremiah G., March 11, 1812. m. Mary Ford.
(2058) Charles G., February 21, 1814. m. Sarah Flanders, May, 1837.
(2059) Hannah D., March 26, 1816. m. Cyrus Ford, March 11, 1844.
(2060) James S., February 28, 1822. m. Clarissa Ford, April 29, 1847.
(2061) Gustavus C., October 19, 1838. d. at Hilton Head, March 26, 1862. Company D, 3d N. H. Vol.

Mary d. April 19, 1882. Stephen d. February 17, 1873.

---

808 Joseph and Susan Dearborn had :

(2062) Joseph, June 7, 1820. d. young.
(2063) Joseph, June 21, 1821. m. Clara Butler, October 17, 1843. Served in War of Rebellion.
(2064) Chas. D., September 20, 1822. m. Harriet N. Buck, December, 1845.
(2065) Julia A., August 25, 1829. m. Micah Dyer, May 1, 1851.
(2066) Thomas, January 25, 1831, in Concord, N. H. d. young.
(2067) Susan D., August 8, 1836. m. Dr. Joseph Gerland, May 3, 1870.

Joseph was a soldier in the War of 1812. He d. May 31, 1865. Susan was a lineal descendant of General Dearborn of Bunker Hill fame.

---

809 Ebenezer and Lydia Harris had :

(2068) James.
(2069) Hosea C.
(2070) Charlotte.
(2071) Sally.
(2072) Nancy.
(2073) Betsey.
(2074) Ruth.
(2075) Lydia.

Ebenezer d. March 22, 1888.

---

810 Charlotte Knowlton and Nathan Hoyt had :

(2076) Eliza, November 19, 1807. m. Nathaniel Knowlton.
(2077) Hannah, February 19, 1809. m. David Robinson of Candia, N. H.
(2078) Harriet, September 16, 1812.
(2079) Nathan, November 15, 1814. m. Emily Bennett, of Woonsocket, R. I.

(2080) John S., March 16, 1816. m. Louisa Foss, of Chichester, N. H.
(2081) Hosea C., June 14, 1819. m. Mary W. Durgin, Newton, Mass.
(2082) Abigail, January 21, 1821 m. John Chesley.

---

811 James and Sally Demerritt had:

(2083) Betsey, April 23, 1816. m. Andrew Woodman.
(2084) Gilbert G., June 10, 1818. m. Olive Batchelder, January 12, 1842.

James d. Septemer 2, 1824. Sally d. December 22, 1865.

---

816 Hosea C. and Betsey Seavey had:

(2085) Melissa, April, 1828. m. F. H. Jones, March 18, 1860.
(2086) Alonzo, March 29, 1831. d. 1841.
(2087) Sally, November 21, 1833. m. C. Drake, August 13, 1862.
Residence in Chichester, N. H.

Betsey d. December 1, 1861.

---

821 Mary Knowlton and Thomas Blake had:

(2088) David.
(2089) Jemima.
(2090) Marian.
(2091) Hannah.
(2092) Betsey.
(2093) Ithamar.

Mary d. December 12, 1846. Thomas d. April 14, 1844.

---

824 (Rev.) David and Hannah True had:

4 chil., all d. young.

He was b. in Pittsfield, N. H., and ordained in Bernstead, N. H. His wid. m. Jonah Fogg.

---

825 Ebenezer and Abigail True had:

(2093 A) Daniel, November 18, 1803. d. 1815.
(2093 B) Betsey, April 27, 1806. m. John Chase; m. 2d John Madden.

(2093 C) David, July 13, 1813. m. Mehitable Lane.
(2093 D) Ebenezer, December 6, 1815. m. Phoebe True, August 16, 1840. He d. September 10, 1874.
(2093 E) John C., October 10, 1822. m. Sarah Webb.

Ebenezer was a Representative for nine years. Rem. from Pittsfield, N.H., to Montville, Me., and d. November 18, 1841.
Abigail d. November 22, 1868.

---

828 Benjamin and Abigail Wright, of Hollis, N. H., had:

(2094) Abigail, June 23, 1777. m. Joseph Stevens, February 10, 1795.
(2095) Charlotte, October, 13, 1778. m. Dr. John Rexford, August 27, 1794. 9 chil.
(2096) Benjamin, August 10, 1780. m. Lucy Campbell.
(2097) Amos, January 16, 1783. d. February 9, 1864.
(2098) Lucy, January 13, 1786. m. John Chamberlain.

Benjamin was a soldier of the Revolution, and served in the Lexington Alarm, at Charlestown, siege of Boston, and at Fort Ticonderoga, in Capt. Heald's company, Col. Reed's regiment, from New Ipswich, N. H.
He rem. to Sangerfield, N. Y., in 1808; and thence to Manlius, N. Y., where he d. February 13, 1810.

---

829 Henry and Sibyl——had:

(2099) Henry, September 20, 1779. m. Rebecca Southwick; m. 2d Matilda Moore.
(2100) Sibyl, August 18, 1781. d. 1793.
(2101) Ruth, January 25, 1783. d. young.
(2102) Charles, November, 13, 1784.
(2103) William, September 11, 1786. d. 1791.
(2104) Timothy, July 2, 1788.
(2105) Eunice, July 3, 1793.
(2106) John, May 10, 1790; d. young.

Henry was a soldier of the Revolution, in the same company as his brothers Benjamin and John, and in the same engagements. Of the 150 volunteers from New Ipswich, the names of only 65 have been preserved in the State Rosters. The record of the services of Benjamin, Sen., and his sons has been preserved in the history of the town.

832 Sarah Knowlton and Obadiah Coolidge had:

(2107) Benjamin.
(2108) Obadiah.
(2109) John.
(2110) Harriet.
(2111) Hannah.
(2112) Esther.

Res., Potsdam, N. Y.

The father and sons were in the battle of Plattsburgh, N. Y.

833 John and Sally Holden had:

(2113) Joseph, July 19, 1795. m. Harriet Jane Temple, October 24, 1821. He d. 1867. She d. 1855.
(2114) Sally, May 11, 1797. m. F. G. Temple, August 17, 1829.
(2115) Eliza, July 12, 1799. m. Shubal Shattuck, May 14, 1830. d. January 23, 1863. 7 chil.
(2116) John H., August 19, 1802. m. Mary Rodgers, April 10, 1834.
(2117) Sophronia, September 18, 1805. d. March 8, 1806.
(2118) Sophia, September 18, 1805. d. March 10, 1806.
(2119) Almira, January 15, 1808. m. Daniel Nutting. 1 chil.

Res., New Ipswich, N. H.

John served in the Lexington Alarm.

840 John and Mary Gott had:

(2120) John L., 1789. Drowned in 1806.
(2121) James, October 23, 1796. m. Sarah Lane, February 18, 1821.
(2122) Mary, 1799. m. —— Griffin. 4 chil.
(2123) Epps, November 10, 1801. m. Elizabeth Bridges, January 11, 1825.
(2124) Joseph, 1803. m. Mary Remick; m. 2d Lydia Remick.
(2125) Ammi L., January 20, 1806. m. Maria Lond.
(2126) Josiah, 1809. d. March, 1875.
(2127) Judith, 1813. m. Joseph Berry.
(2128) Lydia, 1815. m. —— Wendell. d. February 23, 1877. 4 child.

John d. 1825. Mary d. 1827.

843 Johnathan and Dolly Prouty had:

(2129) Erastus, 1795. m. Res. in Toronto, Canada.
(2130) Faxon, 1797. m. Elizabeth Buck.

(2131) Dorothy.
(2132) Eunice.
(2133) Lina.

Dolly d. and Jonathan m. 2d and had:

(2134) Charles.
(2135) Barnabas. Supposed to have perished with all his family in the Peshtigo, Mich., fire.
(2136) Hannah.
(2137) Clarissa.

Johnathan was b. and lived in West Brookfield, Mass., whence he removed to Canada. He was a land speculator, and in his expeditions through the wilderness he discovered the lake which now bears his name. After accumulating a large property, he removed to Livingston Co., N. Y. In 1811 he returned to Canada to settle up his affairs, and when the War of 1812 broke out he was impressed into the British service. He escaped with his two sons by night in a boat; and, breaking his way through the ice, reached the American shore, and at once enlisted in the U. S. service.

---

844 Mary Knowlton and James Bush had:

9 chil. After Mary's death, James m. the widow of John Knowlton, who was then living on a farm near East Brookfield, Mass.

---

848 Judith Knowlton and Bela C. Stoddard had:

(2138) Charles K.

She was his 3d wife.

---

849 Capernium and Marshall P. Wilder had:

(2139) Chas. K.
(2140) Mary B.
(2141) James M.
(2142) Sally. m. Elijah Nichols. West Brookfield, Mass.

---

851 John and Betsey Curtis had:

(2143) Betsey. m. Amasa Nash. 3 chil.
(2144) John, December 29, 1789. m. Ruth Holmes, March 15, 1816. Res. in Minot, Me.

(2145) Ephraim. m. Sarah Braglin. He d. January 7, 1849.
(2146) Mercy. m. Phineas Curtis. 8 chil.
(2147) Jane. m. Enoch Ellis. 2 chil.
(2148) Mary, March 16, 1802, m. John Kimball, November 14, 1821.
(2149) Delilah. m. Josiah Seekens.
(2150) Ann. m. John Seekens.
(2151) Lucinda. m. Jacob Peavey.
(2152) Charlotte. d. young.
(2153) Elepha. m. Joel Proctor.
(2154) Zina, September 20, 1813. m. Betsey Proctor, November 24, 1838.

John d. April 14, 1844. Betsey d. May 12, 1853.

---

852 Andrew and Olive Curtis had:

(2155) Benjamin. m. Res. in Kennebec, Me.
(2156) Stephen, November 3, 1803. m. Res. in Brooklyn, N. Y.
(2157) a dau. m. —— Weevell.

Andrew rem. to Kennebec, Me., about 1807. He was lost at sea.

---

853 Stephen and Betsey Curtis had:

(2158) Betsey, September 7, 1797. m. Amos Knowlton, 1820.
(2159) Mercy, January 6, 1799. m. Lemuel Curtis. 4 chil.
(2160) Avis, November 22, 1801. m. Reuben Colsin. She d. January 1, 1849. 1 son, Reuben.
(2161) Henry, November 16, 1804. m. Betsey York. Res. in Maine. Lost at sea.
(2162) Mary, 1806. m. Nathaniel Greer.
(2163) Lydia, January 14, 1807. m. Joseph Batchelder.
(2164) Stephen, July 19, 1812. m. Susan Pottle. Drowned in Bedford Harbor, 1875.
(2165) Reuben, May 18, 1814. d. December 17, 1831.
(2166) Julius W., January 19, 1817. d. in California, 1855. Res. in Maine.
(2167) William M., January 19, 1820. m. Patience Sprague.
(2168) Charles.

---

856 Annie Knowlton and William Flanders had:

(2169) Jane.
(2170) Myer.
(2171) Hezekiah. m. Mary Thomas.

(2172) William. m. Martha Whitney.
(2173) Lucy.
(2174) Benjamin.
(2175) Eliza.

---

857 Anna Knowlton and Lieut Amos Atkinson had :

(2176) Chas., January 2, 1786. d. unm.
(2177) George, November 17, 1788. m. Eliza Rider. Eliza wid., m. —— Gordon of Boston, Mass.
(2178) Amos, May 10, 1792. m. Anna G. Sawyer.
(2179) Nancy, July 22, 1797. m. Alfred Johnson, Belfast, Me. Res. Roxbury, Mass.

---

858 John and Elizabeth Parker had :

(2180) Nancy, September 1, 1791. m. Samuel Baker of England, 1831.
(2181) Martha, May 7, 1800. m. Samuel Baker.
(2182) Jane. m. Alvin Burby.
(2183) William. d. young.

John m. 2d Martha Parker, who, after his death. m. —— Townsend, of White Creek, N. Y.

John d. at White Creek, 1824. Elizabeth d. in Newburyport, Mass., May 1, 1808.

---

860 William and Lucy Woodley had :

(2184) Betsey, June 22, 1800, d. young.

Lucy d. 1800. aged 26, and William m. her sister Sally, September 25, 1812. He was lost at sea, 1813, and his wid. m. Joseph Patch, Jr.

---

861 Daniel and Lucy Freeman had :

(2186) Amos, December 6, 1792. m. Eunice Blood, April 1, 1812 ; m. 2d Mrs. Rhoda Bull, September 29, 1845.
(2187) Elisha, April 1, 1796. m. Sophia Turner.
(2188) Josiah, August 18, 1798. m. Eunice Knight. He d. August 23, 1846.
(2189) Polly, March 19, 1801. m. L. Baker, December 9, 1851.
(2190) Sylvia, May 3, 1803. d. young.
(2191) Parker, June 20, 1804. m. Rebecca Wright, July 13, 1834. He d. October 26, 1864.

(2192) Eliza, July 13, 1806. d. young.
(2193) Thomas C., December 28, 1807. m. Louisa Sampson, March 24, 1832.
(2194) Daniel, October 16, 1810. m. Belinda Liscomb, January 3, 1840. Res., Moline, Ill.
(2195) Lucy, December 23, 1812. m. Lewis Vaughn. d. October 30, 1887.

Daniel was with his father, Amos, at the battle of Bunker Hill, being then but eight years old. After the war he removed to N. Y., and lived with Nathan Warren, brother of his mother, learning the nail-maker's trade. He ran away, went to sea on a whaling voyage, and on his return married Lucy Freeman in Middlebury, Mass. Thence he removed to Hartland, Vt., became a farmer, and d. there, November 7, 1842. Lucy d. from insanity, May 25, 1826, and Daniel m. 2d —— Liscomb, by whom he had no children.

---

865 Polly Knowlton and Ebenezer Moulton had :

(2196) Lydia, 1802. m. —— McDermitt.
(2197) Ebenezer, 1803.
(2198) Mary, 1807. m. Amos Wilkins.

Polly d. August 10, 1858. Ebenezer d. May 31, 1847.

---

871 Robert and Sarah Buckmaster had :

(2199) William.
(2200) Robert.
(2201) Thomas.
(2202) Abigail.
(2203) Enoch.
(2204) John.
(2205) Daniel.
(2206) Henry.

---

872 Benjamin and Esther Lindsey, of Deer Isle, Me. had :

(2207) Timothy.

---

873 Joseph and Rhoda Buckmaster had :

(2208) Stephen, June 9, 1823. m. Hannah Coombs.
(2209) Margaret, May 24, 1826. m. —— Moody.
(2210) Mary J., June 6, 1827. d. September 12, 1852.
(2211) Ann S., November 17, 1839. m. —— Haynes, July 21, 1860.

(2212) Elizabeth, September 30, 1841. d. November 2, 1861.
(2213) Ellen, December 20, 1843. m. Watson Coombs, January 2, 1868.

---

874 Elizabeth Knowlton and Solomon Hamilton had:

(2214) Solomon.
(2215) Rebecca.
(2216) Daniel.
(2217) John.
(2218) Betsey.

Elizabeth d. at the age of one hundred.

---

875 Nancy Knowlton and Aaron Matthews had:

(2219) Aaron, 1808.
(2220) Sally, 1810.
(2221) Annie, 1812.
(2222) Esther, 1814.
(2223) Elizabeth, 1816.
(2224) Joseph, 1818.
(2225) Levi, 1820.
(2226) John, 1822.

---

876 Jane Knowlton and Joseph Curtis had:

(2227) Joseph.
(2228) Jane.
(2229) Leonard.
(2230) Sarah.

---

877 Sarah Knowlton and George Smith had:

(2231) Sally, 1806.
(2232) Sophia, 1808.
(2233) George, 1810.
(2234) Nancy, 1812.
(2235) Harriet, 1814.
(2236) Abiatha, 1816.
(2237) Barbara, 1818.

877 (A) John and Isabella Bailey had:

(2237 A) Matilda, 1797. m. Samuel Moore. Had dau. Mary M. who m. —— Lyon.

(2237 B) John, 1798. m. Chloe Meeker Carman.

(2237 C) William, 1800. d. about 1821.

(2237 D) Isabella.

John was b. in Beverly, Mass. Isabella, his wife, was the daughter of a wealthy English squire, and John met her on a voyage to America in his brother Mark's ship. He d. in 1805, in New York City, and was buried in Old Trinity Churchyard. In his will, probated March 27, 1805, he made Isabella, his widow, his executrix, leaving all his property to her in trust for herself and children, and making liberal provision for her in the event of her remarriage. At her death in 1861, she left a handsome property (will probated June 4, 1861) to her children and grandchildren in nine equal shares.

---

877 B Mark Knowlton

was a sea captain, and resided in Beverly and Boston, Mass. Had children by his first and second wife, all of whom d. young. Nancy, 3d wife, by whom he had no children, was the widow of Col. Thorndyke. Mark left a large estate.

---

883 Cyrus Knowlton and Celia Bostwick had:

(2238) Arezilla, April 19, 1821. m. W. H. Wiggin, March 25, 1844. d. December 23, 1881.

(2239) Julia, August 27, 1823.

(2240) Caroline, May 29, 1825. m. W. M. Drury, March 9, 1845.

(2241) Celia, October 25, 1828. m. Samuel Tibbets, April 1, 1849.

(2242) Cyrus, February 7, 1831. m. Sarah Taylor, October 3, 1853. He d. July 19, 1855.

(2243) Daniel, June 3, 1833. m. Sarah Rodgers, June 8, 1856. d. September 25, 1876.

---

885 David F. and Susannah Knowlton had:

(2244) Nancy. m. Daniel Black.

(2245) Hannah.

(2246) Susan. m. John Davis.

(2247) David.

(2248) Lucinda. m. Henry Brown.

(2249) Amanda. m. Had. S. Herbert.

(2250) Caroline.

888 Jeremiah and Betsey Rhodes had:

(2251) Jeremiah, April 15, 1816. m. Beatrice Whitney.
(2252) Harriet, October 31, 1817. d. January 8, 1831.
(2253) Lucy A., September 25, 1818. m. Dexter Farrar, May 10, 1846. Res. in Northport, Me.
(2254) Lucinda, October 31, 1821. m. Geo. L. Phillips. July 13, 1853.

Jeremiah was a sea captain. He. d. February 21, 1851. Betsey d. March 4, 1878.

---

889 Amos and Betsey Knowlton had:

(2255) Mary E., June 16, 1821. m. Unah Allstine.
(2256) Amos, July 23, 1823. m. Esther Robinson, 1835. d. August 22, 1876.
(2257) Caroline, August 9, 1825. d. May 16, 1844.
(2258) Joanna, July 21, 1827. m. Joel Nasebury (?).
(2259) Lydia, September 30, 1828. m. Melvin Thomas, in 1856. 3 chil. d. April 3, 1871.
(2260) Susan, April 18, 1832. m. C. F. Wellington, September 30, 1852.
(2261) Ruth, March 23, 1835. d. October 4, 1852.
(2262) Harriet, November 9, 1836. m. Ezra Matthews, 1856.

Amos was killed by lightning June 29, 1837.

---

890 Harriet Knowlton and Robert Moore had:

(2263) Joanna.
(2264) Susan.
(2265) Harriett.
(2266) Daniel. d. in War of the Rebellion.

---

891 Lewis Knowlton

served on a man-of-war in the War of 1812. Having been wounded in the arm, he was requested to go below and have the wound dressed. He replied:

"No! Not as long as I have an arm or leg to give to my country."

In the next round from the enemy, a ball pierced his body, and he fell dead.

892 George and Ruth Holmes had :

(2267) Thomas, February 4, 1818. m. Sarah Prescott, April 8, 1845.
(2268) Sarah J., February 14, 1820. m. O. B. Robinson, October 15, 1844.
(2269) George, April 23, 1822. d. 1823.
(2270) Eliza M., July 25, 1828. m. Martin S. Cottrell, 1846. m. 2d Dexter McLellan.
(2271) Ruth, January 30, 1824. d. young.
(2272) George, October 10, 1825. d. 1826.
(2273) Mark, August 13, 1830. m. Mary E. Shaw, November 30, 1852.
(2274) Harriet, December 7, 1832. m. Fred. A. Dickey, November 2, 1852. 3 chil.
(2275) Hiram, March 11, 1835. d. 1836.
(2276) Helen, May 3, 1837. m. A. A. Fletcher, February 10, 1859. d. November 6, 1870.
(2277) Malvena, October 15, 1839. m. Alonzo E. Fletcher, November 3, 1862. Had 3 chil. m. 2d R. D. Fish, 1874.

894 Nathaniel and Rachel Pottle had :

(2278) George M., August 15, 1835. m. Nellie Matthews, December 9, 1866.
(2279) Julia A., January 24, 1837. m. David H. Rose, July 17, 1861.
(2280) Albert H., September 17, 1840. m. Judith M. Nelson. 2 chil.
(2281) Byron O., July 16, 1843. m. Hannah J. Doane, August 23, 1868.
(2282) Chas. A., October 2, 1841. m. Hattie Bacon, February 2, 1870. res., Malden, Mass.
(2283) James, November 17, 1846. d. young.
(2284) Clara, December 6, 1847. m. Christopher Cottrell.
(2285) Rachel, December 23, 1849. d. January 25, 1870.
(2286) Vinal, April 30, 1852. d. December 16, 1879.
(2287) Nathaniel, January 17, 1854. d. October 10, 1871.

Rachel d. August 31, 1872.

895 Abraham and Lucinda Billings had :

(2288) Lewis, February 21, 1825. m. Lizzie Pendleton, December 25, 1848. Res. in Bedford, Me.
(2289) Fred. A., October 23, 1826. m. Lizzie Rhodes, January 14, 1855.
(2290) Cyrus, February 22, 1828.
(2291) Abraham, January 16, 1830. m. Jeanette Wylie.
(2292) Abina, August 2, 1831. m. —— Tyler.
(2293) Franklin, August 8, 1834. m. Mary Winslow.
(2294) Lucinda, September 4, 1836.

896 Bernard and Betsey Sargent had:

(2295) Barnet S., February 26, 1812. m. Elizabeth Pulsifer.
(2296) John C., 1813. m. Hannah Allen.
(2297) Betsey, July 7, 1814. m. —— Douglass.
(2298) George W. m. Harriet Rust.
(2299) Mehitable.

Betsey d. June 22, 1876.

---

897 Benjamin and Lydia Haskell had:

(2300) Lydia, June 16, 1814.
(2301) Elizabeth, August 31, 1817.
Residence, Ipswich, Mass.

Lydia d. 1876.

---

902 Johnathan and Molly Knowlton had:

(2302) Polly, September 4, 1802.
(2303) Sophronia, December 20, 1804.
(2304) Jonathan, August 5, 1807.
(2305) Anna, August 8, 1810. m. Henry Dodge, August 20, 1831.
(2306) Ebenezer, May 2, 1812.
(2307) Abraham, September 19, 1821.
(2308) Ann Maria, April 19, 1823. m. Joseph Simonds, 1841.

---

905 Josiah and Miriam Draper had:

(2309) Alvan, December 22, 1797. m. Lucy Perry, 1822. He d. August 7 1867. She d. October 21, 1868.
(2310) Charles. m. Adaline Weatherbee.
(2311) William. m. Sarah Farnham.

Josiah d. August 6, 1829. Miriam d. February 21, 1809.

---

907 Oliver and Mary Dodd had:

(2312) Almira, February 5, 1803. d. 1813.
(2313) Walter, February 27, 1805. m. Harriet Carter, May 7, 1834. He d. April 8, 1885.
(2314) George, September 25, 1810. d. young.

(2315) Mary, December 23, 1814. m. Wm. Flagg.
(2316) Eliza, August 20, 1818. m. Theodore A. Barton, July 27, 1837. 4 chil. Res., Middlebury, Mass.
(2317) Charles, September 2, 1820. m. Maria L. Bullard, December 25, 1845. He d. 1887.

Oliver d. May 24, 1854. Mary d. October 14, 1868.

---

908 Asa and Alice Divoli had:

(2318) Joseph, June 1, 1805. m. Louisa Swallow; m. 2d Nancy Upton.
(2319) Sarah, January 23, 1807. m. Albert Merrill, November 13, 1841.
(2320) Emily, October 9, 1809. m. Thomas Hammons, September 30, 1832.
(2321) Joel, November 6, 1811. d. March 14, 1858.
(2322) William, March 28, 1814. m. Emeline Shutleff, October 15, 1855.
(2323) Delnah, June 12, 1816. m. Chas. Gillis, October 31, 1837.
Residence, Sterling and Lancaster, Mass.

Asa d. July 13, 1857.

---

912 Elisha and 2d wife, Polly Chamberlain, had:

(2324) Hannah, July 18, 1812. m. Joseph Appleton, November 3, 1829.
(2325) Mary, July 18, 1812. m. Reuben Thwing.
(2326) John T., December 20, 1813.
(2327) Elisha.
(2328) Emeline. m. J. W. Larned, October 23, 1834. Res., St. Johnsbury, Vt.
(2329) Harriet, 1820. m. Prentiss W. Greenwood.
(2330) Andrew.
(2331) Helen M. m. Joseph W. Russell.

Polly d. December 5, 1835. Elisha was a blacksmith.

---

914 Daniel and Lucinda Blake had:

(2332) Daniel, February 11, 1804. m. Lucy Dodd, March 8, 1827.
(2333) Jeremiah, August 17, 1805. m. Jane Stoddard.
(2334) Maria, June 4, 1809. m. Winslow Fairbanks, October 13, 1829.
(2335) Caroline, December 16, 1813. m. Chas. C. Green, July 4, 1840.
(2336) George, February 4, 1816. m. —— Flagg.
(2337) Franklin, June 12, 1819. d. young.

(2338) Louise. m. Morrill Abbott, October 8, 1840.
(2339) Susan. m. B. W. Abbott, January 15, 1845.
(2340) Austin, December 9, 1824. m. Abby H. Crosby, November 27, 1845.
(2341) Angeline, 1829. d. June 7, 1845.
Residence, Holden, Mass.

Daniel d. July 14, 1877. Lucinda was from Holden. She d. April 30, 1861.

---

915 Jesse and Polly Blake had:

(2342) Betsey, October 24, 1794. m. Seth Clapp, Jr., November 26, 1812.
(2343) Leonard, May 30, 1796. Sand Lake, N. Y.
(2344) Polly, December 19, 1797. m. —— Paterson.
(2345) Susan, October 5, 1799. m. —— Greenwood. d. 1888.
(2346) Harriet N., September 9, 1814. m. W. E. Minturn, May 16, 1825. Res., Boston, Mass.
(2347) Curtis, 1805. m. Amanda Butcher, 1834.
(2348) Lucy. m. —— Walker.
(2349) Jason. m. Adeline Partridge, November 11, 182–. He d. June 9, 1844. Res., Worcester.
Alona. m. —— Stow.
Residence, Holden, Mass.

---

916 Luther and Prudence Dadman had:

(2350) Pauline, November 1, 1801. d. August 31, 1831.
(2351) Eunice, March 8, 1803. m. Mark Webster, July 3, 1832.
(2352) Luther D., April 1, 1806. m. Mary A. Derby.
(2353) Charles, March 8, 1809. d. young.
(2354) Elias W., October 8, 1811. m. Margaret Cannon.

Luther d. February 8, 1857. Prudence d. October 13, 1843.

---

919 Simeon and Hannah Wrisley had:

(2355) Asa, September 15, 1821. d. young.
(2356) Simeon, August 25, 1822. d. August 8, 1859.
(2357) Lydia, July 10, 1824.
(2358) Josiah, January 25, 1827.

Hannah d. February 22, 1827, and Simeon m. Content Wrisley, March 26, 1829. They had:

(2359) Olive, August 10, 1830.
(2360) Deborah, November 2, 1832.
(2361) Elias, June 18, 1834.
(2362) Asa, March 14, 1836.
(2363) Mary, March 1, 1837.
(2364) James, May 28, 1839. m. 1864. d. December 14, 1876. Residence, Dublin, N. H.

Content d. March 30, 1840, and Simeon m. Caroline Hortley, December 3, 1843. He d. September, 1877.

---

923 Leonard and Angeline Coleman had;

(2365) Ezra, October 9, 1825. m. Elizabeth Gabler, June 12, 1858.
(2366) Ansel, August 27, 1827. m. Rebecca Carman, December 23, 1851.
(2367) Orville, July 31, 1829. m. Charlotte Bronson, July 18, 1857. Res. in Durhamville, N. Y. 3 chil.
(2368) Eliza, March 11, 1831. m. Wilson Gillett, December 15, 1850; m. 2d —— Gabler.
(2369) Isaiah C., June 18, 1835. m. Maria Cummins, May 7, 1857. Res. in Troy, N. Y. 4 chil.
(2370) Royal H., July 19, 1837. m. Susan Maxwell, June 26, 1860. Res. Canastota, N. Y.
(2371) Minton, July 19, 1837. Killed at Turkey Bend, August 12, 1863.
(2372) Harriet A., December 26, 1846. m. Ferdinand Truell. Res., Lincoln, Neb.

Leonard was born in Worcester, Mass., and removed to Willett, N. H., thence to Sand Lake, N. Y., in 1830, and d. July 15, 1875. Angeline d. January 30, 1879.

---

929 Micah and —— had;

(2373) Albert.
(2374) Charles. Res., Ashland, Mass.
(2375) A dau. Marlborough, N. H.

---

935 Nathan and Eunice Randall had:

(2376) Warren. m. —— Gorgan. Res., Hoosac, N. Y.
(2377) Mary. m. —— Reynolds.

(2378) Pauline.
(2379) Harriett.
(2380) A. B. m. Martha ——. Res., Sand Lake, N. Y.

Nathan d. at Sand Lake, N. Y., 1873. Eunice d. February 1, 1864.

---

936 Martha Knowlton and Isaac Hunt had:

(2381) Moses, December 22, 1788.
(2382) Aaron, October 10, 1790.
(2383) David, December 26, 1792. d. young.
(2384) Isaac, February 4, 1795.
(2385) Betsey, July, 1802.
(2386) Harriet, July 3, 1805.
(2387) Hannah, August 13, 1807.
(2388) Sarah, May 28, 1809.
(2389) David, October 12, 1811.
(2390) Alvira, October 12, 1813.
Residence, Hancock, N. H.

---

940 Abigail Knowlton and Samuel Moore had:

(2390 A) Letitia, January 13, 1816. m. Horace Butterfield, June 11, 1837.
(2390 B) James, March 13, 1818. m. Almira Knowlton, September 24, 1846.
Residence rem. from Londonderry to Dublin, N. H. in 1812.

---

941 Betsey Knowlton and Samuel Derby had:

(2391) Elvira, December 8, 1806. m. Harvey Learned, December 20, 1825.
(2392) Mary A., May 17, 1808. m. Luther D. Knowlton, February 4, 1832.
(2393) Dexter, July 10, 1810. m. Julia Davis, December 17, 1840.
(2394) Franklin, May 20, 1812. m. Susannah ——, 1835. He d. September 6, 1836.
(2395) Webster, July 28, 1814. d. April 22, 1835. unm.
(2396) Betsey J., November 27, 1819. m. Charles Whittemore of Ravenswood, L. I., January 29, 1839.
Residence, Clearwater, Minnesota.

Betsey d. March 28, 1833.

942 Thaddeus and Rebecca Bishop had:

(2397) Eliza. m. Simon Flagg.
(2398) Lyman. m. Jane Grey, of Petersham.
(2399) Sylvia. m. John Todd; m. 2d George Todd; m. 3d —— Chandler.
(2400) Dexter, 1813. m. Mary Newell, December 2, 1834.

Rebecca d. January 14, 1826.

---

944 Henry and Polly Leonard had:

(2401) Levi, June, 1831. m. Caroline Simonds. Rem. to Chester, Vt.

---

947 Luke and Mercy Bemis had:

(2402) James, December 20, 1828. m. Amelia Mason, 1854.
(2403) Luke, Jr., September 5, 1830. m. M. J. Pierce, 1854.
(2404) Eli B., December 8, 1833. m. Elmira Stone, January 11, 1858.
(2405) Caroline E., January 27, 1836. m. W. M. Mason, June 6, 1855. She d. December, 1862.
(2406) Charles, June 23, 1838. He d. in Poolesville, Md., June 6, 1864. Soldier in the Rebellion, 14th Regiment, N. H. Volunteers.
(2407) Lois J., March 10, 1842. d. young.
(2408) Sarah, November 27, 1843. m. W. M. Nason, November 27, 1862.
(2409) Maria J., September 30, 1847. d. young.

Residence, Marlborough and Nelson, N. H.

---

949 Mary Knowlton and Cornelius Towne had:

(2410) John P.
(2411) Cornelius.
(2412) Hannah C.
(2413) Gilbert.
(2414) Mary E.

Residence, Dublin, N. H.

Mary d. May 19, 1836.

---

950 Levi and Mrs. Lucy Hadley had:

(2415) Mary H., April 7, 1833. m. S. Nixon.

951 Isaiah and Clarissa Spooner had:

(2416) Clarissa, January 17, 1822. m. Robert Lamphier, 1848.
(2417) Royal, June 9, 1823. m. Mercy Whitman, 1849.
(2418) Eunice, August 9, 1824.
(2419) Leonard, February 4, 1826. m. Lauretta L. Lowe, December 19, 1852.
(2420) Isaiah S., October 11, 1827.
(2421) Cyrus, March 9, 1829. d. September 26, 1848.
(2422) Sarah, July 11, 1830. m. Stephen Lamphier, January, 1852.
(2423) Henry, December 17, 1831. m. Lucretia Harlow, 1855.

Clarissa died March 6, 1837, and Isaiah m. Lydia Pollard. They had:

(2424) Kendall, April 15, 1838. m. Mary A. Butcher, March 3, 1860.
(2425) William, October 21, 1839. m. Ellen C. Flanders, 1867.
(2426) Croyden, February 4, 1841. m. Lucy Noble, April 11, 1860.
(2427) Thomas, March 8, 1842. m. Rosilla Pratt, 1864.
(2428) Lydia, April 20, 1846. d. young.
(2429) George, July, 14 1847. d. young.

Isaiah d. March 5, 1875.

---

953 William and Jeanette Waterman had:

(2430) Aaron, May 29, 1830. m. Ianthe Harlow, 1867; m. 2d Ruth Davis 1863.
(2431) Mary L, October 25, 1831. m. Abel Oakes, November 15, 1854.
(2432) Chas. H., November 15, 1833. m. Grace Howard 1866.
(2433) Susan F., July 13, 1836. m. Henry C. Parsons, 1857.
(2434) Emily J., July 28, 1841. m. Freeland W. Thompson, December 3, 1871.

---

954 Nancy Knowlton and Asa Jackson had:

(2435) Alden, August 29, 1831. d. 1834.
(2436) Prentiss, September 3, 1832. d. 1847.
(2437) William, December 7, 1833.
(2438) Edwin, January 1, 1836.
(2439) Ann M., March 4, 1839. d. young.
(2440) Martin H., May 1, 1840.
(2441) Alden, July 1, 1843.
(2442) Lorene, March 31, 1847.

955 Henry and Hannah Downs had:

(2443) Maria L., November 30, 1832. m. Josiah Herdsly, March 23, 1859.
(2444) Harriet, July 1, 1835. d. March 27, 1860.
(2445) Harrison, December 1, 1840. d. June 9, 1852.
(2446) Amelia, November 23, 1847. d. April 17, 1870.
(2447) Margaret, May 25, 1843. m. L. T. Waterman, June 23, 1869.

---

956 Mary Knowlton and Wm. Burgess had:

(2448) John C., April 5, 1831. m. Betsey A. Merrill, December 14, 1852.
(2449) Hannah, November 14, 1833. m. S. T. Merrill, December 31, 1860.
(2450) Jemima S., August 9, 1835. m. A. M. Ayer, April 16, 1867.
(2451) Mary E., September 14, 1837. m. J. B. Harlow, March 14, 1860.
(2452) William, June 17, 1839. m. Anna Barrett, September 2, 1868.
(2453) Mattie A., April 7, 1843. d. December 20, 1869.
(2454) Charles A., August 5, 1847.
(2455) Susie M., December 28, 1848. d. 1873.

---

961 Ebenezer and Nancy Knowlton had:

(2456) Irene M., 1809. m. Emelyn Leland, 1843.
(2457) Susanna, 1812. d. young.
(2458) Daniel, 1814. m. Rebecca Sleeper; m. 2d Hannah Davis.
(2459) Henry, 1816. m. Angeline Hubbard.
(2460) Susannah, 1818. d. 1841.
(2461) Alpheus, 1822. m. Eliza Snow.
(2462) Eliza M., 1825. m. Daniel Metcalf.
(2463) Nason, 1827. d. young.

Res., Hopkinton, N. H.

Ebenezer d. July 20, 1871.

---

962 Jesse and Sarah Wight had:

(2464) Mary W., February 18, 1817. m. J. Phelps, September 1, 1840.
(2465) Jabez, March 9, 1822. m. Joanna ——

Sarah d. February, 1829.

---

963 Silas and Susannah Nutting had:

(2466) Benjamin F., December 1, 1818. d. August 18, 1826.
(2467) Asa H., September 8, 1820. d. young.

(2468) Elmira, October 23, 1823. m. James Moore, September 24, 1846; m. 2d Rufus Cogswell, September, 184-.
(2469) Susan, September 1, 1825. m. Phineas Hemmingway, April 18, 1844.

Susannah d. January 1, 1832, and Silas m. 2d Elizabeth Hardy, May 26, 1832, and had:

(2470) Harriet, March 10, 1833. m. Minot Hemmingway, March, 1856.
(2471) Asa, March 2, 1834. m. Lydia Darling, 1859.

---

964 John and Lois Bemis had:

(2472) Sylvester, November 22, 1817. m. Maria Rowell, 1848.
(2473) Josiah, March 14, 1819. m. Rachel Powers, 1845.
(2474) James M., November 16, 1821. m. Olive Palmer, 1849. Res., Dublin, N. H.

John d. December 12, 1824. (Another date given 1831.)

---

965 Jeremy and Elizabeth Farnham had:

(2475) Jeremy, February 19, 1820. m. Jeanette Marsh, December 4, 1850.
(2476) Joseph, June 2, 1823. m. Martha Weaver, 1847.
(2477) Louisa, August 27, 1826. m. Israel Green, December 1, 1847.
(2478) Levi, February 1, 1830. m. Mrs. Martha Knowlton.

---

966 Eunice Knowlton and James Upton had:

(2479) Daniel, September 29, 1828. m. Lovinia Ludwig, December 18, 1856.
(2480) Susannah, February 12, 1831.
(2481) Algina, August 26, 1833. m. Frank Bidwell.
(2482) Martha, June 30, 1837. d. April 30, 1850.
(2483) Francis F., March 15, 1841. d. 1852.

---

970 Dr. Benjamin and Polly Jackman had:

(2484) Mercy, February 14, 1794. m. Warren Clough, November, 1825.
(2485) Enoch, May 14, 1796.
(2486) Elizabeth, February 20, 1799. m. Andrew Clark, December 26, 1826.
(2487) Mary, March 24, 1803. m. Warren Smith, June 10, 1829.
(2488) Hannah, July 17, 1808. m. Geo. Jessamine, January, 1832. She d. July 23, 1833.

(2489) Charlotte, May 11, 1811. m. Cyrus Richards. d. November 21, 1821.
(2490) Annette, September 27, 1815.

---

971 Joseph and Lois Flanders had:

(2491) John, December 11, 1801. m. Eliza Burpee. He d. August 3, 1838.
(2492) Eunice, March 6, 1803. d. September 30, 1849.

---

972 Rosel and Prudence Conkling of Pelham, Mass., had:

(2493) Susannah.
(2494) Mercy.
(2495) Sarah.
(2496) Chloe.
(2497) Jason.
(2498) Rosel.

---

973 Rev. Warren and Mary Dunbar had:

(2499) Josiah, August 20, 1815. m. Sarah Lippett, August 14, 1838.
(2500) Emeline.
(2501) Roswell A., November, 1819.
(2502) Hiram. d. young in Va.
(2503) William. d. young in Va.
(2504) Mary. m. Albert Lawson, of N. Y. City.
(2505) Nancy, August 22, 1823. m. W. S. Burt, November 30, 1843.

Rev. Warren Knowlton removed to Virginia in 1817, and cleared a good farm there, which he subsequently lost through a defective title.

In 1843 he removed to Cumberland and engaged in mercantile business. He was also a minister of the Baptist Church. His wife, Mary, was the dau. of Capt. Josiah Dunbar, a native of Scotland, and an officer in the U. S. service during the Revolutionary War.

---

974 Nancy Knowlton and James Bartlett had:

(2506) Carlisle.
(2507) Sophia.
(2508) Harriet.
(2509) Henry D.

(2510) Elisha.
(2511) Rebecca.
(2512) George.
(2513) Elmira.
(2514) Mary.
(2515) Susannah.

Nancy d. January 27, 1877.

---

975 Elisha and Nancy Hubbard had:

(2516) Lucy.
(2517) George.
(2518) Warren.

---

976 Susannah Knowlton and Josiah Dunbar had:

(2519) Nancy.
(2520) Mary R.
(2521) Elizabeth.
(2522) Marion.
(2523) Linus.
(2524) Emeline.

---

978 Rev. Gideon and Polly Hayden had:

(2525) Ackley. m. Lydia Sherman.
(2526) Henry. m. Tryphena Armstrong.
(2527) Polly. m. Gilbert Robinson. 4 chil.
(2528) Sally. m. Saul Williams. 6 chil.
(2529) Betsey. m. Selden Rathbone. 5 chil.
(2530) Lydia. m. John Renigan. 2 chil.
(2531) Mercy.
(2532) Elbridge.
(2533) Henry.

Rev. Gideon res. in Belchertown, Mass. He d. August 15, 1810. Polly d. August 29, 1822.

---

980 Roswell and Lydia Stone had:

(2534) Jared. m. Charlotte Burright.
(2535) Alonzo de Castor, October 31, 1804. m. Margaret Parkinson, 1828.
(2536) James. m. Delia Bennett.

(2537) John. m. Pauline Hough.
(2538) Lucy. m. Hiram Burroughs. 3 chil.
(2539) Jane. m. Jeremiah Pierce. 3 chil.

Resided in Belchertown, Mass., and removed to Troy, N. Y. Roswell d. 1839.

---

998 Friend and Alice Hammen had:

(2540) Nathan.
(2540 A) Joshua.

---

999 Betsey Knowlton and Martin Wheelock had:

(2541) Willis.
(2542) Samuel.

She d. June 8, 1874.

1000 John and Roxana Wheeler had:

(2543) Caroline.
(2544) Marietta.

1001 Sylvia Knowlton and Samuel Bradford had:

(2545) Ansel.
(2546) Fidelia.
(2547) Edward.

Sylvia d. November 16, 1851.

1002 Oren and Jane Fulton had:

(2548) Fidelia.

1004 Sally Knowlton and Joshua Shumway had:

(2549) Harrison.
(2550) Harriet.
(2551) Oren.
(2552) Luther.
(2553) Laura.
(2554) A dau.

1005 Polly Knowlton and John Bidwell had;

(2555) Betsey.
(2556) Amanda.
(2557) George.
(2558) A dau.

1006 Elijah and Sally Brown had:

(2559) Maria.

1007 Ebenezer and Mehitable Welch had:

(2560) Ebenezer, 1800. Drowned in Echo Lake, Hopkinton, Mass., April 21, 1821.
(2561) Joseph, August 5, 1802. Drowned in Echo Lake, Hopkinton, Mass., April 21, 1821.
(2562) Eliza, January 23, 1807. m. Daniel J. Coburn.
(2563) William, June 29, 1809. m. Caroline Taft, January 1, 1833.

Ebenezer was b. in Medway, and went, when young, to Rowe, Mass. He was a surgeon in General Dearborn's division, War of 1812, was taken prisoner and sent to Dartmoor, England. Term of service four years. He d. 1826. Mehitable d. 1845.

1008 Joseph and Betsey Johnson had:

(2564) Charlotte, March 6, 1807. m. Asaph Munson, February 22, 1824. She d. May 8, 1885. Res., Clarkson, N. Y.
(2565) Emily, November 17, 1808. m. Abraham Countryman, September 17, 1826. She d. May 16, 1895. Res., Clarkson, N. Y.
(2566) Betsey, January 30, 1811. m. Morgan Barnes, February 24, 1828. She d. May 24, 1893.
(2567) Seneca, December, 1812. m. Polly Maria Stevens, March 10, 1833.
(2568) Sidney, October 30, 1813. m. Sarah Barnes, May 13, 1841; m. 2d Elizabeth Foster, 1853.
(2569) Angeline, January 10, 1818. m. Wm. Greene, May 30, 1839; m. 2d James Billings, 1856.

Joseph was b. in Mass., removed to Salisbury, Vt., married there his wife Betsey, of Leicester, Vt., and thence emigrated to Leroy, N. Y., finally settling in Clarkson, N. Y. He was a farmer, and he made the then long journey in an ox cart. He d. 1823 and Betsey d. at Parma, N. Y., September 20, 1863.

1009 Benjamin and Betsey Grant had:

(2571) Betsey, 1808.
(2572) Hannah, 1810.
(2573) John R., 1812. m. Mrs. McFalls, June 14, 1865.
(2574) Stephen, 1814. d. 1858.
(2575) Benjamin.
(2576) Polly.
(2577) Charles, d. 1864.
(2578) Phoebe J. m. —— Woodman.
(2579) Milo A. d. March 17, 1867.
(2580) Sophie.
(2581) Franklin.
(2582) William. m. —— ——.
(2583) An infant. d. young.

Benjamin rem. to Le Roy, N. Y., where he kept a hotel for many years. He finally disappeared, and his relatives have no knowledge of his subsequent residence and history, except that he is reported to have d. at the house of Robert McFalls, Ashtabula, O.

1010 Mary Knowlton and James Clark had:

(2584) John.
(2585) Sallie.
(2586) Katie.
(2587) Daniel.
(2588) David.
(2589) Huldah.

1012 Hannah Knowlton and —— Keyes had:

(2590) Eli.
(2591) Sallie.
(2592) Hannah.
(2593) Ruel.
(2594) Ezra.
(2595) Polly.
(2596) Nathan.
(2597) Lawton.
(2598) Azuba.
(2599) Daniel.

Residence, Reedsboro, Vt.

1013 Paul and Eunice Shaw had:

(2600) Comfort, January 9, 1804. d. young.
(2601) William, June 7, 1806. m. Charlotte Haskell, May 31, 1825.
(2602) Paul, June 28, 1809. m. Susan Beckley, December 15, 1836.
(2603) Daniel, February 2, 1810. d. July 28, 1855.
(2604) Eunice, January 17, 1813.
(2605) Sally, September 14, 1815.
(2606) Napoleon, August 8, 1817.

Paul d. July 20, 1817.

1015 Huldah Knowlton and Wm. Bratton had:

(2607) Lydia.
(2608) David.
(2609) Robert.
(2610) Sallie.
(2611) Henry.
(2612) Joseph.

1019 Timothy and Eunice Rice had:

(2613) Timothy, May 23, 1792. m. Unity Plimpton, 1821; m. 2d Lydia Todd, 1831.
(2614) John, January 11, 1794. m. Ruth Stone, 1819. He d. March 19, 1869.
(2615) Ephraim, June 7, 1795. m. Sally Eldridge of Deerfield, Mass.
(2616) Eunice, December 4, 1796. 4 chil.
(2617) Nancy, March 26, 1798. m. —— Stone.
(2618) Mary, December 13, 1799. m. —— Blakeslee. Had s. Dr. Edwin. Res., Los Angeles, Cal.
(2619) Aaron, September 10, 1801. 5 chil.
(2620) Polly, April 27, 1803.
(2621) Abigail, April 22, 1805. m. Dexter Moore, 1827.
(2622) Rhoda, April 27, 1807.

Eunice was drowned August 12, 1808, and Timothy m. 2d Sarah Baxter, and had:

(2623) Daniel, April 11, 1810. d. arch 27, 1818.
(2624) Sarah, January 29, 1812. d. August 17, 1815.
(2625) Anna, July 11, 1813. d. August 20, 1816.
(2626) Wm. Rice, March 1, 1815.

(2627) Sarah, February 2, 1817. m. —— Holcombe.
(2628) Joseph M., June 12, 1818. m. Hannah Wheeler. He d. April 8, 1872. Hannah res. in Whittingham, Vt
(2629) Horace, June 12, 1818.

Residence, Rowe, Mass.

Sarah, 2d wife, d. October 24, 1859.

1020 Samuel Brooks and Eunice Bass had:

(2630) Juliana. m. Danforth Armour.
(2631) Lucy Knowlton.
(2632) Maria.

1028 – ([illegible] sheet)

1032 Joshua Knowlton,

b. October 21, 1760, is thought by some to have been killed in the Revolutionary War. As a possible refutation of this belief, the following will be interesting to the reader. Many years since, a man of about forty years of age called on Mr. Geo. H. Knowlton, of Lowell, Mass., introducing himself as Carl Knowlton, from Vienna, Austria, claiming to be a son of Joshua, who fought in the Revolutionary War. He presented a letter from his father, in which the writer claimed to be the identical soldier, and said that at the close of the war he had left the country with the German troops, having formed intimate friendships with some of them, and settled in Germany, where he had married a native. He was anxious to have his son visit his relatives in Connecticut, and he was liberally supplied with funds for that purpose. Mr. Geo. H. Knowlton gave him suitable letters for that purpose, from which nothing further was heard. There can be but little doubt that Joshua, not returning to Ashford, was believed to have been killed in the war, and that Carl was his son.

1033 Harney and —— Wheeler had:

(2633) Fanelia, September 2, 1765. m. —— Hill. 2 chil.

Residence, Ashford, Conn.

1034 Fanelia Knowlton and —— Wheeler had:

(2633 A) John.
(2634) Polly.
(2635) Permelia.

Residence, New York City.

1028

On page 180, Julia a Brooks [2630] (who married Danforth Armour); and Lucy Knowlton Brooks [2631]; and Maria Brooks [2632] were not the children of Samuel Brooks [1020] (who married Eunice Bass), but were the children of his younger brother, Simon Brooks [1028], b. 22 Dec., 1767, d. 4 June, 1844, listed on page 82. However, Simon is a misspelling and should read Simeon.

The "American Dictionary of Biography" shows that Lucy [Lucinda] Knowlton [1051], (page 89 of Knowlton Genealogy) who was youngest daughter of Col. Thomas Knowlton [425] married Simeon Brooks.

This agrees with the family traditions of their descendants, one of whom is Mr. Simeon Brooks Chapin, banker and broker of Chicago and New York City. His mother was Marietta Armour Chapin, who was daughter of Danforth and Juliana Brooks Armour.

Signed,
Jennie B. Chapin

1036 Stephen and Eunice Swan had:

(2636) Joshua, August, 1797. m. Eliza Holmes, March 13, 1821.
(2637) Ephraim, April 13, 1800. m. Irene Butler; m. 2d Mrs. Barbery Berry.
(2638) Hannah. m. A. H. Adams; m. 2d D. C. Clinton.
(2639) Lucinda. m. George Holmes.
(2640) Ann, February 3, 1806. m. Judge Samuel H. Dowden, June 1, 1843.
(2641) Stephen, 1810. m. Almira Finch.
(2642) Renselliaer, April 15, 1811. m. Marilla Caulkins.
(2643) Schuyler. d. young.

Stephen rem. from Stonington, Conn., to Berne Township, N. Y., where all his children were b., and thence to Indiana in 1818.

1041 Daniel and Betsey Burchard had:

(2644) Nathaniel, January 17, 1794. m. Temperance Day, October 6, 1818.
(2645) Clarissa, May 15, 1795. d. young.
(2646) Lydia, September 21, 1797. d. young.
(2647) Phineas, November 8, 1800. d. in U. S. Navy, October, 1827.
(2648) Gordon, January 18, 1803. m. Arethusa Atwood.
(2649) Manassah, June 30, 1805. m. Sally Stebbins.
(2650) Calista, December 2, 1807. m. Herman Corbin.

Residence, Ashford, Conn.

1043 Nathaniel and Sarah Leach, of Stonington, Conn., had:

(2651) Rev. Farnham, September 8, 1800. m. Sarah Ingersoll, July 18, 1830.
(2652) Emily A., February 5, 1802. d. April 1, 1880. East Greenbush.
(2653) Hosea, January 6, 1804. m. Sabina Bentley. d. April 4, 1857. Albany, N. Y.
(2654) Dr. Myron, April 12, 1806. m. Melissa Buffum.
(2655) William, May 5, 1808. m. Ann M. Vanderberg, February 11, 1836.
(2656) Nathaniel, July 4, 1814. m. Maria Potts, December 19, 1833.

NATHANIEL KNOWLTON

was the son of Lieutenant Daniel, of Ashford, Conn., and a twin brother of Manassah. When he was but fourteen years old, his father came home on a furlough, and in the course of conversation offered his old French musket to that son who would go back with him. Nathaniel promptly volunteered, and remairied until the close of the war. He rem. to Greenbush, N. Y., in 1800, and carried on farming there. Although a soldier by nature and by profession, he was the peace-maker of the town in all public and private disputes, and his profound Christian character gave has counsels decisive weight. Between him and his brother Manassah there existed a most tender and poetic attachment.

In his old age Nathaniel used to entertain the young people by shouldering his staff, and marching about his home singing patriotic songs with enthusiasm. He served in the War of 1812, was a pensioner, and d. at Greenbush July 6, 1852. Sarah d. February 7, 1844.

1044 Manassah and Lydia Burton had :

(2657) Oren, September 17, 1794. d. young.
(2658) Ephraim, December 9, 1795. d. January 5, 1824.
(2659) Isaac, May 7, 1797. d. May 23, 1883. m. Rachel Whitbeck.
(2660) Orendia, February 20, 1799. d. October 1861. m. Benj. Bradbury, February 20, 1818.
(2661) Almyra, February 1, 1801. d. September 10, 1827.
(2662) Maria, October 13, 1802. d. February 9, 1830.
(2663) George Washington, January 16, 1804. d. October 11, 1884.
(2664) Parmelia, August 16, 1805. d. young.

MANASSAH KNOWLTON

was born in Ashford, Ct., December 24, 1770. His resemblance to his twin brother Nathaniel was so complete that the identity of the two boys could be established only by a dimple in Manassah's cheek, and his own mother was often obliged to excite him to laughter that she might certainly know which of the two he really was. At the age of twenty-one, Manassah settled in Greenbush, N. Y., near the City of Albany, and having learned the blacksmith's trade he opened a shop of his own on the Renssellaer and Columbia Turnpike, the main and post road connecting Albany with N. Y. City and Boston.

The large number of horses used by mail and stage coaches and by travellers of every class—the only means of transit at that time—gave Manassah a flourishing business, and during the War of 1812 it was common enough to see a group of cavalry horses at his shop door at four o'clock in the morning, waiting to be shod by the young Vulcan. In 1798, he purchased a farm of 162 acres, near by, formerly a part of "yé Manor of Rensselaerwyck," of which Stephen Van Renssellaer was the proprietor, and thereafter worked the farm and the shop together. Originally an "Open Communion Baptist" and there being no congregation of this faith at Greenbush, Manassah declined to unite with any church until eight years before his death, when he became a member of the M. E. Church, adorning his profession with "excellency of virtue and innocence of life."

MANASSAH KNOWLTON'S HOUSE,
Greenbush, N. Y.

His patriotic spirit was of the true and historic Knowlton type, and on June 8, 1808, he was commissioned Lieut. in Lt.-Col. Philip Staats's regiment of militia, being promoted to a Captaincy, February 29, 1812.

He was a thrifty, industrious, solid, benevolent man, whose advice young and old sought and followed, and whose character gave him in later years the honored name of "Father Knowlton."

He married 1st Lydia Burton of Schodack N. Y., who d. July 15, 1806; m. 2d Elizabeth Card of Greenbush, N. Y.; m. 3d Clarissa Cogswell, Greenbush, N. Y.

Manassah d. at Greenbush, January 21, 1841.

1045 Ephraim Knowlton and Jemima Farnham had:

(2665) Sidney. Rem. to Utah, and d. there.
(2666) Martha. m. Benj. Hanks. d. January 13, 1861.
(2667) Catherine. m. Wm. Chaffee, Ashford, Conn.
(2668) Lydia. d. 1853. m. Ebenezer Eastman.
(2669) Marcia. d. 1849. m. Benj. Eastman.
(2670) Ephraim, Jr., 1804. m. Mary A. Burgoyne. He d. February 1, 1888.

1046 Martha Knowlton and C. W. Brandon had:

(2671) Charles.
(2672) Rebecca.
(2673) Edward.

Residence, Ashford, Ct.

Martha d. March 30, 1855.

1047 Keziah and Amasa Lyon had:

(2674) Amasa Knowlton, July 4, 1806. d. August 28, 1822.
(2675) Marcus, July 3, 1809. d. April 29, 1810.
(2676) Delotia, October 15, 1811. m. John W. Trowbridge, April 10, 1837.
(2677) Sophronia, January 4, 1813. m. John W. Hasler.
(2678) Lorenzo, February 9, 1815. Res. in Eastford, Ct.
(2679) Elizabeth Ann, November 8, 1816. m. Ebenezer Knowlton.
(2680) Gen. Nathaniel, July 14, 1818. Killed in the Rebellion, August 10, 1861.
(2681) Daniel, November 14, 1819. Res. in Eastford, Ct.
(2682) Lyman, March 30, 1822. Res. in Lowell, Mass.

1049 Erastus Fenton and Waite Windsor had :

(2689) Rebekah, F., August 11, 1817. m. Henry S. Angell, October 12, 1836.
Waite d. April 8, 1819, and Erastus m. 2d Rhoda Gage of Monson, Mass., May 16, 1820. No chil.

1050 Marvin and Calista Leonard had :

(2690) Rebecca F., August 3, 1821. m. Samuel Paul, September 16, 1838. She d. 1840.
(2691) Silence, June 30, 1823. m. Samuel Paul. Res. in Canada.
(2692) Rosina, February 12, 1828. m. Hiram Tufts. She d. 1849. No chil.
(2693) Elbridge, August 27, 1830.
(2694) Marvin, September 16, 1837. unm. Res., Willimantic, Ct.
(2695) Maria B., September, 1837. m. Henry Upton, March 1, 1869.

1051 FREDERIC KNOWLTON.

son of Col. Thomas, inherited his father's spirit. When the first rumor of hostilities reached him, he left home secretly, walked hurriedly as far as New London, and turned back only when he had learned the falsity of the rumor. When but fifteen, he swore that he was eighteen years old, in order to be accepted as a Volunteer. Although strictly forbidden to follow his father to Boston, he disobeyed, and when the men "fell in" at the word of command at Bunker Hill, Col. Knowlton detected his son mustering off to the left of the line. The father gave him a poor musket to discourage him from joining the ranks, but finding his resolution inflexible he substituted a good musket for the bad one, and offered no further opposition. He served under his father at Harlem Heights, after which Washington sent him home to assist in the support of his widowed mother.

1052 Sally Knowlton and Samuel Utley :

(2696) Sally, July 18, 1782, in Ashford. d. young.
(2697) Polly, February 10, 1784, in Ashford. m. Gershom House of Chesterfield, 1803. d. September 13, 1858.
(2698) Frederick, in Dalton (?), April 24, 1787. m. Cynthia Ludden, April 25, 1816. Res. in Chesterfield. d. in Westfield, Mass., April 5, 1856.
(2699) William, in Dalton (?). Res. in Chesterfield. d. in Williamsburg, Mass., December 28, 1871, aged 82 years. unm. Was a soldier in the War of 1812.
(2700) Sally, in Dalton (?). Res. in Chesterfield. d. July 12, 1846, aged 54 years. unm.

(2701) James, in Dalton (?). Res. in Chesterfield. d. December 4, 1817, aged 24 years. unm.

(2702) Ralph, in Dalton (?). m. Zeruah Baker. Res. in Chesterfield and Goshen. d. November 7, 1862, aged 66 years, 7 mos., without chil.

(2703) Samuel, in Dalton (?), February 19, 1798. m. Mary J. Eastman, April 14, 1834. d. August 20, 1883. Clergyman.

(2704) Thomas Knowlton, in Chesterfield, March, 1804. m. Theodocia Knox of Blandford, Mass., January 18, 1834. Res. in Chesterfield. d. November 6, 1847.

1053 Thomas Knowlton and Martha had :

(2705) Martha, December 14, 1811. m. William W. Marcy, 1832. d September 8, 1884.

(2706) Thomas M., September 10, 1808. d. July 5, 1811.

1054 Polly Knowlton and Stephen Fitts had, born in Ashford :

(2707) Christian, August 11, 1794. m. William Loomis, September 14, 1817. d. March 13, 1879.

(2708) Stephen, Jr., October 29, 1798. m. Waty Moore, November 24, 1830. d. October 23, 1875.

(2709) Maria, July 18, 1802. m. Selden Moseley, October 11, 1832. d. April 29, 1889.

(2710) Thomas Knowlton, July 11, 1807. d. February 7. 1831. unm.

1055 Abigail Knowlton and Thomas Chaffee had :

(2711) Sampson Knowlton, August 4, 1792. d. February 19, 1816.

(2712) Frederick, November 25, 1793. d. February 13, 1813.

(2713) Wolcott, May 3, 1795. m. Abigail Kingsley, April 22, 1818. d. November 25, 1870.

(2714) Newman K., December 15, 1796. m. 1st Elizabeth Phelps, March 15, 1820. m. 2d, Olive Abbott, March 1, 1837. d. in West Becket, Mass., December 15, 1858.

(2715) Miner, February 6, 1799. m. Lucy Frary, June 9, 1825. d. September 29, 1880.

(2716) Alma, February 9, 1801. m. W. M. P. Hamblin, November 8, 1830. d. in Lee, Mass., March 6, 1838.

(2717) Anna H., February 4, 1803. m. Justin M. Ames, January 20, 1824. d. August 17, 1859.

(2718) Thomas S., March 24, 1805. m. 1st Betsey Shaw, February 4, 1829. m. 2d Lucy Culver, January 3, 1832. m. 3d Catherine L. Blair, November 2, 1843. d. October 7, 1874.

(2719) Lucinda, January 12, 1807. m. Kendall Baird of Becket, Mass., October 10, 1827. d. April 1, 1863.

(2720) Prentiss, January 1, 1809. m. Betsey Cannon, April 15, 1833. d. April 10, 1892.

(2721) Abigail H., April 12, 1811. m. Wm. Clark, January 8, 1833.

(2722) Sampson Knowlton, July 11, 1814. m. Amelia Shaylor, January 27, 1839. d. November 19, 1891.

1065 Gideon and Mildred Curtis had :

(2723) Abner L. Rem. to California.

(2724) John C. d. U. S. Service, 1863.

(2725) Francis L.

Residence, Stoddard, N. H.

1067 Abner and Nancy Sweet had :

(2726) Jeanette. m. I. D. Woodman.

(2727) Mary F.

(2728) Norris E. d. young.

(2729) Hattie E. d. young.

(2730) Arielle. m. J. R. Putney.

Abner was a brick-maker. He rem. from Hancock, N. H., to Boston.

1068 Anna Knowlton and Ira Moulton had :

(2731) Enoch. Res. and d. in Lowell, Mass.

1069 Louisa Knowlton and George Ring had :

(2731 A) Gordon.

(2732) Mary.

(2733) Harriet.

(2734) Louisa.

(2735) George E.

(2736) Herbert A.

1070 Franklin and Persis Stacey had :

(2737) Albert N.
(2738) Ruel.
(2739) Amorette.
(2740) Annette.

1072 Sophronia Knowlton and Gordon Ring had :

(2741) Gardner W.
(2742) Francis.
(2743) Ida.
(2744) Augustus.

1074 Harriet and Nathaniel Mitchell had :

(2745) Augustus.

1078 Moses and Caroline Whitaker had :

(274) Moses, 1824.
(27) Luther.
(27) Mary.
(2749) Lucy.
(2750) Lucinda.
(2751) Benjamin.
(2752) William.
(2753) George. Last heard from in New Zealand.
(2754) Remembrance. Res. in New York.
(2755) Frederick.

1079 Abraham and Lucy Hildreth had :

(2756) Abraham, September, 29, 1827. m. Sarah White.
(2757) Susan W., May 24, 1829. m. ——— Robins.
(2758) Mary W. m. ——— Lovejoy.
(2759) Elmira.
(2760) Eliza.

1083 Sallie Knowlton and ——— Oliver had :

(2761) Charles.
(2762) Nathaniel.

(2763) Asa.
(2764) Anna.
(2765) Abigail.
(2766) Sarah.

1086 John and Charlotte Holmes had :

(2767) John, Jr., 1808. m.
(2768) Ward.
(2769) Thomas.
(2770) Nathan, 1819. m. Mary A. Stone, 1846. had son Leonard, 1848.
(2771) Hanson.
(2772) Clara.
(2773) Christiana.

The missing marginal numbers from 2774–2785 inclusive designate duplicate names elsewhere referred to.

1092 Calvin Knowlton and Betsey S. Peck had :

(2786) Hiram, April 16, 1813. m. Jane Wire.
(2787) Susan M., October 31, 1814. m. Harvey Watson, May 31, 1834.
(2788) Calvin P., April 15, 1816. m. Jerusha Colwell.
(2789) Erastus R., April 12, 1818. m. Abigail Wire. d. June 9, 1864, in Andersonville Prison. Soldier.
(2790) Josiah P., February 21, 1820. m. Calista House.
(2791) Parney H., January 13, 1822. m. Alvin G. Foote, August 31, 1842.
(2792) Stephen O., February 17, 1824. m. Mary Paine.
(2793) Betsey J., July 18, 1826. m. Abiram Rowley.
(2794) Manly C., December 23, 1829.
(2795) Joseph M., January 8, 1832. m. Anna Billings; m. 2d Charlotte McCormick.

1093 Diodemia Knowlton and Moses Camp had :

(2796) John, September 15, 1806. m. Ursula Whitney. 3 chil.; m. 2d Julia Root.
(2797) Harriett, February 6, 1810. m. Henry Dutton. Both d.
(2798) Adaline, March 11, 1812. d. young.
(2799) Mary, August 3, 1814. m. Elijah White. 2 dau.
(2800) Adaline, January 3, 1817. m. James J. Preston. Res., Winsted, Conn. 3 dau.

(2801) Emeline, June 3, 1819. m. Lewis Loomis. Res., Fulton, N. Y. 3 chil.
(2802) Goodloe, June 28, 1821. m. Hannah Tuttle. 3 chil.
(2803) Moses M., June 30, 1823. m. Amelia Worthington.
(2804) George G., February 11, 1826. m. Lydia Huntley.
(2805) Edgar, April 28, 1828. d. 1833.

"Aunt Demia," as Diodemia was familiarly called, d. in Winsted, Conn., August 11, 1884, lacking but a few days of reaching her one hundredth year, preparations for the celebration of which were making at the time of her death. She was the daughter of Stephen Knowlton, a soldier of the Revolution, who came from Chatham, Conn., to Winsted, and emigrated to Ohio in 1804, taking his large family in ox-wagons. On their arrival at Albany, N. Y., they were overtaken by Moses Camp, who had found that he could not live without Diodemia, and the reluctant consent to their marriage was gained from the parents. The young couple settled in Winsted, where they lived until their death. Diodemia was a woman of extraordinary force of character, and her mind and memory had been so enriched by the great national events of which she had been a witness, that she was a most entertaining conversationalist. She wrote poetry when past ninety years of age, and her wit and vivacity were keen until the last. But a few hours before her death she remarked when sitting in the family circle,

"I am so old that I think I have forgotten everything." "Better join the Know-Nothings, then," remarked a kinswoman. "I would not have far to go," was the ready retort.

She was a staunch Congregationalist, a pattern mother, and a pure soul

---

1094 Laura Knowlton and David Wright had:

(2806) Cornelia, November 10, 1810. d. March, 1887.
(2807) Edward, August 12, 1812. d. February, 1884.
(2808) Florilla, June 21, 1814. m. —— Fenn.
(2809) Harriett, February 26, 1817. d. April, 1830.
(2810) Laura, April 3, 1819.
(2811) Sarah E., October 11, 1822. m. Alexander Osborn, March 13, 1845.
(2812) Eliza, February 7, 1824. m. —— Baldwin. She d. July 1, 1890.
(2813) Amelia, 1826. d. young.
(2814) Mary, January 28, 1828. d. July 17, 1882.
(2815) Martha, January 28, 1832. unm.

David was of Welsh descent. His grandparents, John Wright and Prudence Demming, settled in Winsted, Conn., 1763. Their son John, b. in Wethersfield, Conn., m. Sarah Case. He was captain of the Winsted militia in the Revolutionary War, and rem. to Morgan, Ohio, in 1802, dying there in 1825.

David, his son, was a colonel of the U. S. Army in the War of 1812. He d. May 15, 1879. Laura d. March 4, 1888.

1095 Stephen and Lydia Dudley had:

(2816) George L., 1819. m. Bernice Treadwell; m. 2d Sarah Chapin.
(2817) Philo, October, 1821. Had dau. Mary C. Creth.
(2818) Caroline, 1825. d. young.
(2819) Eliza, 1827. unm. Res. in Hastings. A well known teacher.
(2820) Hiram, 1829. m. Mary Keuk. 3 chil.
(2821) Louisa, 1831. m. Francis Phillips. Hastings, Mich.
(2822) Caroline M., 1832. d. 1846.

1096 Samuel and Fanny Beach had:

(2823) Aaron, August 29, 1814. d. 1819.
(2824) George W., March 1, 1816. d. young.
(2825) Lysander, September 20, 1817. d. young.
(2826) Lydia, May 10, 1822. m. Ira Paine, October 23, 1838.
(2827) Silas.
(2828) George.
(2829) Edward.
(2830) Renny (Rensselaer). d. in the U. S. Army.
(2831) Aaron.
(2832) Jerome B., 1838. m. Catherine Howard. Resided in Ohio.

1110 Monroe and Susan Bryan had:

(2832 A) Ruth M., April 6, 1836. m. Madison Simonds. 3 chil.
(2832 B) Edwin C., April 18, 1841. m. Mary Mc'Wayne, March 14, 1864.

Monroe d. March 19, 1865.

1112 Perry and Caroline H. Weller had:

(2832 C) Julia. m. James Hazelwood.
(2832 D) Ray.

Caroline d. 1864, and Perry m. 2d Delia Hazelwood.

1113 Asa and Rachel Adams had:

(2832 E) Elvira.
(2832 F) Electa. m. William Lee.

1115 Henry A. and Vastaline Alger had:

(2833) Frank.
(2834) Della.
(2835) Vesta.

Vastaline d. 1867.

1116 Benjamin and Eliza Smith had:

(2836) Eliza J., April 5, 1835. d. young.
(2837) Charles Benjamin, September 15, 1836. m. Harriet Lucinda Simonds, July 15, 1879.
(2838) Helen E., February 28, 1839. m. J. Spier Colman, of La Crosse, Wis., November 22, 1862.

Eliza Smith d. January 13, 1841, and Benjamin m. 2d Cynthia H. Waite, August 14, 1842. They had:

(2839) Clark Cecil, May 30, 1843. m. Flora Alice Tillinghast, of Sardinia, N. Y., May 10, 1869. She d. January 24, 1870; He m. 2d. Sarah E. Vredenburg, of Corfu, N. Y., October 26, 1870. She d. August 28, 1888, and he m. 3d Sarah Idella Shourds, of Spencerport, N. Y.
(2839 A) Mary Olive, March 7, 1854. m. Geo. W. Boyer, of Elkdate, N. Y., November 11, 1876.

BENJAMIN KNOWLTON

was b. at Clarendon. Vt. He was educated in part at Brandon (Vt.) Seminary, in which institution he subsequently became a teacher. Removing to Western New York he accepted the position of principal of a public school in Buffalo, retiring from this, after faithful and successful work, to Springville, N. Y. He finally purchased a farm in Elton, N. Y., where he passed the remainder of a happy and useful life. He also studied medicine, and received a license to practice as a botanical physician, but he never made this his actual profession. He was an ardent Methodist, helpful and generous in his support of the work of that denomination, but by no means limited, either in sympathy or practical assistance, to his household of faith. His old saddle-bags are now the valued heirlooms of his son, Dr. Chas. Benjamin.

He d. at Yorkshire Centre, N. Y., March 21, 1876. Cynthia d. June 8, 1890.

Dr. Charles Benjamin Knowlton, (2837) s. of Benj. and Eliza, was born in Buffalo, September 15, 1836. He received his education at the Oberlin (O.,) Institute, the Cleveland, Bryan & Stratton Business College, and under Spencer, the author of the "Spencerian Penmanship." Before entering upon the practice of his chosen profession, the law, he was a professor in the department of commercial education, teaching penmanship, book-keeping, and commercial law, in the Buffalo Bryan & Stratton College, and his skilful and graceful penmanship naturally led to the selection of him as the Superintendent of the Department of Penmanship in the public schools of Buffalo.

He subsequently studied both law and medicine, and on graduating with first honors from the Medical Department of the University of Buffalo, his thesis on "Forensic Medicine" was adjudged the best one submitted, and as such it was ordered to be printed.

Dr. Knowlton has been for many years an active and influential friend to the educational interests of his native city. He is a life member of the Buffalo Society of Natural Science, the Buffalo Historical Society, and the Buffalo Library Association. Aside from his practice at the Buffalo Bar, he is much devoted to agricultural interests, and spends most of his summers at "Idleside," a pretty country-seat on his large farm in Elton, his winters being spent at his city residence, "O-neh-gi-yok" on Massachusetts Avenue, Buffalo.

He m. July 15, 1879. Harriet Lucinda, dau. of Lorenzo H. Simonds, of Ararat, Pa., who d. May 21, 1894.

Clark Cecil Knowlton, (2839) s. of Benj. and Cynthia H., was b. at Springville, N. Y., March 30, 1843. He served in the War of the Rebellion, enlisting in Company F., 5th N. Y. S. V. Cavalry (Ira Harris Guards), September 7, 1861. Captured, first at Hanover, Pa., during the Gettysburg Campaign, paroled after twenty-four hours; captured second, at Stevensville, Va., March 1, 1864, during the Cavalry Raid to Richmond, and was confined in the following Rebel Prisons: Libby, Andersonville, Savannah, Millen, Charleston, and Florence, S. C. Escaped at Goldsboro, February 18th, and arrived in the Union lines at at Newbern, N. C., March 1, 1865, making one year in the hands of the enemy. He was discharged from the service at Elmira, N. Y., April 30, 1865, by reason of expiration of term, having served three years and eight months. He is now President and Manager of the Merchants' Mutual Association of Chicago, Ill.

1136 Robert and Sally Brown had:

(2840) John E. m. Lucretia Knowlton, his cousin.
Res., Bethlehem, N. Y.

He was b. in Clifton Park, N. Y., was by trade a blacksmith, and a soldier of the Revolution.

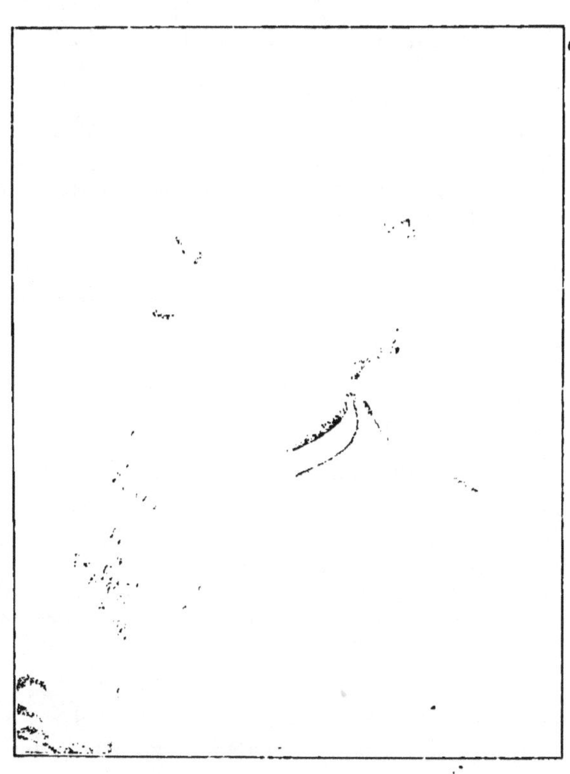

Charles Benjamin Knowlton, M.D.,
Buffalo, N. Y.

1138 John and Louisa Evans had:

(2841) Louisa M., March 12, 1811. m. —— Donnelly. 5 chil.
(2842) Ephraim, 1812. m. Eveline ——. He d. January 18, 1873.
(2843) Thomas E., July 23, 1813. m. Jane Wickman, March 17, 1842. He was drowned, September 14, 1849.
(2844) Elijah.
(2845) John J.
(2846) Daniel H., m. ——. He d. in Colorado, 1860. Had 1 son.
(2847) Esther H.
(2848) Lucretia A.

John d. August 15, 1854.

1139 Daniel and Susannah Vedder had:

(2849) Lucretia, October 1, 1813. m. John Knowlton.
(2850) Sarah, August 15, 1816. m. Peter Palmer, November, 1838.
(2851) Eliza, June 29, 1819. m. Munson Dotey.
(2852) David, March 15, 1820. m. Mary Smith, September 10, 1848.
(2853) Daniel, June 17, 1825. m. Ellen Marcellus, September, 1863. He d. April 14, 1864.
(2854) Harriet, August 15, 1829. m. Wm. Hicks.

Susannah d. October 21, 1828, and Daniel m. 2d Mrs. Judith Knowlton, March 27, 1830. They had:

(2854 A) Charles, October 31, 1831. d. 1852.

Daniel was b. in Clifton Park, N. Y., and d. there July 8, 1839. Judith d. there August 31, 1879.

1142 Esther Knowlton and John Evans had:

(2855) Agnes.
(2856) John J.
(2857) Caroline.
(2858) Eveline.
(2859) Ephraim K.

1143 Mary Knowlton and Jonah Townsend had:

(2860) Sarah.
(2861) Joseph.

1144 John B. and Polly Rexford had :

(2862) Alexander, January 20, 1807. m. Hannah Hayes. Res., Rexford Flats, N. Y.
(2863) Amelia, September 7, 1810. d. March 18, 1852.
(2864) Maria, February 14, 1820. d. November 27, 1842.

John B. res. in Schenectady, N. Y., and d. in N. Y. City, September 26, 1826.

1145 David and Achsah Barnes had :

(2865) Sophronia, March 5, 1806. m. Isaac Andrus, May 29, 1823. She d. June 10, 1888.
(2866) Achsah, March 23, 1809. d. young.
(2867) David, February 15, 1810. d. young.
(2868) Dexter A., March 3, 1812. m. Evaline Arnold, January 15, 1834. He d. March 10, 1876. She d. August 19, 1874.
(2869) Betsey A., May 3, 1820. m. Lewis Morgan. She d. November 16, 1882.
(2870) Dyer, May 11, 1822. d. young.
(2871) Wm. Alfred, August 4, 1831. m. Matilda Hitchcock, January 21, 1857. He d. 1892

Residence, Fairfield, N. Y.

Achsah d. April 19, 1843, and David m. 2d Electra Luce. He d. November 25, 1857.

1146 Ephraim and —— had :

(2872) Myron.
(2873) Byron.
(2874) James H., February 24, 1814. m. Agnes Flanders, who d. January 29, 1879.

Residence, Wheaton, Ill.

Ephraim rem. to Janesville and thence to Middleford, Wis., where he died.

1147 William and Almira Parkhurst had :

(2875) Oren. m. ——. 3 chil.
(2876) Lydia. m. ——. Had 3 chil.
(2877) Robert. m. ——. Had 4 chil.

Residence, rem. to Perrysburgh, N. Y.

1149 Dyer and —— had:

(2878) John D., June 15, 1821. m.
(2879) Jonathan, February 15, 1824.

Residence, rem. to Canada.

1152 Robert Woolsey Knowlton and Miriam Gaylord had:

Robert H., October 18, 1817. m. Had chil. George, Lansing, and Gertrude. He d. 1891.
Charles A., October 30, 1820. d. 1832.
George Gay, March 22, 1805. m. Had chil. Chas. G., Frank E., Hattie M. He d. 1868.
Aurelia Lyons, October 12, 1826. m. Chas. P. Clark. Had son, Dr. Gaylord P. Clark. She d. 1891.
Eliza Starin, December 9, 1830. d. 1836.
Hiram, November 14, 1833. d young.

Robert Woolsey was b. in Greenfield, Saratoga Co., N. Y., whence he removed to Fairfield, N. Y., where, at the age of 21, he established himself in the business of carriage making. In 1824 he removed to Syracuse, N. Y., where he carried on the same business, and also that of salt manufacturing. He d. August, 1876.

1156 Daniel and Catherine Burrell had:

(2883) Henry D., December 15, 1827. m. Caroline E. Hamlin, September 19, 1833.
(2884) Jane, September 25, 1829. d. young.
(2885) George B., June 29, 1831. m. Elizabeth Robbins.
(2886) Mary, December 11, 1833. m. Geo. B. Robbins.
(2887) Daniel, June 26, 1836. d. of yellow fever, in Memphis, Tenn. Lawyer.
(2888) Katherine J., June 2, 1838. m. John W. Wood.

Catherine d. June 1, 1841, and Daniel m. 2d Angeline H. Fox. They had:

(2889) Clara A., October 19, 1843. d. June 2, 1890. unm.
(2890) Julia E., June 18, 1845. m. Myron Willard.
(2891) Charles F., September 14, 1847. m. Mary Pettingill, of Holland Patent, N. Y.

Daniel was a farmer, and resided in Fairfield and Holland Patent, N. Y. He d. February 2, 1890.

1157 Jerusha Caroline Knowlton and Henry Graves had:

(2892) Robert. m. Annie Cadwallader. Had dau. Elvira.
(2893) Henry. m. Harriet B. Hale. Res., Orange, N. J.
(2894) Annie. m. Edward Benedict.
(2895) Ella S. m. Robert Barton.
(2896) Helen A. m. Alfred W. Taylor.
(2897) Lizzie. m. Abram Baldwin, October 29, 1867. Residence, Orange, N. J.

1158 Stephen and Phoebe Russell had:

(2898) James R., 1795. m. Harriet Merritt.
(2899) Robert, 1798. m. Margaret Lounsberry.
(2900) Ephraim, 1801. m. 2 chil.
(2901) Stephen, 1806. m. Harriet Dibble; m. 2d ——— Dana.
(2902) Elizabeth, 1808. d. young.
(2903) Phoebe, 1810. m. ——— Raymond.
(2904) Pamela, 1812. m. Samuel Haight.

Phoebe d. 1858. Stephen owned an estate of 1500 acres of land in Westchester Co., N. Y., of which he gave two hundred acres to each child at marriage.

He was a man of unusual physique, over six feet tall, genial and courtly, full of energy until his death, and honored by a wide circle of relations and fellow-citizens.

1159 Abijah and Abigail Ann Russell had:

(2905) Phoebe. m. ——— Cotterell, of N. Y. 2 chil. m. 2d Justus Barrett of Putnam Co., N. Y.
(2906) Stephen, October 2, 1808. m. Eliza Clarke. m. 2d Mary A. Wycoff.
(2907) Isaac, 1810. m. Hannah Hippen of N. Y. 3 chil.
(2908) James Russell, 1809. m. Ann Eliza Von Bos Kirk of N. Y. 1828.
(2909) Abigail, April 15, 1815. m. N. B. Lane of N. Y. m. 2d Isaac Weeks.
(2910) Eliza J. m. James Vantine.

Abijah owned a large farm in White Plains, N. Y., an inheritance from his father, and on which the battle of White Plains was fought. He d. in 1810, and Abigail in 1848, in Brooklyn, N. Y.

1162 Stephen Williams and Elizabeth Longfellow had:

(2911) Lorenzo D., September 9, 1813. Lost at sea, 1838.
(2912) William L., February 10, 1815 m. Mary A. Hardy. m. 2d Mary Clough. d. May 19, 1882, Canaan, N. H.
(2913) Abraham L., August 24, 1818. m. Christina Burnham, February 13, 1845. She d. August 23, 1861.
(2914) Samuel, May 18, 1820. m. Ursula Day, of Canaan, N. H.
(2915) Susan L., June 25, 1824. m. James Eastman.
(2916) Mary G., January 24, 1826. d. September 22, 1886.
(2917) Stephen, March 14, 1828. m. Rebecca S. Case, of Nashua, N. H. Residence in Canaan, N. H.

1166 Ebenezer and Margaret Bass had:

(2918) Margaret, November 21, 1803. m. Samuel W. Hall, April 26, 1830. She d. September 21, 1883.
(2919) Ebenezer, November 23, 1805. d. October 13, 1845.
(2920) Lucy Lakeman, January 2, 1806. m. Alfred A. Wellington, December 4, 1832. She d. December 22, 1871.
(2921) Mary Elizabeth, September 26, 1809. m. James W. Whiton.

1167 Lucy Knowlton and Richard Lakeman:

(2922) Eben Knowlton, December 10, 1799.
(2923) Lucy. m. Ami Smith.
(2924) Susan, December 29, 1802. m. Abram Lord.

Lucy was b. in Ipswich, in 1772. She was a great beauty, celebrated for her tall, commanding figure and graceful manners.

1170 Daniel and ——— had:

(2925) Thomas. m.

Daniel was a soldier in the War of 1812, and served at Fort Montgomery on the Hudson.

1171 Sylvia Knowlton and Caleb Maxham had:

(2926) Phœbe A., January 15, 1828. m. Oramul Averill, May 19, 1853.
(2927) Stephen Knowlton, February 19, 1831. m. Frances A. Pinney, September 18, 1866. Had Harriet and Walter.

Sylvia was a tailoress. When her father died, she bought her brother's share of the farm, and paid for the whole property by the earnings of her needle. She d. June 3, 1863, thrifty and honored.

1176 Ezra and Anna Loomis had:

(2928) Ezra, 1821. m. Rosanna ——; m. 2d Emeline Billings, 1851.

Anna dying, Ezra m. 2d Abigail Hoar, and had:

(2929) Almena. m. Nathan Lyon. Res., New Haven, Conn.
(2930) Hannah.
(2931) Rufus E. m. Samantha Bowen, 1851.
(2932) Edwin Onias. m. Caroline M. Hoar.

1178 Achsah Knowlton and Jesse Marsh had:

(2933) Danforth, June 20, 1826.
(2934) Miner P., October 9, 1827.
(2935) John B., May 26, 1830.
(2936) Maurice, June 14, 1833.
Residence, Ashford, Conn.

1180 John and Almira Chaffee had:

(2937) John Marvin, December 10, 1817. m. Anna ——.
(2938) Almira Calista, August 8, 1820.

Almira d. February 17, 1821, and John m. 2d Polly Crab. They had:

(2939) Henry, March 26, 1822.
(2940) Royal, June 26, 1823. m. Had son, Frank, 1862.
(2941) Mary.
(2942) Hannah.
(2943) Lucretia.
(2944) Achsah.
(2945) Warren.

After the death of his wife Almira, John rem. from Ashford, Ct., to Windsor, Broome Co., N. Y., where he d. October 8, 1864.

1181 Guerdon and Laura Pickett had :

(2946) Elvira, August 25, 1822. m. Oren Doolittle, January 1, 1839.
(2947) Sarah, June 17, 1831. m. Dr. J. C. Edson, October 20, 1852.
(2948) Laurina. m. Oliver Winsor, October 31, 1861.
(2949) Alma. m. Walter Hoadley, January, 1861.
(2950) Alanson. m. Malinda Crofut, July 4, 1857.
(2951) Miles. m. Nancy Wooster, April 10, 1861.
(2952) Hansen.
(2953) Clara. m. Eugene Bronson, September 12, 1869.

1182 Tamsen and Ezra Crawford had :

(2954) Laura, January 19, 1831.
(2955) Almira, June 17, 1832.
(2956) Oren, February 6, 1835.
(2957) Charles, February 3, 1839.
(2958) William.

Residence, Ashford, Conn.

1183 Laura Knowlton and Washington Blakely had :

(2959) Jemima, March 8, 1829.
(2960) Angeline, May, 1831.
(2961) Otis, October 5, 1832.
(2962) Delilah, August 22, 1836.

Residence, Ashford, Conn.

1185 Armanda Knowlton and Daniel B. Reed had :

(2963) Daniel K., January 22, 1826. m. Matilda Gibson.
(2964) William P., October 23, 1828. m. Annette Park.
(2965) Almira, April 2, 1830.
(2966) Eliza, July 2, 1831. m. Alonzo Cheever.
(2967) Jeremiah, August 26, 1833.
(2968) Elvira, January 4, 1836. m. Chas. H. Moulton.
(2969) Henry, July 14, 1839. m. B. Austin.
(2970) Darwin.
(2971) Myron, 1843.
(2972) Herbert, 1845.
(2973) Louisa, 1848.

Residence, Mansfield, Conn.

1186 Palmer and Harriet E. Conant had :

(2974) David P., November 16, 1833. m. Elmira Simonds.
(2975) John E., February, 16, 1839. d. June 6, 1847.
Residence, Ashford, Conn.

Palmer d. there December 29, 1844. Harriet was from North Haven, Conn.

1188 Johnathan W. and Harriet M. Bottom had :

(2976) Chas. C., September 22, 1844. m. Isabel M. Howard, May 12, 1870.
Res., Brooklyn, N. Y.
(2977) Mary E., April 23, 1846. Res., Ashford Conn.
Residence, Ashford, Conn.

1192 Laura Knowlton and Rev. A. W. Baker had :

(2978) James, May 21, 1840.
(2979) Lafayette, January 17, 1843.
(2980) Addie, May 25, 1844.
(2981) Lewis, January 28, 1846.
(2982) Maria, August 23, 1849.
(2983) Oliver, April 13, 1853.
(2984) Frank, January 22, 1855.

1193 Philena Knowlton and Wm. A. Locke had :

(2985) Orlando, May 23, 1836.
(2986) Mary E., January 24, 1838.
(2987) Francis, March 9, 1840.
(2988) Eliza J., July 1, 1842.
(2989) Adaline, January 25, 1845.
(2990) Helen C., September 27, 1848.
(2991) William, August 22, 1850.

1194 Minerva Knowlton and Henry C. Locke had :

(2992) Fernando, October 7, 1835. m. Ellen Rugby.
(2993) Caroline, July 24, 1844. m. Wm. H. Ashley.

1195 Sophronia Knowlton and John C. Lamberson had:

(2994) Martha, 1841. d. June 4, 1853.
(2995) Imogene, 1848. d. June 5, 1860.

1197 Orissa Knowlton and Chas. Torrey had:

(2996) Helen C., May 16, 1846.
(2997) Mary A., June 25, 1851.
(2998) Harriet, August 10, 1858.
(2999) William, April 24, 1861. d. young.

1198 Jane Knowlton and Dorester Torrey had:

(3000) Adelbert, November 4, 1847.
(3001) Herbert, October 3, 1851. m. Lottie Derbyshire.
(3002) Allen, January 3, 1861.

1199 James and Clarinda Wheat had:

(3003) Ellen M., March 20, 1846. m. H. G. DeGroot, December 28, 1869.
(3004) George F., May 20, 1851.
(3005) Walter, August 15, 1855. d. young.
(3006) Milton, August 15, 1855. d. young.
(3007) Mary P., October 18, 1858.

1200 Adelia Knowlton and Isaac Torrey had:

(3008) Carlton, June 13, 1849.
(3009) Ella, September 16, 1852.

1201 Elizabeth and Wm. H. Ashley had:

(3010) Carrie, January 17, 1863.
(3011) William, October 20, 1864.
(3012) James M., November 3, 1866.
(3013) Herbert, April 9, 1869.

1207 Merrick and Fatima Perrin had :

(3014) William M., October 30, 1829. m. Elizabeth Parker Guiberson, October 20, 1862.
(3015) Fidelia H., January 22, 1833. m. Freeman E. Eno, Somers, Conn.
(3016) Marens P., February 3, 1839. m. Sophia Ritchie, July 18, 1867.
(3017) Mary A., February 19, 1843. m. Achille E. Eastman, May 21, 1871.
Residence, Palmer, Mass.

Fatima d. August 2, 1876. Merrick d. January 25, 1864.

1208 Persis Knowlton and Mace Moulton had :

(3018) Orson, August 10, 1825. m. Maria T. Butler, October 13, 1847.
(3019) Mace, June 29, 1827. m. Mary A. Burr, Wilbraham, Mass.

Persis m. 2d. Truxton Squire, 1829, and had :

(3020) Elvira, March, 1830. d. young.
(3021) Lucinda, July, 1831. d. young.
Residence, Monson, Mass.

Mace d. June 7, 1827. Persis d. July 6, 1836.

1212 Stephen and Cassandra Hester had :

(3022) Orson, June 3, 1822. m. Frances Wilde, January 28, 1855.
(3023) Fernando, August 8, 1824.
(3024) Porter, September 29, 1826.
(3025) Almira, August 11, 1828. m. Henry Kilburn.
(3026) Marcus L., March 16, 1831.
(3027) Minerva, March 31, 1833. m. Hiram Griffin.
(3028) William S., June 30, 1839. m. Sarah Harrity.
(3029) Giles H., August 9, 1842.

Stephen d. April 28, 1893. Cassandra d. November 13, 1864.

1213 Arnon and Susan Wentworth had :

(3030) Ezra L., March 21, 1831. m. Ann E. Coman, March 22, 1857.
(3031) Lydia M., November 9, 1832. m. Wm. R. James, October 16, 1853.
(3032) Henry E., April 12, 1834. d. young.
(3033) Ralph, June 19, 1835. d. January 18, 1860. Shot while hunting.
(3034) Maria J., September 10, 1836. d. August 10, 1870.
Residence, Ashford, Conn.

Arnon d. December 6, 1874.

1217 Ebenezer and Elizabeth Lyon had :

(3035) Henry E., November 1, 1839. m. Hattie S. Ballard, January 15, 1871.
(3036) Hannah, January 18, 1842. m. John Church, March 31, 1864.
(3037) Nathaniel, May 19, 1843. m. Sarah E. Wright, April 5, 1868.
(3038) Mary E., May 24, 1845. m. C. W. Thomas, November 24, 1870.
(3039) Adaline, November 30, 1853.
(3040) Lillian, December 30, 1859.

Ebenezer d. August 13, 1866.

1218 Samuel and E. Fay Woodward had :

(3041) Albert D. July 4, 1840. m. Frances Whittaker, March 18, 1868.
(3042) Sarah M., May 26, 1842. m. D. P. Woodman, December 22, 1869.
(3043) Ellen S., January 21, 1844. m. Frank O. Sanger, March 16, 1872.

Samuel d. September 21, 1845, and Fay m. 2d P. C. Higgins, November 6, 1846.

1219 Hannah Minerva Knowlton and John S. Dean had :

(3044) Charles L. m. Juliette Fuller.

Residence, Boston, Mass.

1220 Abraham and Huldah Hastings had :

(3045) Waldo, 1831. d. young.
(3046) Knox, July 11, 1833. m. Huldah Alexander, April 16, 1872.
(3047) Emily, October 13, 1837. m. J. H. Coleman.
(3048) Leone, July 14, 1839. d. young.
(3049) Elizabeth, June 2, 1840. m. J. Stafford, November 25, 1875.
(3050) Bersheba, August 6, 1842. d. 1848.
(3051) John, January 21, 1845. m. Melissa Oliver, January 10, 1870.
(3052) Paul, November 17, 1847. m. Eunice Stafford, 1877.
(3053) Cephas, November 17, 1849. d. October 11, 1877.

Abraham d. October 11, 1850.

1221 Lucinda Knowlton and David Mufford had :

(3054) Laura, 1830.
(3055) Sarah.
(3056) George.

Residence, Arkansas.

Lucinda had four other children whose names are not known. She d. 1863.

1224 Miles and Mrs. Tucker had :

(3057) Robert, August 8, 1838. m. Ivy Smith, 1867. 2 chil.
(3058) Melissa, August 20, 1841. m. Wm. Hewitt.
(3059) Oregon, May 25, 1849. m. 2 chil.
Residence, Arkansas.

Miles d. 1866.

1225 Cephas and Julia E. Ludlow had :

(3060) Miner, March 13, 1854. m. Mary A. Booth, March 23, 1877.
(3061) Cephas, October 25, 1856.
Residence, Arkansas.

Cephas d. 1864.

1235 Permelia Knowlton and Lysander C. Frost had :

(3062) Ashbel, December 11, 1821.
(3063) Lyman, May 20, 1823.
(3064) Daniel, February 2, 1826.
(3065) Reuben, November 26, 1833.

1236 Dennis and Eliza Weatherby had :

(3066) Miriam, April 27, 1830. d. September 8, 1846.
(3067) Henry L., June 12, 1832. d. August 13, 1841.
(3068) Emma C., November 18, 1834.
(3069) Charles D., August 10, 1837. d. July 1, 1861.
(3070) William M., February 14, 1840. d. July 8, 1858.

Elizabeth d. December 16, 1847, and Dennis m. 2d Laurana Loomis.

1237 Hesse Knowlton and Wm. S. Barker had :

(3071) Lybenah, April 8, 1834.
(3072) Lusette, January 1, 1838.
(3073) William, August 5, 1842.
(3074) Wesley, August 5, 1842.
(3075) Sherrod, September 10, 1844.
(3076) Delbert, February 1, 1847.

Capt. Miner Knowlton, U. S. A.,
West Point Military Academy, 1804–1870.

1239 Lydia Knowlton and Thomas Glover had:

(3077) Jane E., October 20, 1832. m. Elisha B. Boomer.
(3078) James N., August 15, 1835.
(3079) William H., December 30, 1837.
(3080) Harriet A., September 24, 1845.
(3081) Thomas N., October 29, 1852.

1241 Abraham and Emily Witt had:

(3082) Sarah J., January 29, 1846. m. Chas. J. Smith, March 19, 1874.
(3083) Susan E., January 12, 1848.
(3084) Danforth A., November 9, 1850. m. Stella M. Graves, November 14, 1874.
(3085) Alfred N., February 13, 1852.
(3086) James E., June 5, 1856.
(3087) Jane E., June 5, 1856. m. Edward Noble, January 3, 1875.
(3088) Rufus E., July 6, 1858.

Residence, Wilbraham, Mass.

Abraham d. March 1, 1871. Emily d. February 26, 1866.

1242 CAPTAIN MINER KNOWLTON, U. S. A.

Captain Miner Knowlton was a grandson of Lieut. Daniel Knowlton, a grandnephew of Col. Thomas Knowlton, and first cousin of Gen. Nathaniel Lyon, an officer of the Regular Army of the United States, and instructor at West Point Military Academy. At the last officers' mess he attended, when ending his long and arduous duties at West Point, in 1844, he was stricken with epilepsy. He was always an ambitious student while performing his duties as Instructor in Mathematics, French, Artillery, and Cavalry, and he finally broke down through overstudy.

For this reason he obtained a furlough, and visited many foreign countries in the hope of overcoming the malady, yet always striving to inform himself in military affairs, and giving to the Government the benefit of all information he acquired of foreign armaments and methods. Thus, after leaving West Point, we find him in the French Army in Algeria, and later on in Bermuda, and in Havana, Cuba, on delicate and special service for the Government, and doing recruiting service and engineering work on the Rio Grande, although incapacitated through disease for service in the field, during the Mexican War.

The "falling sickness" never left him, and at the breaking out of the war in 1861, being then 57 years old and the oldest captain in the Artillery, he retired from the service, and spent the remainder of his life at Burlington,

N. J., where he had gone to secure necessary quiet, and where he organized a company of home guards known as the "Knowlton Rifles."

He was the instructor of Lee, Grant, Beauregard, Lyon, and many of the prominent West Point officers, both Union and Confederate, who took part in the Civil War.

An ardent Republican, he was always courteous to those who differed from him in politics.

He was more the student than the fighter, and, adding to the inborn courtesy of the old school the trained etiquette of the Regular Army officer, he had the breadth of view and the charity of a highly educated and liberal-minded man.

Captain Knowlton was never married. He is buried in St. Mary's Churchyard, Burlington, N. J., and his monument is capped with a fac-simile in stone of a mortar ready for discharge and the inscription reads: "Our aim is always heavenward—for God and for our country."

Ashbel Woodward inscribed his "Life of General Lyon" to Captain Knowlton as a tribute

"to patriotism, integrity and distinguished attainments, and a memorial of old and uninterrupted friendship."

Captain Knowlton fostered the military instincts of the descendants of Lieut. Daniel Knowlton, and it is believed that his example largely influenced Lyon in adopting a military career, and that, thereafter, Lyon was guided in military and other matters by the precepts and opinions of the relative and friend who, fourteen years his senior, was his instructor and the respected comrade of the older and then more distinguished officers of the Army.

The publication of the "Life of General Lyon" for distribution among his relatives, and for the public libraries, was mainly due to Captain Knowlton, and it is probable that it was at his request that his friend, Ashbel Woodward, edited the pamphlet with miniature engraving of the battle of Bunker Hill, in memory of Col. Thomas Knowlton.

Captain Knowlton built a beautiful home for himself in Burlington, N. J., where he entertained his friends and his old Army comrades, and in spite of a generous expenditure of money and of his many silent charities, such were his habits from the early training in Connecticut that, through good management and intelligent investment of accumulated savings from the modest pay of an Army officer, he left a handsome fortune at his death.

1244 Miriam Knowlton and Hiram Cady had:

(3089) Mary A. H., November 9, 1832. m. Philo Chaffer, August, 31, 18 .
(3090) Hiram, February 17, 1837.

Residence, Ashford, Conn.

Miriam d. August 28, 1895.

Danforth Knowlton,
New York City, 1811-1890.

1245 Danford and Miranda H. Rockwell had:

(309) Maria R., June 6, 1842. d. April 29, 1848.
(3092) Danforth Henry, April 18, 1846. m. Mary B. Johnes, August 21, 1873.
(3093) Miner R., June 6, 1847. m. Hattie Hull, September 17, 1867.
(3094) Gertrude M., July 14, 1858. m. J. B. Van Schaick.

DANFORD KNOWLTON.

was born at Ashford, Windham County, Conn., May 5, 1811. His father and mother were Daniel and Hannah Knowlton, both of the same name, and from families remotely connected. On the paternal side they were farmers in comfortable circumstances, having influence in the community, and filling places of trust and responsibility. On the maternal side they were also farmers, the grandfather of the subject of the present sketch, Daniel Knowlton, and Thomas Knowlton, his brother, being conspicuous while quite young in the war against the French and Indians, serving with General Putnam, and in the early struggles for national independence.

In the autumn of 1832, Mr. Knowlton left a happy paternal home with a desire to find some occupation more congenial to his taste than farming. On April 10, 1833, he entered into an existing firm doing a wholesale grocery business in Hartford, Conn. Continuing the same class of business until December, 1843, he removed to New York, looking for a wider field of operations. With some changes of partners, the wholesale grocery business was continued until 1852, when he visited the island of Cuba and united the importation of its products with the existing enterprise. This mixed class of business was continued until 1861, when the firm confined itself to importation only, from the West Indies and South America. In 1855 Mr. Knowlton retired from business, after fifty-two years of successful mercantile life, in which he earned an enviable reputation for business enterprise and commercial honor.

During the continuance of the importing business, a good deal of controversy arose between importers and refiners of sugar respecting the proper duty to be placed upon various classes of sugar, the latter desiring so to discriminate against the better classes suitable for consumption as to prevent their importation.

These controversies led to various appeals to Congress, in which the importers generally found the champagne and good dinners of the refiners more effective than the solid arguments and cold water of the importers. Thus that "infant industry" was so protected as to lead to colossal fortunes among the refiners of sugar, at the expense of the consumers, resulting in the exclusion from the country of all sugars except such as are required for refining. In these controversies Mr. Knowlton took a prominent part, appearing before committees of Congress and contributing many articles on the subject to the press, and otherwise securing the attention of the members of Congress.

Danford Knowlton was first cousin and life-long friend of Gen'l Lyon, and on the receipt of the news of the hero's death at Wilson's Creek, he started from New York at once to secure the body. At St. Louis he secured a metallic coffin, and after much delay there, caused by General Fremont, he succeeded in obtaining permission for an ambulance and an escort to pass under flag of truce inside the rebel lines to Springfield, Mo. At Rolla he met our army, August 20, 1861, and from Emmett MacDonald, Captain Com'd'g C. S. A., who was there to exchange prisoners, he obtained permit to pass inside the rebel lines. After a rough ride to Springfield he found the body there tenderly cared for by Mrs. Phelps, a loyal Connecticut woman. It had been left on the field of battle ; then recovered by our retreating army under flag of truce, and again left at Springfield in the hurried retreat from that place. Danford Knowlton brought the body to Eastford, Conn., where it was buried.

In his matrimonial experience, Mr. Knowlton was one of the most fortunate of men. Married to Miss Miranda H. Rockwell, the daughter of Park and Esther Rockwell of Stafford, Conn., September 26, 1837, he passed almost forty-nine years of a most happy union with one whose amiable character rendered her beloved by all who had the pleasure of her acquaintance. Previous to retirement from business, Mr. Knowlton built a fine country residence in Stafford, at the birthplace of his wife, with a view of spending at least his summers in that delightful locality. He died there in December, 1890, and was buried in the family lot in Greenwood Cemetery, Brooklyn, Long Island, N. Y.

1246 Elvira Knowlton and Asher Knowlton had :

(3095) Nancy M., January 23, 1841. m. James F. Chamberlain.
Residence, Ashford, Conn.

Asher d. May 10, 1883. Elvira d. January 28, 1887.

1247 Edwin and Mary F. Woodward had :

(3097) Robert D. W., November 18, 1860.
(3098) George B. M., March 3, 1863.
(3099) James E. A., April 28, 1866.
(3100) Hattie E., October 26, 1868.

Edwin Knowlton was born in Ashford, Conn., June 24, 1835. His education was limited to that of the public schools, and though desirous of a wider business sphere, his filial duty kept him on the farm of his parents, which he brought to a high state of cultivation, and greatly extended its area. It has been in the possession of the Knowltons for a century and a half, being now

Edwin Knowlton,
Ashford, Conn., 1825–1884.

Hon. Jabez Knowlton,
Newburgh, Me., 1809–1895.

owned and worked by Robert, the eldest son. Edwin's industry and enterprise made him prominent among his townsmen, and he was at various times Selectman, Highway Surveyor, and Representative. His good judgment and sterling integrity made him in constant request for the settlement of estates, and when the old Baptist Society decided to distribute an accumulated fund among the members and heirs of deceased members, he was selected to make the distribution.

He married Mary, dau. of Otis and Eliza Woodward, and d. September 11, 1884. Mary d. April 29, 1895.

1248 Sally and Chauncey Warren had:

(3101) Amos K., February 24, 1824. m. Helen Moore.
(3102) Calvin, March 27, 1825. d. young.
(3103) Jabez, March 19, 1830. m. Myra Groot.
(3104) Lucian C., May 2, 1833.

1250 Jabez and Susan M. Bickford had:

(3105) Amos W., April 27, 1845. m. Annie H. Church, November 10, 18 .

Jabez Knowlton was born in Ashford, Conn., where he worked on his father's farm during the summer, attending the public school during the winter months. This limited education was about all that the average New England boy received at that time, but it proved to be serviceable and effectual when supplemented by native shrewdness and personal industry. At the age of twenty-two Jabez removed to Maine, where he conducted a thrifty business in books and clocks. When in Newburgh, he always stopped at the Bickford Tavern, a notable hostelry on the turnpike between Bangor and Augusta, where he met Susan, the landord's daughter, whom he soon after made his happy wife. He went into the business of a "General Store" then owned by his father-in-law, and when this was burned he erected one of his own, where he continued business for the rest of his active life, accumulating a handsome fortune. His suavity of manner, generosity to debtors, and geniality to everyone made him a great favorite. He was a prominent member of the old Whig party, and, though living in a Democratic district, was sent to the State Legislature in 1849. After the dissolution of his party, he became a Democrat, but his popularity so far prevailed over partisanship that both parties joined in making him Postmaster and Selectman for forty years, and Town Treasurer for thirty-seven years. He died at Newburgh, June 3, 1895, beloved and regretted by all.

1256 Sally Goulding and —— Warren had :

(3105 A) Waterman.
(3105 B) Elbridge G., 1810.
(3105 C) John.
(3105 D) George.
And three others.

1257 Sarah Knowlton and —— Gleason had :

(3106) One child.

He dying, she m. 2d Aaron Sibley and had :

(3107) F. Knowlton Sibley, 1825.
Res., Waltham, Mass.

She d. April 10, 1861.

1258 Benjamin and Olive Stone had :

(3108) Tryphena, September 17, 1807. d. August 22, 1840.
(3109) Mary A., January 20, 1810. d. November 12, 1846.
(3110) Abigail M., June 24, 1812. m. Jonathan Drury.
(3111) Israel S., January 22, 1815. m. Hepsibeth C. Fisk ; m. 2d Mary F. H. Cochrane.
(3112) Candace, December 25, 1817. m. Jeremiah Young.
(3113) Marcia, January 20, 1821. m. W. S. Erenbrach, January 1, 1836. He d. 1891.
(3114) Benjamin L., September 26, 1824. m. Eliza Ann Maclay.
Res., Salem, Mass.

Benjamin d. August 23, 1865. Olive d. December 13, 1865.

1259 Nathan and Sally Gates :

had many children. He rem. to Pennsylvania and d. there, March 12, 1846.

1261 Abigail Knowlton and Johnathan Stone had :

(3115) Oliver, August 22, 1815. d. February 4, 1863.
(3116) Joseph J., December 26, 1816. d. October 2, 1833.
(3117) Prescott B., July 13, 1819. d. May 21, 1886.

(3118) Sarah L., February 1, 1822. d. August 4, 1885.
(3119) Lewis, April 21, 1823.
(3120) Emory, March 9, 1827.
(3121) Marshall, April 19, 1828.
Residence, Auburn, Mass.

Abigail d. February 15, 1884.

1263 Joanna Knowlton and David Rockwood had :

(3122) Joanna, October 10, 1815.
(3123) David, November 29, 1816.
(3124) Chester, March 27, 1818.
(3125) Nancy, March 29, 1820.
(3126) Charles, August 10, 1821.
(3127) Joseph, February 20, 1823.
(3128) Samuel, March 10, 1823.
(3129) Hermann, March 10, 1827.
(3130) Nathan, June 14, 1829.
(3131) Martha, April 1, 1831.
(3132) Laura, April, 1, 1834.
Residence, Bennington, Vt.

Joanna d. August 16, 1857. Daniel d. January 12, 1857.

1264 Pomeroy and Marcia Palmer had :

(3133) Sarah.

He d. January 1, 1874.

1266 Olive Knowlton and Curtis Fay had :

(3134) Chandler, October 25, 1826.
(3135) Augustus, January 25, 1828.
(3136) Elizabeth, September 13, 1829.
(3137) Ann Eliza, March 29, 1831.
(3138) Henry B., December 22, 1832.
(3139) Martha, January 28, 1835.
Residence, Lawrence, Mass.

Curtis d. February 2, 1876. Olive d. March 3, 1886.

1267 Arad and Sophia Wilkinson had:

(3141) Norman W., September 3, 1825. d. 1893.
(3142) Nancy S., May 5, 1830. d. November 14, 1874.
Residence rem. from Townsend, Vt., to Brockton, Mass.

Sophia d. May 1875, and Arad, February 17, 1877.

1269 Lucy Knowlton and N. S. Clark had:

(3143) Henry S.
Residence, Worcester, Mass.

Lucy d. 1882.

1270 Asahel and Sophronia C. Cummings had:

(3144) John P., October 8, 1833. m. Jane Shumway, November 29, 1859.
(3145) Sarah S., October 19, 1836. m. Wm. S. Wood, August 7, 1856. Had son, Wm. C.
(3146) Marcia A., January 20, 1842. m. M. A. Harrington, November 28, 1872.

Asahel was b. in Newfane, Vt., in 1803, and is the only survivor of a family of sixteen children. In 1826 he removed to Auburn, Mass., where he worked on a farm. By his industry and frugality he purchased, in 1835, the Jonas Stockwell farm, where he resided until 1856. He then removed to Boylston, where he was Warden of the Town Farm for four years, after which he returned to Auburn, serving the town successively as Tax Collector, Assessor, Selectman, and Excise Agent under the old prohibitory law. In 1868 he purchased the John Shumway place in Webster, Mass., and since that time he has acted as janitor of the court and school houses, and of the Bank Block. He is now 94 years old and in fair health. Sophronia was born in Auburn, Mass., October 17, 1809, and d. August 12, 1893.

1271 Swan and Mrs. Sarah Eddy Baird had:

(3147) Sarah Ann, January 4, 1832. m. Wm. R. Barrett of Barre, Mass., September 12, 1851.
(3148) Nathan M., December 5, 1836. m. Harriet E. Bailey, November 22, 1862. Westboro.
(3149) Maria A., April 6, 1840. m. Albert L. Smith, Worcester. 1 child.

Swan was a farmer. For many years he was Deacon in the Congregational

Church in Ward, now Auburn, Mass. He served during the Rebellion as a member of the Christian Commission in the camps before Richmond. The last twenty years of his life were spent in Worcester, Mass. He d. November 27, 1883. Sarah d. June 29, 1893.

1272 Luthera Knowlton and Ezra Rice had:

(3150) Susan, August 19, 1834. d. 1851.
(3151) Emily, July 27, 1838. d. August 9, 1865.
(3152) Nancy F., July 28, 1840. m. Rev. C. C. Carpenter, May 1, 1862.
(3153) George D., April 16, 1842. Soldier, Co. C, 51st Reg't, Mass. Vol. d. in hospital at Newberne, N. C., March 9, 1863.
(3154) Selina, June 20, 1844. m. S. Augustus Perrin, June 20, 1871. 1 child.
(3155) Abbie L., July 5, 1844. m. S. A. Sinnicks, May 14, 1885. She d. August 8, 1892.

Residence, Auburn, Mass.

Luthera d. February 28, 1881. Ezra d. April 13, 1884.

1298 Calvin and Abigail Powers had:

(3156) A dau. m. Alonzo Farrar.

Calvin d. in Rye, N. H., January 30, 1878. Abigail was from Rye and d. in Hardwick, Mass., September 24, 1822.

1301 Maria Knowlton and William Dexter had:

(3157)
(3158) Samuel W., March 8, 1829. d. young.
(3159) Lucy M., August 21, 1831. m. J. B. Wiggin, September 17, 1856.

1303 Timothy and Susan Locke had:

(3160) Mary E., December 20, 1838.

Susan d. July 17, 1842, and Timothy m. 2d Augusta Locke, September 10, 1843. They had:

(3161) Susan A., January 9, 1849.

Timothy lived in Rye, N. H. and d. there July 9, 1869.

1308 Thomas and Eliza A. Brand had:

(3162) Walter S., December 28, 1846. d. 1850.
(3163) Henry H., November 26, 1849.
(3164) Lizzie S., December 1, 1851.
Residence, West Brookfield, Mass.

1309 Amos S. and Mary J. Hodge had:

(3165) Lucy M., October 12, 1851.
(3166) Gerald, December 2, 1853. d. young.
(3167) Amos H., June 19, 1855. m. Addie Patch. 1 child. Res., Littleton, Mass.
(3168) Wm. F., December 14, 1857.
(3169) Frederick, February 13, 1860. d. May 29, 1875.
(3170) A dau. d. young.
(3171) Mary L., December 7, 1865.
Residence, Woburn, Mass.

Mary d. February 29, 1844, and Amos m. 2d Ann M. Stone, January 12, 1851.

1310 Susan Knowlton and Francis Gerald had:

(3172) Fannie, February 8, 1846. m. Ezra S. White, August 26, 1873.

1312 Charles H. and Annie C. Root had:

(3173) Annie S., January 27, 1861.

1313 Polly Knowlton and Artemas Mann had:

(3174) George H.
(3175) Rosanna.
(3176) Joseph H.
(3177) Algeria.
(3178) Henry.

1315 Cynthia Knowlton and Jason Goulding had:

(3178 A) Agnes S., August 7, 1830. unm. Res., Springfield, Mass.
(3178 B) Cynthia K., November 16, 1833. unm. Res., Mills College, Cal.

(3178c) Abigail C. D., August 10, 1835. m. Rev. J. P. Kremler, of Pittsburg, Pa., October 1, 1856.

Cynthia was the 2d wife of Jason. She d. January 23, 1845, and Jason m. 3d Mrs. Harriet Bowker Knowlton, widow of Joseph Knowlton, his brother-in-law.

1317 Joseph and Abigail Canuth had no children. He m. 2d Harriet Bowker, June 16, 1836, and had:

(3179) Abigail C., May 28, 1837. m. J. C. P. Chapin. Had dau. Charlotte, who m. Dr. V. P. Gibney of N. Y. City.
(3180) Cynthia Eva, April 13, 1839.
Residence, Phillipston, Mass.

Joseph was a Deacon in the Congregational Church, a Selectman, and Town Treasurer. He d. March 6, 1840. She d. February 13, 1834.

1318 Francis E. and Rev. J. W. Chickering had:

(3181) Prof. John W. Res., Washington, D. C.
(3182) Frances, April 25, 1834.
(3183) Prof. Joseph, July 20, 1836. Res., New Haven, Conn.
(3184) Mary G., February 24, 1841.

1319 Stephen S. and Sally Atwood had:

(3185) Harriet, November 3, 1827. d. May 3. 1857.
(3186) Stephen, January 20, 1831. m. Frances Kent, August 25, 1858. A Congregational minister in Danville, Vt.
(3187) Susan E., October 10, 1833. d. April 7, 1877.
(3188) Mary F., June 8, 1839.
(3189) Eliza A., August 3, 1841. d. December 20, 1860.
Residence, Pittsfield, Vt.

Sally d. July 28, 1861. Samuel was a Deacon in the Congregational Church. He d. February 24, 1865.

1321 Jonas and Eliza Pinney had:

(3190) Joseph, October 22, 1873. m. Sarah Hansell, September 17, 1867.
(3191) Henry. m. Georgiana Penny, October 19, 1870.

(3192) William, November 9, 1839. d. February 14, 1849.
(3193) Fannie, January 18, 1851. m. Jacob Keslur.
Residence, Portage des Sioux, Mo.

Jonas d. December 3, 1876.

1323 Emmons and Abigail Taggart had:

(3194) Albert F., February 21, 1841. m. Maria Cozzens, December 19, 1867.

Abigail d. March 19, 1841, and Emmons m. Hattie A. Taggart, October 9, 1844. They had:

(3195) John R., January 5, 1846. m. Emma C. Cornell, January 13, 1870.
Soldier during the whole War of the Rebellion from 1861.
(3196) Abbie, March 10, 1848. d.
(3197) Carrie, July 15, 1858. d. April 7, 1864.

1325 Phoebe (or Phila) Knowlton and Joseph Taggart had:

(3198) George, April 26, 1851. Res., Royalton, Vt.
(3199) Charles, August 1, 1855. d. December 14, 1865. Res., Royalton, Vt.
(3200) Flora, November, 1858. Res., Royalton, Vt.
Res., Stockbridge and Royalton, Vt.

1326 Abigail Knowlton and Alonzo Keyes had:

(3201) Willie, November 18, 1863. d. young.
(3202) Alonzo, April 6, 1865.

1327 George and Betsey Brummell had:

(3203) Mary.
(3204) Sarah. m. Had Harriet A., March 29, 1849.
(3205) George.
(3206) Laura.

1328 John and Rebecca Sperry had:

(3207) George. m. Henrietta Webber.
(3208) Julius S., 1816. m. Res., Meriden, Conn.
(3209) Mary J., 1820. m. W. N. Porter. Res., Beach Pond, Pa.
(3209 A) Moses, 1822. Res., Harpersfield, N. Y.

John d. 1853.

1330 Betsey Knowlton and Joel Finch had:

(3210) Maria.
(3211) Harriet.
(3212) Mary A.

1331 Polly Knowlton and John Sanford had:

(3213) Augustus.
(3214) Albert.
(3215) Lysander.

1335 Erastus and Mary Moore had:

(3216) Samuel, October 24, 1833. m. Mary Kenworthy, October 28, 1858.
(3217) Fannie, May 20, 1836. m. Wolstan Dixie, May 20, 1858.
(3218) Henry M., March 30, 1840. d. young.
(3219) Mary E., January 8, 1844. m. C. H. Sturtevant, October 6, 1860.

Erastus res. in Brookfield, Mass. He drove for many years the mail and passenger coach on the old stage road between Springfield and Worcester. In 1837 he entered the service of the Boston & Albany R. R., and was baggage master on the first train that ran between the above cities. He was promoted for his efficiency, and was for a long time, and until his death, December 31, 1848, the head of the baggage department at Worcester station, invaluable to the company and to the travelling public by reason of his experience and affability. Mary d. October 19, 1858.

1336 Sewell and Maria Quance had:

(3220) Julia M., September 8, 1834. m. H. H. West, July 3, 1850.
(3221) James M., December 4, 1835. m. Sophia Drake.
(3222) John C., January 5, 1839. m. Tamsen Ingles, September 3, 1860.
(3223) George H., August 26, 1840. m. Phoebe Evans, 1862.

(3224) Mary A., September 21, 1841. m. James Strickland, 1862.
(3225) Helen H., April 3, 1851. m. Franklin Clark, February 29, 1868.
(3226) Sophia, June 20, 1854. m. William Smith, May 8, 1873.
(3227) William, July 18, 1855. d. April 10, 1867.

Sewell d. March 21, 1869.

1341 Fannie Knowlton and A. B. Jones had:

(3228) Edward, March 22, 1839.
(3229) Eliza, January 11, 1841. m. —— Stacey. Res., Springfield.
(3230) George, October 23, 1844.
(3231) Frances, July 18, 1849. m. —— Fass. Res., Springfield.

Residence, Chicopee Falls, Mass.

1342 James M. and Nancy Kendall had:

(3232) Jane.
(3233) Mary.

1343 Samuel and Marietta Howard had:

(3234) Marietta, August 26, 1844. m. W. H. Grath, November 27, 18[illegible]7.
(3235) Albert W., May 5, 1846. d. June 3, 1865.
(3236) Lucy E., September 5, 1850. m. Fred C. Hyde, February 2, 1871.

1345 Catherine Knowlton and Levi Whitcomb had:

(3237) Calvin H., March 8, 1828.
(3238) Rosina, June 29, 1830.
(3239) Joel A., September 12, 1832.
(3240) Eliza A., June 18, 1838.

They rem. to Simms Co., Iowa, 1847.

1346 Levi W. and Amanda Hollister had:

(3241) Levi, May 2, 1834. m. Fannie C. Alsdorf, May 13, 1861.
(3242) Amanda, November 25, 1836. m. Zenophon Wheeler, 1862. She d. in Chattanooga, Tenn.
(3243) Mary A., April 25, 1838. m. Henry Baker, 1861. Res., Trenton, Mo.

Levi rem. to Utica, Ohio, in 1832. d. there September 18, 1870. Amanda was from South Glastonbury, Conn. d. October 25, 1868.

1349 Lucy Knowlton and Thomas Carter had:

(3244) Emeline L., August 13, 1832. m. —— Bleeker, September, 1870. Residence, Chatham, Medina Co., Ohio.

Thomas d. June 24, 1876. Lucy d. October 24, 1865.

1350 Orilla Knowlton and John Luck had:

(3245) Orilla F.

Orilla d. October 22, 1842.

1352 Edward and Abigail F. Williams had:

(3246) Ella L., November 9, 1851. m. John M. Hales, September 25, 1872.
(3247) Frederick, January 28, 1854. m. Ida Shirley. Residence, Marion, Iowa.

1353 Francis P. and Nancy Wilson had:

(3248) Clara E., May 11, 1850.

Francis d. May 11, 1871.

1354 Mary Knowlton and Edward Wright had:

(3249) Jerome, July 18, 1826. m. Hannah Almy, October 7, 1845.
(3250) Mary, March 11, 1828. m. Robert Daggett, October 17, 1847.
(3251) Hollis, September 13, 1829. d. March 27, 1854.
(3252) Polly, October 30, 1832. d. July 30, 1883.
(3253) Fannie, May 29, 1834. m. Philip Phelps, February 16, 1856.
(3254) Addie, December 15, 1835. m. Cyrus Nichols, April 9, 1854.
(3254 A) Pamela, September 17, 1837. m. Giles Austin, April 4, 1860.

1356 Adaline Knowlton and Apollos Kenny had:

(3255) Amelia, September 24, 1835.
(3256) Jasper, September 8, 1837.
(3257) Samuel, May 10, 1845. m. Julia Starkweather.
(3258) Daniel, March 1, 1848. m. Elsie Norton, December 18, 1868.

1358 Daniel and Chlorine Bowker had:

(3259) Jennie, December 25, 1851.
(3260) Florence, May 28, 1854. m. W. H. Sheldon, February 8, 1874.
(3261) Alice S., October 18, 1857.
(3262) Adaline, January 30, 1859.
(3263) Azor S., January 28, 1861.
(3264) Mary E., November 6, 1863.
(3265) Thaddeus, January 28, 1866.
(3266) Maud J., May 27, 1868.
(3267) Edith, June 27, 1870.
(3268) Fannie, March 15, 1873.

Residence, Waterloo, Wis.

Daniel d. March 22, 1875.

1359 Hepsabeth Knowlton and E. D. Wright had:

(3269) Fortescue, November 3, 1837. m. Chlorena Knowlton.
(3270) Carter E., March 24, 1842. m. Althea Wright, May 9, 1858.
(3271) Gesler K., June 13, 1843. m. Julia Pike, November 16, 1864.
(3272) Silas F., February 28, 1845. m. Ella Baker, February 8, 1865.
(3273) Louisa, May 9, 1848. m. Wm. Partridge.

1360 Thaddeus and Mary Stewart had:

(3274) Daniel S., September 30, 1853. m. Nelly Verney, January 27, 1876
(3275) Frank J., December 25, 1856. d. young.
(3276) Eva F., October 18, 1860. unm.

Res., Batavia, N. Y.

Thaddeus was b. in Bethany, N. Y., where he lived until 1885, removing then to Batavia, N. Y., where he d. after a long illness in 1896. Accounts differ as to the name of his wife, but his own daughter reports her mother's name as Mary Stewart, and not Phœbe Stevens.

1361 Levi P. and Alicia Dickerson had:

(3277) Martha, June 27, 1853. d. young.
(3278) Ezra D., January 8, 1856.
(3279) Elizabeth, June 22, 1858. d. August 27, 1863.
(3280) Ruel, August 22, 1862.
(3281) Jeremiah, August 8, 1867.

1362 Elbridge and Artelissa Robinson had:

(3282) George F., October 30, 1832. m. Lovie Mason, September 15, 1858.
(3283) Ellen M., August 3, 1834. m. Thos. Hodgkins, Northfield, Mass., March 16, 1856.
(3284) Lizzie, May 27, 1836. m. A. G. Stockwell, February 17, 1870.
(3285) Frances J., September 13, 1838. m. Warner Hodgkins, Rochester, Vt., November 27, 1860.
(3286) Elbridge G., July 2, 1840. m. Addie Burnham, January 11, 1869. Soldier in the Rebellion.
(3287) Hermann L., June 11, 1842. m. Hattie Blodgett, December 24, 1870. Soldier in the Rebellion.
(3288) Horace R., October 24, 1844. m. Ada Blodgett, April 21, 1880.
(3289) Katie A., November 18, 1846. m. Eli Cook, of Halifax, Vt., March 1, 1876.
(3290) Harlan P., January 19, 1849. m. Hannah Kaye, September 14, 1876.

Residence, Guilford, Vt.

1363 Diodema Knowlton and Elijah Wyman had:

(3291) Sarah A., June 1, 1833. m. Henry Lewis, February 12, 1865.
(3292) Cyrus, October 4, 1835. m. Ellen Washburn, January 10, 1859.
(3293) John K., April, 1, 1838. m. Alice Nason, May, 1869.
(3294) Lucien, 1842. Commissary clerk in Army of Potomac. d. at Fort Slocum, October 16, 1863.

Residence, Rochester, Vt.

1364 Sarah D. Knowlton and D. Franklin Dortt had:

(3295) Luella, June 10, 1834.
(3296) Parthenia, November 30, 1835.
(3297) Lucy Ann, February 20, 1837.
(3298) Elizabeth, January 26, 1840.

D. F. Dortt d. in Rochester, Vt., October 19, 1840.

1366 Ruel and Sarah Luther had:

(3299) Sarah J., March 19, 1837. m. John W. Bigelow.
(3300) Charles J., November 12, 1842. d. August 8, 1861.

1369 Daniel and Aurilla Pinkham had :

(3302) Lucius H., August 16, 1845. d. young.
(3303) Clara A., May 20, 1847. m. S. B. Slate, September 1, 1866.
(3304) Julia F., July 29, 1849. m. Eben C. Hunter, July 31, 1872.
(3305) Myra F., February 25, 1851. d. young.
(3306) C. Adora, April 15, 1852. m. Dyer Murphy, January 15, 1873.
(3307) Stella, January 9, 1854
(3308) Eli, February 3, 1856.
(3309) Ida J., June 19, 1858.

Residence rem. from Worcester, Mass., to Michigan, in 1854, thence to Gordon Plains, Ill., in 1859.

1370 Elijah and Mehitable Hall had :

(3310) Samuel H., February 9, 1844. m. Flora Dadman, August 31, 1876.
(3311) Mary C., March 30, 1846. d. August 18, 1865.
(3312) Calvin, January 27, 1648. d. January 30, 1859.

1371 Charles H. and Martha Boyden had :

(3313) Charles L., March 15, 1851. m. Had son, Frank E., 1873.
(3314) Albert B., September 20, 1855.
(3315) Edwin C., January 26, 1857.

1375 Perrin and Elizabeth Carter had :

(3316) Mary E., February 2, 1827. m. Dr. Sylvester F. Mixer, February 23, 1853.
(3317) Rev. Chauncey Carter, June 23, 1832. m. Sarah Hastings of Richwood, Ohio.
(3317 A) Annie Carter, May 23, 1837. m Townsend Davis, of Buffalo, N. Y.

Perrin was born in Shrewsbury, Mass., whence he rem. to Mt. Vernon, Ohio, and thence to Cincinnati.

He was a man of such striking appearance as to arrest the attention of strangers, who involuntarily turned about to get a second look at him. Very tall, erect, and remarkably handsome, with jet black hair and eyes, he was altogether a stately figure among his fellow-citizens, and his great natural intelligence, mental force, and physical energy gave him an undisputed influence over his associates.

Elizabeth, was the daughter of Chauncey Carter, Esq., of Brooklyn, N. Y. She d. August 24, 1884. Perrin d. in Buffalo.

1374 Irene Knowlton and Washington Wakefield had:

(3318) Callista,
(3319) Charles.

1376 Newell and Sophia Wallace had:

(3320) Moses A., February 26, 1828, m. Sarah J. Wright, March 23, 1851. She d. March 12, 1858.
(3321) Newell F., August 30, 1832. m. Mary J. Matthews, July 22, 1852.
(3322) Mary L., July 18, 1836. m. Thomas Paxter, July 21, 1856.
(3323) Grover W., February 26, 1838. d. April 28, 1858.
(3324) Adelaide S., June 25, 1842. m. M. W. Brigham, December 25, 1861.
(3325) Marcia E., June, 1, 1848. d. September 9, 1857.

1378 Lydia B. Knowlton and Elisha A. Briggs had:

(3325 A) Otis C.

1387 Julia A. Knowlton and Seth Baker had:

(3326) Benjamin F., April 28, 1817. m. Delinda Hagar, October 17, 1839.
(3327) Winfield S., September 23, 1819.
(3328) Lucy C., April 19, 1822.
(3329) Edmund, April 26, 1824.
(3330) David, May 28, 1827.
(3331) Jerome, July 8, 1831.
(3332) Marietta, April 27, 1833.
(3333) Cynthia, December 17, 1838.

1389 Artemus and Fanny Spencer had :

(3334) Melvin, February 22, 1826. M. Jane E. Morrell, September 6, 1847 ; m. 2d Mrs. Elizabeth Compton.

(3335) Charles B., June 20, 1827. m. Ellen M. Grover, December 11, 1855.

(3336) Henry, June 16, 1829. d. September 25, 1849. Law student.

(3337) Harriet, June 12, 1833. m. Meredith Thomas.

(3338) Josephine. m. Carlos Sharp, Lockport, N. Y.

(3339) Walter. d. young.

Fanny was b. in Sempronus, Cayuga Co., N. Y., August 30, 1865. d. November 17 1865.

1391 Abraham and —— had :

(3340) Oscar.

(3341) Egbert.

1393 David and Harriet L. Hamilton had :

(3342) Mary A., June 16, 1835. m. William J. Wood, January 15, 1867. 4 chil.

(3343) Ella A., January 4, 1851. m. John Adams, December 28, 1869.

Residence, Battle Creek, Mich.

1394 Marietta Knowlton and Chester Keyes had :

(3344) Jerome C., February 26, 1839. d. July 8, 1869.

(3345) Lucy C., October 24, 1841. d. young.

(3346) Nellie F., September 6, 1844. m. Henry Dickerson ; m. 2d Henry Bangs. 2 chil.

(3347) Mary G., December 28, 1846. d. young.

(3348) Ellis B., September 25, 1842. d. young.

1396 Mary E. Knowlton and Louis Brown had :

(3349) Henry L., February 13, 1830.

(3350) Waldo F., October 24, 1832.

(3351) Edwin W., March 26, 1837.

(3352) Emma A., October 10, 1841. m. Ezra F. Peabody.

(3353) Myra A., February 3, 1844.

(3354) Benjamin H., September 6, 1846.

Residence rem. from Worcester, Mass., to Reedsburg, Wis., and thence to Oxford, Ohio, where Mary d. May 25, 1874, and Louis, March 3, 1876.

1397 James F. and Olive Brown had :

(3355) George F., April 30, 1836. d. March 16, 1865.

Olive d. February 4, 1838, and James m. 2d Margaret Dickey, September 27, 1838. They had :

(3356) Olive B., November 30, 1840. m. Geo. M. Latham, April 10, 1865. 1 child.

(3357) Emily J., November 13, 1843. m. Geo. M. Latham, April 28, 1870. d. December 9, 1872.

(3358) John D., June 15, 1847. m. Irene Evans.

(3359) Charles L., June 23, 1849. m. Emma Denny, December 5, 1872.

(3360) Warren M., July 2, 1852. m. Emma F. Lee, September 27, 1877.

(3361) Mary J., June 25, 1855. d. young.

Residence, Geneva, Kansas.

1398 Nancy Knowlton and Chas. N. Ide had :

(3362) Ella C., May 11, 1843. m. Philetus Martin.

Residence, Oxford, Ohio.

1399 Sarah W. Knowlton and John Brown had :

(3363) Margaret, April 14, 1842. m. Geo. F. Ward, September, 1863.

(3364) Agnes, April 10, 1844. m. Wm. Ford, February, 1876.

(3365) Lucy, June 18, 1848.

Residence, Brownsville, Ind.

1401 Charles A. and Sarah Crouch ; m. 2d Caroline E. Crouch ; m. 3d Nancy Cooper. They had :

(3366) Emma C., October 10, 1846. m. Casper Crist, 1870.

(3367) Charlotte, July 22, 1848. m. Wm. Macy, 1868.

(3368) Nathan, December 25, 1850. m. Sett. in Texas. An engineer.

Residence, Liberty, Ind.

1402 Charlotte Knowlton and Williamson D. Vanoter had :

(3369) Emma K., September, 1853.

(3370) Charles K., September, 1855. d. September 27, 1879.

Residence, Santa Monica, Cal.

Williamson D. d. July 1, 1894. Charlotte d. December 27, 1893.

15

1403 Harry G. and Martha Miller had:

(3371) Albert, July 16, 1847. m. Had dau., Maud P., November 13, 1874.
(3372) William, June 23, 1850. m. Had dau., Mertie, June 15, 1875.
(3373) Emily, December 20, 1852.
(3374) Chas. E., June 8, 1855.
(3375) Sanford, June 8, 1858.
(3376) Marian L., March 31, 1862.
(3377) Olive, March 9, 1866.

1406 Lucy Knowlton and Moses Haskell had:

(3378) Sylvia.
(3379) Charlotte.
(3380) Jane.
(3381) Waldo.

1408 Stillman and Lydia Cheney had:

(3382) Chas. H., 1828. d. 1842.

Lydia d. 1829, and Stillman m. 2d Emily Thorpe, December 29, 1831. They had:

(3383) Nathan, 1830.
(3384) Emma J., 1837. m. Had Eva, Grace, and Samuel.
(3385) Josephine, 1841. m. Had Henry H. and Fred H.
(3386) Charles W., August 21, 1844. Res., Brooklyn, N. Y.

Stillman was a man of remarkable physique, being 6 ft. 2½ in. tall. He d. May 18, 1874.

1411 Elizabeth Knowlton and Joseph Blood had:

(3387) Edward J., April 1, 1852.
Residence, Groter, Kansas.

1413 Emery and Polly Fisher had:

(3388) Ezekiel, November 12, 1823. d. young.
(3389) Mary, October 20, 1825. d. young.
(3390) Ezekiel A., August 26, 1826. d. March 24, 1830.
(3391) Leander, November 21, 1828. m. Nancy Kelton, January 10, 1854.

(3392) Augustus, October 14, 1831. m. Martha Putnam, April 2, 1862.
(3393) Henry C., December 24, 1833. m. Mary A. Eaton, January 5, 1857.
(3394) Mary A., May 19, 1836. m. Charles Whitney, December 2, 1857.
(3395) Chloe, January 23, 1838.
(3396) Lyman, April 26, 1842.

Emery was a manufacturer. He d. July 1, 1857, in Gardner, Mass.

1414 Charles and Tabitha Stewart had:

(3397) Charles L., May 3, 1824. m. Rebecca Williams.
(3398) Lucy M., August 5, 1827. m. S. W. Faber, May 2, 1843.
(3399) Owen S., October 29, 1828. d. 1849.
(3400) Augusta C., November 25, 1831. m. A. H. Thompson, November 15, 1854. She d. July, 1892.
(3401) Willis, May 2, 1837. m. Mary H. Holten, May 15, 1858.
Residence, Ashfield (Winchendon), Mass.

Dr. Charles Knowlton was b. in Templeton, Mass. He worked on his father's farm in summer, and attended school in winter until eighteen years old. He was graduated from Hanover Medical College in 1824, practised medicine in various towns, and finally settled in Ashfield, Mass. As a physician and a writer on medical science he showed talents of a high order, and many of his publications were widely circulated and highly prized. He d. February 10, 1850.

1415 Augustus B. and Anna M. Simms had:

(3402) Dr. Augustus Barton, June 23, 1827. Augusta, Ga.
(3403) Stephen, May 15, 1840. m. Eliza Hallett.
(3404) Anna Simms, July 27, 1844. m. Chas. L. Colby, May 10, 1864.

Augustus Barton Knowlton res. in Ashfield, Mass. He was greatly interested in the Knowlton genealogy, and made a considerable collection of family records, all of which were destroyed by fire.

1417 Justus and Chloe Hanruven had:

(3405) Permelia, November 21, 1816. m. Dr. Joel Holton, December 3, 1839.
(3406) Melvin, August 7, 1818. m. Orendia Sabin, December 2, 1841.
(3407) Lucy F., July 24, 1820. m. D. Dobbins, September 16, 1842.
(3408) Miles J., February 28, 1825. m. Lucy St. John, July 10, 1853.
(3409) Jason S., June 8, 1827. m. Cornelia Thompson, May, 1850.

1418 Sullivan and Isabel Begold had:

(3410) A son, September 23, 1818. d. young.
(3411) Philomela, August 21, 1819. d. young.
(3412) Amelia, October 14, 1820. m. C. P. Pierce, May 15, 1844.
(3413) Lyman S., February 12, 1822. m. Mary J. Boyle, September 16, 1850.
(3414) Elizabeth S., June 10, 1826. m. Alden Wakefield, June 9, 1849. She d. January 29, 1854.
(3415) Lucretia, June 1, 1832. m. Geo. M. Bissell, October 5, 1865.

1419 Chester and Sally Bixby had:

(3416) Rosina, April 18, 1818. d. April 12, 1839.
(3417) Tryphena, April 8, 1820. m. Isaac W. Fero, January 9, 1842.
(3418) Jeyhendra, April 30, 1821. m. Wm. Blandon, July 6, 1843.
(3419) Sarah D., February 22, 1823. m. Daniel Chapman, May 30, 1841.
(3420) Calista, February 20, 1824. d. young.
(3421) Mary R., January 22, 1826. m. Alfred Robson, September 20, 1855.
(3422) Philura, April 5, 1827. m. Daniel Clark, November 30, 1848. She d. February3, 1872.
(3423) Louisa, January 27, 1829. m. Wm. Culver.
(3424) Malvina, July 20, 1832. d. young.

Sally d. October 25, 1841, and Chester m. 2d Susan Underwood, June 5, 1842. They had:

(3425) Lodemia, April 4, 1851.

Chester d July 9, 1867.

1420 Samantha Knowlton and Luther Johnson had:

(3426) Arvilla, October 27, 1821.
(3427) Chandler, October 29, 1822.

1421 Miles J. and Lemyra Bartlett; m. 2d Abigail Howard; m. 3d. Betsey Jones. They had:

(3428) Frank. m. Sarah Gillson, of Hinsdale, N. H.
(3429) Henry. m. Eliza Prouty.
(3430) William. m. ——. d. in Baltimore, 1885.
(3431) Adaline. m. Wm. B. Prouty. He d. 1863.

1422 Tryphena Knowlton and Nathaniel Kidder had :

(3432) Elvira, March 16, 1821.
(3433) Catherine, July 23, 1822.
(3434) Francis, February 1, 1924.
(3435) Jerome, March 11, 1826.
(3436) Albert, January 10, 1828.
(3437) Tryphena, December 4, 1830.
(3438) Roxalina, September 5, 1832.
(3439) William, March 18, 1834.
(3440) Harriet, August 27, 1836.
(3441) Sarah P., September 7, 1838.
(3442) Lucinda, September 10, 1840.

1423 Roxanna Knowlton and Simeon Hungerford had :

(3443) Angeline, July 8, 1840.
(3444) Nelson, January 14, 1842.
(3445) Samantha, January 1, 1846.

Simeon d. February 20, 1877.

1435 Miles and Belena Ellis had :

(3446) Lyman, 1834. m. Maria S. Patton, 1856.
(3447) Melinda, 1842. m. Osgood P. Brown. Had chil., Nellie and Winthrop.

Miles d. in Canada, P. Q., 1876.

1438 Hannah Knowlton and Amasa Lewis had :

(3448) Mary E.
(3449) Betsey L.
(3450) Cynthia.
(3451) Amasa E.
(3452) Hannah H.
(3453) Silas.
(3454) Ezekiel.
(3455) Asaph K.
(3456) George.

Hannah d. April 27, 1888, in Waterloo, P. Q.

1439 Amasa and Harriet Lewis had:

(3457) Stillman, February 19, 1837. m. Cornelia Hyatt, September 14, 1858.
(3458) Caroline E. October 9, 1838. m. Wm. F. Kent, August 9, 1857.
(3459) Alfred S., April 8, 1842. m. Mary Hamilton, December 27, 1864.
(3460) Laura S., March 11, 1845. m. Hiram Kent, December 29, 1862.
(3461) Abigail C., February 15, 1850. m. Samuel Porter, October 1, 1873.
(3462) Sarah M., November 5, 1855. m. Wm. Christie, March 5, 1875.
Residence, Stukely and Waterloo, P. Q.

Amasa d. January 18, 1885. Harriet d. November 25, 1875.

1441 Harriet Knowlton and Hial Curtis had:

(3463) John, December 30, 1839. m. Myra Knowlton.
(3464) Amos B., September 11, 1843. m. Mary E. Willard.
(3465) Ezra N., October 19, 1854. m. Emma Batchelder, February 12, 1880.
(3466) Homer, September 20, 1848. d. 1853.

1442 Asaph A. and Mary Peasley had:

(3467) Mary L., July 1, 1846. m. Wm. A. Geddes, June 1, 1864.
(3468) James A., March 9, 1848. m. Ella Wilder, March 14, 1877. He. d. November 18, 1883.
(3469) Harriet A., January 22, 1850. unm. Res. Oldfield, Iowa.
(3470) Marion B., March 9, 1857. d. young.

Asaph rem. from Canada, to Mitchellsville, Iowa, and d. June 1, 1886, at Oldfield, Iowa.

1443 Luke Holland and Elizabeth Spinney had:

(3471) Mark A., August 19, 1841. m. Josephine Hyatt, May 15, 1867.
(3472) Myra C., September 10, 1843. m. John C. Curtis, February 3, 1864.
(3473) Luke W., December 6, 1845. m. Sophie Willard, October 7, 1886.
(3474) Armina, December 6, 1845. unm.
(3475) John A., January 22, 1848. unm.
(3476) Jane E., June 3, 1853. d. 1856.
(3477) Levi M., February 26, 1856. d. 1856.
(3478) Walter M., August 27, 1857. unm.

Luke Holland was a farmer and merchant. He was very prominent in public and political affairs, and for over thirty years he held the offices of Secretary-Treasurer of the school and municipal funds of South Stukely, P. Q. He d. July 13, 1892. Elizabeth d. 1895.

1444 Cynthia Knowlton and Roswell Sargent had :

(3479) Prosper, August 22, 1836.
(3480) Sarah W., November 27, 1840.
(3481) Aretta, June 7, 1846.
(3482) Alfred, July 4, 1851.
(3483) Myron K., May 18, 1856.

Residence, So. Stukely, P. Q.

Cynthia d. August 7, 1893. Roswell d. at So. Stukeley.

1445 Ezekiel and Nancy Bryant had :

(3484) Betsey A., July 18, 1843. m. Chas. A. Savage, January 1, 1863. She d. June 8, 1865.
(3485) Holey A., September 12, 1844. m. Delia Smith, October 4, 1870. Res., Plainview, Minn.
(3486) Nancy L., June 12, 1846. m. Chas. A. Savage, June 17, 1868. Res. Leominster, Mass.
(3487) Amasa J., February 10, 1848. m. Ellen Rixford, May, 1872.
(3488) Loella, March 3, 1850. m. Frank Eaton, January 22, 1875.
(3489) Lyman E., December 7, 1851. m. Eleanor Stone, June 14, 1878.
(3490) Albert C., March 4, 1854. m. Lydia Giddings. Res., Knowlton.
(3491) George, October 4, 1855. m. Res., Dakota.
(3492) Hattie A., April 23, 1857. m. Res., Manchester, Mass.
(3493) Amos C., August 9, 1859.
(3494) Chas S., June 12, 1861. unm.

Residence, So. Stukely.

Ezekiel d. January 31, 1889.

1447 Czarina Knowlton and Shepard Parker had :

(3495) Shepard Pratt, November 14, 1817. m. Elizabeth Harris.
(3496) Helen M., January 26, 1822. m. Julius Shepherd.
(3497) Cynthia, December 15, 1823. m. Joseph Palmer.
(3498) Danford, November 11, 1825. m. Sophronia Lewis. Killed in the battle of Gettysburg.

(3499) Luke, September 8, 1827. Died from effects of a fall.
(3500) Enos, October 27, 1829. m. Ellen Gould. Killed by fall from horse.
(3501) Mark, January 13, 1833. Res. in California.
(3502) Leander, August 29, 1837. m. Ellen Oakley, February 9, 1864.
(3503) Elizabeth, October 23, 1839. m. Edward Hinckley.

They rem. from Canada to Wisconsin, where Czarina d. at Hartford, September 6, 1846. Shepard P. d. August 23, 1846.

1448 Rosetta Knowlton and Aaron Frost had:

(3504) William.
(3505) Harriet.
(3506) Matilda.
(3507) Martha.
(3508) Mary W.
(3609) Caroline.

Residence, rem. from Frost Village, P. Q., to Lowell, Mass., where Rosetta d. January, 1829.

1449 Lee and Maria Sargent had:

(3510) Eliza M., June 9, 1829. m. Wm. M. Atwood, November 9, 1852.
(3511) Horace L., September 6, 1831. m. Caroline Goff, September 28, 1852.
(3512) Sophia S. S., October 17, 1835. m. James Channell, March 31, 1857.
(3513) Amanda M., July 13, 1841. m. Gilbert M. Willey, March 18, 1873. One son d. young. Res., Boston, Mass.

Residence, So. Stukely and Magog, P. Q.

Lee was engaged in insurance, manufacturing, and railroad enterprises. He d. March 8, 1854.

1450 Stephen and Elizabeth Hiliker had:

(3514) Rosetta M., January 22, 1834. m. George I. Shepherd, December 23, 1839.
(3515) Hannah M., April 22, 1836. m. James Rooney, December 27, 1859.
(3516) Stephen, February 14, 1838. m. Margaret Rooney, December 24, 1863.
(3517) Lyman, March 30, 1840. m. Catherine E. Martin, January 11, 1864.
(3518) William Keene, March 27, 1842. m. Annie P. Day, May 17, 1870.
(3519) Alfred, November 19, 1845. m. Charlotte Coburn, February 6, 1870.

(3520) Melinda, June 2, 1848. m. Franklin Martin, March 1, 1869. She d. June 9, 1873.
(3521) Merinda, June 2, 1848. d. young.
(3522) Merinda, August 25, 1852. m. Robert Savage, January 5, 1876.

Stephen P. d. July 10, 1866. Elizabeth d. March 4, 1887.

1451 Jane Knowlton and Jacob Shepherd had :

(3523) Stillman K., August 22, 1826.
(3524) Thomas L., August 22, 1828.
(3525) William H., October 13, 1830.
(3526) Sepha J., October 28, 1833.
(3527) Ezekiel H., May 5, 1835.
(3528) Symira, August 30, 1837.
(3529) George A., June 30, 1840.
(3530) Helen L., November 23, 1842.
(3531) Ambrose, April 23, 1845.
(3532) Roxanna C., April 19, 1847.
(3533) Flora A., June 20, 1849.
(3534) Frederick, October 5, 1851.
(3535) Ida M., January 13, 1853.
(3536) Jonathan.

Residence, So. Stukely, Canada, P. Q.

Jane d. December 24, 1895. Jacob was a tanner. He d. June 1, 1889, in Osage, Iowa.

1453 Newton and Laura Turner had :

(3537) Stillman N., November 17, 1840. m. Sophia Libbey, August 16, 1860.
(3538) George W., January 1, 1843. m. Melissa Schoolcraft, December 7, 1864.
(3539) Arthur A., September 9, 1845. m. Lizzie M. Boynton. Res., Magog, P. Q.
(3540) Paul H., January 13, 1848. m. Lizzie Keezer. Res., No. Hatley.
(3541) Jessie M., September 10, 1850. m. —— Shaw.
(3542) Cynthia M., June 19, 1853. m. C. M. Keezer, November 25, 1875.
(3543) Lee H., February 19, 1856. unm.
(3544) Whitcomb, December 3, 1858. d. November 25, 1870.

Residence, Magog, P. Q.

Ne[illegible]n d. February 2, 1862.

1454 Anna Knowlton and Luther Libby had :

(3545) Lucy M.
(3546) David G.
(3547) Harriet S.
(3548) Mark.
(3549) Elizabeth.
(3550) Almira.
(3551) Lyman M.

Anna d. September 25, 1864.

1455 George Willard and Elizabeth Carroll had :

(3552) Sophia W., June 9, 1831. m. Chas. Perkins, November 20, 1852. She d. June 12, 1853.
(3553) Maria C., April 26, 1833. m. John Rice, November 30, 1852. She d. 1884.
(3554) Elizabeth, December 3, 1834. d. August 16, 1847.
(3555) John C., February 22, 1837. m. Susan Fiske, December 3, 1863.
(3556) George W., August 17, 1839. m. Frances G. Clark ; m. 2d Gertrude S. Ely.

George Willard Knowlton was b. in Newfane, Vt., and rem. to Brattleboro, thence to Watertown, N. Y., in 1825. In 1824 he organized the firm of Knowlton & Rice, for manufacturing paper, and he continued actively in this business until 1854, when he retired, leaving the business to his two sons. The goods manufactured by this firm have always held a first position in the market.

Elizabeth d. in 1896. Geo. W. d. October 18, 1886.

1457 Sally Knowlton Warner and James Miller had :

(3557) James Warner Miller, July 8, 1807. m. Mary G. Bryant. Residence, Newark, O.

Residence rem. from Dummerston, Vt., to Ohio. The Millers were of Scotch descent, and furnished soldiers for the French and Indian, Revolutionary, 1812, Mexican, and Civil Wars of America.

1460 Willard Warner and Elvira Williams had :

(3558) Anna E. m. Hon. —— Woods, Justice Supreme Court, U. S. Wid. Anna E. res., Vineyard Haven, Mass.

1465 Paul Holland and Laura Moss having no children, they adopted several of the children of Luke, son of Silas.

HON. PAUL HOLLAND KNOWLTON.

Paul Holland, son of Silas and Sarah was born in Newfane, Vt., and was, therefore, but a lad when his parents invaded the wilderness. He was old enough, however, to remember that he was left with his mother in a temporary log cabin on the way while his father and Capt. John Whitney went off to hunt game for supper, and to procure fodder for their oxen; the women keeping off the wild beasts by lighting fires around the cabin, and hanging blankets before the door and windows. Young Paul was sent back to Newfane three years later to be educated, and while attending the academy he boarded with his grandfather Luke, and his uncle, Luke, Jr. From these two kinsmen and rare men he daily drew an inspiration that determined his future career. He returned to Stukely in 1807, and when but twenty years old married Miss Laura Moss, a school teacher of Bridport, Vt. After spending six years in farming, he purchased another large farm in Brown Township in 1834, and also engaged in mercantile pursuits on an extensive and varied scale. He built mills, stores, and a church, and threw himself with characteristic energy into every possible effort to promote the public and private interests of the infant community.

The permanent result of his creative genius and public spirit is seen to-day in the town of Knowlton, named from its founder, charmingly situated at the head of Brome Lake, and a centre of business, social, and religious activity. It was inevitable that the first permanent settler in, and founder of, Knowlton should become a prominent factor in the larger problem and sphere of provincial development, and this he became, giving his services for the most part without fee or reward. He was a prominent member of the Historical and Literary Society of the Province of Quebec; a member of the Provincial Parliament in 1827, and he served as a member of the Special Council for Lower Canada, and also of the Legislative Council for thirty-five years, until his death in 1863. He was commissioned Lieut.-Colonel of Militia in 1837, and by his personal force and military skill the Canadian troops subdued the Papineau rebellion incited by religious fanaticism. For this public service he received the thanks of Parliament, and his reputation passed over to the mother country. Henceforth his life was tinged with something of romance. The honorable mention in the English papers attracted the attention of Miss Knowlton of Darley Dale, and led first to a correspondence, and then to an invitation to visit her. The invitation was accepted, an intimate friendship resulted, and in April, 1845, he opened an English letter to learn that the celebrated Devonshire beauty had died, leaving him heir to her entire and handsome fortune.

Hon. Paul Knowlton and Laura, his wife, having no children, adopted three of his brother Luke's children.

1466 Luke and Mary Ware had:

(3559) Sarah, April 20, 1822. m. Hiram S. Foster.
(3560) Sophia M., December 21, 1824. m. Samuel P. Wood, May 25, 1851.
(3561) Laura, January 25, 1826. unm.
(3562) Amanda, February 5, 1828. d. July 7, 1853. unm.
(3563) John Holland, January 30, 1830. m. Alena Gleason, December 10, 1856.
(3564) Luke H., December 24, 1831. unm. d. 1852.
(3565) Silas W., January 27, 1834. m. Susan Randall, December 4, 1861. No chil. He d. October 6, 1865. She m. 2d —— N. Currier, and d. in Illinois.
(3566) Rotus P., January 11, 1836. unm. Res., Montana.
(3567) Alice M., May 18, 1837. m. James C. Reed, August 4, 1859. She d. December, 1866. He d. March 12, 1867.
(3568) Jane E., September 13, 1839. m. Arad F. Foster, October 3, 1859. She d. 1878. He d. March 29, 1894. 2 chil.
(3569) William S., September 22, 1841. m. Jane Ingalls.
(3570) Thomas Anson, August 22, 1843. m. Sarah D. Foster, February 26, 1868.

Residence, Knowlton, P. Q.

1467 Samantha Knowlton and Samuel Stone had:

(3571) Melissa.
(3572) John.
(3573) William.
(3574) Simon.
(3575) Lucy.
(3576) Ellen. Res., California.
(3577) Adaline.
(3578) Fitch.

Res. rem. to Michigan in 1837, where five of her children died.

1468 Samuel W. and Amanda Loomis had:

(3579) Anna.

Residence, So. Stukely, P. Q.

1469 Patty Holbrook and William Fessenden had:

(3580) Sarah. m. Hon. Elisha H. Allen, Chief-Justice of the Sandwich Islands.
(3581) Ellen. m. John S. Blake, of Boston.
(3582) William W. unm.
(3583) Sophia K. unm.

Patty Holbrook and Wm. Fessenden res. for a time in Warehouse Point, Conn. William was a printer, book-binder, book-dealer, publisher, and paper-maker, carrying on an extensive business which the reputation of his product had built up for him. The development of the business compelled Mr. Fessenden to return to Brattleboro, where he d. at the age of 36, widely lamented. He published the first newspaper, "The Reporter," ever issued in Brattleboro.

1472 Sally Holbrook and Geo. W. Hall had:

(3584) Edward, and three others. Res. in Philadelphia.

Sally m. 2d Isaac Crale, and had:

(3585) Dau. m. —— Hyde, of Visaba, Cal.
(3586) Belle.
(3587) William. Res. in N. Y. City.

Sally d. September 5, 1849.

1476 Rev. John C. Holbrook and Cynthia Tuttle had:

(3588) ——
(3589) ——

He res. in Stockton, Cal.

1478 Frederick Holbrook and Harriet Goodhue had:

(3590) Franklin Fessenden, March 1, 1837. m. Res. in Boston. 4 chil.
(3591) William Cune, July 14, 1842. m. M. Chalmers. Res., N. Y. City. 6. chil.
(3592) John Calvin, July 17, 1852. unm. Res., Clearfield, Pa.

HON. FREDERICK HOLBROOK

is historically known as the distinguished "War Governor" of Vermont. He was the great-great-grandson of Thomas Knowlton, who married for his first wife Margery, daughter of Joseph Goodhue, and four generations later the Knowlton and Goodhue bloods again unite in Frederick Holbrook and his wife, the daughter of Col. Joseph Goodhue. Mr. Holbrook was b. in 1813, in Brattleboro, Vt., where his parents had settled in 1795. Natural genius had been assisted by a good education when young Holbrook began the work of practical life. At eighteen years of age, he was captain of a company of State Militia. Before he was of age he had learned a good deal of business matters and methods in the book store of Richardson, Lord, & Holbrook, Boston, but preferring agricultural life he returned to Brattleboro, and for many years was a practical farmer. He began his political career in 1847 as Register of Probate, and in 1849 and '50 was a State Senator. Chiefly by his efforts a joint committee was appointed at this time to consider the expediency of forming a National Bureau of Agriculture, and as Chairman of such committee he prepared a memorial to Congress which found prompt support in a recommendation in President Taylor's Message to Congress, that the proposed Bureau be organized. The recommendation was adopted, and the Bureau became a fact. From 1850–1861, Senator Holbrook was President of the State Agricultural Society, a member of the Board of Trustees of the Brattleboro Retreat, and President of the Vermont Savings Bank.

At the outbreak of the Rebellion, Senator Holbrook was nominated for Governor in a notable convention of men of all political creeds, who forgot party interests in the greater question of the preservation of the Union, and in September, 1861, he was elected by an overwhelming majority. He proposed and carried through a financial measure which enabled the State to equip and send into the field a larger number of troops, it is said, than any other State, in proportion to its population.

When President Lincoln was almost bewildered by conflicting opinions of politicians, he turned, in his anxious search for a clear and judicious estimate of duty, to Governor Holbrook, and the letter written by the latter being laid before Gen. Simeon Draper, Provost Marshal-General, and the Secretary of War, on a Tuesday night, solved the President's difficulties, and resulted in the call for 300,000 volunteers. To Governor Holbrook's courage and faith is due, in large part, the splendid record of the State in the war for the Union. In the face of opposition and honest doubts, he pushed through his own plan for a military hospital in Vermont, and the surprising cures wrought on the sick and wounded in the hospital at Brattleboro, and the conservation of the splendid material in the Green Mountain soldiers, placed the State far ahead of all other States in her successful treatment of sick and disabled soldiers.

The term of Governor Holbrook's official service was a most memorable one. And in private life he is an illustration of the symmetrical statesman, the zealous patriot, the modest gentleman, and the genial friend.

1491 Seleucia Knowlton and Hezekiah Robinson had:

(3593) Charlotte K., November 28, 1818. m. Roswell Ellis, February 26, 1839.
(3594) Jonathan, November 4, 1820. m. Emily Dampier.
(3595) Rev. Frederick, February 20, 1823. m. —— Johnson. Rector of Abbotsford, and Canon, Diocese of Montreal. d. 1893.
(3596) Seleucia, November 2, 1824. d. 1839 (or 1835).
(3597) Luke H., January 1, 1827. m. four times. One son, George.
(3598) Sarah M., December 5. 1828. m. —— Chandler. Son, George M., is a professor in Magill University, Montreal.
(3599) Rev. George C., August 25, 1831. m. Emma Whitten.
(3600) Abigail K., April 31, 1834. m. J. D. Parsonage, merchant.
(3601) Edward, September 6, 1837. m. Emily Dunning.

Seleucia d. December 8, 1876. Hezekiah was one of the most influential men in the Province of Quebec, and connected with its agricultural, commercial, and financial development, a devoted churchman and an upright citizen.

1492 Marcia Knowlton and Clarke Fisher had:

(3603) Katherine, September 3, 1821.
(3604) Marcia, June 10, 1823.
(3605) Sarah J., May 8, 1825.
(3606) Charlotte, March 18, 1827.
(3607) William S., February, 1829.
(3608) Marion, April 12, 1831.
(3609) Daniel, March 31, 1834.
(3610) Henry, October 27, 1836.

Marcia d. in Ohio, July 19, 1849.

1493 Sally Knowlton and Daniel W. Sanborn had:

(3611) Myron, November 23, 1820. m. Julia Westover.
(3612) Luke, April 29, 1822. unm. d. in Michigan.
(3613) Julia, November 15, 1823. m. Wm. Damphier. She d. in Los Angeles, Cal., January 11, 1897.

Daniel d. September 7, 1827, and Sally m. 2d Dr. Rotus Parmalee, and had:

(3614) Mary, January 3, 1836. m. Prof. Joseph Marsh, Forest Grove, Oregon.

(3615) David, March 10, 1838. d. in California.

Dr. Rotus d. in Forest Grove, Oregon, and Sally d. there, May 20, 1896.

1495 Charlotte and Austin Wheeler had:

(3616) Abigail S., September 3, 18 7. m. Bethuel Ranger, June 26, 1851. Brattleboro, Vt.
(3617) Susan W., February 14, 1829. m. J. C. Pettes, September 26, 1849.
(3618) Thomas W., November 16, 1830. m. Anna Duboise. Res., Knowlton.

Residence, Knowlton, P. Q.

Charlotte d. December 29, 1831. Austin d.

1496 Luke M. and Laura A. Wheeler had:

(3619) Luke W., October 6, 1833. d. young.
(3620) Infant son, August 11, 1834. d. same day.
(3621) Ellen M., February 8, 1836. m. John M. Fisk, June 5, 1860.
(3622) Henry C., June 20, 1838. m. Alma J. Corey, December 25, 1864.
(3623) A dau., August 8, 1848. d. young.
(3624) Lucia A., November 15, 1841. m. James Carter. Res., Missawippi, P. Q. No chil.
(3625) Luke L., July 21, 1843. m. Julia M. England, October 1, 1868.
(3626) Franklin, May 29, 1845. d. young.

Laura d. June 4, 1845, and Luke M. m. 2d Emma Peters, October 28, 1847. They had:

(3627) William M., July 24, 1849. d. young.
(3628) Mary E., April 12, 1850. m. Richard L. Carter, June 1, 1869.
(3629) Myron M, December 5, 1851. m. Susan Wheeler.
(3630) Charles R., December 14, 1853. m. Emily Crawford. He d. 1894, in California.
(3631) Frederick A., June 10, 1855. m. Sarah A. J. Corey. Res., Knowlton.
(3632) Walter H., March 8, 1858. d. April 14, 1864.

Emma d. January 20, 1876, and Luke M. m. 3d. Mrs. Chase. No chil.

Residence, Knowlton, P. Q.

Luke d. May 15, 1890. He was, at his death, the oldest inhabitant of Knowlton, a Justice of the Peace, Commissioner, and Councillor for many years, and was the father of the Liberal Party.

1499 Katherine and Merrick Cummings had :

(3633) Helen Warner, May 1, 1841. m. Chas. A. Wood, March 12, 1860. Res., Faribault, Minn.
(3634) Julia E., August 17, 1843. d. 1846.
(3635) Charles M., December 5, 1845. d. May 2, 1896.
(3636) Louisa, March 8, 1848. m. Chas. M. Starr, November 23, 1876.
(3637) George F., October 15, 1850. d. 1854.
(3638) Edward W., February 24, 1854. Druggist, Tower, Minn.
(3639) Abbie E., November 18, 1856. d. March 23, 1893, in Montreal. Residence, Granby, P. Q.

1500 Hanson and Mary Soles had :

(3640) Charlotte M., February 3, 1840. m. Asaph K. Lewis, March 16, 1869.
(3641) Agnes A., October 3, 1841. m. Almus Rexford, November 6, 1864. Res., Minneapolis, Minn. 1 dau., d.
(3642) Willard W., January 2, 1845. m. Isabella Elliot, September 14, 1868.
(3643) Warren H., April 29, 1847. m. Frances Cummings, June 16, 1874.
(3644) Hanson L., November 19, 1849. d. young.
(3645) Calvin H., June 2, 1852. d. young.
(3646) Emma A., January 30, 1854. m. Ernest Drake, January 20, 1873.
(3647) George A., May 26, 1855. m. Mary Clark, June 22, 1886. d. at So. Stukely.
(3648) Hanson E., June 26, 1858. d. 1861.
(3649) Arthur R., June 26, 1860. m. Ellen Howe, December 22, 1881.

Hanson rem. from Canada to Mitchell, Iowa, in 1865, and thence to Minneapolis, Minn.

1501 Patty Knowlton and John A. Jackson had :

(3650) Charles J., June 29, 1853. m. Julia Sanborn. 1 dau. Res., Montreal.
(3651) Frederick, June 29, 1858. d. young.

1502 Merab Knowlton and Wm. W. Willard had :

(3652) Charlotte, April 18, 1844. m. —— McLaughlin. Res., Sweetsburg, P. Q.

(3653) Samuel R., August 26, 1845. m. Emma Hill of Waterloo. 3 chil. Res., Brooklyn, N. Y.
(3654) Mary E., August 7, 1847. m. Amos B. Curtis.
(3655) Sophia A., October 7, 1851. m. Luke W. Knowlton.
(3656) Merab K., November, 1853. unm.
(3657) George, March 15, 1856. m. Jennie Spinney. Res., So. Stukely. 2 chil.
(3658) Elizabeth, July 25, 1863. unm.

Residence, So. Stukely.

Merab d. July 13, 1887.

1503 Goodloe and Julia Duboise had:

(3659) Lyman W., June 10, 1846. m. Nellie Ryerson, July 16, 1872.
(3660) Emily, February 24, 1848. d. 1854.
(3661) Luke G., June 12, 1862. d. October, 1896.
(3662) Martin H., June 12, 1862. m. Flora V. Detchemeudy.

Residence rem. from Canada to Iowa in 1867, where he d. November 7, 1894.

1506 Asa and Damaris Howe had:

(3663) Adaline, June 2, 1820. m. Simon Newton. She d. 1846.
(3664) Charles, January 4, 1822.

Residence, Shrewsbury, Mass.

1511 Seth and Volma (or Vilma), Shepard had:

(3665) Otis S., February 22, 1831. m. Mary Miller, January 11, 1854. Res., Clinton, Iowa. Furniture dealer and undertaker.
(3666) Artemus, May 20, 1839. m. Lavinia Bennett. He d. at Monson, Mass., June 10, 1874.

Seth was b. in Charleston, Mass. He rem. to Clinton, Iowa, where he d. Januaiy 21, 1887. Vilma d. at North Wilbraham, Mass., December 13, 1843.

1513 Huldah Knowlton and John Hart had:

(3667) Martha.
(3668) Mary.
(3669) Seth.

(3670) Phoebe.
(3671) Waldo C.
(3672) Vilma.

Residence, Sutton, Mass.

1516 Artemus and Maria Kenny had :

(3673) Joseph, September 11, 1838. d. young.
(3674) Eliza, April 10, 1840. d. 1845.
(3675) Caroline, August 19, 1842. m. Loren Howell, March, 1864.
(3676) Marion, September 6, 1846. d. young.
(3677) Harriet, April 23, 1849.
(3678) Ella, October 18, 1855. m. Anton Knowlton.
(3679) Clara, December 3, 1857. m. L. C. Phillips.

Residence rem. from East Douglass, Mass., to Templeton, Iowa, where Artemus d. 1843. Maria d. at Davenport, Iowa, March, 1894.

1519 Freeman and Hannah Murphy had :

(3680) Catherine A., August 13, 1826. m. Henry B. Winslow.
(3681) Josiah L., January 19 1829. m. Mary Wakefield, April 15, 1852.
(3682) George H., February 28, 1832. m. Abbie Noyes, May 30, 1860.
(3683) Thomas M., June 10, 1836. d. young.
(3684) Walter M. July 15, 1839. m. Adaline Millard, December 25, 1860.
(3685) James A., August 27, 1844. m. Catherine Taylor, December 30, 1871.
Residence, Providence, R. I., where Freeman d. August 2, 1893.

Freeman was a longshoreman. Hannah was from Bedford, N. H. She d. August 9, 1891.

1520 Joseph and Sarah Fitts had :

(3686) Adaline, November 15, 1824, Jamaica. Vt.
(3687) Emory J., March 12, 1826. m. Adaline Pierce. Res., Brattleboro.
(3688) Gilbert N., September 16, 1828. d. December 15, 1847.
(3689) William F., November 7, 1831. m. Ella Brigham. Res., Colorado.
(3690) Orrin F., February 4, 1836. m. C. J. Haskell. Res., Windsor, Vt.
(3691) Laura, March 30, 1838. m. Wm. H. Carr. Res. Jamaica. She d. 1873.

(3692) Julia H., August 30, 1840. m. Chas. S. Clark. Res., Jamaica. She d. April 22, 1876.

(3693) Edwin S., May 13, 1844. d. young.

Joseph d. at Jamaica, Vt., November 24, 1894. Sarah d. there August 12, 1883.

1525 Darwin and Sarah N. Harrington had:

(3695) Chas. F., June 7, 1829 m. Lucy M. Temple, July 18, 1855.

(3696) Relief, January 21, 1831.

(3697) Hannah, October 11, 1832. m. W. G. Holt, July 22, 1851.

(3698) Daniel, June 25, 1835. m. Elizabeth Temple, August 31, 1852.

Residence, Shrewsbury, Mass.

1528 Artemus and Emeline Smith had no chil. She d. November 2, 1837, and Artemus m. 2d Mary Ewell, August, 1841.

Residence, Marlboro, Mass.

1529 William and Hannah Harrington had no chil. He m. 2d Miriam Dresser, August, 1837. They had:

(3699) Julius W., November 28, 1838. m. Jane E. Fairchild, December 17, 1866.

Miriam d, March 4, 1847; and William m. 3d Stella Brooks, October 2, 1850. They had:

(3700) Stella L., March 28, 1854. d. young.

(3701) Stella B., February 15, 1857. d. young.

William rem. to Bridgeport, Conn., where he d. March 22, 1880.

1530 Eunice Knowlton and E. G. Putnam had:

(3702) Ann E.

(3703) William H.

(3704) William H. 2d.

(3705) John E.

(3706) Francis M.

(3707) Abbie M.

(3708) Charles H.

1531 Nancy Knowlton and Horace Stowe had:

(3709) Walter H., January 11, 1834. m. Mary Ogden, 1854.

Horace d. March 23, 1839, and Nancy m. 2d E. B. Rice, July 3, 1843; m. 3d C. C. Felton.

1532 Calvin and Mary C. Warren had:

(3710) Henry C., April 29, 1842. m. Sophia Lippincott, November 22, 1870.
(3711) Edward R., January 23, 1844. m. Alice Wheeler, January 11, 1865.

Calvin was b. in Shrewsbury, Mass. He was engaged in railroad business for twenty-five years, and in banking for seventeen years. He d. in Santa Barbara, Cal., March 6, 1880. Mary C. d. in Joliet, Ill., June 24, 1886.

1533 Dolly Knowlton and Joseph P. Leland had:

(3712) Nancy H., June 30, 1838.
(3713) Marion P., April 26, 1848.
(3714) Stella, October 6, 1861.

1534 William H. and Susan Brigham had:

(3715) Susan E., December 26, 1828. m. Elnathan C. Wheeler, May 25, 1859.
(3716) Mary A., May 19, 1831. m. Joseph Nourse, April, 1855.
(3717) Everett W., September 26, 1832. m. Mary E. Brown, January 7, 1856.
(3718) Lucy M., May 25, 1835. d. September 30, 1880.
(3719) William E., September 26, 1836.
(3720) Eliza G., October 18, 1837. d. November 26, 1855.
(3721) Martha B., October 6, 1839. d. young.
(3722) Caroline E., April 13, 1843. d. January 9, 1868.
(3723) Walter B., December 2, 1845. d. January 3, 1866.

Residence, Shrewsbury, Mass.

William d. August 5, 1852. Susan d. September 25, 1871.

1535 Hannah W. Knowlton and S. Haven had:

(3724) Oscar D., May 29, 1830.
(3725) Joseph S., October 9, 1833.
(3726) Ward R., October 3, 1837.

(3727) George F., October 5, 1843.
(3728) Charles M., March 29, 1849.

1537 Joseph and Huldah Newton had:

(3729) Mary E., August 8, 1835. d. July 7, 1849.
(3730) Susan M., May 27, 1837. d. August 30, 1889.
(3731) Joseph H., April 25, 1839. m. Helen Lowell, November 22, 1866.

Huldah d. August 2, 1839, and Joseph m. 2d Sarah E. Johnson, November 26, 1840. They had:

(3732) Frederick, February 23, 1842. m. Catherine E. Allen, May 16, 1867.
(3733) Greenville, March 24, 1844. d. young.
(3734) Lorenzo, October 19, 1846. m. Mary F. Brigham, August 31, 1870.
(3735) Francis A., January 7, 1849. m. Lucy J. Stratton, April 26, 1871.
(3736) Herbert J., July 5, 1851.
(3737) John F., September 18, 1852. m. Carrie Plasted, February 6, 1879.
(3738) George W., September 26, 1854. d. 1857.
(3739) Sarah E., October 19, 1856.
(3740) George W., May 20, 1858.
(3741) Walter C., July 20, 1860.
Residence, Shrewsbury, Mass.

1538 Susan W. Knowlton and John Rice had:

(3742) Emily A., December 1, 1838. m. Rufus C. Eldridge, March 4, 1861.
Residence, Northbridge, Mass.

Susan W. d. March 16, 1842.

1543 Lincoln B. and Charlotte Spooner had:

(3743) Eleanor B., 1835. m. William Shepard, Springfield, Mass. She d. 1889.
(3744) William S., 1841. m. Anna Negus, of Rock Island, Ill., November, 1875.

Charlotte d. 1841, and Lincoln m. Lucretia Wolcott. August, 1842. They had:

(3745) James W., May 1, 1843. m. Mary Riddle, June, 1873.
(3746) Louise Wolcott. m. Wm. H. Brown, November 15, 1888.
(3747) Elizabeth P. m. Harrison Dodge, June 1, 1875.

LINCOLN B. KNOWLTON

was b. in Shrewsbury, Mass. He graduated from Union College, under the presidency of Dr. Nott, studied law in the office of Governor Davis of Massachusetts, and opened a law office in Peoria, Ill. He was an intimate friend of Abraham Lincoln, David Davis, Stephen A. Douglas, and other noted men of his time. His natural eloquence as a speaker, and his vigorous presentation of his legal cases, were made all the more forceful by his striking personality.

Over six feet in height, and remarkably well proportioned, he towered above his fellows physically as well as mentally, and he easily won the name of "the Henry Clay of the Illinois Bar." He was a delegate to the Baltimore Convention in the interest of Henry Clay, and was nominated for Congress, but died before the election. Being asked to name his successor in the canvass, he named his friend James Knox, who was elected. In the history and traditions of the Illinois Bar, Lincoln B. Knowlton will always hold a prominent place, and it was not an extravagant estimate of his extraordinary abilities and sterling character that made his friends predict for him an illustrious national career. His sense of justice called him promptly to the side of an injured or oppressed defendant, often without fee or reward, and his only weakness seems to have been a too implicit confidence in the honesty of others, a confidence which involved him in large financial losses. He married in 1834 Charlotte Spooner, and after her death Lucretia Wolcott, a lineal descendant on the maternal side of Governor William Bradford and Alice Southworth, his wife, of the Colony of Massachusetts Bay, and, on the paternal side, of the Plymptons and Peabodys of England, and Governors Rogers and Oliver Wolcott, prominent in the settlement of the Colony of Connecticut, and Signers of the Declaration of Independence.

Mrs. Knowlton survives her husband in a green and genial old age that is a benediction to all the members of a large social and domestic circle.

Lincoln d. in Peoria, Ill., June, 1853.

1553 Rebecca W. Knowlton and Dr. A. Brigham had:

(3748) Fred A., April 1, 1835.
(3749) Franklin W., September 3, 1841.
(3750) Arthur K., December 13, 1850.

1555 Harriet A. Knowlton and John Hatton had:

(3751) William L., February 15, 1843.
(3752) Charles L., April 6, 1845.
(3753) Horace K., March 10, 1847.
(3754) Martha, April 17, 1849.

1558 George L. and Olive Haskins, (or Haskell), had:

(3755) Mary R., November 1, 1849. d. 1852.
(3756) James L., November 21, 1851. m. Ella Chamer, December, 1875.
(3757) Katie E., March 12, 1854.
(3758) Belle, December 21, 1856. m. Henry Englebeck, May 4, 1876.

1560 Sarah E. Knowlton and Rufus Blood had:

(3759) Sarah A., July 17, 1849. m. Chas. E. Ingalls, May 30, 1870.

1561 Catherine Knowlton and Osman S. Rice.

Had no children. He d. February 25, 1849, and she m. 2d Moses ——, January 14, 1859. He d. February 17, 1871.

1564 Caroline Knowlton and George Stebbins had:

(3760) Charles H., September 13, 1849. m. Emily D. Chase.
(3761) Anna, July 20, 1854.
(3762) Emily, September 8, 1860. d. young.

1566 Nancy M. Knowlton and Horace Nichols had:

(3763) Walter, June 6, 1862.
(3764) Herbert.

1571 Jonathan and Molly Knowlton had:

(3765) Polly, September 4, 1802.
(3766) Sophronia, December 20, 1804.
(3767) Jonathan, August 5, 1807.
(3768) Anna, August 8, 1810. m. Henry Dodge, August 20, 1831.
(3769) Ebenezer, May 2, 1812. Res., Newburyport, Mass.
(3770) Abraham, September 19, 1821.
(3771) Ann M., April 19, 1823. m. Joseph Simonds, October 26, 1841. Residence, Wenham, Mass.

1572 Caleb and Anna Sargent had:

(3772) William, 1802. m. Eliza Bedney, of Salem, Mass.

(3773) Isaac, 1805. d. April, 1840.
(3774) Willis S. m. Agatha ——. Res., Salem, Mass. 3 chil.
(3775) James.

Anna d. 1808, and Caleb had by 2d wife:

(3776) Andrew, November 28, 1811. m. Mary Benson. Child. b. in Michigan.
(3777) Eliza, February 13, 1810. m. Justus Benson. Child. b. in Iowa.
(3778) Mary, November 15, 1814. m. Ephraim Webster. Child. b. in Springfield, Mass.
(3779) Isaac, December 15, 1815.
(3780) Cyrus, May 14, 1822. m. Adaline Dodge, December 31, 1851.
(3781) Martha, April 15, 1818. m. Chester Kingsley.
(3782) Allen, March 8, 1820. d. October 31, 1839.
(3783) Amanda, May 6, 1824. d. August 18, 1840.
(3784) Daniel, October 17, 1826. m. Julia Schofield, September 4, 1849. Child. b. in Newton, Kan.
(3785) Jane, April 20, 1828. m. Henry C. Martin, July 6, 1847.
(3786) Maria, August 27, 1830. d. young.
(3787) Caleb C., September 21, 1831. d. young.

Caleb rem. from Manchester, Mass., to Brandon, Vt. Anna d. October 5, 1808.

1573 William and Betsey Andrews had:

(3788) William F., November 9, 1804. Wenham, Mass.
(3789) Betsey, April 16, 1806. m. Jonah Carver, August 26, 1827.
(3790) Sally, May 19, 1808. m. Sylvester Spooner, December 15, 1830.
(3791) Mary, July 14, 1810. m. Homer Hart, September 18, 1830.
(3792) Albert, March 23, 1812. m. Sarah Whitcomb, 1833.
(3793) Nancy, January 5, 1817. m. Zebulon Crane, December 6, 1836.
(3794) Adaline, January 7, 1819. m. Austin Williams, January 7, 1841.
(3795) Alonzo, January 1, 1821. m. Eliza De Peyster, December, 1845.
(3796) John, July 2, 1823. m. Lois Crittenden, 1847.
(3797) Ephraim, December 25, 1824. m. Jane Alvord. rem. to Coldwater, O.
(3798) Ann E., March 7, 1836.

William d. August 12, 1866. Betsey d. March 24, 1878.

Residence in Gloucester, Mass. Rem. to Brandon, Vt., thence to Cleveland, Ohio, and to Kent, Ohio, where the parents died.

1575 Anna and Mark Sexberry had :

(3799) Maria, October 3, 1804.

1579 John and Betsey Buckley had :

(3800) Julius A., May 1830. m.
(3801) Gardner J., June 8, 1839.
Residence, Brandon, Vt.

John d. August 24, 1793.

1598 Polly Knowlton and Asa Fogg had :

(3802) Ezekiel. Res. Freedom, Ill.
(3803) Nelson.
(3804) Miranda.
(3805) Mary Ann.
(3806) Martha.
(3807) Jane.
(3808) Leander (or Lucinda).
Residence, New Sharon, Me.

Polly d. 1872.

1599 Sally Knowlton and Henry Erskine had :

(3809) Rev. Justus, June 3, 1822. m. Martha True ; m. 2d Hattie B. Rand. 1 son.
(3810) Roselinda, March 30, 1824. d. 1874.
(3811) Sally, January 27, 1833. d. 1846.
Residence, Palermo and Montville, Me.

1600 Hiram and Lorena Hunt had :

(3812) Benjamin O., December 12, 1838. d. January 23, 1849.
(3813) James S. April 30, 1840. m. Mary E. Chase, July 13, 1868. Res., Camden, Me.
(3814) Thomas Oakes, January 4, 1843. New Boston and Oil Mills, N. H. Lawyer.
(3815) Claudius B., October 7, 1845. Res. Menominee, Mich.
(3816) Benjamin O., April 5, 1850. State Farm of Mass.

Hiram d. [illegible], in Camden, Me., on the old Knowlton Homestead.

1601 Amy Knowlton and Edward Stevens had:

(3817) John. d. young.
(3818) Abigail. d. young.
(3819) Mary. m. Enos Harding.
(3820) John.
(3821) Edward.
(3822) Isaac C. d. young.
(3823) Abbie. m. —— Daniels. Res., Montville.
Residence, Montville, Me.

1602 Joseph W. and Julia Davis had:

(3824) Placentia, June 18, 1833. unm.
(3825) Infant, 1834. d. young.
(3826) Joseph E., February 16, 1835. m. Joanna Gridley. Res. in Duluth, Wis. m. 2d Joanna Crandall.
(3827) Acca L., November 22, 1838. m. Elbridge C. Norton. She d. 1877. Res., Liberty, Me.
(3828) Edward P., April 10, 1842. m. Lizzie A. Worth.
(3829) Frederick, May 30, 1845. m. Abbie M. Sanborn, February 14, 1870.
(3830) Francis Wayland, December 23, 1846. m. Belinda Wentworth, October 16, 1870. Lawyer and editor. Res., Belfast, Me.

Joseph W. is a lawyer, and has been Probate Judge.

1603 Lucinda Knowlton and Daniel Carey had:

(3831) Mary E. m. Calvin Hubbard. Res., Belfast, Me.
(3832) Daniel Warren. m. —— Chapman; m. 2d Luella Bean.
(3833) John C. m. Francis Dickson. Res., Mountville, Me.
(3833A) Fred E. Drowned when young.

Lucinda d. 1860, at the old farm in Maine.

1605 Rev. Isaac C. and Mary S. Wellington had:

(3834) Hosea Morrill, May 30, 1847. m. Sylvia Bassett Almy, May 22, 1873.
(3835) Mary Alice, February 7, 1850. m. Edward S. Rich, June, 1874.
(3836) Frank Warren, October 2, 1851. d. January 20, 1871. West Acton.
(3837) Wellington Case, May 14, 1858. d. 1861, in Keene, N. H.

REV. ISAAC CASE KNOWLTON, D.D.,

son of Ezekiel and Mary Knowlton, was b. at Liberty, Me., September 6, 1819, and d. at West Acton, Mass., March 23, 1894. His father and mother died in his infancy, and he was brought up by his oldest sister, Abigail. At an early age he began earning his livelihood by coopering, making lime casks at Rockland and Thomastown, Me. Early in life he formed the purpose of entering the Universalist ministry, and while engaged in coopering he studied Latin and Hebrew. With the exception of a brief pupilage in the Academy in China, Me., he was entirely self-educated. He first preached at Albion, Me., about 1844. His first settlement was in Lincoln, Me., in 1843. His several settlements were in Lincoln, Me., 1843; Durham, 1845; Auburn, 1850; Hampden, 1851; Oldtown, 1853; Keene, N. H., 1860; South Boston, Mass., 1863; New Bedford, Mass., 1865; Calais, Me., 1870; West Acton, Mass., 1875. His pastorate at West Acton continued for eighteen years, or until 1893, when, after having completed fifty years' work in the ministry, he formally retired. During the whole of his ministerial life he was active in literary work, being a frequent contributor to the Universalist papers and magazines. He was also the author of two books, "History of Calais, Maine," published in 1873, and of a denominational work entitled "Through the Shadows," published in Boston in 1885. The degree of Doctor of Divinity was conferred upon him by Tufts College in 1889.

He was m. at Albion, Me., November 27, 1845, to Mary Smith Wellington, daughter of John and Mary Smith (Winslow) Wellington. He d. April 17, 1894, and his widow is still living in West Acton.

1606 George and Louisa Bowker had:

(3838) Ellen.
(3839) Helena.
(3840) Orestes.
(3841) Marcia.
(3842) Lucia.
(3843) Josephine.
(3844) Alice.

Residence; Johnstown, Pa.

1607 Roxanna Knowlton and James Grant had:

(3845) Mary L., October 8, 1832.
(3846) James A., May 10, 1849. d. 1853.

Reverend Isaac C. Knowlton, D.D.,
Liberty, Maine, 1819–1894.

1608 Freeman and Abbie Bowker had :

(3847) Emily F., October 3, 1836. m. Ariel Fogg, December 12, 1860.
(3848) John W., June 22, 1838. m. A. E. Prow, January 10, 1861.
(3849) Chester F., November 2, 1840. d. young.
(3850) Wm. Wesley, September 16, 1842. m. Nellie Garland, November 20, 1867.
(3851) Chester L., August 9, 1845. d. young.
(3853) Mark L., January 23, 1847.
(3854) Frank E., December 7, 1851. d. young.
(3855) Neddie E., November 28, 1854. d. young.
(3856) Chas. E., August 14, 1857.
(3857) Edward W., July 2, 1858.

Residence, Liberty, Me.

Freeman d. August, 1864.

1609 Martha Knowlton and —— Prince had :

(3858) Laura, April 16, 1835.

She m. 2d —— Johnson and had :

(3859) Ralph, March 29, 1841.

She m. 3d John Safford.

1610 John C. and Eveline Bacon had :

(3860) Dallas, October 2, 1844. m. May Rhodes, August, 1877.
(3861) Albertus, 1845. m. Martha W. Angell, October, 1877. Res., Hutchinson, Me.
(3862) Georgianna, June 10, 1847. m. A. W. Young, December 25, 1868.
(3863) Maria, 1849.
(3864) Willis J., 1855. Farmer, Liberty, Me.
(3865) Kleber J., 1856. Res., Waterville, Me.

Residence, Liberty, Me.

JOHN C. KNOWLTON

was b. and for many years resided, in Liberty, Me. He was a lumberman, and prominent in political circles. When but twenty-two years old, he was a Representative in the State Legislature, serving three terms in that body, twice in the State Senate, and in the governor's Council. In 1864 he was commissioned by the Governor of Maine to receive and carry to the State capital the votes of the Maine soldiers in the field. He served three years as Asst. Doorkeeper of the U. S. Senate, and two years as the Supt. of the Seed Room in the Department of Agriculture at Washington. He d. at Brantford, Ont., in March 1888.

1611 Ann Knowlton and Kendall Brown had:

(3866) Fidelia, May 17, 1836.
(3867) John H., May 22, 1840.
(3868) C. Wesley, January 28, 1842.
(3869) Caroline, November 18, 1844.
Residence, Liberty, Me.

1612 David and Susan French had:

(3870) Viola G., August 5, 1847. m. C. A. Buckland, August 7, 1867.
(3871) Joseph A., July 22, 1849. m. Nellie Crosby, October 1, 1874.
(3872) John D., August 7, 1851.
(3873) Frank E., May 10, 1856.
(3874) Willis D., June 9, 1859.
(3875) Mary E., July 10, 1860. d. young.
(3876) George W., May 8, 1862. d. young.
(3877) Susie E., Ausust 7, 1865.
Residence, Camden, Me.

1614 Charles H. and Delinda Davis had:

(3878) Freeland, February 22, 1849. Served in U. S. Navy.
(3879) Freeman P., January 3, 1854. Res., Michigan.

Delinda d. January 23, 1854.

Chas. H. m. 2d Victoria Speer and had:

(3880) Chas. F., November 14, 1859.
(3881) Nellie, September 29, 1866.
Residence, Rockland, Me.

1619 Alfred and —— had:

(3882) Mary F., September 26, 1841.
(3883) Adoniram.
(3884) Walter. Res., Nevada.

1622 William A. and —— had:

(3885) George.
(3886) A son.
(3887) A daughter.

Residence, Lincoln, Neb.

1623 Samuel and Hannah B. Lewis had:

(3888) James L., February 24, 1845. m. Sarah Chapman, April 1867.
(3889) Joseph F., October 21, 1847. d. in War of the Rebellion, 4th Maine Regiment.
(3890) Rosetta, January 16, 1850. m. Chas. F. Thompson, August 29, 1870.
(3891) George F., July 10, 1855.
(3892) Neddie, April 16, 1859.
(3893) Aurilla, September 26, 1860. m. Geo. W. Stevens.

1626 Lot and Alice Dolen had:

(3894) S. Byron, October 13, 1857.
(3895) Hollis F., December 6, 1859.
(3896) Winfield, March 12, 1862.
(3897) Carrie B., January 2, 1865.
(3898) Arthur M., March 22, 1873.
(3899) Lillian G., November 14, 1875.

Residence, Camden, Me.

1627 Bainbridge and Augusta Ozier had:

(3900) Chas. H.
(3901) Franklin.
(3902) Blanche.
(3903) F. Llewellyn.
(3904) Henry B.
(3905) Ernest L.

1629 Henry and Mary A. Semms had:

(3906) Maurice, November 20, 1862.
(3907) Herbert, June 30, 1865.

1631 Julia Knowlton and —— Davis had:

(3908) Mary K., February 6, 1864.
(3909) Julia, December 7, 1865.

1632 Angeronia Knowlton and —— Cotton had:

(3910) George E., November 24, 1865.
(3911) John F., January 13, 1867.

1633 Carrie B. Knowlton and A. A. Brown had:

(3912) Lizzie, October 11, 1868.
(3913) Mary, April 17, 1870.

1637 Sarah A. Knowlton and Everett Stetson had:

(3914) Henry C., June 28, 1854. d. 1872.
Residence, Damariscotta, Me.

1638 Martha Knowlton and Abner Robinson had:

(3915) Martha S., August 27, 1857.

1641 Mary H. Knowlton and Capt. Martin Tukey had:

(3916) Fred, February 18, 1862.
(3917) Corinne, August 2, 1866.
(3918) Alice, March 17, 1870.
(3919) Frank, June 2, 1872.
(3920) Mary M., October 22, 1874.

1655 Sally Knowlton and Benjamin B. Barstow had:

(3921) Ida L. m. Fred Weeks.
(3922) Mary Isabel. m. —— Coombs.
(3923) Lillie.
(3924) Celia.

1657 Rufus M. and Mary A. Hodgkins had:

(3925) Rufus A.
Rufus Sen. d. 1852.

1659 Martin and Nancy Dunbar had:

(3926) Ruth A., May 10, 1848. d. young.
(3927) Althea A., March 20, 1859.
(3928) Martin, May 16, 1861. d. young.
(3929) Lina, December 29, 1866.
(3930) Irvin L., December 29, 1866.
(3931) Cyril, February 4, 1869. d. young.
(3932) Iona Belle, April 16, 1870.
(3933) Edwin A., December 14, 1871.
Residence, Belfast, Me.

Nancy d. December 19, 1871.

1660 Mary M. Knowlton and Nelson Glidden had:

(3934) Mary A., 1857.
(3935) George, 1859.
(3936) Willis, 1861.
(3937) Anna, 1863.
(3938) Julia. 1877.

1672 Josiah B, and Deborah Weeks had:

(3938 A) Isaac.
Res., N. Chesterville, Me.

1673 Rebecca Knowlton and Francis Butler had:

(3939) Caroline E. m. A. W. F. Belcher.
(3940) Hiram H.
(3941) Margaret J. m. F. F. Belcher.

Rebecca m. 2d Eliphaz Gray, April 28, 1846, and had:

(3942) Mary J. (Gray). m. Geo. W. Rainer.

1674 Caroline Knowlton and Ephraim Butler had:

(3943) Julia W.
(3944) Charles F.

Residence, Farmington, Me.

1676 Sumner and Mariana Gilbert had:

(3945) Charles.

1679 Selden and Abigail Hodgkins had:

(3946) Henry T., May 6, 1844. unm.
(3947) Ann R., October 13, 1846. m. James F. Gower, October 3, 1870. Res., Pendir, Neb.
(3948) Abbie R., October 12, 1849. m. C. Asa Talbot, November 24, 1870. Res., East Wilton, Me.
(3949) Selden H., May 28, 1852.
(3950) Julia G., June 28, 1854. m. Jacob Alexander, March 6, 1881. Res. Cisco, Texas.
(3951) J. Preston, November 6, 1855. m. Louisa C. Baker, May 26, 1880.
(3952) Margie E., September 26, 1855. m. C. Frank Fogg, June, 1881. Res., Gray, Me.
(3953) Augustus E., August 31, 1862.

Selden was for many years a school teacher, and he was noted as a Shakespearian scholar. Resides in Farmington, Me.

1680 Edward A. and Cornelia A. Backus had:

(3954) Cora Blanche, October 14, 1857. Res., Dorchester, Mass.
(3955) Harriette, April 12, 1859. m. Wm. R. Pitman, February, 1885. Res., N. Y. City.
(3956) Harry May, May 1, 1864.

Edward rem. from Farmington, Me., to Boston, Mass., where he d. of heart disease, July 5, 1883. Cornelia res. in Boston. She was the dau. of Zenas Backus, Esq., of Farmington, Me., and on her mother's side a lineal descendant of Hon. Thomas Hinckley, the last Governor of Plymouth Colony, an office which he held for nearly twenty years.

1681 Francis H. and Fannie Foster had:

(3957) Daniel S., December, 1842. Soldier in Civil War. Merchant and Banker.
(3958) John, 1845. Lumber business, Milan, Ind.
(3959) Francis, October, 1854. Money lender in Chicago.

Francis went overland to California in 1849, returned in 1851 by the Isthmus, and contracted a fever from which he d. in Milan, Ind., July 15, 1854. His widow d. April, 1870.

1682 Hon. Hiram and Mary Stephenson had:

(3960) Elizabeth, June, 1836. m. J. S. Stiles, June, 1860.
(3961) Olive, October, 1842. m. Dr. W. H. Jeffries, 1870. 2 chil.
(3962) Hiram, April, 1844. m. Lucy Connelly, November, 1867. He served in 83d Regiment, Indiana Vol., War of Rebellion.
(3963) Mary, May, 1845. Res., Indianapolis.
(3964) Edwin F., September, 1846. m. Elizabeth Hall. Had 2 chil., Annie and Edna.

Residence, Indianapolis, Ind.

Hon. Hiram d. February, 12, 1878. Mary d. September 10, 1885, at Milan, Ind. Hiram was a Representative and State Senator. Moved to Indiana 1843.

1683 Permelia Knowlton and Benjamin Tufts, Jr., had:

(3965) Elial L., August 17, 1834. Soldier in the Rebellion.
(3966) Mary J., February 11, 1839. m. Reuben Deems.
(3967) Benjamin, October 16, 1841.
(3968) Olive, January 16, 1844.
(3969) Cornelia B., March 15, 1849. m. Dr. L. W. Bishop, 1874.
(3970) Chas. W., October 30, 1855. Res., Hartwell, Ohio.
(3971) Lewis George, August 20, 1858.

Residence, Maineville, Ohio.

Benjamin was a farmer.

1684 Sherman m. Dorcas Monahan, May 13, 1848. She d. January 1849, and Sherman m. 2d Martha Stevens, August 23, 1850. He d. of cholera July 9, 1850.

Residence, Cincinnati, Ohio.

1685 Samuel and Julia Hadley had:

(3972) Olive A., October 31, 1846. m. W. H. Needham, December 20, 1866. 1 child.

(3973) Sherman, May 3, 1848.

(3974) Simon H., May 16, 1849. m. Susan Nordycke, September 29, 1871. 3 chil.

(3975) Mary M., February 24, 1851. m. K. C. Naylor, October 4, 1870.

(3976) Charles F., May 16, 1853. m. Anna Arnold. Res., Chicago.

(3977) Emma H., March 18, 1855. m. J. C. Gritman, May 17, 1876. She d. July 14, 1878.

(3978) Edwin S., March 2, 1857. m. Sylvia Hunt, February 1, 1888.

(3979) Annie P., May 17, 1859. m. L. B. Christman, June 9, 1880.

(3980) Rosa L., June 9, 1861. m. George A. Webster, August 28, 1883. d. March 15, 1886.

(3981) Julia E., January 3, 1864. m. Otis Noel, September 15, 1892. d. 1880.

(3982) Minnie B., June 27, 1866. m. D. E. Whitehill, September 3, 1891.

(3983) Cora M., March 10, 1869. m. A. F. Styles, September 13, 1893.

1686 Sarah Knowlton and Temple Fouche had:

(3984) Hiram T., May 20, 1850.

(3985) George B., October 11, 1851.

Residence, Foster's Crossing, Maineville, Ohio.

1687 George W. and Nancy Hunter had:

(3986) Francis S., February 28, 1866.

(3987) Mary O., June 17, 1869.

(3988) Samuel B., July 27, 1872.

Residence, Rising Sun, Ind., and thence rem. to Cunningham, Kansas.

1703 Jeremiah and Sarah Fassett had:

(3989) Samuel F., May 17, 1853. m. Isabella Towle.

(3990) Lovie B., March 1, 1859. d. December 6, 1880.

Residence, Strong, Me.

Jeremiah was an extensive farmer.

1704 William and Irene Carrick had:

(3991) Francis W., August 24, 1864.
(3992) Martha A., January 22, 1866.
(3993) Frederick J., November 15, 1867.
(3994) Maud M., November 15, 1871.
(3995) Ada L., 1879.
(3996) Grace I., 1881.

Residence rem. to St. Cloud, Minn.

1705 Rev. Francis B. and Mrs. Louisa Butterfield had:

(3997) Lillian E., June 30, 1867. d. young.
(3998) Ellen F., June 3, 1869.
(3999) Irwin L., July 17, 1876.

Present Residence, Athol, Mass.

Rev. Francis B. prepared for college at the Farmington Academy, and was graduated from Bowdoin College in 1858. He taught in the Classic Grove Seminary at Oxford, Pa., for two years, after which he entered the Bangor Theological Seminary, and was ordained to the Congregational ministry, August 29, 1865. He has had the charge of churches in South Paris, Alstead, and Oxford, N. H.

1706 David and Clara Hinckley had:

(4000) Clarence H., September 19, 1876.
(4001) Helen, October 9, 1879.

Residence, Farmington, Me.

DAVID KNOWLTON

prepared for college at Lewiston Falls Academy, and graduated from Bowdoin College in 1869. He has been a prominent educator, and is deeply interested in literary pursuits. In 1871 he founded the steam-printing and publishing house of Knowlton, McLeary & Co., which has become a strong and reputable establishment, David Knowlton being the senior partner.

He was Town Treasurer for four years, and is one of the representative men of his native State.

1707 Mary B. Knowlton and Henry C. Johnson had:

(4002) Ruth I.
(4003) Mary.

1712 Robert and Betsey Bixby had:

(4004) Almira, August 31, 1820. m. Solomon Sutton, March 6, 1838.
(4005) Missouriana, January 26, 1823. m. Adam Cowan.
(4006) Narcissa, September 23, 1825. m. Isaac Miles, 1840.
(4007) Margaret, December 6, 1827. m. Daniel Hoffman.
(4008) Jerome, June 21, 1830. d. young.
(4009) Elizabeth, March 5, 1833. m. Walter Blakely.
(4010) Rebecca, December 29, 1836. m. Jonah Crouse.
Residence, Vevay, Ind.

Robert d. December 29, 1836. Betsey d. September 3, 1859.

1713 Samuel and Elizabeth Pike had:

(4011) Dennis G., m. Elizabeth Chase.
(4012) Moses F., July 7, 1716. m. Elizabeth Bailey.
(4013) John P., September 1, 1821. m. Abigail S. Morgan.
Samuel rem. to Sunapee, N. H. He was a State Legislature.

1714 Josiah and Sarah Smith had:

(4014) Catherine, January 31, 1824. d. young.
(4015) Mary L., November 5, 1725. d. young.
(4016) George C., September 28, 1834. m. Mary Ann Higbee. He d. November 30, 1896.
(4017) Eliza J., May 3, 1837. m. Joseph Bryest.

Sarah d. September 11, 1836, and Josiah m. 2d Rosanna Wilcox, March 15, 1839. She d. May 15, 1871. Josiah twice represented Herkimer, N. H., in the Legislature. He was Capt. in the State Militia, and for twenty-five years a Deacon in the Baptist church, succeeding his father who held the same position for the same number of years.

1715 Sophronia Knowlton and Jonathan Flanders had:

(4018) Thankful, March 7, 1822.
(4019) Philip, January 6, 1825. m. Elsie A. Richards.
(4020) Jonathan P., January 2, 1826. m. Mary Brooks.
(4021) Euphonius, September 18, 1828. d. young.
(4022) Robert L., May 8, 1830. m. Almira Holden.
(4023) William W., January 15, 1833. m. Eliza Handel.

(4024) Martin B., January 1, 1835. m. Tryphena Murray.
(4025) Samuel K., February 14, 1837.
(4026) Sophronia A., August 23, 1839. m. Roswell Appleton.
(4027) John K., August 29, 1842. d. January 14, 1866.

1724 Ezekiel K. Trussell and Emily Colburn had:

(4028) Marcia J., November 12, 1826. m. W. W. Boardman, August 1854. She d. April 1891.
(4029) James H., September 28, 1828. m. Mary E. Hill, of Champlin, Minn., November 18, 1857. d. March 15, 1895.
(4030) Charles F., November, 1831. m. M. A. Goodhue, of Boscawen, N. H., March 18, 1857. She d. August 20, 1861.
(4031) Marietta S., September 6, 1833. m. 2d C. B. Martin, of Grafton, November 7, 1861,

Residence, New London and Lebanon, N. H.

1725 Luther Trussell and Eliza Story had:

(4033) Sarah E., July 30, 1845. m. John W. Morse, April 8, 1875. d. at New London, N. H., August 5, 1881.
(4034) Mary K., January 8, 1849. m. Rev. Chas. P. Bennett, June 17, 1882. She d. May 28, 1883, at Shapleigh, Me.

Residence, New London, N. H.

1725 A Nathaniel and Ruth Herrick had:

(4035) Nathaniel C., March 16, 1820. m. Caroline Chadwick, October 20, 1850.
(4036) Caroline R., December 2, 1821. m. Elbridge Haynes, November 3, 1840.

Capt. Nathaniel rem. from Newbury, to Sutton, N. H., in 1825. He d. there July 14, 1879. Ruth d. March 29, 1867.

1725 B Samuel S. and Martha Witherspoon had:

(4037) Andrew, 1823. d. young.
(4038) Betsey, 1825. m. John Cutler; m. 2d C. Messer, October 14, 1858.
(4039) Samuel, March 28, 1827. m. Sabrina Morrill; m. 2d Allora Winchester. He d. in California.

(4040) James, December 7, 1828. m. Mary F. Marshall, January 9, 1855.
(4041) Ezekiel, December 7, 1828. d. 1857. School Teacher in Baltimore.
(4042) John, February, 1831. m. Susan Harvey, of Sutton, N. H.
(4043) Mary, 1832. d. young.
(4044) George, December 28, 1833. m. Laura Goodrich.
(4045) Martha, June 2, 1837. d. January 18, 1860.
(4046) Nathaniel, March 28, 1838. m. Elizabeth F. Hill. March 10, 1864.
(4047) Mary, 1841. d. May 20, 1867.

Samuel resided on the home farm which he purchased from his father in 1834, to which he subsequently added other valuable property, becoming a prosperous and representative farmer. He was of striking physique, being over six feet tall, weighing two hundred and thirty pounds, and his many physical feats were the foundation of many interesting anecdotes still current in his native town. His farm was noted for the size of its huge stone fences, which he called "Jackson Walls" out of admiration for the hero of New Orleans. His wife Martha was a noble woman, taking unusual and intelligent interest in public affairs, ruling also her household well, and her death which occurred July 10, 1881, was the occasion of a general demonstration of regretful regard. Samuel d. May 12, 1852.

1741 Benjamin and Lucinda Allen had :

(4048) D. L. B.
(4049) Samuel.
(4050) Mary L. m. —— Porter.
(4051) Sarah A. m. —— Clements.

Benjamin d. February 2, 1844.

1743 Daniel and Rhoda Abbott had :

(4052) Rhoda, 1818. m. Jeremiah Abbott.
(4053) Adaline. d. young.
(4054) Adaline A., 1825. m. Jeremiah Abbott. Had dau. who m. D. K. Abbott.
(4055) Mary F., 1830.

Daniel d. March, 1873.

1745 Nathaniel and Ruth Sargent had :

(4056) William C., October 8, 1822. m. Roxana Kidder, August 27, 1842.
(4057) Hazen, May 23, 1824. m. Eliza Shedd, November 27, 1850.
(4058) Robert. m. 3 chil.

Nathaniel d. March 18, 1870. Ruth d. July 17, 1877.

1746 Gilman and Sarah Sargent had:

(4059) Ellen A., September 30, 1825. m. Hon. Richard Potter. Res. Holyoke Mass.

(4060) Ann M., October 7, 1828. m. J. P. Beverly, September 29, 1847.

(4061) Nancy I., June 17, 1830. m. Pliny B. Young, October 25, 1849.

(4062) Edwin G., September 14, 1838. m. Belle Benham, December 3, 1867.

(4063) Joseph A., September 10, 1848. m. Fanny Brown, September 10, 1871.

Gilman d. April 2, 1874. Sarah d. March 22, 1875.

1759 Benjamin Leach and Susan Cheever had:

(4064) John, June 24, 1813. m. Ann Black, 1843.

(4065) Benj. B., November 8, 1815. m. Cynthia Hall, June 25, 1848.

(4066) Susan C., February 6, 1819.

(4067) Sarah, April 16, 1821. d.

(4068) Elizabeth C., January 7, 1825. m. John A. Gould, October 5, 1845.

Susan d. June 7, 1829, and Benj. m. 2d Lucy, Widow of Nathan Allen, and dau. of Aaron Allen, January 7, 1830. They had:

(4069) Richard, December 31, 1830. m. Sally Moody, October 20, 1855.

(4070) Henry C., October 9, 1832. m. Caroline E. Roberts, July 30, 1866.

(4071) Aaron A., January 26, 1836. d. young.

(4072) Samuel, August 29, 1837. m. Helen F. Wheaton, April 13, 1870.

(4073) Lewis, December 13, 1839. m. Ellen Ward, September 20, 1862.

Benj. d. October 10, 1859. Lucy d. March 26, 1889.

1770 Ariel and Abigail Lee had:

(4074) Edward L., April 17, 1822. m. Frances Kendrick, 1852. He d. December 28, 1881. She d. 1875.

(4075) George C., June 5, 1826. d. young.

(4076) Mary C., October 7, 1827. m. Chas. French, September 25, 1844. She d. October 6, 1852.

(4077) Miranda, June 2, 1833. m. Benj. L. Culver, January 24, 1856. Res. Suncook, N. H. He d. December 4, 1896.

(4078) John H., April 17, 1836. d. young.

(4079) John H., November 12, 1838. Res. Hopkinton, N. H. Merchant.

Ariel d. September 2, 1866. Abigail d. December 17, 1874.

1772 John S. C. and Anna W. Hartwell had:

(4080) Frank, September 12, 1830. d. young.
(4081) Helen M., August 16, 1832. unm. An artist.
(4082) Francis A., November 13, 1834.
(4083) Lucy E., December 12, 1837. Res., Worcester, Mass. A music teacher.
(4084) Elizabeth C., December 10, 1840. d. 1845.
(4085) John A., May 23, 1843. m. Fannie Phelps, August 30, 1870.
(4086) Frederick, February 26, 1846. m. Annie J. Rice, September 20, 1869, He d. July 19, 1873.
(4087) Edward H., October 29, 1848. m. Josie E. Sprague, October 18, 1872; m. 2d Harriet Utley, September 27, 1882.
(4088) Charles F. June 16, 1852.

John S. C. d. June 11, 1871. Annie W. d. May 25, 1892.

He resided the greater part of his life in Worcester, Mass., of which city he was Mayor. He edited and published the *Worcester Palladium* for thirty-eight years, was a member of the State Senate, and High Sheriff of Worcester Co. for sixteen years.

Anna was dau. of Dea. John Hartwell, of Littleton, N. H.

1774 Daniel and Anne Billings had:

(4089) Mary F., November 29, 1833. m. Henry B. Adams, June 8, 1871. Res. Fitchburg, Mass.
(4090) George B., January 10, 1836. unm. Res. Fitchburg, Mass. Merchant.

Daniel d. April 17, 1837, and Ann m. 2d Waldo Wallace.

Daniel was the Editor and Publisher of the *Lowell Journal*.

1175 Lucy P. and John M. Bailey had:

(4091) George H., July 14, 1829. m. Helen Young, October 15, 1860.
(4092) Fred H., September 18, 1832. m. L. G. Jones; m. 2d Sarah M. Knowlton.

John M. d. January 18, 1886. Lucy P. d. November 17, 1891.

Residence, Hopkinton, N. H.

1776 William and Mary L. Ferguson had

children whose names have not been ascertained.

William was a Professor of Music. He d. in Pontiac, Mich., January 15, 1848.

FRANCIS P. KNOWLTON,
Littleton, Mass.

1777 Francis P. and Mary Hartwell had:

(4093) George Hartwell, November 6, 1839. m. Isabel J. Johnson, January 1, 1868.

(4094) Ellen F., October 16, 1844. m. Robert A. Johnson, May 1, 1870.

(4095) Sarah M., January 29, 1849. m. Fred H. Bailey, January 1, 1885. Res., Chicago, Ill.

(4096) Mary Dix, December 12, 1852. unm. Res. in Littleton, Mass.

FRANCIS KNOWLTON

was a jeweller. He resided in Hopkinton, N. H., until 1834, and from 1837-55 when he rem. to Littleton, Mass. He was Town Clerk for seven years, and a Representative to the General Court in 1850-52, and, as may be inferred from these public and political honors, a man of ability and deserved prominence.

He was indefatigable in his genealogical researches among the Knowltons of America, and to his patience and zeal is due no small portion of the Records of this history. His residence in Hopkinton was burned after he left it, and his Littleton residence was also destroyed by fire after his death, which occurred, March 14, 1887. Mary d. April 16, 1892.

1781 Coolidge B. Murphy and Mary A. Atkins had:

(4097) Erskine C. m. Mary Hardy.
(4098) Elijah M. m. Helen A. Hurlburt.
(4099) Thomas A. m. Mary E. Whipple.
(4100) Sophia L. m. Dr. Harmon Waterman.
(4101) Harriet E. m. David Burr.
(4102) Mary K. m. Chas. B. Howe.
(4103) Martha B.

1787 John and Lucy Vaughn had:

(4104) S. A., 1851. d. October 22, 1893.

Lucy d. 1861 and John m. 2d Romelia Connor, who d. November 4, 1876. They had:

(4105) Belle. m. —— Collins.
Residence, No. Chesterville, Me.

1792 Samuel and Hepsie M. Mitchell had:

(4106) Frank H., May 28, 1858.

(4107) Mabel L., May 23, 1862. m. Albert Morrow, December 8, 1880.

(4108) Dana A., July 19, 1865. d. young.
(4109) Walter E., March 10, 1868.
Samuel was a farmer and carriage maker. Hepsie d. August 27, 1870. He d. June 6, 1884.

Residence, Farmington, Me.

1794 Ebenezer and Emily A. Perry had :

(4110) Augusta, August 18, 1857. m. Frank Burbank, January 10, 1883.
(4111) Eben A., April 5, 1859. d. 1864.
(4112) Harnden J., February 21, 1861. d. 1867.
(4113) William H., February 4, 1866. d. 1869.
(4114) Eben C., December 8, 1867.
(4115) Emily F., December 8, 1867.

Ebenezer was a farmer and carriage maker.

Residence, Farmington Centre, Me.

1800 Sylvanus and Rebecca Colburn had :

(4116) Emily L., May 24, 1854. m. Elbridge Allen, June 10, 1877.
(4117) Newell R., April 30, 1856.
(4118) Frederick, November 2, 1862.
(4119) Sylvanus, Jr., June 15, 1864. m. Jennie S. Mason, December 25, 1881.

Sylvanus was formerly a farmer, but subsequently an inn-keeper in Farmington, Me.

1811 Caroline Knowlton and John B. Bass had :

(4120) Arthur, September 19, 1854. d. young.
(4121) Edward C., September 24, 1858. d. October 13, 1865.
(4122) George S., July 5, 1860.

Residence, Quincy, Mass.

John B. was Postmaster for twenty years, and d. February 19, 1859. Caroline d. July 23, 1890.

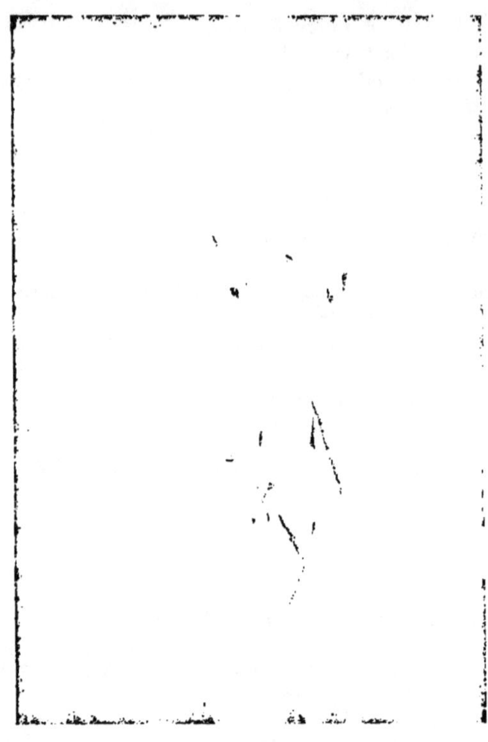

Mark D. Knowlton,
Rochester, N. Y.

1812 Nancy J. Knowlton and Elnathan P. Brewer had:

(4123) Charles W., July 4, 1855.
(4124) Elizabeth M., January 19, 1862.
(4125) Harry G., June 9, 1865.

Elnathan d. in Worcester, Mass., December 5, 1890. His widow resides in Milford, Mass.

1813 William M. and Smyra J. Brown, of Lowell, Vt., had:

(4126) Hattie E., January 30, 1855. d. young.
(4127) Isabel M., March 4, 1861. m. Fred. Goss.

William is a banker in Milford, Mass.

1815 Harriet E. Knowlton and Andrew Fuller had:

(4128) Helen M., April 24, 1865.
(4129) Caroline K., June 16, 1868.
Residence, Needham, Mass.

Andrew d. May 6, 1861, and his widow resides in Milford, Mass.

1816 Mark D. and Abbie E. Currier, of Methuen, Mass., had:

(4130) Annie D., March 25, 1865.
(4131) Grace E., December 2, 1866.
(4132) Hattie G., October 27, 1868.
(4133) Kirk, February 23, 1879.
(4134) Ola, July 17, 1888.

MARK D. KNOWLTON

was b. in Milford, N. H., October 5, 1840. He received the education common to the average New England lad; and at the age of seventeen went to Nashua to learn the trade of a carriage maker. In 1861 he went to Camden, N. Y., to assist his brother in the management of his farm, and in the following year entered the service of Rice, Barton & Co., Paper Machinery Manufacturers, Worcester, Mass.

In 1863 he was in charge of a prosperous business in the manufacture of carriage hardware, in Nashua, N. H., from which he withdrew to become the owner of a paper box manufactory a year later. In 1867 his interest in the extraordinary business development and future promise of the great West induced him to remove to Chicago, where he was the first to apply modern methods and mechanical improvements in his growing business. The prosperity which at once rewarded his foresight and enterprise was rudely interrupted by the great Chicago fire, which left of his flourishing business only a heap of ashes. Having located his residence at the neighboring suburb of Evanston, he promptly assisted in organizing a relief association and mounted patrol for the assistance of refugees and the protection of the homes and property of his fellow-citizens, filling his own house with the unfortunate and the destitute, his family, with equal benevolence, cooking the necessary food for the famishing, and clothing the almost naked victims of that tragic horror. Mr. Knowlton was the first to re-establish his business while the city was still burning.

In 1873 the second fire swept away every vestige of his manufactory, but with characteristic energy he again rebuilt, and in 1878 was as prosperous as ever, employing over four hundred operatives, and producing a daily average of over four tons of boxes. His early mechanical experience was so assisted by his inventive genius that in 1890 he was furnishing both new machinery and finished products throughout the country.

As most of the manufacturers in his line were East of the Alleghanies, he concluded to confine himself to the manufacture of machinery, and the business was divided, he removing to Rochester, N. Y., and his partner continuing to manufacture goods in Chicago.

Since March, 1891, Mr. Knowlton has resided in Rochester, where he now continues his business, protected by many U. S. Patents which he has secured by his own inventive genius, and which have given him an enviable footing in the great American and European markets.

He served for two years as Justice of the Peace in Evanston, Ill., declining re-election, and has devoted himself to business anu philanthropic interests since that time. An ardent Republican in politics and a devout and loyal Presbyterian in religious faith, he serves his country with conscientious citizenship, and his fellow-men with modest benevolence that commend him to the love and regard of all.

His only son, Kirk K., is in Purdue University, La Fayette, Ind., of the class of 1900, taking a full course in electrical engineering. His grade of scholarship in previous years gives full assurance of distinction in his chosen profession.

1817 George P. and Helen B. Gibbs, of Brighton, Mass., had :

(4135) Lillian S., March 24, 1869. d. young.

(4136) Samuel D., June 10, 1871.
(4137) George F., April 11, 1873.

George was in the leather business, and was burned out by the great Boston fire. He subsequently opened a hotel, and finally settled down in a prosperous grocery business in North Cambridge, Mass.

1839 Willis and Ida L. Orr had:

(4138) Dean Owen, May 25, 1876.

Ida d. April 13, 1885.

1840 Chas. M. and Martha J. Bradley had:

(4139) Daniel C.
(4140) Infant son. d.
(4141) Esther B. } Twins.
(4142) Mary R. }
(4143) C. Milton.
(4144) Willard. d. young.
Residence, Cazenovia, N. Y.

1841 Annie R. Knowlton and E. Bowen Crandall had:

(4145) Ruth K.
(4146) Bowen.
(4147) Eugene B.
Residence, Cazenovia, N. Y.

1842 Mary A. Knowlton and Walter C. Jackson had:

(4148) E. Steele.
(4149) Annie F.
Residence, Cazenovia, N. Y.

1844 William and Mary Chapman had:

(4150) Hiram, August 17, 1823. m. Salina W. Chapman, March 11, 1846.
(4151) Elvira, April 13, 1825. d. young.

(4152) A. K. P., December 10, 1827. m. Mary McGuire, May 23, 1859; m. 2d Almira Chase, December 13, 1864.
(4153) William A., April 5, 1830. m. Hannah Kimball, January, 1853.
(4154) Isaac, June 10, 1833. m. Eliza Blanchard, December 17, 1858.
(4155) Mary E., March 31, 1836. d. 1839.
(4156) Martha H., August 29, 1839. m. Joseph W. Methuen, September 4, 1859.
(4157) Mark L., January 10, 1843. m. Emma Savage, February 5, 1864.

1845 Joseph and Hannah Sanborn had:

(4158) Leonard, October 14, 1830. m. Caroline Bartlett, October 9, 1853; m. 2d Laura Knowles, February 3, 1864; m. 3d Mrs. Emma Pierce.
(4159) Lucy, January 19, 1832. d. May 23, 1843.
(4160) Nancy, January 12, 1836.

1847 John and Caroline Churchill had:

(4161) Asa, January 15, 1845. d. August 22, 1856.
(4162) Asa H., March 16, 1847. m. Eliza Hutchins.
(4163) Alice, October 15, 1848. d. September 26, 1865.
(4164) Nancy, November 26, 1850. d. young.
(4165) Juliette, January 24, 1852.
(4166) John, October 7, 1854.
(4167) Jennie, March 26, 1857.
(4168) Berthia, December 23, 1864. d. 1869.

Residence, East New Portland, Me.

1848 Martha Knowlton and George Howes had:

(4169) Wm. Joseph H., December 17, 1834.
(4170) Mary, June 16, 1836.
(4171) George, May 18, 1837.
(4172) Mary E., February 17, 1839.
(4173) George F., March 7, 1842.
(4174) Carrie P., August 17, 1844.
(4175) Wm. H. H., October 4, 1845.
(4176) John A., February 12, 1850.
(4177) Edmund G., December 5, 1855.

1850 Sarah Knowlton and David McKenney had:

(4178) Joseph, December 17, 1843.
(4179) William, September 17, 1845.
(4180) Winfield, November 8, 1847.
(4181) James, February 19, 1850. d. young.
(4182) Hannah, April 26, 1856.

1852 Albion and Ellen Poland had:

(4183) Mary D., August 16, 1847. m. Herbert M. Daly, August 1, 1869.
(4184) Eliza C., August 20, 1849. m. Thomas Merchant, November 22, 1868.

Albion d. February 8, 1857, and his wid. m. 2d Moses Parsons, June 1, 1864.

1854 David and Vienna Holbrook had:

(4185) David A., June 24, 1857.
(4186) George H., August 21, 1859. d. 1865.
(4187) Charles, January 20, 1867.
(4188) Edith, December 6, 1868. d. young.
(4189) Charles, March 16, 1874. } d. young.
(4190) Anna, March 16, 1874. }

1856 John and Adelaide Marshall had:

(4191) Annie, May 17, 1849.
(4192) John D., October 21, 1852.
(4193) Mary E., June 22, 1854.
Residence, Boston, Mass.

1858 Joseph and Adeline Preston had:

(4194) George R., November 9, 1857.
(4195) Nellie P., November 26, 1860.
(4196) Frank L., April 7, 1867.
(4197) Fannie P., August 10, 1870.

1861 George K. and Irene M. Pullins had:

(4198) Lucretia M., May 31, 1862.
(4199) Odella E., July 11, 1864.
(4200) Charles, December 9, 1867.

1863 Isaac and Sarah W. Dodge had:

(4200 A) Gertrude F., June 24, 1873.

1865 John H. and Sarah A. Knowlton had:

(4201) Orendia, July 12, 1872.
(4202) Clarence D.
(4203) Grace A.

1866 Joseph and Esther Knowlton had:

(4204) Eliza P., March 15, 1837.
(4205) Martha M., June 10, 1838. m. H. P. Witham, November 25, 1875.
(4206) Esther A., November 19, 1839. d. young.
(4207) Isaac P., March 4, 1843. m. Georgiana Brackett.
(4208) Joseph F., October 13, 1844.
Residence, Hamilton, Mass.

1867 Edmund and Amanda Saunders had:

(4209) Levi, March 18, 1838. m. Rosanna Dudley.

Edmund d. March 12, 1866.

1889 James A. and Clarinda M. Fuller had:

(4210) Austin A., March 18, 1848. d. July 18, 1876.
(4211) James B., September 14, 1855. m. Fannie Seavey, September 15, 1893.
(4212) Edward F., March 9, 1858. m. Martha N. Marsh, November 16, 1882. Res., Salem, Mass.
(4213) Daniel F., October 31, 1860. m. Mary Lansing, October 4, 1892.
(4214) Nellie M., March 16, 1863. m. Arthur Widger, October 30, 1889.
(4215) Charles F. January 31, 1865. Supt. Public Works, Quincy, Mass.
(4216) Hattie F., March 31, 1872. Unm.

JAMES A. KNOWLTON

was born in Gloucester, Mass., in 1821. When but a small boy he removed to Salem, where he was apprenticed to a ship-builder, and before many years he had founded a business of his own, in which he was eminently successful. In 1844 he removed from Salem to Gloucester, becoming the proprietor of a ship-yard from which craft of all sorts have been launched. He inevitably became one of the most widely known and respected of the citizens of his native town, taking great interest in local and political matters, and serving as overseer of the poor, assessor, selectman, and, in fact, in nearly every office in the gift of his fellow-citizens. For about forty years he spent his winters at Norfolk, Va.

Clara M., is the daughter of William and Marion Fuller, b. at Swampscott in 1823. This worthy couple recently celebrated their golden wedding, surrounded by numerous descendants.

1890 Allen and Frances Farr had:

(4217) Johnnie, June 18, 1870.
(4218) Warren.

Frances d. November, 1888.

1892 Ira P. and Esther Appleton had:

(4219) Mary E., January 10, 1847. m. Rufus Benham, September, 18, 1870.
(4220) Sarah A., May 22, 1849. m. J. H. Knowlton.
(4221) Mary E., November 18, 1854.
(4222) Ellen H., February 13, 1859.

Residence, Salem, Mass. A farmer.

1894 Richard and Mary Means had:

(4223) Mary E., October 5, 1852.
(4224) Charles H., October 30, 1854. d. young.
(4225) Reuben, April 23, 1856. Killed by lightning the same year.
(4226) Alice H., March 31, 1858. m. George M. Low, November 29, 1879.

1896 Charles and Mary W. Tuttle had:

(4226 A) Lucy N., 1826. m. Thos. Hale, June 17, 1847.

Charles d. September 15, 1850.

1897 Timothy and Hannah Farr had:

(4227) Martha, October 8, 1826.

Timothy was the s. of Neamiah (735) and Patience Parsons, (accidentally omitted). He d. March 1, 1826.

1898 Harvey and Lucy Davis had:

(4228) Lucy H., April 3, 1825. m. Allen Pettingill, 1857.
(4229) Harvey, October 6, 1828.
(4230) Cordelia, February 12, 1830. d. young.

Harvey m. 2d Elizabeth Webber, 1839.

1899 Neamiah and Harriet Coley had:

(4231) John C., October 15, 1839. m. Mary Mc'Ennis, December 19, 1865.
(4232) Harriet, August, 1842. d. 1851.
(4233) Harriet L., 1851. m. Frank H. Dennis, February 20, 1873.
Residence, Rockport, Mass.

1901 Asa, Jr., and Eliza A. Porter had:

(4234) Frances A., July 19, 1833. m. D. S. Watson, May 4, 1856.

Asa, Jr., m. 2d Anna E. Trask, 1842. Residence, Gloucester, Mass. Asa, Jr., d. June 25, 1878.

1905 Hannah Knowlton and Joseph Andrews had:

(4235) Joseph Warren. m. Agnes Burnham of Gloucester, Mass.
(4236) Susan Elvira. m. Luther F. Allen of Manchester, Mass.
(4237) Francis Marion, September 29, 1831. m. Mary P. Morrill.
(4238) Horatio N. m. Helen Story.
(4239) Maryline. m. Chas. Prindall.
(4240) Elias C. m. Florence Forst.
(4241) Hannah, M., January 31, 1846. m. Noah Burnham.
(4242) Horace M., January 10, 1849. m. Ida A. Scoville.
Residence, Essex, Mass.

1906 Abigail Knowlton and Noah Story had:

(4243) Abbie.
(4244) Albert.
(4245) Clement A.

1907 Susan Knowlton and Jeremiah Henderson had:

(4246) Abbie L. m. Albert F. Low.
(4247) Susan M. m. Charles Burnham.
(4248) Moses K. m. Isabelle Richardson. m. 2d Anette Hobbs.
(4249) George W. d. Served in the U. S. Army during the Rebellion.
(4250) Fannie H. m. Elias Crocker.

1908 Moses and Mary Lufkin had:

(4251) Alphonso, 1840. d. 1846.
(4252) Elizabeth, November 14, 1843. m. David B. Burnham.
(4253) Lydia, October 22, 1845. d. young.
(4254) Alphonso M., June 21, 1848. m. Susie F. Andrews, December 6, 1871.
(4255) John C., March 23, 1850.
(4256) George, August 5, 1853. d. young.
(4257) Mary L. m. Thomas Morgan.
(4258) Lydia C., July 3, 1857. m. Chas. S. Marston.

Moses is a prominent citizen of Essex, and a director in the Cape Ann National Bank of Gloucester, Mass.

1909 Esther and William A. Andrews had:

(4259) Leonard.
(4260) Oscar A.
(4261) Edmond.
(4262) William A. Jr., 1846. d. in the army, during the Rebellion.
(4263) Zylpha H.

Residence, Essex, Mass.

1911 David and Anstice C. Norton had:

(4264) Herbert A. m. Nancy G. Story, February 4, 1870.
(4265) Webster. d. young.

(4266) Perry B. m. Emma A. Howes, March 10, 1876.
(4267) Annie C. m. Ephraim Dane.
Residence, Essex, Mass.

1912 Aaron and Harriet Choate Norton had:

(4268) Charles L., December 29, 1854.
(4269) Edward F.
(4270) Sarah Eva.
(4271) Alva L.

Harriet d. and Aaron m. 2d Emma F. Andrews, June 21, 1876. They had:

(4272) Jessie A., June 30, 1877.

Aaron is a farmer on the old paternal estate.
Residence, Essex, Mass.

1913 Elizabeth Knowlton and John P. Lufkin had:

(4273) Chas E.
(4274) Charles Perry, 1843. Killed in the War of the Rebellion.
(4275) John E.
(4276) Abbie L.

John P. d. and Elizabeth m. Jesse Burnham. They had:

(4276 A) Edward Burnham. m. Abbie A. Hill
(4276 B) Sarah L. Burnham. m. Joseph Brown.

Elizabeth res. in Essex, Mass.

1914 Minerva Knowlton and Johnathan Richardson had:

(4277) Frank Chester. m. Myra Etta Davis of Essex, Mass.
Residence, Danvers and Essex, Mass.

1915 Perry and —— had:

(4278) George.
(4279) Evelyn.
(4280) Florence.

1916 Cassandra Knowlton and Chas. T. Littlefield had:

(4281) Charles W. m. Eva D. Mannell.

1919 Michael and Louisa Hodgkins had:

(4282) Sidney D., October 18, 1850.
(4283) Almeda, April 16, 1852. m. L. G. Pool, December 18, 1876.
(4284) Isaac D., November 15, 1855.
(4285) Louisa, May 14, 1858.
(4286) Albert.
(4287) Frank.
(4288) Eva, August 5, 1866. d. young.

Louisa d. April 1, 1877.

1923 Addison and Mercy Willey had:

(4289) Thomas F., February 3, 1838. m. Olive A. Walker, August 17, 1858.
(4290) Melville, August 18, 1843. m. Rebecca Grimmings, February 3. 1863.
(4291) Orlando, January 26, 1846. m. Rhoda Pool, January 29, 1868.
(4292) Edgar, May 5, 1851. d. 1859.
(4293) Mary L., April 18, 1854.
(4294) Edgar, December, 20, 1859.

1926 George W. and Mary Dodge had:

(4295) Adaline, September 30, 1836.
George F.
(4296) George W., September 10, 1838. m. Olive J. Foster, April 28, 1859.
(4297) Mary E.
(4298) Frank D., April 21, 1843.
Residence, Salem, Mass.

1927 William H. and Mary Clarkson had:

(4298 A) William J., August 31, 1846. Res. in Boston.
(4299) Margaret, December 5, 1847.
(4300) Alona L., April 5, 1849.

1928 Andrew and Mary O. Fulton had:

(4301) Jackson. m. Catherine ——
(4302) John T., April 28, 1841. d. 1849.
(4303) Edwin H., November 14, 1843.

1929 Azor and Martha Tower (or Turner), had:

(4304) Edwin L., October 22, 1845. d. young.
(4305) John, November 27, 1854.

Azor d. February 23, 1879.

1931 Eben and Elizabeth Matthews had:

(4306) Eben S., June 9, 1851.
(4307) Rebecca, April 11, 1853. m. W. H. Colby, January 16, 1875.
(4308) Forrest H., August 10, 1854.
(4309) ——, July 10, 1856.
(4310) Herbert, July 10, 1858. d. 1861.
(4311) A son, December 26, 1862.
(4312) James A., January 14, 1867.

1936 Frank P. and Phoebe —— had:

(4313) Addie A., March 14, 1867.
(4314) Mabel A., September 24, 1869.
(4315) Blanche B., December 25, 1871.
(4316) Frank W., October 18, 1875. d. young.

1937 Martha L. Knowlton and Augustus Dodge had:

(4317) Martha A., September 21, 1835. m. Samuel R. Prime, of Salem, January 1, 1856. 9 chil.
(4318) Sarah P., September 11, 1837. d. in Wenham, March 13, 1893.
(4319) George A., March 21, 1842. d. in Wenham, December 15, 1879. He was a soldier in the Civil War, Company F., 23d Regiment, Mass. Vol., 1862-4. He m. Elizabeth G. Dodge, February 16, 1865.
(4320) Frances E., March 30, 1850.

Martha L. was from Hamilton, Mass.

1938 Sarah D. Knowlton and Zebulon Burnham had :

(4321) Sarah A., June 21, 1837.
(4322) Ives D., September 10, 1838.
(4323) John C., July 3, 1840.
(4324) Anna P., August 14, 1842.
(4325) Calvin, January 4, 1844.
(4326) Otis, December 30, 1845.
(4327) Frank, March 3, 1847.

1949 Ephraim and Catherine Holmes had :

(4328) Caroline.
(4329) Mary A., 1838. m. Finley Bond.
(4330) Ellen M., 1842.
(4331) Anna E., 1846.
(4332) Ephraim, 1851.
(4333) Clara B., 1857.

1950 Benjamin and Mrs. Caroline (Gray) McMullen had :

(4334) Franklin, July 4, 1852. m. Evie Ward, April 23, 1879. Had son Clarence F., 1876.
(4335) Emma, May 28, 1854. m. Benj. Thomas.
(4336) Maria A., June 10, 1861. res. Warren, Maine.
(4337) Bennie, September 17, 1867. res. Warren, Maine.

Benjamin was born in Rockland, and rem. to Warren, Maine, April, 1876.

1955 Thomas and Lucy Blanchard had :

(4338) William B., July 21, 1817. m. Alma Persons.
(4339) Lucy M., March 2, 1819. m. Royal Barrow.
(4340) Thomas J., July 21, 1821. m. Laura Beecher.
(4341) James S., February 6, 1823. m. Had 4 chil.
(4342) George W., November 12, 1824. m. Ellen Peck.
(4343) Henry, November 14, 1825. m. Laura Goodwin.
(4344) Ephraim, October 3, 1830.
(4345) Amos A., July 25, 1833.
(4346) Charles P., June 15, 1835.
(4347) John C., November 20, 1837. m. Celia Caulkins, November 9, 1859.
(4348) Byron P., August 20, 1841. m. Kitty Graham.
(4349) Alvira, December 21, 1842. d. February 25, 1863.

Thomas d. February 25, 1859.

1957 William and Maria Barney had:

(4350) Augustus E., December 11, 1819.
(4351) Lucy, December 27, 1821.
(4352) Marian, December 29, 1823.
(4353) Julia, October 3, 1825.
(4354) Sarah J., July 13, 1829.
(4355) John B., July 28, 1857. m. —— Clymer of N. Y., October 16, 1852.
(4356) Wm. W., September, 6, 1831.
(4357) Harriet, May 29, 1833. d. May 5, 1870.
(4358) Hiram, June 29, 1835.
(4359) Emily, October 3, 1837. d. December 16, 1863.
(4360) Maria, July 6, 1840. She d. February 11, 1874.

1969 Samuel Stearns and Mary Fitch Moore had:

(4361) Mary Elizabeth, August 18, 1832. m. Hon. James Vanderveer, of New Jersey, December 29, 1864.
(4362) Ezra Scollay, September 1, 1838.
(4363) Samuel H., July 27, 1840.
(4364) George, August 16, 1842.

Samuel and Mary (Moore) Stearns removed in 1834 to Rindge, N. H., and he at once took a very prominent part in the civil and religious affairs of the town. Among the various positions of public trust to which he was repeatedly elected were those of Selectman and Representative. His wife Mary died August 28, 1849, and Samuel m. 2d Almira Hale, daughter of John and Betsey (Bennett) Hale, of Ashburnham, Mass., who died in 1877.

1973 Nathaniel and Rosanna Goodwin had:

(4365) Sarah, August 22, 1817. m. George W. Emery, January 1, 1845. Res., South Berwick, Maine.
(4366) James, September 2, 1819. m. Harriet Hanscom, in 1846. Res., Portland.
(4367) John, December 18, 1820. m. Elizabeth C. Ham, September 4, 1845. Res., in Portsmouth, N. H.
(4368) Jeremiah, July 30, 1822. m. Eliza Goodwin, January 26, 1851. Res., Salmon Falls.
(4369) Hannah, December 24, 1824. m. H. D. Walker. Settled in Berwick, Maine.

(4370) Carrie, August 20, 1826. m. Isaac P. Yeaton. Res., at So. Berwick, Maine.
(4371) Nathaniel, May 11, 1830. m. Addie Goodwin. Res., So. Berwick, Maine.

Nathaniel was a cabinet-maker, res. in Eliot, Maine, where he d. March 17, 1864.

1974 James and Isabel Tobey had :

(4372) Nathaniel, July 4, 1822. d. October 4, 1867.
(4373) Mary, September 20, 1826. d. young.
(4374) Isabel, March 1, 1824. m. Jefferson Pratt, (or Raitt), November 17, 1868. She d. January 9, 1856.
(4375) Mary F., April 7, 1828. d. 1848.
(4376) Jas. H., October 20, 1831. m. Matilda Bartlett.
(4377) Hannah A., January 15, 1834. m. C. H. Daniels, June 8, 1848.
(4378) Lucy J., February 8, 1837. m. J. D. Frost, November 14, 1859.
(4379) Sarah, December 6, 1839. m. M. L. Hatch. 4 chil.
(4380) George W., February 18, 1843. m. Sarah E. Monroe.

Residence, Eliot, Me.

James was a Farmer. He d. June 13, 1880. Isabel d. January 11, 1895.

1975 John and Nancy I. Frye had:

(4381) Annie E., November 6, 1836. m. Rev. Geo. E. Sanborn, June 10, 1858. Res., in Hartford, Conn.
(4382) Sarah A., March 18, 1839. m. Horace E. Robinson, September 18, 1861. 4 chil.
(4383) Mary. H., July 15, 1842. m. Chas. E. Lane, October, 1863. She d. 1865.
(4384) Wm. H. H., June 28, 1841. m. Mary L. Butcher, November 9, 1865.
(4385) Eliza W., March 1, 1848. Unm. Res., in Hartford, Conn.

Residence, Portsmouth, N. H.

John d. August 1, 1870.

1976 Lucy Knowlton and James Bartlett had :

(4386) John. Residence, in Milwaukee, Wis.
(4387) Lucy. m. —— Thompson.
(4388) Edwin. Res., in New York City.

(4389) Sarah. m. —— Johnson. Res., Baltimore.
(4390) Margaret. d.
(4391) James P. Res., Portsmouth, N. H.
(4392) Louisa. m. —— Goodale.

1977 Hannah Knowlton and Joshua W. Kenney had:

(4393) Joshua, August 27, 1826. d. August 6, 1852.

1979 Abigail Knowlton and Joseph G. True had:

(4394) Elias F., November 13, 1828. m. C. G. Crossman, November 11, 1855.
(4395) Mary R., February 20, 1830. m. Hannah Staniels, January 27, 1860.
(4396) Jacob R., September 11, 1831. m. Annie R. Pierce, October 21, 1852.
(4397) Lewis P., January 15, 1833.
(4398) Abbie J., November 18, 1835. m. Wm. Snow, January 16, 1862.
(4399) Joseph E., September 2, 1837. m. Hattie Tibbets.
(4400) Ora A., December 15, 1839. m. Susan Staniels, May 25, 1871.
(4401) Annie, September 20, 1841. m. J. Cushing Bartlett; m. 2d Jesse F. Bartlett.

1980 Thomas and Cynthia Savage had:

(4402) Augusta, 1835. Res., Brunswick, Maine.
(4403) Emily, September 7, 1836.
(4404) Chas. T., February 7, 1838. m. Martha Hoagdon.
(4405) Chauncy, July 3, 1840. Killed in the Civil War, October 16, 1862.
(4406) Josephine, November 11, 1841. Res., Watsonville, Cal.
(4407) Wesley, 1845. d. young.
(4408) Isadore, January 4, 1848.

Thomas d. June 16, 1863, in San Francisco. Cynthia d. March 18, 1888.

1982 Joseph and Rachel Lowe had:

(4409) Infant. d.
(4410) Abby. m. —— Peterson.
(4411) Isabel. m. Theodore Wilder.
(4412) Lucy. m. Geo. D. Card.
(4413) Joseph. m. Lizzie Doolittle. 2 chil.
(4414) Annie E. m. —— Osborne.

1893 Jacob and Mary Rogers had:

(4415) George, March 11, 1838. d. January 26, 1864.
(4416) Abby, January 23, 1840.
(4417) John R., October 26, 1842. m. Sarah M. Kidder, June 2, 1870.
(4418) Sarah, March 19, 1844. m. John H. Bowditch, April, 1864.
(4419) Beatrice, January 1, 1846. d. young.
(4420) Frances, January 11, 1850. m. Chas. L. Nichols, June 27, 1871.

Jacob d. May 21, 1867. Mary d. March 6, 1874.

1985 Francis and Caroline Billings had:

(4421) Mary, 1839. m. Ferdinand Hall. He d. in California.
(4422) Emily, January 18, 1842. m. Robert C. Smith, December 30, 1860.
(4423) Edward, April, 1844. m. Lucy Annis.
Rem. to Michigan.

2013 Jonathan and Lydia Palmer had:

(4424) Mayhew C., April 3, 1823. m. Had s. Everett. Lynn, Mass.
(4425) Alonzo, October 11, 1824. m. Had s. Walter F.
(4426) George H., April 21, 1838. m. Hannah Cilley, February 4, 1869.
(4427) Mary, September 8, 1830.

2014 Miles and Nancy M. Demeritt had:

(4428) Henry, June 25, 1819. m. Mary Morrison, February 14, 1841.
(4429) James, August 5, 1821. m. Jane M. Morrison, September 3, 1844.
(4430) John, March 26, 1831. d. young.
(4431) Daniel C., December 15, 1832. m. Mary Dearborn, March 5, 1857.
(4432) Alfred, December 2, 1824. d. young.
(4433) Angeline, April 19, 1827. m. J. B. Morrison, October 28, 1852. Res., Northwood, N. H.
(4434) Elizabeth, October 15, 1828. m. Eben James, of Deerfield, N. H., June 14, 1851.
(4435) Roxana, April 21, 1823. m. Stephen Tuttle; m. 2d W. H. Furber, of Boston. She d. 1869.
(4436) Gardner, June 25, 1834. d. August 17, 1858.
(4437) Chas. E., June 25, 1836.
(4438) Annie M., April 30, 1837. m. Jonah Morrison, July 2, 1855.
(4439) Olive J., February 7, 1839. m. N. J. Tilton, of Deerfield, Mass.

Miles d. February, 1874. Nancy d. July 3, 1870.

2017 William and Betsey Drake had:

(4440) Chas. B. m. Eleanor Norris.
(4441) James W.
(4442) Mary W. m. William Hodgman.
(4443) Helen. m. Hon. L. Clark.
(4444) Adaliza. m. John M. Kane.
(4445) Josephine.
(4446) Emma F. m. Geo. M. Teele.
(4447) Jonathan.
(4448) Miles.
(4449) William.
(4450) Nathan.

Residence, Northwood, N. H.

2019 Jane Knowlton and Miles Durgin had:

(4451) Woodbury M., June 8, 1825. m. Abbie E. James, December 16, 1847.
(4452) Mary J., May 13, 1827. m. W. H. Simmons, June 14, 1848.
(4453) William T., February 13, 1833. m. Hattie Stewart, February 8, 1863.
(4454) Amos S., February 2, 1837. m. Annie Batchelder, November 29, 1859.
(4455) John A., May 15, 1839. m. Mary E. Webster, 1859.

2020 Nathaniel and Eliza Hoyt had:

(4456) Emery M., September 16, 1831. d. 1840.
(4457) Mary, October 3, 1836. m. C. H. Robinson, July 1, 1857.
(4458) Eliza, December 18, 1837. m. A. G. James, November 16, 1858.
(4459) John B., April 6, 1838. m. Mary A. Harvey, September 22, 1860. 1 son.
(4460) Melissa, May 22, 1844. m. B. P. Giles, August 6, 1864.
(4461) Francenia, September 23, 1846. m. John H. Thompson, August 22, 1874.
(4462) Plummer, May 3, 1848. m. Mary A. Thompson, 1866.

Residence, Chichester, N. H.

2026 Oliver and Lucinda Batcheller had:

(4463) George, February, 25, 1827. m. Mary J. Demerritt, December 19, 1853. Soldier in Civil War.

(4464) Charles, November 9, 1829. Res. in Miles City, Montana.
(4465) Kirk, February 24, 1836. m. Susan Clark, 1865.
(4466) John, May 25, 1832. m. Rachael Batchelder, May 2, 1858.
(4467) Frank, August 12, 1834. Killed at Battle of Gettysburg, July 2, 1863.
(4468) Mary, April, 20, 1840. m. Geo. Sanborn, February 9, 1861. Residence, Sanbornton, N. H.

Oliver was a teacher, Selectman, and Representative in the Legislature.

2027 Mehitable Knowlton and Lewis Fiske had:

(4469) Oliver, January 22, 1819.
(4470) Amos, July 5, 1821.
(4471) Charles, September 9, 1827.
(4472) Daniel, November 22, 1829.

Mehitable d. July 10, 1873.

2028 Samuel and Sally Danforth had:

(4473) George W., December 19, 1818. m. Sophronia Evans, June 28, 1840.
(4474) Mary J., March 25, 1820.
(4475) Warren, October 13, 1821. d. 1825.
(4476) Emeline, December 25, 1824.
(4477) Lucy A., September 17, 1826.
(4478) Sarah O., December 25, 1828. m. H. H. Channell, March 20, 1862.
(4479) Oliver, April 16, 1834. m. Ellen ——.
(4480) Abigail, April 13, 1836.
(4481) Andrew, August 12, 1839.
Res., Northwood, N. H.

Sally d. September 17, 1859.

2031 Harriet Knowlton and F. C. Morrill had:

(4482) Samuel G., August 19, 1828.
(4483) Harriet, February 24, 1830.
(4484) Lydia, February 10, 1833.
(4485) Drusilla.
(4486) Charles.

Harriet d. July 31, 1877. He d. 1840.

2032 Lydia Knowlton and Jacob C. Harvey had:

(4487) Susan, January 2, 1826. m. J. H. Winslow, December 26, 1859.
(4488) Francis, August 6, 1827. m. Annie Robinson, December 4, 1853.
(4489) George J., January 12, 1829.
(4490) Louisa A., May 8, 1830. m. Paschal Sturtevant, March 1, 1849.
(4491) Merilla, June 20, 1832. d. 1839.

Lydia d. October 1, 1848.

2034 George W. and Eliza W. Garland had no chil. He m. 2d Mary A. Virgin, and had:

(4492) Olive, April 4, 1840. m. Wm. F. Hill, January 25, 1858.
(4493) George, September 22, 1844. m. Olive A. Cate, February 10, 1866.
(4494) Ursula, November 5, 1846. m. Chas. Batchelder; m. 2d John Smith, 1877.
(4495) Winfield, October 17, 1848. m. Ellen M. Clark, December 4, 1869.
(4496) Lizzie, June 21, 1853. m. George M. Morse, July 10, 1872.
(4497) Frank P., December 29, 1858.
(4498) Sarah K. February 8, 1860.

Residence, Lowell, Mass.

2043 Asahel and Eliza Shaw had:

(4499) John, January 9, 1841.
(4500) Lizzie, November 27, 1842.
(4501) Hosea C., October 9, 1844. m. Ellen Flagg. 1 child.
(4502) Edwin, October 16, 1846.
(4503) Frank, November 9, 1850.

Eliza d. December 27, 1850, and Asahel m. 2d. Mary D. Clark, April 1851, and had:

Chas. F., September 17, 1886.

Residence, Chichester, N. H.

(2044) SAMUEL KNOWLTON

enlisted in the United States Army, and served in the Florida War. His regiment having been so invested by the savages that provisions and war material could no longer be had, and the troops being on the verge of starvation, the commanding officer called for volunteers in a "forlorn hope," and who would risk their lives in an attempt to reach the next garrison and obtain relief. Samuel Knowlton was the only volunteer. He threaded the dense forest by night, hiding and sleeping by day; and for several days he eluded the vigilance of the enemy. He finally lost his way, was captured by the savages, and flayed alive.

2045 James and —— had:

(4504) Amanda. m. George Diamond.
(4505) Adaline. m. John Danforth.
Residence, Danbury, N. H.

2046 Asa and Lydia —— had:

(4506) Marietta, January 7, 1854. m. James P. Reed, 1870.
(4507) Kinsman, September 12, 1850. d. 1854.
(4508) George, September 30, 1853. m. Lucy Bennett, 1875. Had dau. Lillian.
(4509) Olive, March 10, 1862. d. young.

2047 Andrew and Mary Blake had:

(4510) Charles, November 23, 1847.
(4511) Nellie, May 3, 1850.
Residence, Nashua, N. H.

2049 William and Merinda Bailey had:

(4513) Charles B., April 12, 1856.
(4514) Sarah, November 25, 1857. m. Frank Webster, November, 1877.
(4515) George, July 20, 1860. d. 1864.
(4516) Henry, June 9, 1863.
Residence, Lawrence, Mass.

William m. 2d Lydia Currier, 1847.

2056 William H. H. and Eleanor Norris had:

(4517) Blake N., 1831. d. 1863.
(4518) Martha A., February 25, 1833. m. J. M. P. Batchelder, February 17, 1859.
(4519) Susan, January 23, 1831. m. Dr. N. Clarke, June 15, 1859.

2057 Jeremiah and Mary Ford had:

(4520) Edward.

Residence, Danbury, N. H.

2058 Chas. G. and Sarah Flandors had:

(4521) Frances, December, 1838.
(4522) Amasette, April 16, 1843. m. Ezekiel S. Waldron. m. 2d Geo. H. Waldron. m. 3d James M. Abbott.
(4523) George, 1845.

Sarah d. June 27, 1845. Chas. m. 2d Mrs. Mary A. Robson. m. 3d Mrs. French and had:

(4524) Mary. m. Brooks. Res., Independence, Ia.
(4525) Eliza.
(4526) Martha.
(4527) Charles.
(4528) Anna.

Chas. d. November 19, 1871, in Maysville, Iowa.

2060 James and Clarissa Ford had:

(4529) Sarah J., January 22, 1850.
(4530) Alma A., October 12, 1851.
(4531) Anna, November 15, 1852.
(4532) James, June 27, 1854. m. Carrie E. Gordon. res. in Lebanon, Ind.
(4533) Clara E., November 21, 1859. d. November 23, 1883.

Clarissa was from Orange, N. H., whence the family rem. to Danbury, N. H.

2063 Joseph and Clara Butler had:

(4534) Horace, March 18, 1846. m. Ella Dobbins.
(4535) Frank, December 14, 1847. m. Clara Powell. 1 child. d. young.
(4536) Joseph, January 16, 1857.
(4537) Thomas E., January 3, 1860. m. Maude ——.

Residence, Manchester, N. H.

Joseph, Senr., was a soldier in the War of the Rebellion.

2064 Chas. D. and Harriet Buck had:

(4538) Ellen W., March 1, 1846. m. Chas. Green, of Springfield, Mass.
(4539) Chas. E., 1847. d. 1857.

Chas. D. rem. from New Boston, N. H., to Mexico.

2065 Julia Ann Knowlton and Micah Dyer had:

(4540) Willard K., April 1, 1852. m. Sarah Holmes; m. 2d Georgie Dunham.
(4541) Walter R., m. Mabel Cross; m. 2d Martha Houston. He d. April 20, 1855.
(4542) Mabel, October 16, 1857. d. young.

JULIA KNOWLTON DYER

was b. in Deerfield, N. H., August 25, 1829. She is a lineal descendant of Gen. Dearborn, of Bunker Hill fame, and of Col. Thomas Knowlton of Maine.

Her infancy was spent in Concord, N. H., and in 1839 she was taken to Manchester, and educated under private teachers, and in boarding school. At the age of 18, she was graduated from New Hampton Institute, with first honors, and became a teacher of French, English Literature, and Higher Mathematics.

On her marriage to Micah Dyer, Esq., a lawyer of high standing, she removed to Dorchester, on the old and attractive Clapp estate, where she still resides. Her career has been so marked that few women in Massachusetts society are better, or more honorably, known than she. In 1864, the Dedham Home for Discharged Soldiers was founded through her personal efforts, and she has for thirty years made monthly visits to the Institution.

In 1882, she was chosen President of the Ladies' Aid Association. She founded the Women's Charity Club for the benefit of females needing surgical treatment, starting the enterprise with faith and courage, though without one dollar of capital, and made it a permanent success and blessing.

She organized the Wintergreen Club for women over fifty years of age, became its President, and has been the V. Pres. of the W. T. U., and an active member and officer in not less than twenty-five different charitable, philanthropic, and patriotic societies. Her extraordinary ability as an organizer, a speaker, and an administrator has made her an indispensable factor in the working out of many problems of modern society.

2067 Susan Knowlton and Dr. Joseph Garland had:

(4543) Ethel E.
(4544) Alice.
(4545) Roy.

Residence, Springfield, Mass.

2084 Gilbert and Olive Batchelder had:

(4546) James F., December 25, 1854.
(4547) Carrie, January 4, 1858.
(4548) Addie, February 25, 1860.
Residence, Nottingham, N. H.

2093 C David and Mehitable True had:

(4549) Ebenezer, November, 1835. m. Lizzie Johnstone. Rem. to San Francisco.
(4550) David M., July 3, 1837. d. May 30, 1877.
(4551) Chas., 1839. d. young.
(4552) Sarah G., 1841. d. young.
(4553) Charles, March 1843. d. 1848.
Residence, Monteville, Maine.

2093 D Ebenezer and Pheobe True had:

(4554) Ellen, August 27, 1843. m. Chas. A. Milliken, May 21, 1875. He was Mayor of Augusta, Maine.
(4555) Hattie, August 14, 1847. m. Lyman G. Jordan, December 24, 1871.
(4556) Abbie, August 5, 1849. d. August 31, 1874.
(4557) Eben, November 23, 1859. d. young.

Widow Phoebe resides in Lewiston, Me.

2093 E John C. Knowlton and Sarah A. Webb had:

(4558) Charles, August 29, 1843. m. Helen Blood, 1867.
(4559) Mary, April 17, 1845. m. Daniel Farr, 1869.
(4560) Carrie, December 5, 1848. m. F. C. Keating, 1875.
(4561) J. Frank, March 19, 1856. m. Josie Merservy, December 4, 1878.

Widow Sarah lives in Lewiston, Me.

2094 Abigail Knowlton and Joseph Stevens had:

(4562) Jared, September 10, 1795.
(4563) Hattie B., June 1, 1797.
(4564) Permelia, March 20, 1799.
(4565) Amos, May 31, 1801.
(4566) Jonas, March 13, 1803.
(4566 A) Benjamin, May 12, 1805.
(4567) Joseph, August 20, 1809.

(4568) Ralph, December 2, 1811.
(4569) Marcus, February 20, 1814. m. Mary Erwin, December 26, 1854.
(4570) Almond, June 12, 1816. m. Martha Gates.
(4571) John, February 19, 1819. m. Mary B. Covert, October 8, 1845.
(4572) Millicen A. m. Joseph Pratt.
(4573) A daughter. d. young.

Abigail d. December 19, 1864. Joseph d. December 1, 1846.

2095 Charlotte Knowlton and Dr. John Rexford had:

(4574) Calista, January 28, 1796.
(4575) Polly, October 8, 1798.
(4576) William, July 25, 1800.
(4577) Daniel, April 21, 1802.
(4578) Abigail, April 1, 1804.
(4579) John, July 7, 1806.
(4580) Charlotte, July 1, 1808.
(4581) Lucy, May 10, 1810.
(4582) Ensign, March 13, 1812.

2096 Benjamin and Lucy Campbell had:

(4583) Ursula, June 25, 1804. d. November 29, 1837.
(4584) Charlotte, July 3, 1806. d. 1809.
(4585) Benjamin, December 8, 1809. d. July 17, 1833.
(4586) Charlotte, October 17, 1811. m. Dr. P. W. Belknap, January 9, 1837. and had son, Noyes.
(4587) Emeline, November 16, 1813. m. Freeman Smith. Res. and d. in Cato, N. Y.
(4588) Oliver J., January 6, 1816. d. July 3, 1840. Res., Portage, Michigan.
(4589) Ernest J., February 11, 1818. m. R. A. Potter.
(4590) Maria, November 29, 1822. m. M. M. Emerson. She d. March 19, 1874.

Benjamin was a captain in the war of 1812. He resided for several years in Portage, Mich., removing thence to South New Lyons, Mich., where he d. February, 1864.

2098 Lucy Knowlton and John Chamberlain had:

(4591) Destimony, July 8, 1806. m. Amos Cornell, January 15, 1824.
(4592) Isabella. unm.

2099 Henry and Rebecca Southwick had:

(4593) Chas. A., August 14, 1810. m. Ruby Ingraham, March 7, 1835.
(4594) Leander, May 7, 1814. m. Matilda Monroe.
(4595) Henry, May 24, 1819. m. Harriet N. Dodge.
(4596) Clark, 1821. m. Jemima ——.
(4597) Hannah, 1811. m. Had 4 chil.
(4598) Caroline, 1817. m. Nathaniel Crofut. d. in the War of the Rebellion. 3 chil.
(4599) Harriet, 1823. m. E. B. Burt, of Oswego, N. Y. 3 chil.
(4600) Ruth, 1825. m. Had 2 chil.
(4601) Eliza, 1827. d. 1845. Had 4 chil.

Henry m. 2d Matilda Moore, who d. June 26, 1844. Residence, New Ipswich, N. H., where Henry d. 1838.

2113 Joseph and Harriet Jane Temple:

(4602) William, September 10, 1822.
(4603) Sarah E., 1825. m. John B. Fuller, 1844.
(4604) Benjamin, November 2, 1828. m. Grace Nichols, May 29, 1853.
(4605) Laura J., 1832. d. young.

Joseph is said to have been an adopted son, his surname being Dorling.

2114 Sally Knowlton and F. G. Temple had:

(4606) John, December 19, 1831.
(4607) Charles, February 14, 1833.
(4608) George, October 11, 1835.
(4609) Ira, December 19, 1837. d. 1842.

Sally d. April 15, 1848.

2115 Eliza Knowlton and Shubal Shattuck had:

(4610) Edward, December 6, 1831. m. Lizzie Cruen, 1861.
(4611) Elmira, January 26, 1833. m. J. W. Crosby, 1861.
(4612) John, October 24, 1834. Killed at Morris Island, S. C., in the Civil War, August 5, 1863.
(4613) Eliza, December 22, 1835. m. Chas. Simonds, 1865.
(4614) Harriet C., December 9, 1837. d. young.
(4615) George W., December 18, 1838.
(4616) Harrison H., May 15, 1851. m. Clara Palmer, 1870.

2116 John H. and Mary Rogers had:

(4617) Mary, 1836.
(4618) Martha, June 7, 1840. m. C. H. King, October 11, 1872.
Residence, Williamstown, Mass.

2121 James and Sarah Lane had:

(4619) Sarah E., January 22, 1824. m. Maurice Hodgkins, December 24, 1847.
(4620) John J., July 26, 1826. m. Susan A. F. Dennison, April 27, 1856.
(4621) Joseph L., July 26, 1829. m. Clara F. Thomas, September 23, 1851.
(4622) Daniel W., November 2, 1831. m. Lucy Cloudman, September 15, 1871.
Residence, Annisquam, Gloucester, Mass.

2123 Epps and Elizabeth Badger had:

(4623) Sarah A., October 12, 1825. m. Caleb Prouty, Jr., March 14, 1855. He d. at Vicksburg, 1863. 4 chil.
(4624) James J., October 3, 1827. m. Lucy Welsh, June 26, 1849. 10 chil.
(4625) John W., December 3, 1830. d. in Illinois, September 22, 1862.
(4626) Ann E., December 5, 1833. m. W. H. Sturtevant, June 24, 1855.
(4627) Joseph S., May 8, 1836. m. Mary Morgan, October 28, 1857.
(4628) William H., July 4, 1841. m. Sarah J. Rowlee, November 14, 1869.

Epps res. in Gloucester, Mass., during a portion of his life, and d. of yellow fever near Savannah, Ga., 1844. Elizabeth was from Badger's Island, Me., and d. March 2, 1875.

2124 Joseph and Mary Remick had:

(4629) Joseph B., January 12, 1828. m. Louisa Brewer, February 20, 1862.
(4630) Hannah, October 21, 1830. m. Albert R. Walker, March 4, 1864.
(4631) William, September 13, 1832. m. Ellen M. Prindall, June 19. 1860.
(4632) Reuben, July 30, 1834. d. young.
(4633) Annie, September 4, 1836. m. Frank B. Hanson, May, 1861. He d. at Newbern, N. C., 1862.

Mary d. May 19, 1852, and Joseph m. 2d Lydia Remick, who d. July 10, 1860. He d. January 8, 1876.

2125 Ammi L. and Maria Lond had :

(4634) Frank, October 21, 1836. m. Victoria Morton.
(4635) William, August 15, 1839.
(4636) Mary, October 25, 1842.
Residence, Portsmouth, N. H.

2126 Josiah and Lucy —— had :

(4637) Clara.
(4638) Lucy, November 18, 1832. m. James H. Adams.
(4639) George, April 11, 1835. d. January 3, 1871.

2129 Erastus and —— had :

(4640) Charles B., February 18, 1810. m. Harriet Evans, July 9, 1837.

Erastus res. in Toronto, Canada.

2130 Faxon and Elizabeth Buck had :

(4641) Frederick B., 1822. A Methodist preacher.
(4642) Louisa, 1825. m. John Spafford who d. 1890.
(4643) John H. Res., Vermillion, N. Y.
(4644) Calvin H. Res.. Vermillion, N. Y.

Faxon was b. in Canada. He resided there most of his life, and was killed by the falling of a tree, in 1830. Elizabeth d. 1888.

.2144 John and Ruth Holmes had :

(4645) William H., February 4, 1818. m. Betsey Bruce. m. 2d Sarah Allen, 1837.
(4646) Mary J., September 26, 1820. m. William Knowlton.
(4647) John W., August 11, 1822. m. Elmira Ames, May 11, 1845.
(4648) Ruth, May 27, 1824. m. George Groover (or Grover).
(4649) George T., May 11, 1826. d. May 12, 1842.
(4650) Sally A., March 21, 1829. m. Watson Curtis, November 4, 1845.
(4651) Susan A., March 11, 1830. m. Joseph Morrison, February 5, 1850.
(4652) Ezra T., February 17, 1833. m. Eliza Quimby, August 30, 1858.
(4653) Rebecca, December 4, 1835. m. John Bunce.

(4654) Elisha P., January 17, 1838. m. Susannah Lenfest. He d. in the War of the Rebellion.

(4654 A) Adamizer, November 2, 1839. m. Lucy Nash, 1860.

Residence, Minot, Me.

2145 Ephraim and Sarah Braglin had:

(4655) William. m. Mary J. Knowlton, October 8, 1837.
(4656) Aaron. m. Mary Curtis, September 18, 1839.
(4657) Amasa. m. Olive M. Howard.
(4658) Ephraim. m. Sally A. Allen, September 17, 1839.
(4659) Thomas. m. Mehitable Nash.
(4660) Mary Jane. m. Jere Small, October 30, 1845.
(4661) Sally. m. Watson Reaney.

Ephraim d. January 7, 1849.

2151 Lucinda Knowlton and Jacob Peavey had:

(4662) Watson, April 28, 1828.
(4663) Hollis M., July 7, 1830.
(4664) Washington, December 13, 1833.
(4665) Mary J., April 19, 1835.
(4666) Emory, October 26, 1838.
(4667) Rosella, May 3, 1841.
(4668) George, July 8, 1843.
(4669) Fannie, April 29, 1846.
(4670) Columbus, December 31, 1848.

2154 Zina and Betsey Proctor had:

(4671) Andrew, February 12, 1835. m. Ann Curtis, August 6, 1853.
(4672) James, January 18, 1837. m. Harriet Martin, June 6, 1858.
(4673) Jane C., April 24, 1839. m. James C. Gray, October 2, 1859.
(4674) Charlotte, August 8, 1841. m. Samuel Stevens, August 16, 1857. ✓
(4675) Joshua, January 1, 1843. m. Phoebe Bates, December 10, 1865.
(4676) Caleb, October 4, 1846. m. Jennie Putnam, October 23, 1866.
(4677) John, January 5, 1850. m. Ann Mason, December 25, 1870.
(4678) Zina, October 2, 1852. d. young.
(4679) Rose, August 10, 1855. d. September 2, 1872.

Residence, Maine.

2161 Henry and Betsey York had:

(4680) Rebecca.
(4681) Georgiana.
(4682) Lucy.

2164 Stephen and Susan Pottle had:

(4683) Amanda. m. Rev. A. Perkins. She d. 1865.
(4684) Edwin. m. Maria Case. Res. in West End, Alameda Co., Cal.
(4685) Faustina. m. George Batchelder.
(4686) Emma.
(4687) Eugene.

Stephen was drowned in Belfast Harbor, Me.

2167 William and Patience Sprague had:

(4688) Wm. W. m. Sarah Batchelder. He d. 1877.
(4689) Alonzo.

They res. in Troy, Me.

2178 Amos Atkinson and Anna G. Sawyer had:

(4690) William F. d.
(4691) George.
(4692) Elizabeth Parsons.
(4693) Edward. m. Mary C. Heath.
(4694) Henry. d.
(4695) Annie. m. Richard M. Stagg. d.

2180 Nancy Knowlton and Samuel Baker had:

(4696) Elizabeth, November 1, 1819. m. Michael Pond, 1839. 2 chil.
(4697) Samuel, July 1, 1826. d. May 24, 1852.

Nancy d. before September, 1829. Samuel Baker was from Wallingford, Berkshire Co., England. He d. in Mineral Point, Wis., January, 1846.

2181 Martha Knowlton and Samuel Baker had:

(4698) William, September 5, 1832. m. Adelaide Ortman, July 28, 1861. 1 dau. Res., Boston, Mass.

(4699) John H., March 1, 1835. m. Jessie Sumner, of Tiffin, O., July 31, 1867.
(4700) George A., September 2, 1837. unm. d. at Sacramento, December 19, 1890.

Martha d. at Madison, Wis., November 3, 1866. Samuel d. May 24, 1852, of yellow fever, when en route for California. His s. William res. in Hoboken, N. J.

2186 Amos and Eunice Blood had:

(4701) Lucy, December 28, 1812. m. Ralph Hatch, October 7, 1847.
(4702) Mary, August 2, 1814. m. John Phelps, March 5, 1835. She d. November 8, 1851.
(4703) Patience, December 1, 1815. m. Geo. Miller, December 12, 1839. She d. December 24, 1896.
(4704) Eunice, August 20, 1817. m. Lucius Bradley, July 4, 1843.
(4705) Angelette, June 15, 1819. m. John Bègole, October 6, 1842. 1 child.
(4706) Hannah, September 25, 1822. unm. Res., Olean, N. Y.
(4707) Frederick, November 17, 1826. m. Althea Van Deusen, October 18, 1855.

Amos m. 2d Rhoda Ann Ball and had:

(4708) William H., April 22, 1848. m. Mary E. McConnell, September 24, 1878.

Amos rem. from Hartland, Vt., to Moreau, N. Y. in 1810, and d. August 21, 1864.

2187 Elisha and Sophia Turner had:

(4708 A) Emily, March 21, 1821. m. Joseph Hascall.
(4709) Alfred, August 11, 1823. m. Aurelia Atwill.
(4710) Minerva, April 14, 1825. m. Lorenzo Kenney.
(4711) Lucy, November 9, 1827. m. Elias Ward.
(4712) Harriet, July 2, 1830. m. Oren Grimes.
(4713) Augusta, 1831. d. young.
(4714) Orville, May 10, 1833. m. Jennie Crawford. Res., Hartland, Vt.

Elisha d. July 19, 1861.

www.ingramcontent.com/pod-product-compliance
Lightning Source LLC
Chambersburg PA
CBHW021111270326
41929CB00009B/821

* 9 7 8 3 3 3 7 2 5 7 4 7 7 *